# Time and Value

# Time and Value

*Edited by*
Scott Lash,
Andrew Quick
and
Richard Roberts

Institute for Cultural Research at
Lancaster University

Blackwell Publishers Ltd

Copyright © Blackwell Publishers Ltd 1998

ISBN 0–631–21003–2

First published in 1998

Blackwell Publishers Ltd
108 Cowley Road, Oxford OX4 1JF, UK
and
350 Main Street,
Malden, MA 02148, USA

*British Library Cataloguing in Publication Data*

A CIP catalogue record for this book is available from the British
Library.

*Library of Congress Cataloguing-in-Publication Data*
applied for


This book is printed on acid free paper.

# Contents

# Preface

The chapters in this volume are drawn from papers presented at an international conference held in 1997. The conference, 'Time and Value', was organized by The Institute for Cultural Research at Lancaster University. Founded in 1996 and inheriting the work of Lancaster's Centre for the Study of Cultural Values, the Institute provides a means of enhancing, co-ordinating and promoting interdisciplinary research on culture and facilitates a range of activities across the University including seminar series, lectures, workshops, postgraduate research, conferences and publications. The Institute also produces an international journal *Cultural Values* (Blackwell) in which all the chapters of this volume first appeared in a themed issue (Volume 2, Nos. 2 & 3) in June of 1998.

Unfortunately, it is impossible to acknowledge all those who contributed to the conference (it lasted for three days and included over 130 speakers). Particular thanks, however, goes to the planning committee with whom we worked to manage the conference: Barbara Adam, Mick Dillon, Paul Heelas, Jeffrey Richards, Rob Shields, Jackie Stacey, John Urry, Jeremy Valentine and Emily Lomax. The success and the smooth running of such a large event would have been impossible without the hard work, dedication and wit of June Rye, Assistant to the Institute. We would also like to express our gratitude to the editorial board of *Cultural Values*, the many distinguished readers who commented on the contributions and also to the Managing Editors of the journal, Mick Dillon, Paul Heelas and Scott Wilson and the Assistant Editor, Tom Cahill, for their advice and support in the development and completion of this project.

The editors would also like to acknowledge the support afforded by Blackwell Publishers Ltd, Lancaster University's Committee for Research, René Lacombe (French Cultural Attaché) David Martin and the Department of Theatre Studies.

# Introduction:
# Millenniums and Catastrophic Times

Scott Lash, Andrew Quick, Richard Roberts
Lancaster University

The approaching Millennium is an appropriate moment for the publication of a volume addressing time, and particularly apt for a wide-ranging collection that addresses time and value. The current millennial sensibility has been characterized by varieties of apocalyptic thinking among the general public: a thinking that in inchoate ways connects impending futures with the destruction, even the dissolution, of value. This kind of thinking, which associates these new times with the destruction of value, is apparent in the widespread resistance to the incursion of the new global and technological order. This resistance is present among the identitarian, sometimes fundamentalist politics of groupings in the interstices of the 'glocalized' world system. It is a form of thinking that has strong reverberations – expressed in fears of multiculturalism and a general disintegration of value – in the very heart of Western Capitalist culture. Fear of the dissolution of time and value in the face of the Millennium pertains not only to those who experience apprehension and *ressentiment* at the implosion of tradition, but also to a younger generation – in the most 'wired' zones of our global cities. These neo-tribalists and techno-anarchists, who would applaud the collapse of received values after the year 2000, and who might thus celebrate apocalypse, nonetheless register the insidious inevitability of ecological degradation. It is difficult to confront planetary catastrophe as a Millennium to be greeted with the *amor fati* of Nietzschean laughter.

At the end of the first Millennium in a Christendom infused with sacramental values, there was widespread anxiety and some disorder as the promissory judgement threatened in the Second Coming became once more imminent. This end of history implied both destruction and completion in an individual and collective salvation and a New Heaven and a New Earth. Now, once again there is another sense of the end of history. Confronted with the Third Millennium there is foreboding at the dissolution of intelligible time, the time of Western order. On the one hand, there is anxiety about the emergence of the as-yet unintelligible catastrophic times in which values are seen to disappear. On the other, there is unease that the ends of history and of intelligible time could bring with them uncharted revivals of value and of the sacred. Such new sacralities may no longer fit the received categories of the immanence and transcendence of the West, nor indeed those of migrant world religions in a global religious market. The new sacred inhabits a spectrum that extends from chthonic immanence and matriarchal nurturing of a battered earth to virtual and cyborgic paradisal longings seemingly extending beyond all societal and biological construction. Presaged by Nietzsche, the new sacred can be a return of the primordial, a reality seemingly before and beyond Christianity, which brings with it its own modes of judgement. Such transformed anxiety assumes that we must judge ourselves. For the 'ancients' of the first Millennium, value might be said to have been inscribed in the temporality of everyday life. In the modernity of the latter centuries of the second Millennium, time and value were sharply and dichotomously counterposed as abstract, empty frame and the instrumental striving of the market place.

The third Millennium appears to inaugurate the collapse of dualisms between time and value. It heralds new questions that interrogate new temporalities and new values. In Britain, a prime site of this renegotiation is the Millennial Dome at Greenwich. Astride the meridian, time's bisector, it lies at the historical origin of modern, abstract, empty and global time. As millennial metaphor, the Dome is a metropolitan enterprize, but is an as-yet empty signifier awaiting its signified. Conceived on a vast scale, it echoes Wren's dome at St Paul's Cathedral, a stone-built, perduring symbol of a Christian England. By contrast, the Millennial Dome as national space seeks content through calculated impermanence. Recycling the novelty of the Festival of Britain (1951) and its dome and skylon, the tent-like structure of the New Dome is reminiscent of Gaddafi's Bedouin tent, and of the transience of postmodern nomadism. In more distant terms, such a construction resonates with Coleridge's 'pleasure dome' of Kubla Khan, apostrophized by Stewart Clegg as the multi-dimensional pleasure dome of postmodern society. In this space, 'the canvas is not fixed; the palette is not given; the style not dictated. Representations can be fixed anywhere, anyhow, anyway' (Clegg, 1989, p. 275).

In the quasi-sacrality of the Dome, a 'New Britain' is invited to invent itself within the (fluid) cultural-symbolic logic of New Labour. A tentative, transitory project, the Millennium Dome takes up the national/cosmic potential of an identity created in the image/space of the hemisphere, but it crucially avoids the trammels and burdens of tradition and the imagic sources that might have been implied by a millennial celebration in St Paul's. If, however, the image of the Millennium Dome gains access to the memory bank of globalized symbolization, then it will have achieved its purpose in creating a globally projected 'New British' identity. The physicality of the Dome will be an irrelevance. In effect, it has to be impermanent in order to symbolize the transience of the Millennium itself (what will be remembered of it in 2005?); the Dome needs to be physical only to the extent that it can gain virtual existence. It is the retort in which a Durkheimian 'social effervescence' can take place.

## Catastrophic Time, Intelligible Time

The sort of apocalyptic temporality suggested by the Millennium and the Dome is given theoretical flesh in Chapter one of this volume, in Alphonso Lingis's discussion of 'catastrophic times'. Here Lingis juxtaposes intelligible time with catastrophic time. Intelligible time is moulded, is shaped in the face of, in the encounter with, catastrophic time. According to Lingis, intelligible time takes its shape according to the logic of work. Work activities are shaped by perception, by the 'order of means and foreseen results', causes and effects, a sense of purpose and a consciousness which is subordinated 'to an anticipation of the future'. For Lingis, the individual's efforts, 'his enterprize', requires 'the future to make sense'. Work is 'possible only in intelligible time' and time becomes intelligible through work. Catastrophic time, for its part, emerges with the imminence of disaster. It erupts in the imminence of death, of astonishment in the face of the sublime, in 'exhaustive' love, in violence. Yet the very imminence of catastrophic time drives us into intelligible time. Thus, we shape intelligibility in the face of our ultimate disappearance. A sense of value connects to this shaping sense of catastrophe. The sense of what is of value 'endures across time' and yet it is always undermined by time. For Lingis, the 'possibilities of the future and the resources and momentum of our past are drained into the present' thus bringing about the coincidence of being and value. As such, catastrophic time, its very value, is both devastating (dropping us into the 'time of the empty endurance of void') and impels us to think of a time after disaster, to rebuild our world in the aftermath of catastrophe, in the 'intelligible time of futurity'.

In Chapter two Elizabeth Grosz, drawing on the work of Jacques Derrida, shows that one cannot speak of temporality, without first addressing violence and politics. Hence for her, catastrophic time would have to emerge in an originary violence of difference itself. A second and subsequent order of violence would then yield the intelligible time that conceals originary violence. The ordering of violence has strong political implications. For Grosz and Derrida, the first order of violence is 'bound up with the structures of equivocation and undecidability that radically unhinge discourse, representation and other modes of self-presence'. It comprizes an 'arché-writing' which is the very condition of writing in which violence is inscribed by the trace. The second order of violence entails the 'containment and ordering of things to give up their very thingness and submit themselves to the levelling of representation'. This 'reparatory violence' – identified with reason, right and the law – denies originary violence of becoming, of appearance. The third order of more 'empirical' violence is directly related, and indeed, made possible, by the previous two orders of violence. The political and ethical implications are that each order of violence contains its own implicit temporality, its own implicit value.

Lingis and Grosz work from a distinctly Kantian, aporetic notion of temporality. Here, the condition of the intelligibility of enlightenment is the unintelligibility or limited intelligibility of the deeper layers of being and existence. Here, being is the precondition of knowing: ontology is the condition of epistemology. The *aporia* lies in the fact that this difference cannot be resolved. In Chapter three, Roy Boyne points to the possibility of a perhaps more threatening, and indeed Millennial scenario, in which the boundaries between ontology and epistemology are subverted. Boyne draws on Michel Serres, who implodes the transcendental aporetics of catastrophic and intelligible time into a flattened and immanent scenario 'of connections, fluxes, and objective intensities'. Serres's notion of the present is singular and is seen as 'a given assemblage of particularities'. Resisting discourses of rupture which attempt to order and categorize thought, history, science and notions of temporality, Serres formulates a metaphysics of 'angelic' connectedness. This unusual conjuncture accounts for the characteristics and potential of 'singularities', beyond any construal in terms of their causes or qualities. On this view singularities have their own principles and resist the homogenization of scientific or philosophical inscription.

Serres's notion of the angel is particularly adroit. The 'angelos', or messenger, appears as the angelic figures in the Hebrew Bible who bring to Sarah and Abraham the message that they will have a child. The archangel bears to the Virgin Mary the tidings of the Annunciation. In the Gospel of Luke, Satan is glimpsed as the falling angel, as an indifference consistent with Serres's scenario. Angels are not substance, they exist as beings without ontological structures occupying a space of indifference rather than difference. Hermes – the messenger – operates in a universe that is constructed not so much from the classical time of past, present and future, but rather from one that is formed out of the simultaneity of speed. His etymology figures in hermeneutics. Hermes and the angels operate in a universe in which the aporetic dichotomies of alienation and freedom, of pure and practical reason have been displaced in favour of a swirling vortex of semantics. A hermeneutic universe of actor-networks is connected by information and communication flows. They operate in a flat world in which subjects and substances are dissolved. Angels are messengers in a universe of interpretation and translation. They are bearers of connectivity, circulating as actor-networks without subjects or objects in a digital Millennium. Angels have neither substance nor gender, they are neither humans nor deities. Derrida's (and for that matter Foucault's) space of the irreconcilable difference between ontology and epistemology is, as Boyne notes, tantamount to an archive. This space buckles into Serres's flat assemblage of flows and messages; here are Boyne's poignant 'angels in the archive'.

In Chapter four, Andrew Quick addresses the experience of catastrophic time in a problematics of performativity and 'the event'. In the event, intelligible time collapses into unintelligible time. This amounts to a displacement of performativity into the space of 'pedagogy', whereby in the experiencing of events the individual is forced to relinquish what is known and create new rules that might (for a time) account for the encounter. Quick's text is itself a reflective performance which recapitulates the enactment of 'the event(s)' and 'tumbles' out its happening and its own representations of space and time. Drawing upon the conscious affinity between Lyotard's account of the event and the aesthetics of performance, Quick shows how 'speculation' and imposition of the figural upon space and time is the product of the synergetic interaction of the latter, which brings about 'an effect greater than their attempted synthesis'. His account of the performance of *Black Works* by Station House Opera draws the reader into a claustrophobic spatio-temporal visualization of the complexity of multiple social constructions, the result of instructions heard by the performers (but not by the audience/witnesses). The performers are driven into a frenzy of uncoordinated performativity 'witnessed' both by the audience and a suspended 'observer'. The constantly obliterated and renewed 'traces' left on the stage by the movements of the performers are all that remains (temporarily) of and within the mutually-witnessed spatio-temporal matrix. The climax is catastrophic in that, in a movement of self-ingestion, 'events absorb their own meaning'. Quick's reflected recapitulation of *Black Works*, his (re)performance of the impermanence, endorses the return of the same that renders all events catastrophic: newness, originality such as it is, is enactable only in the difference trapped/released in the drama of repetition.

Intelligible time also describes the rhythms of the ego, catastrophic time those of the id. Thus, in Chapter five, Monica Greco addresses the nature of disease in terms of this unintelligible time of 'the real'. Here the real erupts as event in the heart of the logic of intelligible time. Greco addresses an immanent link between time, value, and disease, by questioning the logic of 'presence' and 'absence' as a way of relating to the reality of illness. These questions are explored by juxtaposing aspects of the work of Viktor Von Weizsäcker and Sigmund Freud, both central figures in the debates on 'psychosomatic' research. While Von Weizsäcker drew attention to the implications of the 'logic of the unconscious' for general medicine, Freud deliberately contained these implications by establishing psychoanalysis as a 'legitimate scientific endeavour'. Drawing on conceptual slippages in Freud's writings on neurosis, Greco's paper explores the negotiation of two questions. The first is: 'Under what circumstances, and for what conditions, is disease interpretable as to its meaning, purpose and value?' The second probes consequences: What happens when we open 'disease' to this task of interpretation? Greco argues that Freud reduces the unconscious dimension of disease to a psychological symptom which effaces the temporality that would permit us to acknowledge the unintelligibility of 'real' disease: a disease whose being is entirely visible in the body, without residue' and without 'interpretable meaning'.

## Tribal Time, Compressed Time

The time of modernity is ideal and transcendental (its paradigm being Newtonian time). As an abstract homogenous time, it is dualistically separated from space, things, people and values. It is not the lived time of things and people, but an empty time in which things happen and people act out their 'times'. In classical discourse, modernity is constructed from Newton's time in which things relate to each other as cause and effect. It includes Marx's time of equally abstract and homogenous proletarian labour, a time in which value is suborned to the instrumental rationality of exchange-value. By contrast the Third Millennium appears to herald the displacement of these dualisms into the simultaneity of Serres's communicational assemblage, implying a certain dissolution of time and value. It also proclaims a resurrection of values in an integral and organic sense. As such, the New Millennial world-view seemingly gropes back into the past for pre-modern juxtapositions of time and value. Some hungrily probe the value integralism of traditions, hence the proliferation of literature on 'community' and collective memory, and the patterns of the resurgence in the world religions. Most strikingly, this sensibility extends its search even further into archaic, *pre*-traditional cyclic, tribalistic time. This is not postmodern de-differentiation, but pre-traditional undifferentiated time, an aeon described by Max Weber in terms of magic, enchantment and the 'plurality of gods and demons'. This is a time prior to the distinctions of signifier and signified, of words and things, a time in which, as Durkheim and Mauss noted, gods, demons, social classifications and logical categories become indistinguishable. This was neither the backward linearity of tradition nor the forward linearity of modernity. It was a cyclical time, visible in, but not yet separated from, the shift of seasons and the motions of sun, moon and stars. It was the time of the animism and totemism described in Durkheim's *Elementary Forms of Religious Life*, and now speculatively adumbrated in the cultural borderlands of megalithic science and astro-archeology.

Few analysts have been more influential in exposing the pre-traditional reworking of time and value than Michel Maffesoli, whose 'neo-tribalism' depicts a radical cultural politics of relatively disorganized and fluid 'sects' engaged in a struggle against the institutions (or 'churches') of modernity in a radical repositioning of both time and value. In Chapter six, Maffesoli further reflects on the contrast between linear and cyclical time. In this instance, linear time involves the trajectory of the bourgeois order in its progress from the Hegelian dialectic, through class struggle. Cyclical time begins to emerge in the street theatre of contemporary life where it expresses a growing passivity in the face of the relativism of the 'return of the same'. It is this repetition that constitutes the present, or 'present-dayness', which should be the centre of attention. Maffesoli, inspired by Nietzsche, explores the ways in which past, present and future are culturally constructed in a sociality, whose life-force is structured through 'cyclical relativism'. Myth and the imagination (*l'imaginaire*) now play a central role in the production of sociality through ludic national events and public spectacles (*le ludisme public*) as emotion and affectivity inhabit a cyclic time that overwhelms rationalized constructions. Maffesoli argues for a new empiricism, a spiral of knowing. This informed knowing, a thinking of everyday life, takes place through the invocation of the idea of 'encyclopaedia', suggestively interpreted as a gyration that constantly relates phenomenal experience to the paradigmatic framework of theory. The cyclic view may seem to banalize daily existence, but this is misleading. It is possible that *the* world ceases to exist, since it submits to a sensual orgy that disrupts the serenity necessary to envisage it as a singularity. In the erasure of *the* world, new worlds become exposed.

In Chapter seven, through an analysis of the temporal dimensions of the contemporary religious field, Richard Roberts shows how under postmodernising conditions a complex, polyvalent polarity is emerging within the religious *imaginaire*. First, he outlines how the category of time has functioned in twentieth century Western theology and religious thought as they have reacted to modernity. Then Roberts draws upon Helga Nowotny's account of the transformations of time under postmodernising conditions in order to amplify the theoretical setting in which to understand how new temporal values are clustered around a complex polarity between virtual and chthonic imperatives. As the drive for ever greater speed of circulation informs use and exchange values, so the colonisation of virtual time-space and cyborgic enhancement offer gendered value recompositions and ambiguous realisations of value, exemplified in, and even driven by William Gibson's *Neuromancer*. In conscious counterpoise to virtual flight and cyborgic emancipation, the reappearance of cyclic and tribal time in the 'chthonic', earth-centred time of the Great Mother (Gaia), becomes the Goddess who bears a mythopoeic, cyclic crown of (essentialist) values. Thus as the banalised *chronoi* of tradition and modernity decompose, so significant new times, the epiphanic *kairoi* of New Millenial consciousness irrupt - and disrupt. As time implodes - and 'dies', so new value-bearing patterns of ultimacy, new 'uchronias' appear.

In Chapters eight and nine, Luiz Soares and Scott Lash point to the continued critical nature of memory and tradition. Without memory, would mourning be possible? In these chapters they cast a different light on the temporality of traditional values. Soares's interest is in how we 'stage ourselves by performing the other', which he pursues through two case studies. The first is of cosmopolitan business visitors in a provincial South American hotel. The visitors ask for a wake-up call. The hotel promises one, but does not deliver it. The visitors order from a menu. The hotel waiter notes their order, and then brings them entirely different dishes. The visitors object and order more from the menu. The waiter produces something new, but this is once again at variance with the order. This hotel in a small town in the developing-world, stages 'the self through performing the other'. It performs the other as cosmopolitan modernity, replete with wake-up service and cosmopolitan menu, but this is conducted as an instance of what Soares calls 'the migration of the projective imagination'. The hosts 'stage' their own traditions; they embody values such as honour and hospitality to outsiders as they perform the other. These are the activities that the anthropologist James Clifford (1997) describes as re-routed 'roots'. Soares's second vignette counterposes a Swedish couple visiting a Brazilian couple in Rio de Janeiro and then in Stockholm. The 'Apollonian' Swedes never miss a chance to get up and party as they perform the 'Dionysian' rites they ascribe to the putatively carnivalesque Brazilian 'other'. But at the same time as acting out the 'migratory' and 'projective imagination', the Swedes perform their own traditions, their own roots. Soares's point, made in a debate with notions of cosmopolitanism produced by such in analysts as Richard Rorty, is that our millennial temporality is not only a question of groundlessness, of movement, or of attitude constructed from an experience that 'all that is solid melts into air'. It is also a matter of roots, groundedness and traditions: a complex and irresolvable dialectic of routes and roots.

Lash starts out from a sociological critique of Heidegger's transcendental claim that time is the horizon upon which the concept of 'being' is conceptualized. Lash proposes that we contextualize this position as a creation made of, and through, modernity. The chapter foregrounds an idea of temporal experience prior to the modern notion of time which is understood as tradition or 'history', and proposes an idea of temporality posterior to the present notion of time which he characterizes as an epoch, or age, of 'speed'. Politics, in such an epoch of speed will, Lash argues, break with notions of difference such as those proffered by Heidegger and Derrida. Instead, Lash suggests a politics of melancholy. Locating his argument in analysis of Walter Benjamin's 'The Storyteller', Lash identifies three modes of temporal operation: the story (in connection to history and tradition), the novel (whose characteristic temporality is 'time') and information (the dynamics of which create or impel the epoch that is named as speed). In this new era, time resists both the reversibility promised by the notion of history and the irreversibility designated in the novel and in narrative. According to Lash, ours is the time of 'hypersurveillance', where the new chronology is 'the speed of light', and where the symbolic and imaginary are 'exploded into fragments' and disseminated outside of the subject into what he identifies as a 'space of indifference'. In this age of speed, within this space of indifference, emerge new politics, new values, where subjectivity itself is put into question as a post-human world is seen to emerge. For Lash, in the age of speed, we are positioned like Benjamin's melancholic angel: we look back at the objects of history, to the discarded fragments of civilization, to the ruins of the city, to tradition. This looking back is not a gaze of mere retrieval but is also the glance of invention, the look that might imagine something anew.

In Chapters three, seven and nine, Boyne, Roberts and Lash write in terms of a temporality of difference and a time of 'indifference'. Here the time of difference – associated most prominently with thinkers such as Derrida – works from the aporetic and irreconcilable distinctions between same and other, between epistemology and ontology, between time and value. The time of indifference emerges with the machinic intelligence of the information age, and it tends to reduce all distinctions into the flat and immanent plane of assemblages described in the work of Serres and Deleuze. In Chapter ten, Timothy Luke pursues these reflections on millennial indifference as he develops implications drawn from Paul Virilio's work on the idea of speed. Luke begins with a brief description of the 66 satellite, Motorola-led Iridium project, which will provide large-bandwidth digital communications facilities at 3 dollars a minute (available anywhere throughout the world) to any user with the basic technical facilities. Whilst this project does not in itself effect a new revolution, it nonetheless highlights the increasing compression of time and value in an 'omnipolitan' society of completed modernity, where 'nature is gone for good'. Luke explores the cultural consequences of this 'flowmational' acceleration. For him, reality melts down into a 'just in time' fluid environment, in which binaries of animate and inanimate, factual and virtual, implode into a 'sharing of perception'. The flow of acceleration diminishes the temporal space essential for judgement and discrimination. Luke works through a series of examples in which a second and third 'nature' fuse and challenge all somatic limitations: the identification of humankind with motor and the total institution become normative in the deterritorialized habitation of 'uprooted man'.

In Chapter eleven, Hilary Radner challenges the idea that ethics must be based in a static and considered space of judgement, and argues instead for the possibility of an ethics of speed. Drawing on Foucault's later work, she locates ethics, not in a transcendental moment of judgement, but in our fleeting forms of life, in ever faster changing forms of life. For Radner, slowing down and freezing a transcendental space of judgement is impossible. There is no turning back from the present age of compression and of constant change. Given this condition, the central question for Radner is where the ethical might be located. Radner's particular focus is on feminism and fashion. Drawing on analyses of cultural artefacts ranging from CNN to MTV, from *Vogue* and *Harper's Bazaar* to Baywatch, Radner takes to task second wave feminism's apparent rejection of consumer and popular cultures and argues that the 1970s second wave endorsement of 'the less the more', a minimalist ethics of consumption, was nonetheless a strategy integral to consumer culture. In discussion of Pamela Anderson (and with reference to Susan Bordo), Radner maintains that feminism can envisage more complex phenomena in popular culture than simple female victimization. Radner then argues with Foucault (and his work on the ethics of the ancients) that the deconstruction of a transcendental subjectivity of judgement still leaves open the possibility of an immanent, self-constructing subjectivity. Thus, in the absence of the possibility of judgement in a timeless auratic culture, Radner conceives an ethics of *'fugit hora'*, an ethics that keeps pace with a constantly changing fashion, an ethics at one with the flight of time.

## History, Time and Spacescapes

In the first of three penultimate chapters, Elizabeth Ermarth points to the culturally-willed indeterminacy of the terms 'modern' and 'postmodern', and to the problematic third term, 'time'. Ermarth seeks to unpack the 'humanist construction' of time as 'neutral' medium through an examination of the art of the *Quattrocento*. She approaches this through consideration of the system of perspective in Renaissance art which provided a neutral spatial common denominator (a single point), to which corresponded 'history' as its temporal counterpart. Ermarth challenges Roland Barthes' reading of the Dutch painter Pieter Saenredam's vacant church interiors as confident nihilism: their very purpose is to act as bearer for overarching generalizations about 'neutral space and neutral time'. This dominant view of history as a neutral time - radically divorced from the heroic narrative - has itself, she argues, undergone deconstruction in the course of the twentieth century. The new temporal regime is bound to the 'phrase'. In the 'grammars' of the *langues* applied and enacted in the *paroles* of life is to be found the potential and raw material of self-construction, in the more modest vision that succeeds the infinite neutralities of modernity.

Further historical reflections are pursued in Chapter thirteen by Roland Robertson, who addresses the recent reconfiguration of world history as *global* history. He develops an historical sociology in which he addresses the following question: should history or sociology become its real focal point? He embarks upon a critique of American global historiography and how it attempts to incorporate 'new imaginings' that might move beyond the sterile juxtaposition of Enlightenment universalism and Third World particularism. Robertson argues against Michael Geyer and Charles Bright's account of a chaotic heterogeneity of all the world's pasts in the simultaneous present of a postmodern globality. He stresses that it is precisely the *interpenetration* of universalising and particularising tendencies that has to be the focal point of understanding. Globalization theory, understood as *glocalization*, should be an indispensable tool for the historian. Geyer and Bright, Robertson argues, 'remain victims of the very form of world history that they have sought to discredit'. He proposes, instead, a distinctive form of reflexive consciousness. Drawing on the work of Georg Simmel, Robertson posits a sociological historiography which occupies a *tertium quid*, a flexible global historical intermediate between history understood as providential or progressive movement, and history as Spenglerian cycle.

In Chapter fourteen, Barbara Adam shifts register from past to future and offers a temporal analysis of science and value. Adam works from a contrast between Max Weber and Ulrich Beck. Initially, she criticizes Weber's separation of fact and value in which science is understood as an autonomous realm, operating in a quasi-Newtonian framework. This placement also assumes a radical dualism between time, on the one hand, and value, on the other. Adam, notes with Beck, a possible emerging 'disautonomization' of science, one in which fact and value, and hence time and value, are no longer separated. If fact and value are separate, then science in association with industry, can deny responsibility for the consequences of both science and technology. Paradoxically, in this context Weber's separation of spheres leads to an ethics of irresponsibility rather than one of responsibility. Only if science becomes reflexive, in looking at its own rootedness in value judgements, and engaging with the consequences of its products for technology and the environment, is any ethics of science possible. This chapter scrutinizes some of the dualistic assumptions associated with the public perception of this valorized knowledge and traces their origins. It shows the limitations of those assumptions for the capacity of contemporary societies to achieve 'true', uncontested knowledge on the one hand, and desired results from action on the other. From a perspective of 'timescape', distinctions between facts and values, objectivity and subjectivity, space and time, past and future, are dissolved in their irreconcilable oppositions: the temporal realm of socio-environmental praxis is thus re-articulated in a new form.

## Reflections on Roots and Options

This volume has come a long way in the relation of time and value to politics, from Grosz's thoughts on violence and the political to Lash's on a Benjaminian politics of melancholy to the much more concrete notions of time and politics expressed by Adam. This juxtapositioning of transmuted times and transformed values is further pursued in the volume's final chapter by Boaventura de Sousa Santos. Santos speaks of a modern dualism between 'roots', on the one hand, and 'options', on the other. It is important to note that Santos's modernity is not Marshall Berman's (and Marx's) 'all that is solid melts into air', a fluidity of options, but comprises of multiple tensions that exist between 'roots' and 'options'. Here, roots tend towards unitary, apparently cohesive origins, whereas options are pluralities. Roots operate in a spatial temporal logic, options melt temporal fixities. Roots look to the past, options towards the future. Roots are fixed, options are open. Roots speak in the idiom of value, options in the idiom of temporality. Two examples follow. In politics, the grounding of the social contract makes possible an open ended political sphere, and in epistemology a Newtonian-Cartesian foundationalism opened up entire continents of scientific exploration. The dualistic temporality of roots and options enters into crisis on the cusp of the new Millennium, where it yields new 'baroque codes' in which roots become options and options roots. Here, what were previously roots, such as national identity and sexuality, become 'overexposed' as options in multiculturalism and sexuality construed as choice. Nature, once conceived in the (option) language of science, is now simultaneously grasped as root. Santos argues that the politics of the conversion of options into roots, of contingency into stability, under postmodern conditions, takes place through a process of 'canonization'. Baroque codes of canonization work, not through overexposure, but systematic 'underexposure'. The 'canonization' of a discourse or practice takes place, Santos notes, through the inclusion and exclusion of rivals, not primarily through argument, but through 'intensification' on 'dogmatic' grounds. This can have deeply conservative implications, such as in the literary canon, whose arbiters include the likes of Allan Bloom. Conversely, progressive and radical initiatives may also be 'canonized' and here Santos gives examples of 'The Common Heritage of Mankind' codified in international law to protect the environment and heritage sites of common value.

# Concluding Timeliness: Third Millennial Geopolitics

What, in conclusion, Santos directs our attention to is highly significant for a rethinking of contemporary politics. Canonization is at the same time institutionalization. The millennial paradigm in which roots become options and options roots, is much more than a mere restatement of contingency. It describes an age that expresses new modes of institutionalization. The 1980s and 1990s bequeath to us a global information culture, in which the order and certainties of an earlier national manufacturing society are thrown into disorder. This disorder was first associated with a reconstructed Right inaugurated by the Reagan/Thatcher compact, in which the free market and instrumental choice were the dominant principles. But in the twilight of the twentieth-century, new leaders command the world stage: Fernando Henrique Cardoso in Brazil, Carlos Salinas in Mexico, Bill Clinton in USA, Tony Blair in Britain, and now it seems Gerhard Schroeder in Germany. These leaders appear comfortable in, and with, the idiom of informationalization. They realize that the global economy is a foregone conclusion and not one that can be resisted. They appear at ease with the expanded role for markets. They seem happy with forms of multiculturalism. They accept and think with the contingency that necessitates chronic innovation in the world economy. Yet there is a certain commitment to equality, toleration and multiculturalism, to openness. These are not figures of the traditional Right; they are prepared to mix and meld.

In an age of chronic change, what sort of *institutions* can provide the best structure for this contingency? In a world in which we are aware that science, the state, the welfare state, the law, urban planning, inevitably produce a host of unintended consequences does not mean we should have followed Niklas Luhmann (or more prosaically Lady Thatcher) and that we should refuse to work out programs for the future. It does not imply that we should refuse or dismantle institutions, but that we should evolve institutions that provide the best possible response for unintended consequences. This, to draw on Barbara Adam in Chapter fourteen, is what institutional reflexivity must become. It involves the disautonomization of institutions, it includes science and government, and the welfare state and law. This is a disautonomization in which institutions are no longer exonerated from responsibility by the metaphysical divorce of fact from value, as in the facts of the law, the facts of science, the facts of a political practice, or even the facts of the market as institution. Institutions must be more embedded in the practice led values of everyday life. This demands that institutions become more reflexive, both in the construal and construction of their own positions and in responsibility for the consequences of their agency – both envisioned and unknown. It involves institutions in examining their own value bases, and not conceiving themselves in terms divorced from these value-groundings. In sum, *it means an end to the separation of time and value.*

These institutions will, of necessity, be supra-national as are the European Union, the United Nations, international law, trade organizations, the International Labour Organisation, the world intellectual property rights organization, and regulation by supra-national accounting and banking bodies. These institutions must, at the same time, instantiate the universal, the global in the particular. At issue are a set of institutions that represent, as Roland Robertson noted in Chapter thirteen, a possible third way between the universalization of the global marketplace, and the untrammelled particularism of the ayatollahs and the irrationalists acting at the 'core'. At stake, therefore, is a third way between the reproduction of the multinationals and the global free market, and the destruction and disintegration occasioned by the irrationalist particularisms. Such a third way of managed chaos in a disordered order should allow not merely the reproduction but, in the words of Alain Touraine, the *'production* of society'. Such a programme will involve the reflexive disautonomization of the universal into the particular, that is into the sphere of values. Historically speaking, chaos and contingency have been relegated to the 'outside', while order has structured the 'inside'. In an age of contingency, we require the chaos of inclusion, and systematically deroutinising institutions. There is a need and future for community, but there is no retreat from individualization. We thus require institutions which simultaneously provide individualization and equality. Hence the overwhelming and central importance of education.

In this collection there are many themes and topics, most of which are frozen for a moment, but which, in reality, are witness to an as yet unconsolidated flux of New Millennial change. At issue is nothing less than a Third Millennial politics. If the first Millennium featured a relatively ordered sphere of the sacred while the profane was steeped in contingency, and in the second Millennium, as Weber noted, order was transferred to the profane, then what will happen in a third Millennium in which contingency triumphs over order and flourishes in new recompositions of 'sacred' and 'profane'? In this 'indifferentiation', such symbols as the Millennium Dome provide theatres of self-definition; but it would be naive to imagine that this is a process that involves a 'forgetting of power' and the absence of 'hegemonic pathways' (Clegg 1989, p. 275). Like the as-yet genderless giant planned for the Dome, much awaits definition; but this definition is, like the managerialization of global society, planned – dictated – from the centre. A Third Millennial politics demands, not only the representation of many 'others', but a hard-won, even ethnographic, illumination of the transforming, temporal textures of such change. This collection, challenging, multi-layered, multi-stranded, finds times and values in their multiple frames: this is one way in which to construe a fluid, yet embedded reflexivity, and to specify millennial modernity.

## References

Clegg, Stuart 1991: *Frameworks of Power*, London, Sage.

# Catastrophic Times

Alphonso Lingis
Pennsylvania State University

## The Order of Time

How strange that the sequoias of California which live 2,500 years, die. The sequoias are gigantic poles which compulsively rise to the very limit (350 feet) beyond which capillary action can no longer pull the weight of a tube of sap. All this to spread to the sun a few scraggly branches and clumps of needles. A few years from their birth they are mostly dead; more than 90% of their weight is the dead wood of the core. Lightning has struck each of them innumerable times, burning at that dead wood, without killing them. For nothing, until humans invented chain saws, can kill a sequoia. When they die, they die of a natural death. Their seeds were, from the start, programmed that they live 2,500 years and then die. There is an inner duration, a lifetime, intrinsic to the natures of all living things. Whenever we see plants or animals we see infancy, youth, maturity, aging, and dying.

The configuration of perception in living things does not solely rely on vision and touch, its formation does not depend upon things at hand. There is no perception without a perception of time. Plants have no recourse but to undergo whatever befalls them (rain and sunshine or scorching sun and tornadoes), but animals which can move can flee. They feel fear, they sense they are vulnerable, they have a sense of the imminence of their death. Those that care for their progeny, as those who do not, have a sense of their own infancy and of the infancy of their offspring. They see, in their own species and in other species, infancy, youth, maturity, aging, and dying. This biological time, intrinsic to their natures, can be transformed into a field of action in some organisms. Work circumscribes and structures time.

A human primate detaches something – a loose stone, a branch, a pipe wrench – from the continuity of the natural or fabricated environment about him. She detaches herself with her tool and shifts her view from the environment continuous with her body to goals or results beyond it. He begins to anticipate and to remember. Between the goals or results and her tool she sees a relationship of means and end, cause and effect. The identification of distinct substances, and the understanding of a relationship between means and ends and between causes and effects, is the core of reason. Everyone who works is rational. Without memory what we call knowledge is not possible; without anticipation action is not possible.

Knowledge is not given to us in a sudden illumination of the mind; to know is to strive, to work. We learn that this stone, chipped, can serve to cut and to chop, that stone, blunted, can serve to grind. We learn that this is iron, that is sulfur, by putting them successively in reactions with other substances. To know is to know how; we do not truly know an object until we know how to make it.

We work in order to maintain, secure, or acquire what we take to be a good. Goods, as the goals and results of actions, are durable goods; they must at least endure the time it takes to reach or take possession of them. And they should contribute to the conservation and preservation of those who acquire them. Something acquires value by being promised in the future, in time, and by withstanding, and helping us withstand, the passing of time, by enduring.

The human primate makes of himself a tool; he inserts himself into the field of work and reason, as an implement that can be used to reach ends, a cause that produces effects. The order of means and foreseen results, of causes and effects, enters into her. His mind turns into a place where his limbs and senses are subordinated to purposes, where his present consciousness is subordinated to an anticipation of the future. What has come to pass in her body (her strength, her skills) and in her mind (her memories) are subordinated to the future. His enterprise, all his efforts, require the future to make sense.

The one who works maintains a sense of individual identity by envisioning herself in the future. I identify what I am doing by specifying what I shall be doing. It is tomorrow that gives its sense to whatever I do today; it is tomorrow that gives its sense to whatever I am today. The one who works envisages the others as collaborators – or as obstructers. Like tools, they stand detached and destined for results and products, for a future. Their tasks, their results and products, their futures, give them individual identities. The others envisage us as collaborators – or as obstructers. They speak to us, envisaging our identity, our future and our past.

Words have valences and extend lines of expectation. The speaker begins with a particle, or an adjective, or a title, which make the listener expect a certain kind of noun or name, which has a valence for certain kinds of adjectives and verbs. As a speaker utters one word after another they extend a narrow and more precise line of cohesion and coherence.

Words designate things that we do not see but could see, things that are only possible, things that we could manipulate or produce. They establish cohesion and coherence between things noted in the past and things anticipated in the future. Words extend the intelligible time, first opened in our field of work, to the fields of work of others, and outward to the limits of the universe. The words addressed to us establish and require cohesion and coherence in us. 'Last week you said you would ... ' 'But you are now a mother ... ' 'But you just said that ... ' The interlocutor seeks coherence, a line of intelligibility, in the phases and states of our duration. He and she seek to link up our past with the present, to know the future as that to which what we say now commits us.

When we respond to these demands, our words bind our past and present to our future. 'I said that, but what I meant was ... ' 'Yes, I am now a mother, but that does not mean I am giving up my course work at the university'. 'Yes, last week I said I would, but here is what I found out that makes me think we should do this instead'.

There is a specific sense of elation in declaring, pledging, committing oneself with such words. We feel the power of words we utter to others, but also implant them in ourselves. We feel their power to remain there, as causal forces, and determine effects, though a profusion of distractions, incidental events, and forgetting of them will intervene until then.

Work extends, circumscribes, and delimits a zone of time. The future is articulated as a field of possibilities, the past as a field of resources retained in our know-how and skills. In work, we perceive processes and transitions in our environment, we envision effects and results. Measurement marks equivalences in the processes and transitions. Work is measurable as a half-day's job, a day's work. The movement of sand down an hour-glass, of a pointer round a dial, can be marked in hours, minutes, seconds, nanoseconds.

Whenever movements and changes are viewed as transitions from one form to another, and transitions that themselves have a graspable form, then it is the forms we envision and not the transitions as such. Time is shut up in the permanence of forms or in changes that are foreseen. Movements inscribed within an order congeal time in a system of measures and equivalences. Equivalences are virtually interchangeable. A day, as a day, is interchangeable with another day, an hour with another hour. This equivalence and interchangeability of measurable segments of time make the events that take place in them appear from the first as repeatable, reversible, repairable. To inspect the time of the world is to see to what extent the succession of things shall be or can be repeated, varied, and reversed. Work is possible only in intelligible time. Time became intelligible through work.

## Catastrophe

Death strikes. Death suddenly strikes down a collaborator. Death does not annihilate him; the body is there and takes up as much space as before. But death, violently and at one blow, destroyed this worker's future and stripped of their meaning not only the task or enterprise she was developing when it struck, but retroactively all the enterprises she had undertaken and which had this task as their result. Death strikes in the now, and immediately drives its shock wave into the future and down the past of that life, rendering not only inoperative but senseless, the order and system that had come to pass, whose endurance and momentum was shaping the emergence of goals and results. Death struck, reducing to nothing the instrument she had made of herself in the world of work, reducing to nothing her individual identity. He fell from the scaffolding of his half-built house. She died from an infection picked up in the emergency room. His half-finished house, her half-finished medical education appear as intensive efforts that, had this outcome been known, would never have been made.

When someone we know dies, we weep: it is impossible that he or she should be dead. We say over and over again, 'I can't believe it'. It is unthinkable that this companion, this associate is dead; to think of him, of what he was, is to think of him as a being whom we identified from the meaning the field of tasks before him and the future ahead of him gave him. Whenever we now think of her, we cannot think of her purely and simply annihilated; we can only think that she, nonetheless, is in some other form. To think of him at all is inevitably to think of his image, his ghost, his soul still involved in his concerns. If we think of our dead parent or lover, we inevitably think of her watching us or speaking to us as she used to do. We think how proud our father would have been to see us at this law school graduation; we see again, in a spasm of horror or shame, our dead lover as we sell his motorcycle to pay for computer programming lessons. But this sense of his or her continuing existence is accompanied by the knowledge that death has annihilated the future and its possibilities and tasks for him or her. The ghost or soul we visualize when we think of the dead one is a trembling, vacillating vision that darkens the world of work and reason.

When death strikes it annihilates a future of possibilities and dangers that was being extended from the present; it annihilates a past that was being retained by memory and that gave force and direction to the movement of the present. It makes the time in which it occurs appear as the empty endurance of the void. The death that strikes this associate of ours, and the death that strikes someone else elsewhere, are events that are separated by stretches of duration. The later death is not the effect or the result of the earlier one. The deaths that come to pass do not come to be, do not accumulate like resources. The expanse of duration between them is empty of them.

Is not duration, beneath or without any things that endure and that pass and without any processes, time itself? But time as the empty endurance of the void is not given in a separate intuition. It is given in an event. A catastrophic event which annihilates a companion and annihilates all his future and also all his past, leaving but his corpse to endure. We can call this sense of the empty endurance of the void, the sense of catastrophic time.

The death of a collaborator also gives us an unnerving premonition of a like violence – a heavy or sharp tool that slips, an automobile collision, a microbe – that can abruptly befall in our time and space of work and reason and annihilate, with our future, all the significance of our past. A violent blow can destroy all our future and past without destroying the present, as when an automobile accident or disease paralyzes the hand of a musician or a young surgeon.

The one who acquires individual identity in his or her work fears for the corner of the world of work and reason upon which he or she was building the project and the enterprises of his or her life. Violence may erupt in a fellow human, a fellow worker, who strikes out amok and abruptly destroys our future. A war breaks out, and we find ourselves drafted into the front lines, or a foreign power, without declaring war, begins shelling and bombing civilian towns and homes about us. A revolution breaks out, and in the fever of revolution, we throw our investments, our homes, our families, our lives into the chaos and violence of revolution.

We cannot imagine our dead companion and imagine him annihilated, but we cannot imagine our death without imagining ourselves cast into the cold brilliance of the empty endurance of the void. But in dying we are not liberated into the abyss of empty time; we sink into the dead weight of a corpse. Fatigue and aging, which make us feel encumbered, held back in the spring of our initiatives by the weight of our bodies, make us feel already the corpse death will turn us into. A wound that infects makes us see, smell, and feel the decomposition and corruption already at work in our bodies. For us to die is to sink into the putrefaction of a corpse which stains and renders foul the environment, its stench filling the choking air. The solid world of things that irresistibly determined one another and that excluded the I that separated itself from those things, now rejects the corpse this I sinks into. We die like dogs, befouling the ground and poisoning the atmosphere.

It is not only our death that destroys all the structure of intelligible time in our lives. Our life can be so allied to our child, where everything we do is energized by the future of that child, that when that child is killed in a hit-and-run accident, not only his future but our own and our past are devastated. Our life can be so allied to our lover, that when a stray bullet in a street leaves our lover paralyzed and in an iron lung, whatever undertakings had extended a future for us, as well as all our strengths for them, are also obliterated. Sometimes it is some nameless and unidentifiable anxiety that cuts an untraversable abyss before any promises or lures beckoning to us from the future and makes of our life an empty desolation.

The time that orders a progression of future, present, and past in which we work appears to us to be linear. It also appears to us to be superficial, to exist on the surface of things and on the surface of earth. It appears superficial when a catastrophe reveals the time of the empty endurance of the void. The empty endurance of the void appears to us to be deep, the void an abyss. This time exists in the core of the earth.

There is the work that detaches things from the surface of the earth – plants, animals, branches and loose stones used as tools. We detach ourselves by standing back, supported by the expanse of the surface of Earth. Work broke through a radically new dimension when we began to work with fire. The first fires to be detached appeared on the surface of Earth, but they came from the storm clouds, and seemed to bring to concentration the inner heat of the ground. At length workers began to disembowel the earth, to pull forth from it ores to be smelted with fire into iron and bronze. Fire and iron made more effective tools, they especially made devastating weapons. Before, individuals had turned their tools as weapons on one another; now a torch thrown burns down a whole hamlet and its field crops, a raid with metal weapons disembowels everybody who fights and also all those who flee. Raids, pillages, disembowelments with fire and iron erupted catastrophe in settlements.

We work on Earth's crust; above us is the sun that radiates, that is in flames, that explodes, and about us the earth's surface is covered with the flowers of plants, of mosses, prairies, and trees, that break forth and brighten the earth with the brief incandescence of their petals. We see that the movements of Earth's substance – shifting continental plates, earthquakes, volcanic eruptions – are catastrophic for all living organisms on them. In earthquakes, geysers, and volcanic eruptions, as in the lightning that sinks into it, we sense all the inner incandescence of our planet. We sense that only on the surface is the earth a crust that can be turned into enduring goods; that beneath the deepest mines there is the incandescent inner core of explosive fire that makes us realize that our Earth is a particle of the sun, separated from the sun by catastrophic explosion. We see that it is in the midst of a cosmic catastrophic time that our work extends its transitory and vulnerable intelligible time.

## Working in the Imminence of Catastrophe

The corpse is there, it has to be washed, the casket has to be selected and paid for, a hall has to be hired and a meal arranged for those who will come to the funeral. A preacher will be hired to extract some real or imagined impulses some of the family and friends recall from the life that was snuffed out before it got anywhere, and deck them with the name of exemplary virtues. Willy-nilly, we bridge over the catastrophe, as though it were but a temporary setback in the open road of intelligible time.

Back from the funeral, we think we felt the grim reaper swing close, and waiting now for us. Anxiety before the imminent and inescapable annihilation awaiting us is warded off by establishing control over our life and field of operations, by projecting an advance representation of what each day brings, and by measuring our enterprises to our forces.

Sensing the inevitable catastrophe ahead of us, we determine to keep its shadow completely out of the intelligible and productive time of work and reason. We arrange our home and our situation and our workday in such a way that those once-in-a-lifetime situations which would require all of our forces, forces which may prove wanting, do not occur. We retain, behind the forms of our routine, a reserve of force for the tasks that will recur the next day. We retain, behind the forms of our thought and speech, a reserve of unused mental energy; we settle into an occupation that presents only mental tasks that we have already contracted the mental skills for. We avoid problems at the farthest limits of mathematics or physics or politics for which no solution has ever been formulated by thinkers, and for which our mind may prove wanting. We retain, behind the coded forms of our feelings, of our pleasures and our angers, our affections and our annoyances, a reserve of force so that we will be able to respond emotionally to like events and like situations that recur. We arrange our zone of activities and our travels in such a way as to avoid once-in-a-lifetime situations that would require all our passion, and which might prove wanting. We avoid going to places utterly unlike any other, which would leave us wholly astonished, with an astonishment that could never recur again. We immediately compare each city and each landscape and each building with cities and landscapes and buildings we have seen before and others we still see, so that we can frame our feeling in the forms and confines of feelings we can repeat indefinitely. We avoid situations and adventures in which we might be overwhelmed with a total and totally new joy, sensing that we could never know such a joy again. We avoid encounters in which we might fall into a total and exhaustive love; we seek out instead people others might also fall in love with, and we love our partner as others love like partners, with a love that we could reactivate for another partner should we lose this one. There are situations that could only be lived once; were we to expend all our forces on an adventure, discharge all our mental powers on a problem, empty out all the love in our heart and sensibility on a woman or a man unlike any other, we die with that adventure, that problem, that love. We sense that; we instinctually arrange our lives so that the tasks and the tools and the problems and the encounters will recur the same each day, we avoid the limits.

The sense of what is of value is what endures across time, but also what may be undermined by time. Goods, as the goals and results of actions, are durable goods; they must at least endure the time it takes to reach or take possession of them. Their endurance should contribute to the conservation and preservation of those who acquire them. But it could also be that all the possibilities of the future and all the resources and momentum of our past are drained into the present. It is then that being and value coincide.

It can be that the sense of imminent (and inevitable) disaster drive us totally and resolutely into the intelligible time of work. Sensing the imminence of a fatal accident that would annihilate all our forces, we resolve to commit them all in the time present. We commit all the forces formed and shaped by events past, and which give their skill, sensitivity, and momentum to the present work. And we make the work before us to be done the condensation of all the works we ever wanted or shall want to accomplish. A jazz musician sets all the concerns of others aside to improvise his own song now, with the sense that he does not have time for concern about business investments, does not have time to spend reading the newspapers about the Japanese economy, does not have time to get a teaching job teaching the music of others to others, has to make his music now, out of the acute sense that he is mortal. He improvises with all the context of his birth in a certain family, a certain ethnic group, a certain neighborhood, and puts into his improvization all the yearnings, hopes, heartbreaks, that have shaped his sensibility. A gymnast goes to the bars and rings each day with the sense that she was born with this exceptional body, in this place on the planet where the gym and the trainer are available, and does not have time to take a full liberal arts course, does not have time this afternoon to go to the picnic with her housemates, because the gymnast in her will be dead by the age of twenty-one.

The guerrilla sees all that is possible for his country in this revolutionary moment, and all that is possible for him, and takes all that he has lived through and suffered and learned from childhood to have prepared him for his decisive and dangerous mission. The one who resolves to act in history determines to fit her own whole field of work, of possibilities and resources, into the broad time of history. The possibilities for which she marshals her own resources are not possibilities that will become actual for her but for her comrades and for the next generation after the victory has been won, perhaps a victory in which she will leave her life.

Thus the sense of the imminence of disaster gives us the sense of the time of our own life. I see the trajectory of time from my birth to my death on which I situate all the initiatives of my life. I act to resolutely bring the momentum of all that has come to pass in me in my acts, and extend my acts until their own ends. What Heidegger called authentic (authentifying) time is a life that lives and works in the imminence of catastrophe. What he calls *Zum-Tode-Sein*, being-toward death, is a living and working in the face of death, despite death, in the postponement of death. It is finding the force to live and work despite the imminence of catastrophe and because of the imminence of catastrophe. The sense of coming to an end, of ending, is what gives my life the sense of ends, and makes me determine initiatives that are determinate. The imminence of catastrophe is what makes me marshal all the resources that have come to pass, come to be in me, and release all my forces in my action.

## The Plunge into Catastrophic Time

Every fatal accident in the factory, or on the highway coming back from the office, we witness, we pull our minds back to where we have to go tonight, and back to steering this car now. We awaken, after the heart attack, and find ourselves paralyzed on one side and half blind; as the shock thins out, we begin to think of how we will manage. In the hospital now, coming to the realization that we will most likely not leave it alive, we think of disposing of our savings for the use of those who will survive us. We lay out works that will consume our lives, and count that there will be others for whom maintaining the fertility of this farm, building these office buildings, writing books will be significant – will be results and goals which will serve as resources for further results and goals. Ecologists today speak urgently of the steps that will have to be taken lest pollution, destruction of the ozone shield, the greenhouse effect, put an end to our life, even all life, on this planet. Astrophysicists, who speak of the inevitable extinction of our sun, hold open the possibility that we may well be able to colonize other planetary systems about other stars by then. They count on thought, on scientific-technological thought, that arose and arises out of work, and thinks in the service of work.

Though the sense of imminent (and inevitable) disaster drive us totally and resolutely into the intelligible time of work, the time of work cannot seal off the heavy or sharp tool that may fall, the automobile collision, the microbe, the violence that seizes a collaborator or a passerby, and that drop us into the time of the empty endurance of void. The catastrophic time does not only devastate us; it can also strangely hold us, and even draw us into it. After a disaster, one rebuilds one's life – in the intelligible time of futurity. But there are drives in us that find the force to let themselves be drawn into catastrophe, that live in catastrophic events.

We had long planned this trip to New Orleans, California, Paris, or India. There, our education would flower, we would find the exciting people, we would find a real life, we would find love or enlightenment. But once there, we found the streets, the buildings, the roads, the landscapes alien and indifferent to us. No opportunities opened up before us. We did not connect with people, find friends or a lover. The streets, buildings, and landscapes looked bleak and harsh to those who lived there. The men and women looked preoccupied and weary, their routine lives without urgency or glamour, empty and sad. We who had left our post at a job and our place in a mediocre community found our life diminished just by observing the barrenness of people living in these narrow confines, the pedestrian neighborhoods and landscapes that had been so mythologized. We found ourselves in a state of detachment and anxiety, disconnected from any initiative or adventure there and feeling the emptiness of our days.

It was the end of the day, it was raining, we were seated in a bus. We were not on a trip to any goal – only having to get to our rented room again this night. We looked out of the bus window into the rain and the fog. And then our eyes got absorbed in the form of the trees emerging from the fog, their branches almost bare of leaves now with the oncoming of the winter. The sprawling of their branches was each time different, not foreseeable, and as they emerged into view they were already passing out of view forever. Memory retained no hold on them. Along with the patterns, without meaning or function, of the trees emerging and passing back into the fog, we feel the empty endurance of the void. The bare branches emerging and fading away filled all our consciousness, such that we no longer felt a separation between them and ourselves. We found ourselves in a kind of spell, from which everything fell away but the emergence of the trees and their dissolution in the fog. We felt desolate, barren, alone, but the strangeness of these barely substantial trees in the fog brought in a sense of gentle melancholy and a kind of wistful serenity.

The Pacific coast of Peru is narrow, walled in on one side by the Andes, and exposed on the other to the Pacific Ocean, kept cold all year round by the Humboldt Current coming up from Antarctica. The air over this coastal strip, heated by the sun, expands out over the cold ocean, such that moisture from the ocean does not drift back over the land. It never rains; most of this coastal plain is drier than the Sahara. To the south the area is geologically very unstable, you cross the stony desert utterly devoid of vegetation, even of cactus, stretches of white volcanic tuff poured out by some 85 volcanoes. You reach the brink of the Colca Canyon; it is the deepest canyon on planet earth. At the bottom winds a river, fed both by melting snows from the Andes and by deep ground water. How wrong Hume was to declare that causality is a mental diagram we construct and project over material reality, which is present and nothing but present. Here one cannot see without seeing causality. Without seeing the successive layering of rock and lava, the cross-sections cut in them and the scalloping of the exposed edges by the shifting of the continental plates and wind and water erosion across millennia. The small crumbling of grit under your shoes, your slow and wearing descent into the canyon measures the time of your effort and of your life against the geological epochs of the planet's crust and rock layers. The scale of the Andes and the canyon diminish you, but also the scale of geological time diminishes you and destines what footprints you leave here, indeed what works you build in your lifetime, to erosion and mineral decomposition.

There are some Indian hamlets at the bottom of the Canyon, Indians who had been passed over by the Inca empire and are too alien and too poor to be enlisted in the Peruvian state today. You are able to find lodging for the night. You are awakened several hours before sunrise, and led by your Indian guide up the river and then up the Canyon wall. By the time the sun has risen you have reached the point where the Canyon is deepest. The Grand Canyon of Colorado is 1,638 meters at its deepest; here the Colca Canyon is 4,174 meters deep. It is also very narrow, a knife cut through twelve thousand feet of granite, at the bottom of which like a mercury wire you see the river. All around, the glaciers of the Andes begin to blaze with the rising sun. Billowing in the sky are the sulfurous fumes of the smoldering volcano you passed hours ago in the dark. You are seated a very long time on a boulder in this arid, uninhabitable, inhuman mountainscape. No human enterprise could take hold here; you yourself could form no project here, not even an exploratory hike. Even if you had any shreds of vocabulary of his language or yours in common, you would not have anything to say to your Indian companion, not even any question to ask him. The discursive movements of the mind, staking out paths, laying out positions, counterpositions, are silenced, deadened. As soon as the sun has emerged over the peaks of the Andes, it turns the whole cloudless sky magnesium-white. Its radiation spreads over your face and hands like warmth, even though the thin air your heaving lungs were pumping in was cold. After a long time spent motionless, you are aware the sun is now high in the sky.

And then, well before seeing them, you are aware of the condors, like a silent drum-roll in the skies over the glaciers. First one alone, a speck that mesmerized your eyes in the empty radiance of the sky, imperceptibly becoming bigger, never once flapping or even shifting its wings, soaring down from a great height and then into the Canyon, coming at eye level in front of you before gradually descending deeper and becoming lost to sight. It is the first time you have seen a condor, with its fifteen feet wingspan the largest flying bird on the planet; this one brown, a young female. From a vast height it was surveying the desolate cliffs and avalanches for carrion. And then, how much later – an hour? two hours? – there were two, again you knew they were there, silent drum roll over the Andes, you knew where they were long before they were visible. They were soaring close to one another, circling one another companionably in the airless heights. When they were overhead, you tried to gauge the depth of the Canyon, and judged they were above you halfway again the depth of the Canyon – that is, some 18,000 feet. You, who could hardly climb much higher than your present 13,000 feet, felt your eyes, your craving, your fascination plunging to their height, falling up into the region of death.

You are nothing but a vision, a longing, a euphoric outflow of life hanging on to the flight of the condors. The soaring of the condors comes from a past without memory and slides into a future without anticipation. You are cut loose, unanchored, without guy wires, drifting in the void of the sky. You know nothing but the flight of the condors, feel nothing but the thin icy air, see nothing but the summits and ice cliffs of the Andes and the granite walls of the Canyon now below your flight. You are alive to nothing but their bodies and their flight, you are alive for nothing but for them.

The catastrophic time, empty endurance of the void, breaks out in nakedness. No doubt the abrupt denuding of someone in our presence is a small hiatus in the time of our everyday work. Yet the dense chains of taboos forged over human nudity in our society, and in all known societies, bear witness to the catastrophic effect denuding has been felt to have, has been found to have on the world of work and reason and on the sane identity of functional citizens.

When we go out in the street, or open our door to someone who knocked, we see someone who has first washed the traces of the night, the anonymity and abandon of the night, from his or her face, has rearranged the turmoil of his or her hair, and has chosen clothing for his or her departure into the public spaces. He and she have selected clothing to identify him or herself under classifications: he or she dresses punk or preppie, worker or executive, inner city or suburban, he dresses up in business suit or dresses down in jeans, she puts on a pearl necklace or a neckchain of Hopi Indian beads. He and she also dress today like he and she did yesterday and last year; she maintains the two-piece crisp look of an active woman with responsibilities, a business executive, he wears a plaid shirt and jeans even when visiting the city or coming to our dinner party. When we see him or her wearing a T-shirt or sweat shirt with Penn State on it, we see someone who is not only dressing in the uniform of a college student, but who has dressed his or her movements, thoughts, and reactions with those of a dormitory rat or a sorority sister. We also see in the uniform the uniformity of a series of actions, undertakings, thoughts, opinions, feelings maintained for weeks, months, years, and predictable for the weeks, months, years ahead. We see the time of endurance, and respond to it.

But she or he undressed before our eyes. Whether in our bedroom with the door closed, or only in the locker room of the gym, she or he exposes a nakedness that we cannot keep our eyes off, even if only with furtive glances. In denuding her and himself, she and he takes off the uniform, the categories, the endurance, and exposes the body substance in the pure chance of its shape and color. Of course in the gym-built musculature we see another kind of clothing, body-armor, uniformization, a body reshaped to fit a model. But in the slight sag of the full or undeveloped breasts, in the smooth expanse of the belly, in the contour of the ass, in the bare expanse of the inside of the upper thighs, we see flesh without memory and without initiatives, without tasks or commitments, flesh meaningless and idle. Flesh in a nudity that, Marguerite Duras writes, 'invites strangling, rape, ill-treatment, insults, cries of hatred, unleashing of whole, deadly, passions' (Duras, 1982, p. 21).

Sexual excitement surges in the shattering of built-up structures. The posture collapses, the manipulative diagrams of the limbs melt, legs and thighs roll about, fingers and hands move in aimless, endlessly repetitive caresses, allowing themselves to be stroked and crushed. The psychic structures with which we screen, block, filter out and channel the superabundance of outside stimuli that flood our senses at all times, are shattered and the stimuli flood us pell-mell. The structures by which we fix an inner ego identity, and censor out a whole underworld of unconscious drives and cravings splinter; in sexual excitement the gates of the lower dungeons are opened and unconscious drives and cravings swarm up and overwhelm our conscious intentions and purposes. Voluptuousness plunges all that is infantile, feral, violent in oneself in the other, seeking all that is disharmonious, predatory, bloodthirsty in the other.

Every breakup of equilibrium, Freud noted, has something orgasmic about it. A child falls into voluptuous abandon when it is rocked on the knees of its father or thrown into the air. You get a hard-on during the solemnity of Christmas high mass and during a funeral. When travelling you always get horny. After an accident in which you got the fright of your life, you can think of nothing but getting into the sack with your lover. In Leonard Cohen's *The Favorite Game*, two men are driving in the country, speeding, suddenly the driver swerves off the road and hurtles the car through a billboard depicting Elizabeth Taylor; on the other side he turns to the other and says: 'Did you come?'.

A year or so back, there was a hurricane roaring up the Atlantic coast, skirting New York, but heading for Boston. A few days later, a woman came up after class to tell me why she missed class. She had heard the news, and suddenly remembered her mother, who was manager of a five-star hotel in the heart of the city. Normally, of course, she did her best to not think of her mother – who wants to think about careerist yuppies? She grabbed her boyfriend, and both leapt into his car and raced to Boston, where her mother, surprised to see her, let them have a room on the top floor for the night. There, against the glass walls of the room, they waited for the eye of the hurricane to reach downtown Boston.

Whenever we witness the breakup of an equilibrium – a revolution that overturns the entire hierarchy of a society, a tornado that sweeps across Miami smashing the windows of all its banks and police stations, an enormous chunk of the ice-shelf extending off the continent of Antarctica, that breaks loose, and with the sound of a cannon-shot slips into the frazzled water into a bobbling iceberg sending a tidal wave far out into the ocean – we feel an exultant wildness churning within. Anguish is not without exhilaration when we suffer revolutions, lightning strikes, floods, shiftings of continental plates, earthquakes, volcanic eruptions within us. It is for this that you take off, leaving everything behind, heading, alone, to countries on other continents where you know nobody and speak none of the languages. Doctors and nurses can tell that few people go into life-threatening operations with nothing but panic. There is resignation, but there is also a heightened intensity of the mind, a curiosity, and an undercurrent of exhilaration. This kind of exhilaration and attraction we feel even when we sense that the catastrophe that looms will plunge us into pain and finally extinction.

There are then the exchangeable values, the goods that endure across time and that contribute to the conservation and preservation of our existence. There are also unexchangeable values, where a value is what one can die for. It is not always an object. It can be a presence, a presence without endurance, without a future. One can prize nudity above all things. One can find it impossible to imagine what it would be to keep on living and being shut off forever from any experience of female, or male, nudity.

To be sure it is strange to speak of valuing catastrophe. But something in us impels us to look beyond the present, future, and past deployed by our work, to let our eyes drift into the abyss beyond. Something in us convinces us that to do so is of value, even though there can be no question of anything being maintained, secured, or acquired.

## Value in Existing in the Universe

Is there not something catastrophic in the very nature of thought? Thought is driven by an excessive compulsion and is itself an excess over and beyond perception. We push ever further into the maelstrom of ignorance. We anticipate the coming consignment of all the psychology and economics and physics of today to the merely literary status which the science of the Middle Ages has for us. We anticipate the coming consignment of all we know to ignorance and superstition. Thought is seeing what exceeds the possibility of seeing, what is intolerable to see, what exceeds the possibility of thinking.

From the most ancient times, sages and scientists found in the stars and planets, in their fixed positions and regular orbits, the immutable order against which the transitions and processes on this planet and the future and past identified within our fields of work could be located and measured. But the factor of unity in the universe, which makes us speak of all the stars, radiations, and black holes as one universe, is only the oneness of the original explosion. The speed of the explosion was, at first, too great to allow any organization to form among the elements, there were just radiations of energy. As the force of the explosion disperses in empty space, stars form galaxies. Molar and molecular organizations appear. Here took form the organization of our solar system, and on Earth, the patterns of strata, continental plates, climate, and, very soon, the first living organisms. As the eons passed more and more complex living organisms, with their development from spores, seeds, or eggs programmed from the start. Before recorded history, we humans already conceived of the growth and reproduction of organisms, but also the movements of inorganic nature, to be regular, governed throughout by detectable and calculable laws of nature.

Yet sudden, uncontrollable events (collisions, explosions that abruptly destroy organizations, patterns, and systems) continue to occur. There are shiftings of continental plates, earthquakes, volcanic eruptions, tidal waves, avalanches, floods, lightning strikes which spread fire across savannah and forest. There are solar storms, there are meteorites that have struck earth, causing massive extinctions of most species of its life, and that may strike again. Earth itself wobbles on its axis and in its orbit, resulting in Ice Ages and massive extinctions of species of life. In outer space there are collisions of heavenly bodies. There are stars that burn out. Our sun is burning itself out as fast as it can, and is today half-way to its extinction.

Astrophysicists Fred Adams and Greg Laughlin, in a paper published in *Review of Modern Physics* (Adams and Laughlin, 1997), have constructed the hitherto most complete scientific analysis on the fate of the universe. The received astrophysical wisdom today is that there is not quite enough gravitational force exerted by all the matter in the universe to cause it to recollapse in a Big Crunch after 60 or a 100 billion years. They have projected its future to the next 200th cosmological decade – 1-followed-by-200-zeroes years from now. The current era, the Stelliferous Era, dominated by stars, began with the Big Bang 10 billion years ago. We are currently midway through this Era. It will come to an end when all the stars burn out. Our sun, 4.5 billion years old, is half-way to burning itself out. It will puff up into a red giant and then collapse into a white dwarf no bigger than Earth. In the process the sun will broil away Earth's oceans, leaving an uninhabitable cinder, which will perhaps spiral into it.

The next Era the astrophysicists name the Degenerate Era. The mass of the cosmos will be locked up in the dim dense hulks of failed, dead, exploded and collapsed stars – white dwarfs, brown dwarfs, neutron stars, and black holes. Galaxies will begin to fall apart. As the degenerate hulks collide or sweep close to each other, some will move out beyond the fringes and go careening through intergalactic space, while others fall toward the galactic centers, perhaps to be eaten by lurking black holes. White dwarfs will capture 'dark matter' particles known as WIMPS (Weakly Interacting Massive Particles), which some theorists believe constitute 90% of the mass of the universe.

Toward the end of this epoch, about 100 trillion trillion trillion years from now, the protons in the heart of every atom will begin to decay. The remaining white dwarfs and neutron stars will dissipate, converting a large fraction of the ordinary mass in the cosmos to radiation and ending the Degenerate Era. The final, Dark Era will consist in a diffuse sea of electrons, positrons, neutrinos and radiation spread tenuously across an infinitely larger region than exists today.

The effect of extending our thought this far is an irremediable desolation. Yet something in us impels us to hurl our thought that far. The thought that follows the cosmic desolation is intoxicated, polluted, infected by that desolation. The cosmic history extends before it with no possible effect on our thought, on us, than this intoxication.

# References

Adams, Fred and Laughlin, Greg 1997: A Dying Universe : The Long Term Fate and Evolution of Astrophysical Objects. *Reviews of Modern Physics*, 69 (2), pp. 337-72.

Duras, Marguerite 1982: *La Maladie de la Mort*. Paris: Editions de Minuit.

**Alphonso Lingis** is a Professor of Philosophy at the Pennsylvania State University. He is author of *Excesses: Eros and Culture* (1984), *Libido: The French Existential Theories* (1985), *Phenomenological Explanations* (1986), *Deathbound Subjectivity* (1989), *The Community of Those Who Have Nothing in Common* (1994), *Abuses* (1994), *Foreign Bodies* (1994), and *Sensation: Intelligibility in Sensibility* (1995).

# The Time of Violence: Deconstruction and Value

Elizabeth Grosz
Monash University

## 1.

In this article I am interested in exploring the ways in which we may see violence both as a positivity, and as the unspoken condition of a certain fantasy of the sustainability of its various others or opposites: peace, love and so on. Rather than simply condemning or deploring violence, as we tend to do regarding the evils of war and suffering and the everyday horrors we believe we can ameliorate, I am interested in raising the question of violence not simply where it is most obvious and manifest – in ˙ the streets, in relations between races, classes, sexes, political oppositions (though I hope what I will raise in this writing does not avoid these issues) – but also where it is less obvious, and rarely called by this name, in the domain of knowledges, reflection, thinking and writing. I pursue this task not simply to condemn violence, but to explore its constitutive role in the establishment of politics, of thought, of knowledge. For this reason: that, as intellectuals or philosophers (they are not always, or are only rarely, the same thing), we play a part in structures of various forms of violence, whether we choose to or not, not only in our daily but also in our professional and intellectual lives, but it is rare that we have the intellectual resources by which to think the level of our investment in the very violences that constitute our relations to work. I want to use some of the rather sensitive and self-conscious resources provided by Jacques Derrida to look at the very violence of writing, of thought and of knowing as the conditions of possibility and of existence of our own immersion in disciplinarity.

Although it has been commonplace to claim that Derrida, and along with him the whole of postmodernism, represents a mode of depoliticization and deflection of feminist, class and post-colonial struggles. Derrida has never written on anything other than politics and violence, even if it is also true that he does not write *only* on politics and violence. [1] I would argue that his are among the most intensely political texts of the late twentieth century, though the language he uses is not one he shares in common with political theory. He is commonly accused of blurring or immobilizing politics, of refusing to provide answers or the conditions of answers to political problems, and of reducing political to theoretical problems. In this vein, Thomas McCarthy's reading of

Derrida's politics is representative: McCarthy argues that in the long run, Derrida produces 'wholesale subversion, with no suggestion of remedies or alternatives' (McCarthy, 1989-90, p. 157), in short, that while critical and perhaps in that sense useful, it remains ironic, parodic, sceptical, negative, deconstructive, perhaps, but never adequately constructive. Able to criticize politics, but never able to positively contribute to it.

I would like to argue, contrary to this prevailing representation of Derrida's politics as a politics of negativism, of nihilism or anarchism, that he offers a profound, if unsettling reconfiguration of political activity that centers on the question of violence. It is true that he refuses to offer political advice, to provide remedies or solutions to answer the pressing needs of today. But it is the very idea that we can find a solution to problems posed by these questions, and to the problem of violence that is put under political interrogation itself. Derrida refuses the kinds of question that McCarthy, Fraser and others use to define the political; which does not mean he abandons or refuses politics but that he engages in different ways and in different questions.[2]

The nature of the violence he both articulates and mobilizes is discernible only through a careful reading of a number of texts in which he appears to be talking of other matters. The question of violence is never very far from these matters. Whenever he talks of force (*The Force of Law* in Derrida, 1990), of discord (*Différance* in Derrida, 1982), of the trace (Derrida, 1976), of dislocation (*Eating Well* in Derrida, 1991), of fraying (*Freud and the Scene of Writing* in Derrida, 1978), as well as in texts more explicitly devoted to the question of violence (*Violence and Metaphysics* in Derrida 1978, *The Violence of the Letter* in Derrida, 1979), it is with the politics of violence that Derrida deals. And moreover, while accused of either political indifference or nihilism, Derrida has addressed the more manifest and concrete political issues of violence – in relation to race and apartheid, in his writings for Nelson Mandela, in his writings on feminist questions, in his discussions of the rhetoric of drugs, and so on – in a much more explicit and direct manner than virtually any other contemporary philosopher one can think of. That his works are seen as apolitical, as lacking a mode of political address, is surely the result of a certain freezing up of politics and an attempt to constrain it to well-known or predetermined forms, the very forms whose naturalness or stability is contestable through deconstruction (See Bennington, 1991).

From the very earliest conceptions of *différance* he develops an understanding of the 'worlding of the world', the marking of the earth, as a mode of cutting. *Différance* is understood as the inscriptive, dispersing dissonance at the impossible 'origin' of any self-presence. As he described it, '*Différance* is the name we might give to the 'active' moving discord of different forces' (Derrida, 1982, p. 18). As 'active' moving discord of forces, or differential forces, one which precedes the opposition between active and passive or moving and stationary, *différance* is the originary tearing of that which, unknowable and unspeakable as it is, was always amenable to inscription, was never 'full' enough to retain its self-presence in the face of this active movement of tearing, cutting, breaking apart. Which is also a bringing together, a folding or reorganizing, and the very possibility of time and becoming.

In *Of Grammatology*, Derrida asks the crucial question, which is, in a sense, what I want to adopt as my own: 'What links writing to violence? And what must violence be in order for something in it to be equivalent to the operation of the trace?' (Derrida, 1976, p. 112). Note that he does not ask the more obvious, and manifestly Derridean question: 'what must *writing* be in order for something in it to be equivalent to violence', but rather, searches for the modes of divergence, ambiguity, impossibility, the aporetic status of violence itself, for a status that it shares in common with the trace, and thus with writing, inscription, or difference. This is, in many senses, a more interesting and complicated question, for it asks: in what ways is violence bound up with the structures of equivocation, of *différance*, of undecidability that so radically structure and unhinge all discourse and all representation, all modes of self-presence? If violence is no longer so simply identifiable and denounceable, if it is not readily delimited in its spheres of operation, if it becomes ambiguous where the divide between violence and its others can be drawn, then violence is a form, possibly the only form, that writing, arche-writing, or the trace can take. Derrida does not ask how violence is like writing, but rather, what is it *in* violence, what operative element in violence, that is equivalent to the trace. Violence is not containable itself, as an identity of the trace: it is its own particularity and excessiveness over and above any conceptual schema, deconstruction notwithstanding. Derrida is inquiring into the allegiance of something in violence with writing, and indeed, with the very operations of deconstruction itself, which can be considered a writing of the violence of writing, and thus a self-consciously violent writing of writing as violence (and production, of violating production).

What makes Derrida's work at once intensely political and ethical, while he remains acutely aware of the problems involved in any straightforward avowal of one's commitments to political and ethical values, is his readiness to accept that no protocol, no rhetorical or intellectual ploy is simply innocent, motivated by reason, knowledge or truth alone, but carries with it an inherent undecidability, and repeatability that recontextualizes it and frees it from any origin or end. His politics is not the espousal of a position, but rather, an openness to a force, the force of *différance*. He lives up to the simultaneous necessity and impossibility of ethics, of politics and of knowledge, the paradoxical binding of that which we must move beyond with how we move beyond.

Derrida outlines his earliest linkage of violence with the structure of writing or difference, in his discussion of Levi-Strauss in a section in *Of Grammatology* called 'The Violence of Writing' (Derrida, 1976). There he argues that the structure of violence is itself marked by the very structure of the trace or writing: a three-pronged process in which concrete or vulgar, everyday writing, or violence, is the reduced and constrained derivative of a more primary and constitutive arche-writing or arche-violence, which is the very condition of both writing/violence and its opposite speech/peace. In 'the beginning' there is an arche-writing, a primordial or constitutive violence which inscribes 'the unique', the originary, the thing itself in its absolute self-proximity, into a system of differentiation, into the systems of ordering or classification that constitutes language (or representation more generally). This violence is the containment and ordering of the thing to give up its thingness and to submit itself to the leveling of representation, a mythical and impossible leveling that assumes a self-identity the thing itself never possessed:

> To think the unique *within* the system, to inscribe it there, such is the gesture of the arche-writing: arche-violence, loss of the proper, of absolute proximity, of self-presence, in truth the loss of what has never taken place, of a self-presence which has never been given but only dreamed of and always already split, repeated, incapable of appearing to itself except in its own disappearance. (Derrida, 1976, p. 112)

Primordial inscription, the ontological equivocation of *différance*, is the rendering of an originary self-presence as impossible: it is the 'production' of presence through the structure of the trace, the binding up of the real in writing or marking. This arche-writing, the writing or violence, inscription or trace, brings about the system of terms, differences that establish oppositions through which structures are made possible. It requires a second, 'reparatory' or compensatory violence, the violence whose function it is to erase the traces of this primordial violence, a kind of counter-violence whose violence consists in the denial of violence. This is a malignant inscription that hides its inscriptive character, that de-materializes and de-idealizes itself, that refuses to face up to its own dependence on, and enmeshment in, the more primordial structure. This is a violence that describes and designates itself as the moral counter of violence. This is the violence that we sometimes name the law, right, or reason.

There is, moreover, a third order violence, one that we can understand in the more mundane and viscerally horrifying, and thus ordinary sense of the word:

> It is on this tertiary level, that of the empirical consciousness, that the common conception of violence (the system of the moral law and of transgression) whose possibility remains yet unthought, should no doubt be situated ... This last violence is all the more complex in its structure because it refers at the same time to the two inferior levels of arche-violence and of law. In effect, it reveals the first nomination which was already an expropriation, but it denudes also that which since then functioned as the proper, the so-called proper, substitute of the deferred proper, *perceived* by the *social* and *moral consciousness* as the proper, the reassuring seal of self-identity, the secret. (Derrida, 1976, p. 112)

This is a dense and difficult discussion and is worth careful investigation. Derrida is suggesting that empirical violence, or 'war in the colloquial sense' rests upon, indeed is made possible by, the two logically prior senses of violence (Derrida, 1976, p. 112). The violence of nomination, of language or writing, is an expropriation, covered over and concealed by the violence that names itself as the space of non-violence, the field of the law (which in its very constitution structures itself as lawful, and thus beyond or above violence, that which judges violence). Empirical violence, war, participates in both these modes of violence (violence as inscription, violence as the containment of inscription, the containment of violence). Mundane or empirical violence reveals 'by effraction' the originary violence, whose energy and form is iterates and repeats; yet it 'denudes' the latent or submerged violence of the law, whose transgression it affirms, while thus affirming the very force and necessity of the law.

If Derrida refuses to locate the 'mundane' violence of 'evil, war, indiscretion, rape' (Derrida, 1976, p. 112) as originary, as the eruption of an unheralded violence upon an otherwise benign or peaceful scene (this is how he locates Levi-Strauss's Rousseauism), he manages to show that everyday violence, the violence we strive to condemn in its racist, sexist, classist and individualist terms, is itself the violent consequence of an entire order whose very foundation is inscriptive, differential and thus violent. It is thus no longer clear how something like a moral condemnation of violence is possible, or at least how it remains possible without considerable self-irony. The very position from which a condemnation of (tertiary) violence is articulated is itself only made possible because the violence of the morally condemnatory position must remain unarticulated. Which is, of course, not to say that moral condemnation is untenable or impossible, but rather, that its own protocols are implicated in the very thing it aims to condemn. Which means that the very origins of values, ethics, morality and law, 'all things noble in culture' (as Nietzsche says) lie in the trace, in the dissimulating self-presence that never existed, and whose tracks must be obliterated as they are revealed. Force, violence, writing not only 'originate', but also disseminate and transform even that violence which cannot be called as such:

> The arche-writing is the origin of morality as of immorality. The nonethical opening of ethics. A violent opening. As in the case of the vulgar concept of writing, the ethical instance of violence must be rigorously suspended in order to repeat the genealogy of morals. (Derrida, 1976, p. 140)

## 2.

Though his work has strayed very far from many of his initial concerns, Derrida returns to a remarkably similar problematic in more recent works, of which a number are clearly linked to the question of violence and its founding role in the constitution of systems of ethics, morality, law and justice, in the operation of modes of gift and hospitality, in the structure of relations to the other, notions of singularity, heterogeneity, the movement of double affirmation, not to mention in his earlier preoccupations with iteration, trace, and undecidability. He gives the name 'violence' a number of characteristic formulations: force, discord, dislocation, anthropophagy, among their more recent incarnations. These terms are not without ambivalence for him insofar as they are both 'uncomfortable' and 'indispensable' (Derrida, 1990, p. 929), paradoxically necessary and impossible: they must be thought, but the terms through which they are thought are complex and overdetermined and bind one to what one seeks to overcome or remove.[3]

Derrida poses the question, one of the crucial political questions of our age:

> How are we to distinguish between this force of the law, ... and the violence that one always deems unjust? What difference is there between, on the one hand, the force that can be just or in any case deemed legitimate, not only as an instrument in the service of law but the practice and even the realization, the essence of *droit*, and on the other hand the violence that one always deems unjust? What is a just force or a non-violent force? (Derrida, 1990, p. 927)

As his ostensive object of investigation, he takes Walter Benjamin's formative paper 'The Critique of Violence' (Benjamin, 1978). He asks, following and problematizing Benjamin, where we can draw the dividing line between legitimized or justified force, and the forces that are either prior to, excessive of, or not obedient to law, legitimation, right or the proper. Can there be a distinction between a constitutive and inscriptive violence, and a gratuitous, excessive violence, between a founding violence and the violence of conservation, that is not warranted or justified? And what provides the force of justification that legitimizes one form and not another? Is it legitimated, if it functions as legitimating?

Derrida suggests, contrary to the characterization of deconstruction as apolitical, as neutral, self-preoccupied or merely formalist and representational in its orientation, that this question of violence and its relation to the law inheres in, is the very project of deconstruction. It is not a peripheral concern, something that deconstruction could choose to interrogate or not, but is the heart of a deconstructive endeavour: the violence of writing, the violence of founding, of in-stating, of producing, of judging or knowing is a violence that both manifests and dissimulates itself: a space of necessary equivocation. The spaces between this manifestation and dissimulation are the very spaces that make deconstruction both possible and necessary and impossible and fraught, the spaces that deconstruction must utilize, not to move outside the law or outside violence (to judge them from outside – which is impossible), but to locate its own investments in both law and violence.[4] Justice, law, right are those systems, intimately bound up with writing. The law is writing par excellence, and the history of legal institutions is the history of the reading and rewriting of law, not just because the law is written, and must be to have its force, but also because law and justice (we will conflate them for only a moment) serve to order, to divide, to cut: 'Justice, as law, is never exercized without a decision that *cuts,* that divides' (Derrida, 1990, p. 963). This, indeed, is the very paradox of the law: that while it orders and regulates, while it binds and harmonizes, it must do so only through a cut, a hurt that is no longer, if ever, calculable as violence or a cut. Deconstruction is not the denunciation of the violence of the law, but rather, a mode of engagement with, a participant in this violence. For it exerts its own modes of judgment, its own cuts on its deconstructive objects, including the law, ethics, morality and is, in turn, subject to other deconstructive and iterative maneuvers. That which makes the law both a part of and that which is inherently foreign to violence is what introduces the structure of *undecidability* into the law, and thus into deconstruction itself:

> The Undecidable remains caught, lodged, at least as a ghost – but an essential ghost – in every decision, in every event of decision. Its ghostliness deconstructs from within any assurance of presence, any certitude or any supposed criteriology that would assure us of the justice of a decision, in truth of the very event of a decision. (Derrida, 1990, p. 965)

The undecidable is not a thing, a substance or self-presence that inhabits any situation of judgment, any decision or action; rather it is the very openness and uncertainty, the fragility and force of and in the act of judgment itself: it is the very equivocation of judgment itself, the limit (as Drucilla Cornell puts it) of the law's legitimacy or intelligibility, that is the object of deconstructive interrogation (Cornell, 1992). Deconstruction exploits this undecidability as its own milieu, the fertile internal ground on which it sows disseminating germs and uncertainties. It is not simply critique (as Benjamin conceives it) nor it is prophylactic: there is no 'remedy' or cure (or at least no cure that is not also *pharmakon*) for undecidability. My point is that what is marked, or unmarked, through this equivocation is always the field of violence within and through which the trace weaves its dissimulating web.

Undecidability is the hinge which renders Benjamin's clear-cut distinctions between a founding or constitutive and regulative or conserving justice, between mythic and divine justice, no longer tenable and on the continual verge of exchanging places and identities with each other:

> ... the very violence of the foundation or position of law ... must envelop the violence of conservation ... and cannot break with it. It belongs to the structure of fundamental violence that it calls for the repetition of itself and founds what ought to be conserved, conservable, promised to heritage and tradition to be shared ... Thus there can be no rigorous opposition between positioning and conservation, only what I will call (and Benjamin does not name it) a *différantialle* contamination between the two, with all the paradoxes that this may lead to. (Derrida, 1990, p. 997)

It is no longer clear (if it ever was) that one can distinguish between a 'good' and a 'bad' violence, a violence that is necessary and one that is wanton, excessive and capable of, in principle, elimination; one that is justified by virtue of its constructive force while the other is condemned as destructive, negative. Which is not at all to say that there is no difference between different forms of violence or that we must abandon the right to judge force and violence, whatever force and violence such judgments involve: quite the contrary, it means that we must hone our intellectual resources much more carefully, making many more distinctions, subtleties and nuances in our understanding than any binarized or dialectically structured model will allow. And refuse the knee-jerk reactions of straightforward or outright condemnation, before we understand the structure and history of that modality of violence, its modes of strategic functioning, its vulnerabilities and values.

I do not believe that Derrida abandons the moral and ethical dilemmas raised by very concrete and disturbing explosions of violence in the 'real world', and indeed, much of his work is occasioned by, or is an indirect response to, the question: what is an academic to do? His work sometimes disturbs those concerned by these concrete issues of violence (for example, LaCapra articulates a common fear that in abandoning the right to provide a pure judgement about violence, violence is simply equated with justice and the right to judge, and deconstruction abandons all violences to their own devices): especially because he does not attempt to provide solutions, definite responses or unequivocal judgments (LaCapra, 1990). Is this the abandonment of political judgments, or simply its complexification?

What is it that undecidability changes in our conceptions of law, politics, ethics and epistemology? Why has this concept exercized such terrifying implications for those concerned with moral and political values? It is not the claim that political or conceptual events are *ambiguous*, and thus difficult to judge, nor that they are so complex as to render judgments simplistic or irrelevant (though these may be true as well). Undecidability is probably another name for iteration, for *différance*, for the openness of destination of any articulation, any object or any event, the propulsion of any 'thing' (whether avowedly self-present or not) to a future context or scene where its current meaning, value and status is reread, rewritten, transmuted. Undecidability is precisely the endless iterability of any articulation, the possibility of endless quotation, endless recontextualization where the most crushing defeat is made into the most complex accomplishment, and maybe returned again to defeat. Undecidability dictates that the signification and effect of events or representations can never be self-present insofar as they always remain open to what befalls them, always places them elsewhere: in other words, it dictates that it is only futurity, itself endlessly extended to infinity that gives any event its signification, force or effect. This has terrifying consequences for those who would like to correct situations or contexts here and now, and once and for all. What the principle of undecidability implies is that the control over either the reception or the effect of events is out of our hands, beyond a certain agentic control. This is what an openness to futurity entails: that things are never given in their finality, whatever those 'things' might be. That whatever is made or found, whether it be nature or artifact, must be remade and refound endlessly to have any value:

> What threatens the rigour of the distinction between the two types of violence is at bottom the paradox of iterability. Iterability requires the origin to repeat itself so as to have the value of origin, that is, to conserve itself. Right away there are police and the police legislate, not content to enforce a law that would have had no force before the police. The iterability inscribes conservation in the essential structure of foundation. This law or this general necessity is not a modern phenomenon, it has an *a priori* worth ... Rigorously speaking, iterability precludes the possibility of pure and general founders, initiators, lawmakers ... (Derrida, 1990, p. 1007-9)

Iterability, *différance*, undecidability mean that no founding violence can be contained within the moment of foundation but must endlessly repeat itself to have had any force in the first place; and that any moment of conservation must rely on the repetition of this founding violence to have any force or effect of its own, for it rides on the waves of force that *différance* initiates. In other words, an origin never could infect an end unless it was not simply or even an origin, and an end is always implicated in the origin that it ends. This means that violence and force, indeed law and right, function only in the yet-to-come, the *a-venir*. Which is the unforeseeable, the yet-to-come that diverges from the what is present. This is what futurity is, and the way in which the implosive effects of the 'to-come' generate both the possibility and the undoing of force. Derrida understands the *avenir* as the domain of the new and of surprise, the very condition of iteration and context:

> Paradoxically, it is because of this overflowing of the performative, because of this always excessive haste of interpretation getting ahead of itself, because of this structural urgency and precipitation of justice that the latter has no horizon of expectation (regulative or messianic). But for this very reason, it *may* have an *avenir*, a 'to-come', which I rigorously distinguish from the future that can always reproduce the present. Justice remains, is yet, to come, *à venir*, it has an, it is *à-venir*, the very dimension of events irreducibly to come. It will always have it, this *à venir*, and always has. (Derrida, 1990, p. 969)

There is, in short, no way to decide in advance, through principle or by dint of position, authority or knowledge, the standard by which to judge violence. As Cornell argues, 'there can be no projected standards by which to judge *in advance* the acceptability of violent acts' (Cornell, 1992, p. 167). This, indeed, is the very heart of the deconstructive endeavor: that the status and value of violence – given especially the role of violence in the foundation and maintenance of status and value – is only ever open to a future, and a very particular position within futurity, to decide, which itself is endlessly open to its own modes of futurity, its own disseminating flight either to oblivion (insofar as its force is spent) or to its own endless production (insofar as its force remains virulent and mobilized).

## 3.

What is the counter to violence? What is the other of violence? If it can no longer be seen that the law is the barrier that divides violence from civilization, partitioning the violent, the excessive as either before or outside the law, and thus subject to its judgment, and positing the law as the space of a regulated violence that refuses to see itself as such or call itself by that name, then is there any cultural or natural space outside its ambit or other than its economy of forces? While it is not clear that there is a space before or free from this economy of the cut, the tearing separations of the structures of nomination, Derrida, following Levinas,[5] seems to suggest an alternative economy, which exceeds the very notion of economy. It too, like violence, inscription or writing, goes by many names in Derrida's writings. Among the more resonant of these is the Other, which he also describes, through readings of Mauss and Benveniste, in terms of the gift, hospitality, donation, generosity, or ethics; these themes are developed in 'Plato's Pharmacy' (Derrida, 1981), *Glas* (Derrida, 1986), *The Post-Card* (Derrida, 1987), *Psyché: Invention of the Other* (Derrida, 1989) and *Given Time* (Derrida, 1992).

The gift is both a part of and, in some sense, always beyond the economy of exchange. It is an impossible (yet imperative) relation in which what is given cannot be what it is: the gift can only function in not being a gift. For the moment an economy of reciprocity or exchange is set up (one gift for another), the gift ceases to be a gift and becomes an object in a system of barter or exchange. To function as gift, it must be given without return, without obligation, without expectation, given 'freely' ñ and moreover, it must be taken without debt, without the need for return or repayment: a pure excess, without accumulation. The gift, thus, cannot be anything that presents itself as gift, anything that is sent or received with a debt or a structure of return. The gift cannot be received as such, for if it is it is marked by debt: but nor can the gift be refused. For the gift is both superfluity and poison.[6] It must be given, but not in excess (for to give in excess is to reinstate the structure of reciprocity), nor in the hope of return or obligation. The gift, in this sense, is outside the law, beyond calculation. But not outside of them altogether. For the gift must not only be given and received while its objectness is annulled, it must also be given *responsibly* according to a logic of temporization, of timeliness. [7]

The gift, as Derrida says, gives time. It does not give itself, an object, the given, to be possessed or consumed: it gives temporality, delay, a calculation of timeliness. This is the very time needed for the time of judgment: the gift gives a possible future, a temporality in excess of the present and never contained within its horizon, the temporality of endless iteration:

> The gift is not a gift, the gift only gives to the extent it *gives time.* The difference between a gift and every other operation of pure and simple exchange is that the gift gives time. *Where there is gift, there is time.* What it gives, the gift, is time, but this gift of time is also a domain of time. The thing must not be restituted immediately and right away. There must be time, it must last, there must be waiting – without forgetting. It demands

time, the thing, but it demands a delimited time, neither an instant nor an infinite time, but time determined by a term, in other words, a rhythm, a rhythm that does not befall a homogeneous time but that structures it originarily. (Derrida, 1992, p. 41)

The gift gives time, not because it is placed in a structure of pre-existing temporization, the rhythms and cadences of economic exchange; rather, it is the object, *the given* that carries with it a force, an impetus of donation, pure expenditure:

... the requirement of circulatory *différance* is *inscribed in the thing itself* that is given or exchanged. Before it is a contract, an intentional gesture of individual or collective subjects, the movement of gift/ countergift is a *force* (a 'virtue of the thing given', says Mauss), a property immanent of the thing or in any way apprehended as such by the donors and donees. Moved by a mysterious force, the thing itself demands gift *and* restitution, it requires therefore 'time', 'term', 'delay', 'interval' of temporization, the becoming-temporalization of temporalization, the animation of a neutral and homogeneous time by the desire of the gift and the restitution. *Différance* which (is) nothing, is (in) the thing itself. It is (given) in the thing itself. It is (given) in the thing itself. It (is) the thing itself. It, *différance*, the thing (itself). It, without, anything other. Itself, nothing. (Derrida, 1992, p. 40)

The thing, like the other, is pure exteriority, with its own order, priority, time and rhythm. Our encounters with it are in part their force or impetus upon us, and in part the force of our inscriptions of them. The problem is that it is undecidable which is which, where one crosses the other and feeds off from it. The thing, whether it is the gift of language, the gift of law or an object, is given as such: the gift to be received must be accepted in its singularity and specificity before it is codified, submitted to economic value and integrated in the circuits of exchange. It gives itself up to be in some sense returned as itself.

Is it then that justice, a justice beyond the legalism and formalism of the law, moves beyond the field of violence to the structure, the non-economy, the pure excess of the gift? Does the idea or ideal of justice, a justice not given in full presence from God nor derived from the Law, provide an other 'logic', 'order' or 'system' outside that of calculation, economy, derivation? Is this another way of asking: is there, beyond violence, a way to love, to give without fear of expending and to take without fear of vulnerability? Derrida writes:

The deconstruction of all presumption of a determinant certitude of a present justice itself operates on the basis of an 'infinite justice', infinite because it is irreducible, irreducible because it is owed to the other, before any contract, because it has come, the other's coming as the singularity that is always other. This 'idea of justice' seems to me to be irreducible in its affirmative character, in its domain of gift without exchange, without circulation, without recognition or gratitude, without economic circularity, without calculation and without rules, without reason and without rationality. And so we can recognize in it, indeed accuse, identify a madness ... And deconstruction is mad about this kind of justice. Mad about this desire for justice. This kind of justice which isn't law, is the very movement of deconstruction at work in law and the history of law, in political history and history itself, before it even presents itself as the discourse that the academy or modern culture labels 'deconstructionism'. (Derrida, 1990, p. 965)

The gift is not outside the economy and expenditure that is regulated law, but operates entwined with and sometimes indistinguishable from it. In this sense, law can only be given and received as gift. But beyond law, where there is 'ideal justice', the structure of the gift can function in a different way, not other than or in difference sphere from violence. Rather, violence, force, disseminates itself into the futurity of the gift, of given time, as its mode of excessive production. It is time itself, only the future, the time to come, *avenir*, that the gift gives, that makes judgment possible (if always provisional), and that converts force into production. The what-is-to-come disseminates with its own force what the gift is. This is a double gift, a double affirmation.

## Notes

1. This is the position adopted by Seyla Benhabib, Nancy Fraser, Linda Nicholson, among many feminist theorists, or Habermas and the followers of the Frankfurt school, or post-Althusserian Marxists. See Fraser, 1984 for a clear example.
2. McCarthy in effect accuses Derrida because Derrida's questions are not McCarthy's, or the critical tradition he represents. Yet this is already the refusal to engage with Derridean questions, a mode of refusal of the possibility of a Derridean politics:

   Although he explicitly eschews any idea of a radical break, the politics of friendship gestures toward a transformation so radical that we can say nothing (positive) about what lies beyond it. I have found nothing in Derrida's writings to persuade me that his quasi-apocalyptic, near-prophetic mode of discourse about politics should displace the more prosaic modes available or constructible in our tradition. (McCarthy, 1989 ,p. 162)

3. As Derrida makes clear:

   For me, it is always a question of differential force, of difference as difference of force, of forces as différance (différance is a force *différée-*

*différante*), of the relation between force and form, force and signification, performative force, illocutionary or perlocutionary force, of persuasive or rhetorical force, of affirmation by signature, but also and especially of all the paradoxical situations in which the greatest force and the greatest weakness strangely enough exchange places. And that is the whole history. (Derrida, 1990, p. 929)

4. Derrida locates violence, law, transgression as the field of deconstructive play:

Deconstruction is justice. It is perhaps because law (which I will consistently try to distinguish from justice) is constructible, in a sense that goes beyond the opposition between convention and nature, it is perhaps insofar as it goes beyond this opposition that it is constructible and so deconstructible. (Derrida, 1990, p. 929)

Derrida, though, is even stronger in his claim: for law, force and violence are the 'proper place' of deconstruction, if this phrase has any meaning:

... it was normal, foreseeable, desirable that studies of deconstructive style should culminate in the problematic of law (*droit*), of law and justice. (I have elsewhere tried to show that the essence of law is not prohibitive but affirmative). It is even the most proper place for them, if such a thing exists. (Derrida, 1990, p. 929)

5. As already outlined in 'Violence and Metaphysics', Derrida wants to suggest that the encounter with the other is somehow outside an economy of the logos – or at the least, that Levinas's understanding of the ethical relation sets up a 'logic' or 'structure' other than the Greek conception of the relation between self and other:

What, then, is the encounter with the absolutely other? Neither representation nor limitation, nor conceptual relation to the same. The ego and the other do not permit themselves to be dominated or made into totalities by the concept of relationship...there is no way to conceptualize the encounter; it is made possible by the other, the unforeseeable and 'resistant to all categories'. Concepts suppose an anticipation, a horizon within which alterity is amortized as soon as it is annulled precisely because it has let itself be foreseen. The infinitely-other cannot be bound by a concept, cannot be thought on the basis of a horizon; for a horizon is always a horizon of the same ... (Derrida, 1978, p. 95)

6. See Derrida's footnote in 'Plato's Pharmacy':

We are asked why we do not examine the etymology of gift, translation of the Latin dosis, itself a transcription of the Greek *dosis*, dose, dose of poison. (Derrida, 1981, p. 131)

7. Derrida explains the relationship between the gift and responsibility in the following way:

> One must – *il faut* – opt for the gift, for generosity, for noble expenditure, for a practice and a morality of the gift (*il faut donner*, one must give). One cannot be content to speak of the gift and to describe the gift without giving and without saying one must give, without giving by saying one must give ... to do more than call upon one to give in the proper sense of the word, but to give beyond the call, beyond the mere word.

> But – because with the gift there is always a 'but' – the contrary is also necessary: It is necessary (*il faut*) to limit the excess of the gift and also generosity, to limit them by economy, profitability, work, exchange. And first of all by reason or by the principle of reason: it is also necessary to render any account, it is also necessary to give consciously and conscientiously. It is necessary to answer for (*répondre*) the gift, the given, and the call to giving. It is necessary to answer to it and answer for it. One must be responsible for what one gives and what one receives. (Derrida, 1992, p. 63)

# References

Benjamin, Walter 1978: *Reflections: Essays, Aphorisms, Autobiographical Writings.* Edmund Jephcott trans New York: Harcourt Brace Jovanovich.

Bennington, Geoff 1991: *Jacques Derrida.* Paris: Seuil.

Cornell, Drucilla 1992: *The Philosophy of the Limit.* New York: Routledge.

Derrida, Jacques 1976: *Of Grammatology.* Gayatri Spivak trans Baltimore: Johns Hopkins University Press.

Derrida, Jacques 1978: *Writing and Difference.* Alan Bass trans London: Routledge.

Derrida, Jacques 1981: *Dissemination.* Barbara Johnson trans Chicago: University of Chicago Press.

Derrida, Jacques 1982: *Margins of Philosophy.* Alan Bass trans Chicago: University of Chicago Press.

Derrida, Jacques 1986: *Glas.* John P. Leavey, Jr, and Richard Rand trans Lincoln: University of Nebraska Press.

Derrida, Jacques 1987: *The Postcard: from Socrates to Freud and Beyond.* Alan Bass trans Chicago: University of Chicago Press.

Derrida, Jacques 1989: Psyché: Invention of the Other. In *Reading de Man.* Lindsey Waters and Wlad Godzich (eds). Minnesota: University of Minnesota Press.

Derrida, Jacques 1990: Force of Law: The 'Mystical Foundation of Authority', *Cardozo Law Review*, 11, pp. 919-1045.

Derrida. Jacques 1991: 'Eating Well' or the Calculation of the Subject: An Interview with Jacques Derrida. In *Who Comes After the Subject?* Eduardo

Cadava, Connor, Peter and Nancy, Jean-Luc (eds.), London: Routledge, pp. 96-118.

Derrida, Jacques 1992: *Given Time. 1: Counterfeit Money*. Peggy Kamuf trans Chicago: University of Chicago Press.

Fraser, Nancy 1984: The French Derrideans: Politizing Deconstruction or Deconstructing the Political. *New German Critique*, 33, pp. 127-54.

LaCapra, Dominick 1990: Violence Justice and the Force of Law. *Cardozo Law Review*, 11, pp. 1065-78.

McCarthy, Thomas 1989-1990 :The Politics of the Ineffable: Derrida's Deconstructionism. *Philosophical Forum*, 21: 1-2 (Fall - Winter).

**Elizabeth Grosz** teaches Philosophy and Critical Theory at Monash University in Australia. She is the author of *Space, Time and Perversion: Essays on the Politics of Bodies* (Routledge 1995) and has edited a number of anthologies on feminist theory.

# Angels in the Archive: Lines into the Future in the Work of Jacques Derrida and Michel Serres

Roy Boyne
Durham University

## Serres

The seemingly unbridgeable space of difference between technoscience and culture can be illuminated by considering the valorization of time which is encountered on each of the opposing sides. On the side of the scientists we find the view that their knowledge is not only up-to-date, but has, in fact, surpassed all previous knowledge. If there is a register of inapplicability for scientific knowledge, it is only to be found in the future, not in any other language game or form of life, and certainly not in the past. In this sense, the general self-understanding of science is the archetype of modernity, and is represented perfectly by Descartes' view that his philosophy was first philosophy, a view which might be seen as parodied in Walter Benjamin's commentary on the small Klée watercolour which he owned, *Angelus Novus* (Benjamin, 1973, p. 259). In short, modernity foreshortens time by denying the past (even though it can see itself being blown by it into the future!). A typical illustration of this denial is given by Michel Serres, in conversation with Bruno Latour:

> Just yesterday I attended a debate on Lucretius at the Centre National de la Recherche Scientifique, where Latin scholars and atomic scientists could not hear themselves talk, with the same schizophrenia as always. On the one hand, those who studied the Latin text – literary critics and philosophers – held forth either on dialectical materialism or on Lucretius' anguish, his heartbreaks, and, on the other hand, the scientists repeated their neutral discourse, launched into orbit without any relation to these soulful matters. Each person was sealed off in his own time. (Serres and Latour, 1995, p. 47)

In the work of Gaston Bachelard, Louis Althusser, Michel Foucault and many others, this gap between two times was called or treated as a rupture, and the idea of the epistemological break was not merely accepted, it gave rise to a style of ruptural thinking, and to an aesthetics of parallel incomprehensibilities. Serres suggests that we might now see the foundation of this notion of rupture as arising from the quasi-religious belief that a new time has come into being, entirely different from the time superseded. Serres argues that ruptural thinking in the humanities and social sciences is actually subordinated to the modernist ideology and spirit of science, asserting that, 'The temporal rupture is the equivalent of a dogmatic expulsion' (Serres and Latour, 1995, p. 50). A consequence of his argument is that Benjamin's interpretation of the *Angelus Novus*, his repudiation of the spirit of the times, enshrined in his view that 'The present defines where the fore-history and after-history of the object of the past diverge in order to circumscribe its nucleus' (Benjamin, 1983-8, p. 25), applies just as much to the Foucault of *The Order of Things* as it does to, for example, Oppenheimer and the scientists of the Manhattan Project.

Serres is suspicious of all ruptures. Even the contrast between, what he calls, 'Newtown' – the single global city of intense communication, with infinite circumference – and 'Oldtown' – demolished, bombed, diseased, and idle – is drawn in terms of a ladder, along which 'angels are constantly rising and tumbling down' (Serres, 1995, p. 87),[1] rather than (even though we are here speaking of Heaven, at least in a sense) as transcendence.[2] In his work he appears to reject such dichotomous schemata as myth or science, fiction or history, ancient or modern. His position is orthogonally opposed to the neo-Kantianism of the dogma of two cultures – recently revived as a subject of discussion. As Latour put it in an article about Serres some ten years ago, 'he goes on digging in the leftovers, as if the world was beginning.' (Latour, 1987, p. 84), and as Latour further explains, this means that Serres rejects the idea of critique as the only path for philosophy. Serres shows that critical philosophy is diremptive, that it divides the world into two, the safe and the unsafe, the true and the false, science and ideology, democracy and totalitarianism, ancient and modern. The critical philosopher is also always paranoid, always in fear of being caught in enemy territory, frightened of being followed home by the transmuting magicians of ideology. For Serres, as Latour put it, 'critique is a long parenthesis that is now put to a close' (Latour, 1987, p. 91).

Serres not only rejects the exclusionary practices of dichotomous categorization, he is also concerned to expose the other major strategy of twentieth century thought: the Heideggerian temptation to find a unique source of wisdom, long lost, but lying dormant and waiting to be recovered, in a historical site such as that occupied by the ancient Greeks. Serres is quite clear that this:

> ... converse prejudice is no more enlightening ... claiming that we have totally forgotten an initial intuition received and developed only by certain pre-Socratics ... This intuition emanates, of course, from the greatest denigrators of science and technology. (Latour, 1987, p. 52)

This does not mean that Serres will not go back to the past – quite the contrary – merely that he rejects the idea that there is some secret key to the meaning of things to be found there, an idea which might seem to be found in Heidegger, when, for example, he writes, 'proper inquiry must be a dialogue in which the ways of hearing and points of view of ancient thinking are contemplated according to their essential origin' (Heidegger, 1975, p. 86).

What, then, is Serres's position? It is against the Kantian heritage. He does not think that the goal of philosophy is the development of an apodictic language: that has already been done, in science: as he said, 'For me, the language of truth, the language of exactitude and rigor, is the language of science, and it has already been found' (Mortley, 1991, p. 52). Furthermore, since the late 1980s, he has been devoted to a 'defence of the qualitative, the empirical, to a defence of the non-reducibility of the empirical to the logical', which emerges as a philosophy of connections, fluxes, and objective intensities, reminiscent of the work of Gilles Deleuze (Mortley, 1991, p. 54). Serres tries to see things from the standpoint of the known, not of the knowing (Latour, 1987, p. 89). As Deleuze put it, 'One becomes a set of liberated singularities, words, names, fingernails, things, animals, little events' (Deleuze, 1995, p. 7). In contradistinction from the reductionism of analytical thought, Serres's project results in emphasis on increase of potentiality rather than on control achieved through diminution of complexity.

Serres regards himself as an encyclopaedic philosopher, in the tradition of Descartes, Diderot and Comte. For him, the goal of philosophy should be synthesis, to open up passages between the sciences and the humanities. It is true that he was known as a structuralist thinker, with a view of structuralism grounded, not in linguistics, but in algebra (Descombes, 1980; Dosse, 1997). His five books, with the collective title, *Hermes: la communication*, were based on the idea that communication in contemporary Western societies had become more important than production. Quite appropriately (since Hermes is the figure of the crossroads), when writing them he was in between a mathematical structuralism and a philosophy of communication. His recent explorations of the nature of communication demonstrate a movement from the economic elegance of asymmetric, non-reciprocating communication between parasite and host to the vitalist vision of a cosmos utterly saturated with communication, which we find in *Angels*. It is with the formulation of angelic connectedness that we may find the links in Serres's work between past, present and future.

*Angels* is an extended conversation which takes place at Charles de Gaulle airport, between Pia and Pantope. The criss-crossing of people and things across the architecture of the central hall of that airport might function, Serres tells us, as a layout for the story. Pia talks of angels. She says:

> I think it's rather important. Unlike you I see something in all that 'transmission' of things. I see angels – which, incidentally, in case you didn't know, comes from the ancient Greek word for messengers. Take a good look around. Air hostesses and pilots; radio messages; all the air crew just flown in from Tokyo and just about to leave for Rio; those dozen aircraft neatly lined up, wing to wing on the runway, as they wait to take off; yellow postal vans delivering parcels, packets and telegrams; staff calls over the tannoy; all these bags passing in front of us on the conveyor; endless announcements for Mr. X or Miss Y recently arrived from Stockholm or Helsinki. Don't you see – what we have here is angels of steel, carrying angels of flesh and blood, who in turn send angel signals across angel airwaves. (Serres, 1995, p. 4)

Pantope thinks it strange to see messages everywhere and to conclude that, since angels take messages, there are angels everywhere. He does, however, enter into the spirit of it, and leading from an exchange about angels hiding in the wind, he parallels the communication richness of which Pia spoke:

> Winds create flows of air in the atmosphere; rivers make flows of water across land; glaciers make solid rivers, cutting their way across mountain and valley; rain, snow and hail are flows of water through the air; marine currents are flows of water within water; volcanoes are vertical flows of fire, from earth into the air, or into the sea, one element passes through others and they, conversely, pass through it. It supports or it transports. These reciprocating fluidities create such a perfect mixing that few places lack at least some knowledge of the state of others. They receive this knowledge by means of messages. (Serres, 1995, p. 26)

Meteorologists, vulcanologists, seismologists, oceanographers define their work by attempting to decode the messages of which Pia and Pantope speak. Pia asks,

> If winds, currents, glaciers, volcanoes, etc., carry subtle messages that are so difficult to read that it takes us absolutely ages trying to decipher them, wouldn't it be appropriate to call them intelligent? How would it be if it turned out that we were only the slowest and least intelligent beings in the world? Tradition says that above us there are the angels. (Serres, 1995, pp. 30-31)

The dialogue which we have been considering exemplifies a number of significant trends in contemporary thought: suspicion of reductionism, the weakening of the privileged position of the human subject as the all-seeing eye, recognition of nonhuman subject positions, environmentalism of various forms, and postphenomenological attempts within philosophy to generate a new theory of objects.[3]

In addition, we find the germ of a new theory of time. As Serres puts it:

> We have to pull together at least three kinds of time: the reversible time of clocks and mechanics, all to do with cogs and levers; then the irreversible time of thermodynamics, born of fire; and, finally, the time of what is called 'negative entropy', which is what gives rise to singularities. (Serres, 1995, p. 46)

We are all familiar with the reversible time of clocks and mechanisms. This is the time of countdown to launch, although the explosion of Challenger might indicate that mechanical time may be overlaid by a more epochal rhythm, giving rise to memories and significance beyond mere arithmetical progression. The time of thermodynamics is the absolute time of modernist, Newtonian-Einsteinian science. While we may borrow from Zizek the suggestion of a link between transcendence and limitation, and take the law of entropy as a form of the Being-of-the-world, we may also link the principle of entropy, by analogy, to Freud's notion of the death drive, tentatively postulated in *Beyond the Pleasure Principle* as comprising those instincts 'which seek to lead what is living to death' (Freud, 1984, p. 318); it may also be said that the notion of entropy is crucial to Bataille's concept of excess, since 'Only the impossibility of real growth makes way for squander' (Bataille, 1988, p. 28). Deleuze and Guattari's judgment completes this soft deconstruction of Serres's temporal categories, with their argument that the principle of thermodynamics is actually a perceptual, experiential observation of a partial observer, and that such partial observers 'belong to the neighbourhood of the singularities' (Deleuze and Guattari, 1994, p. 130). Perhaps, then, the key to the work of Michel Serres, in relation to the possibility of a new concept of time, or, more generally and less ambitiously, to gaining an overall characterization of it, will be gained by understanding the idea of singularities. The obvious first point to make is that they are precisely what Pia refers to as angels. But there is, of course, more to be said.

One source of the idea of singularity in contemporary thought is Spinoza's understanding of substance.[4] Spinoza's *Ethics* has a four-part structure, treating God, the mind, the emotions and the intellect.[5] The seventh of the opening definitions provides a source for the notion of singularity:

> That thing is said to be FREE which exists by the mere necessity of its own nature and is determined in its own actions by itself alone. That thing is said to be NECESSARY, or rather COMPELLED, when it is

determined in its existence and actions by something else in a certain fixed ratio. (Spinoza, 1910, p. 2)

Here we find three characteristics of singularities: first, that they are not properly accounted for in terms of their causes or qualities; second, that they are their own principle, their existence being accounted for by their existence such as it is; third, that they lie at least partly outside the realm of science, there being no fixed ratio. Most analytic philosophers would reject the idea of a thing as its own cause, rejecting this exclusion of scientific reasoning from the realm of singularities.[6] It is likely that the subordination of analytical philosophy to the principle that scientific reductionism is the single path to true knowledge renders such a response to the idea of singularities inevitable. It is therefore quite vital that we recognize that while Serres regards scientific enquiry as the proper pursuit of apodictic truth, he does not regard philosophy as the underlabourer of science. Serres seeks to illustrate the continuing fecundity of apposition, not the overcoming of one narrative by another, but their synthesis in pursuit of temporal and ontological explosion, as singularities are drawn together, transformed and ejected in all directions.

To understand how the notion of vectoring and creative singularities might have come to gain a certain currency, it is helpful to detour a little into the thought of Gilles Deleuze. His philosophical point of departure is neither the past nor the future, but the present as an infinite series of possibilities; as Pia might have put it, a host of angels. This does not mean that all is possible, merely that the range of possibilities extensible from the present is infinite. He understands the present as an infinity of series converging to this point now, and his understanding of the destiny of this time, now, precisely parallels Serres's notion of negative entropy (and, interestingly, matches Benjamin's conception referred to earlier). For Deleuze, the constitutive singularities of the present, angels if you will, are extended in all directions up to the singularities of 'incompossible' worlds, worlds which might have been ours but are not. It is in this sense 'that each individual includes the sum of a compossible world and excludes only the other worlds incompossible with that world' (Deleuze, 1993, p. 63). His focus on singularities and the present means that he understands individuals as flows towards other singularities, thus:

Individuation does not go from a genre to smaller and smaller species, in accord with a law of differentiation, but goes from singularity to singularity, under the law of convergence or of prolongation that ties the individual to one world or another. (Deleuze, 1993, p. 64)

One key then to the thought and philosophical inclinations of both Serres and Deleuze is the flow from the present, the treatment of the present as a bounded infinity and the connection of its singularities into new fields of potentiality. In the field of memory this would mean an inevitable intertwining of memory and forgetting and a refusal to force the future into a certain shape determined by an apodictic reading of the past. Whilst it is clear that Serres rejects the idea that there is a single principle, he does so – as does Deleuze – by embracing multiplicity and by exploring its consequences. Derrida's thought, on the other hand, is defined by its confrontation with the very unavailability of the single principle. This is a dangerous path, for it flirts with recognition at the same time as pursuing denial. This can sometimes appear as a (barely disguised) yearning for the forms of foundation, as the attempt to heal the rupture of history.

## Derrida

Derrida also sees the present as a bounded infinity, but yearns for its foundation rather than its other possible shapes. This leads, in Derrida's thought, to a focus on exclusion and rupture. We can enquire into this a little deeper, if we can find the form of the rupture in Derrida's recent thinking.

One name of this form is 'le secret', the secret. It is in the very form of the secret that we can only say what it is not:

> It would not be a matter of an artistic or technical secret ... such as style, ruse, the signature of talent or the mark of a genius, the know-how that is thought to be incommunicable, untransmittable, unteachable, inimitable ... the art hidden in the depths of the human soul. (Derrida, 1995, p. 24)

This could be the place of rupture, the residual place, the resting place for an otherness otherwise than that which Derrida holds within Reason. This secret, this rupture, would not reside in the subject, either hidden by intention (whether for good or evil, selfish or altruistic reasons) or lodged in the unconscious: 'It would not be ... some secret or mysterious motive that ... the psychoanalyst might have the skill to detect (Derrida, 1995, p. 24). We would not here be concerned with lines of rupture within the subject itself, between conscious and unconscious, between personalities in the postmodern condition of multiple or fragmented identity:

It is not a deprived interiority that one would have to reveal, confess, announce, that is to which one would have to respond by accounting for it and thematising it in broad daylight. (Derrida, 1995, p. 25)

If it is a matter of the principle, it is not within the power of the subject to provide or withhold it. It is not a secret that the subject can have. The secrets that the subject can have are held conditionally, can be asked for by the authorities, in which context:

> The secret becomes simply a problem ... no secrets, only problems for the knowledges which in this respect include not only philosophy, science and technology, but also religion, morality, politics and the law. (Derrida, 1995, p. 24)

If the individual subject cannot have this secret, this site of rupture, perhaps it will be found in community and traditions, but Derrida tells us that it cannot be found there although it makes them possible. In fact, by definition it cannot be found, we simply cannot refer to the other side of the rupture:

> ... the secret will remain secret, mute, impassive ... outside all periodization ... Moreover, no discussion would either begin or continue without it ... the secret remains there impassively, at a distance, out of reach. (Derrida, 1995, p. 27)

The difference between Serres and Derrida pertains to Derrida's noumenalism, his Kantian exploration and assertion of the unreachable presence of the Condition of Possibility. Derrida's concepts of time will be of lived time and of secret time, and his temptation will be that 'secret time' will determine what is to be remembered. The contrast is drawn with the time of singularities as they reach out to other singularities; it is drawn against the time of angels.

Both Derrida and Serres are opposed to the spirit of reductionism that animates modernist science. The thing that sets them apart is, however, pointed out in Felix Guattari's last work, before he died in 1992. He wrote:

> The polyphony of modes of subjectivation actually corresponds to a multiplicity of ways of 'keeping time' ... The simplest examples of refrains delimiting existential territories can be found in the ethology of numerous bird species. Certain specific song sequences serve to seduce a sexual partner, warn off intruders, or announce the arrival of predators. In archaic societies, it is through rhythms, chants, dances, masks, marks on the body ... on ritual occasions and with mythical references, that other kinds of collective existential territories are circumscribed. What we are aiming at with this concept of refrain [is] hyper-complex refrains, catalyzing the emergence of incorporeal universes such as those of music

or mathematics ... This type of refrain evades strict spatio-temporal delimitation. With it time ceases to be exterior ... From this perspective universal time appears to be no more than a hypothetical projection, a time of generalized equivalence, a 'flattened' capitalistic time; what is important are these partial modules of temporalization, operating in diverse domains (biological, ethological, socio-cultural, machinic). (Guattari, 1995, pp. 15-16)

The concept of time advanced here is one of diversion, re-routing and sectoral creativity. It is an understanding of time which is contained also in the work of Michel Serres, but it is foreign to the understanding of Derrida, which would underpin all sectoral temporalizations with a secret form, a universal form (its very unapproachability being for Guattari a sign of its masked partiality, a symptom of its ideological viscosity).

What Guattari is saying is important and original. In pursuit of an understanding of the contemporary subject which gives due regard to complexity, he finds that hyper-complex refrains can create time. For example, the point of time emergence of mathematical universes constitutes the making of an always-having-been-there or, at an individual level, the point of time emergence of newly found self-confidence may mean the arrival of a will-be-there-for-some-time-to-come. Chaosmosis is the modelling of 'ontological heterogenesis', the process of creation of individuals, groups and incorporealities. For Guattari, 'Time is not something to be endured; it is activated [relating to] the invention of new catalytic nuclei capable of bifurcating existence.' (Guattari, 1995, p. 18) We will find Derrida to be unhappy about the idea of a future creation of an always-having-been-there.

Derrida understands time as both given and universal. It is significant that his work on the gift is entitled, in English, *Given Time* (Derrida, 1992). For Serres, time is not universal but is better seen as a given assemblage of particularities. He writes, 'I suspend all judgement ... vortices are pulling ahead of universal attraction ... Time doesn't flow ... [it] is turbulent ... [understood through] the science of nearness and rifts ... called topology (not through) the science of stable and well-defined distances ... called metrical geometry ... ' (Serres, 1995, pp. 53-60). Guattari conceptualizes time as something created in particularities, a conception that runs back to *Anti-Oedipus* and its exhortatory critique of given structures (Deleuze and Guattari, 1984). As for science, if you will forgive the stereotypical and falsely-concretizing straw model approach, its concept of time is universal and also creationist, as cosmologists theorize about n-dimensions and the possibilities of worm-holes and the temporal effects at the edge of singularities.

We can then provide a somewhat up-dated version of the 'two cultures' schema as follows:

|  | Universal | Particular |
|---|---|---|
| Given | *Derrida* | *Wittgenstein*[7] |
| To be Created | *Science* | *Serres* |

What seems clear is that both Serres and Derrida reject epistemological imperialism as we find it in modernist science, but whereas for Serres, the destiny of the present is measured along the lines of potentiality, for Derrida there ought to be more than a little measure of ontological determination, and we find his thought caught between the 'ought-to-be' and its principle. We can explore this further in his *Archive Fever* (Derrida, 1996).

Beginning, as a diagnostician might, with the symptoms of the fever, there is a burrowing into certain words: a concern with etymology, with what the pre-history of word might reveal, and an immediate recognition of the difference between the historico-causal and the legal-political, between what the past or the present lays down: history or *Diktat* as the given truth. Immediately, then, we are faced with an either-or. In either case, we are not dealing here with singularities; there is an account to be given, a theory of institutionalization and its consequences to be articulated. We will not find the secret in the archive. Although the archive may be a perversity, a violation of the law of entropy, of the death-driven destiny of the present as silence, it is an understandable perversity. Archive fever, *le mal d'archive*, derives from the tendency to zero of the present which the feverish activities of historians and politicians try to resist. The provision through science and technology of terabytes of storage will not make a difference:

> One can dream or speculate about the geo-techno-logical shocks which would have made the landscape of the psychoanalytic archive unrecognizable for the past century if, to limit myself to these indications, Freud, his contemporaries, his collaborators and immediate disciples, instead of writing thousands of letters by hand, had had access to MCI or AT & T telephonic credit cards, portable tape recorders, computers, printers, faxes, televisions, teleconferences, and above all, e-mail. (Derrida, 1996, p. 16)

But this would have been another world, incompossible with our own, and would, of course, as Derrida points out, have changed the nature of the whole psychoanalytic enterprise. The mechanics of archiving determines what can be archived, ruling certain memories out of play, adding to the archive fever.

Psychoanalysis is a privileged topic in regard to the question of the archive. Its essence is to trawl the past, to bring to light key events, and held in light these representations will shape the future. It could be the angel Gabriel of communicative highways. The structure of psychoanalysis is, then, precisely archival, and the archive is 'the very concept of the future,' the route for angels (Derrida, 1996, p. 29). Its feverish condition, the fluttering of its wings, is due to the coming of silence. The archive will function to resist this, will take 'responsibility for tomorrow' (Derrida, 1996, p. 36). Derrida himself will add to the archive, underscore it, making his own contribution. This contribution will concern the future of the Jewish people. Derrida, diasporic angel, will send a message to Yosef Hayim Yerushalmi, the author of a book which demands of Freud that he set the record straight on the matter of psychoanalysis as a Jewish science, of the place of psychoanalysis within the archive of the Jews.

Freud knew of the possibility that cultural characteristics might be inherited, or, to use a different language, that individuals are collections of singularities, or, yet again, both culmination and origin of angel tracks. Gilman shows, for example, that Freud did recognize that certain effects might be understood as 'the repetition of some particular experience (which) could only be a very early impression of a very general nature, placed in the prehistory not of the individual but of the species' (cited in Gilman, 1995, p. 139), and he also acknowledged that his being Jewish meant 'sharing many obscure emotional forces' (cited in Gilman, 1995, p. 137), pre-echoing Derrida's citation of Yerushalmi, that 'one's fate in being Jewish was determined long ago by the Fathers, and that often what one feels most deeply and obscurely is a trilling wire in the blood' (Derrida, 1996, p. 35). On the other hand, Yerushalmi refers fully to Freud's secularism, described by Elaine Marks as being 'intelligent, liberal, generous, talented, bright, superior, European, cosmopolitan, and irreligious' (Marks, 1996, p. 145), but he pleads:

> In 1977, Anna Freud was invited by the Hebrew University of Jerusalem to inaugurate an endowed chair carrying the name of her – long dead – father. Unable to go she sends a written statement [which] declares, among other things, that the accusation according to which psychoanalysis is a 'Jewish science,' 'under present circumstances, can serve as a title of honour.' (Derrida, 1996, p. 43)

In the 'Monologue with Freud' which ends his book, Yerushalmi poses this question, 'When your daughter conveyed those words to the Congress in Jerusalem, was she speaking in your name?' He went on to say, 'Please tell me Professor. I promise I won't reveal your answer to anyone' (cited in Derrida, 1996, p. 44).

Derrida makes the point that this final section of Yerushalmi's book is marked by a move away from scholarship, and perhaps it is this move away from familiar territory which results in Yerushalmi's failure to give due weight to both of Freud's answers. The first of these answers is that indeed his daughter was speaking in his name. Had Freud not, on the occasion of his 75th birthday address to the Chief Rabbi of Vienna, said, 'In some place in my soul, in a very hidden corner, I am a fanatical Jew. I am very much astonished to discover myself as such in spite of all efforts to be unprejudiced and impartial' (cited in Gilman, 1996, p. 147). And did not Freud also, in the 1934 preface to the Hebrew edition of *Totem and Taboo*, deny that he had ever repudiated his people, and even predict that some day his substantial Jewishness *'will become accessible to the scientific mind'* (cited in Gilman, 1996, my emphasis). The second of Freud's answers is equally clear, in Freud's letter of June 8th, 1913 to Ferenczi: 'There should not be such a thing as Aryan or Jewish science.' (cited in Gilman, 1996, p. 144); and again, in his analysis of Blanton: 'that psychoanalysis itself is a Jewish product seems to me nonsense. As a scientific work, it is neither Jewish nor Catholic nor Gentile' (cited in Gilman, 1996, p. 143).

It is not difficult to reconcile these superficially conflicting answers: why should any scientist stand accused of repudiating their cultural heritage, why should they not be able to identify and identify with specific cultural inspirations of their work, why should they not be able to stand in community alongside others of that same culture, merely because their work has aspirations to supra-cultural validity? There would be difficulty only if destiny were dictating that there should be just one prime mode of social being. This is the position to which Yerushalmi inclines, and it is the temptation which Derrida faces.

Derrida finds that three doors open onto the future. One door is for Yerushalmi, a historian who will not repeat to anyone what he is told. But this is an imposed silence. A response from Freud would only have come in a dream. How can the historian's responsibility for the future be discharged by reporting on a dream? To work in such a way would break both Yerushalmi's contract with Freud *and* his contract with history, his self-subordination to the productive structures of a discipline (bad enough, Derrida suggests, that Yerushalmi sometimes thinks that he can make history speak for itself – through photographs, for example). The second door is entered holding a promissory note: we will find out the truth at some future point, we must postpone the re-shaping of the future until then. Yerushalmi put it as follows:

Professor Freud, at this point I find it futile to ask whether, genetically or structurally, psychoanalysis is really a Jewish science; ... we shall know, if it is at all knowable, only when much future work has been done.

> Much will depend, of course, on how the very terms Jewish and science
> are to be defined. (Cited in Derrida, 1996, p. 70)

Derrida sees this door as leading onto a complex abyss (never mind that
Freud himself leans through it, that he said that some day his substantial
Jewishness *'will become accessible to the scientific mind'*): how will the terms
be defined; will the answer to the question be learned through
scholarship or revelation, in the latter case messianically revealed in a
way that destroys and re-writes the archive? Derrida's discomfort with
the specter of otherness that is conjured up here has been evident at least
since his essay on Foucault's *L'Histoire de la folie*. All three doors are
Moebian, leading forward to whence we came.

## The Third Door

The third door might have the words 'No matter what' etched into its
lintel. Its frame is shaped out of the 'irreducible essence of Jewishness
(which) is already given and does not await the future' (Derrida, 1996, p.
72). For both Yerushalmi and Derrida (especially for the former, as
Derrida reads him, but subsisting in the tone of the latter's words),
'being-Jewish and the being-open-toward-the-future would be the same
thing' a kind of super-singularity, an unsurpassable facet of the world, a
super-angel at once in past, present and future (Derrida, 1996, p. 74). A
world otherwise than this would be incompossible with our world,
beyond the edge to which singularities might reach, since the injunction
of the archive falls uniquely to this entire people as a religious
imperative continually to remake the same world. Asking whether such
a view could possibly be just (not in the sense of foreclosing the future,
but asking the question whether it would be right that only one people
would have this privilege), Derrida tells us that its logic is 'to call by the
unique name of Israel all the places and all the peoples who would be
ready to recognize themselves in this anticipation and in this injunction'
(Derrida, 1996, p. 77). Thus, it is for Derrida, in a different way to that
meant by Yerushalmi, truly a question of defining what is meant by
'Jewish', and it is, for Derrida, why Freud might not have affirmed the
difference between Jewish and non-Jewish for which Yerushalmi
appealed.

No doubt a definition of Jewishness, as consisting essentially in
living, through the archive, a responsibility for the future, would be
contestable. Politically, such a definition would miss the specificities of
the Jewish people. Empirically, the absolute appropriateness of Derrida's
implication would be powerfully challenged by the histories of
forgetting which too have been a part of Jewishness, past and present.
Finkielkraut's writing has emphasized the way that focus upon the

Holocaust may actually have led away from the reproduction of Jewish culture. Reflecting upon his own experience, he writes, 'A disaster without precedent cut me off from Jewish culture, and I, a simmering rebel, reforged an artificial and reassuring continuity between present and past (Finkielkraut, 1994, p. 36). Boyarin, to take another example, relates a story told to him by a young rabbi on New York's Lower East Side:

> I happened to go to one of the synagogues on a Thursday morning. Maybe fifteen old men were there, and that was it. These people had come in, probably from Long Island – they were obviously people who had a lot of money and weren't involved in *Yiddishkayt* (Jewishness) at all – to make a bar-mitzvah for their kid. The grandfather *davened* (prayed) there. The kid didn't do anything but get an *aliyah* (he was summoned to recite the blessings before and after the Torah reading). He hadn't been prepared at all, so, you know, they wanted to make him a bar-mitzvah, where are they going to take him? To *Zayde's* (grandfather's) synagogue. And this kid didn't even know the *brokhe* (blessing). I mean he's standing up there at the *bime* (lectern), his legs are shaking, and the *shames* (sexton) has to prompt him on each word. (Boyarin, 1992, p. 6)

Boyarin's story and Finkielkraut's recollection illustrate one of the lessons that Derrida's work on the archive has to teach. It is that we 'participate in memory and forgetting simultaneously' (Boyarin, 1992, p. 7). That insight may be developed to demonstrate a weakness which both Serres and Derrida share. As Boyarin puts it:

> The efforts of ethnographers, folklorists, poets, and the like to counter collective forgetting – even when such efforts are archived or disseminated in various ways – do little to change the conditions blocking face-to-face intergenerational transmission of memory. Such efforts are essentially outside the community ... (Boyarin, 1992, p. 7)

Such a conclusion, that Serres's position at an angle to science, and Derrida's location with respect to Jewishness, prevent *a priori* the fulfillment of their respective projects, may be debated. However, this shared exteriority does not obscure the difference between them, that Serres desires to watch the angels in wonder, while Derrida is ultimately concerned to see them on the right path.

## Notes

1. Serres's conception is actually not so far different from Henri Lefebvre's (1962) view of the 'newtown'. Lefebvre contrasts the dream of the mediaeval town, organic, inter-connected, democratic, with the mathematics, boredom

and functionalism of the 'newtown'; but then asks, 'Wasn't your own village a new town once?' He then outlines an analysis which would readily have served as a model for Serres: 'The thing is that men have two different ways of creating and producing, and as yet these have not intersected: spontaneous vitality, and abstraction. On the one hand, in pleasure and in play; on the other, in seriousness, patience and painful consciousness, in toil. Might not the same be true of towns, those products of social living? ... how to reproduce what was once created spontaneously, how to create it from the abstract? ... no matter how immense the gap ... you must make every effort to bridge it'. (Lefebvre, 1995, p. 125)

2. Compare this with Zygmunt Bauman's recent view that the world is dividing into two, creating an absolute division between the desperation of those who have endless time to contemplate their poverty, disease, lawlessness, and stasis, and the inhabitants of the global city whose consumption, work ethic, endless travel, and striving for distinction produce a reduction of time and space to absolute zero (Bauman, 1997).

3. Examples of such attempts to arrive at new perspectives on the object are the work of Zizek: '... what Kant fails to notice is that *das Ding* is a mirage invoked by the transcendental object. *Limitation precedes transcendence*: all that actually exists is the field of phenomena and its limitation ... ' (Zizek, 1993, p. 37, italics in the original) – perhaps we might interpret this as Zizek saying that limitation *is* transcendence); certain attempts in modern art to capture the essence of 'objecthood' (see Fried's repudiation of the work of Judd and Morris in Fried, 1992); Deleuze's attempt to assimilate object and variation (Deleuze, 1993, pp. 18-19); we might add the interest in the body which has developed in philosophy and social science over the last decade, and which might be seen as the becoming-object of the subject; finally (although this does not pretend to be anything like a complete list), we should mention the vital concern within feminism of the objects excluded from the symbolic (Kristeva's notion of the 'abject' being a case in point).

4. In addition to its place in Serres, the idea of singularity is important in the work of Deleuze: 'There are two kinds of concepts: universals and singularities' (1995, pp. 156-7); 'We begin with the world as if with a series of inflections or events: it is a *pure emission of singularities* ... That is the real definition of the individual: *concentration, accumulation, coincidence of a certain number of converging pre-individual singularities* ...' (Deleuze, 1993, pp. 60-63), Probyn, who uses Agamben's notion of singularity to try and grasp the desire for belonging in a non-transcendental way:

> [I] hope to encourage the movement away from thinking and living difference and specificity as negative: to continue with others the task of conceiving specificity as the ground from where we move into the positivity of singularity. Working from desiring identities and belongings then foregrounds the way in which we are propelled into forms of living with ourselves and with others. This is to turn identity inside out so that instead of capturing us under its regime of difference as a negative measure, the desire of belonging becomes a force that proffers new modes of individuation and of being. (Probyn, 1996, p. 23)

and Levinas:

> [The] summons to responsibility destroys the formulas of generality by which my knowledge or acquaintance of the other man re-presents him to me as my fellow man. In the face of the other man I am inescapably responsible and consequently the unique and chosen one. By this freedom, humanity in me – that is, humanity as me – signifies, in spite of its ontological contingence of finitude and mortality, the anteriority and uniqueness of the non–*interchangeable*. (Levinas, 1989, p. 84)

5. Parts III and IV of the book are concerned with the emotions, meaning that it has, formally, a five-part structure.
6. 'I do not see any way of making *better* sense of 'cause of itself' than by equating it with 'necessarily existing'; but like most philosophers today I deny that anything is 'cause of itself' in this sense, i.e. that there are any necessarily existing nonabstract objects.' (Bennett, 1984, p. 73)
7. I place the late thought of Wittgenstein in this cell, following the view that language games and forms of life might be seen as hermetic, so that all one might say to any phenomenologist of time would be that time-consciousness is given in its context, and if I speak of it outside that context, 'it appears in a false light. For then it is as if I wanted to insist that there are things that I know. God himself can't say anything to me about them.' (Wittgenstein, 1977, p. 554)

# References

Bataille, Georges 1988: *The Accursed Share* (Volume 1). New York: Zone Books.

Bauman, Zygmunt 1997: *Glocalisation, or Globalisation for Some*, BSA Conference April 7-10, York.

Benjamin, Walter 1973: *Illuminations*. London: Fontana.

Benjamin, Walter 1983-1984: Theoretics of Knowledge; Theory of Progress. *The Philosophical Forum*, Vol. XV, Nos.1-2, Fall-Winter, pp. 1-40.

Bennett, Jonathan 1984: *A Study of Spinoza's Ethics*. Cambridge: Cambridge University Press.

Boyarin, Jonathan 1992: *Storm from Paradise: the Politics of Jewish Memory*. Minneapolis, MN: Minnesota University Press.

Deleuze, Gilles 1993: *The Fold: Liebniz and the Baroque*. London: Athlone.

Deleuze, Gilles 1995: *Negotiations*. New York: Columbia University Press.

Deleuze, Gilles and Guattari, Felix 1994: *What is Philosophy*. New York: Columbia University Press.

Derrida, Jacques 1995: *On the Name*. Stanford: Stanford University Press.

Derrida, Jacques 1996: *Archive Fever*. Chicago: Chicago University Press.

Descombes, Vincent 1980: *Modern French Philosophy*. Cambridge: Cambridge University Press.

Dosse, François 1997: *History of Structuralism*. Volume 2: The Sign Sets, 1967 – present. Minneapolis, MN: Minnesota University Press.

Finkielkraut, A. 1994: *The Imaginary Jew*. Lincoln, NE: University of Nebraska Press.

Freud, Sigmund 1984: *Metapsychology: The Theory of Psychoanalysis*. Harmondsworth: Pelican.

Fried, Michael 1992: Art and Objecthood. In Charles Harrison and Paul Wood (eds), *Art in Theory: 1900-1990*. Oxford: Blackwell.

Gilman, S.L. 1995: Freud, Race and Gender. In Jonathan Magonet, *Jewish Exploration of Sexuality*, Providence, RI: Berghahn

Guattari, Felix 1995: *Chaosmosis*. Sydney: Power Publications.

Heidegger, Martin 1975: *Early Greek Thinking*. New York: Harper and Row.

Latour, Bruno 1987: The Enlightenment without the Critique: A Word on Michel Serres' Philosophy. In A. Phillips Griffiths (ed.), *Contemporary French Philosophy*. Cambridge: Cambridge University Press.

Lefebvre, Henri 1995: *Introduction to Modernity* (Minuit 1962). London: Verso.

Levinas, Emmanuel 1989: Ethics as First Philosophy. In Sean Hand (ed.), *The Levinas Reader*. Oxford: Blackwell.

Marks, Elaine 1996: *Marrano as Metaphor: The Jewish Presence in French Writing*. New York: Columbia University Press.

Mortley, R. 1991: *French Philosophers in Conversation*. London: Routledge.

Probyn, Elspeth 1996: *Outside Belongings*. New York, Routledge.

Serres, Michel 1995: *Angels: A Modern Myth*. Paris: Flammarion.

Serres, Michel and Latour, Bernard 1995: *Conversations on Science, Culture, and Time*. Ann Arbor, MI: University of Michigan Press.

Spinoza, B. 1910 (1677): *Ethics*. London: Dent.

Wittgenstein, Ludwig 1977: *On Certainty*. Oxford: Blackwell.

Zizek, Slavoj 1993: *Tarrying with the Negative*. Durham, NC: Duke University Press.

**Roy Boyne** holds a Chair in Sociology at the University of Durham, where he teaches courses on European cinema and on risk and surveillance. Since the appearance of his book *Foucault and Derrida* (1990), he has jointly edited a collection on postmodernism, and has published several articles on aesthetics, cinema, structuralism and poststructuralism. His new book, *Weak Subjectivity*, will come out in early 1999. He is a member of the Editorial Board of *Theory Culture and Society*.

# Time and the Event

Andrew Quick
Lancaster University

We don't seek a meaning that has been placed but seek rather a sense of meanings falling into place. A meaning that happens to happen, a feeling that tumbles, a feeling on the very edge of accident. A sense that comes because *that* happened and you were there to see it (but you always knew you could've seen something else, heard another line, caught another gesture). We're seeking a work that values the moment where you saw and connected. Where the job of piecing together torn paper is yours. (Etchells, 1993, p. 3)

I would like to call an event the face to face with nothingness. This sounds like death. Things are not so simple. There are many events whose occurrence doesn't offer any matter to be confronted, many happenings inside of which nothingness remains hidden and imperceptible, events without barricades. They come to us concealed under the appearance of everyday occurrences. To become sensitive to their quality as actual events, to become competent in listening to their sound underneath silence or noise, to become open to the 'It happens that' rather than to the 'What happens', requires at the very least a high degree of refinement in the perception of small differences. (Lyotard, 1988a, p.18)

## Encountering Difference

In the closing Wellek Library Lecture, presented at the University of California in 1988, Jean-François Lyotard observes that the 'so called crisis of foundations' that has disturbed the sciences for the past hundred years has arisen out of a 'questioning of the conditions of time and space.' He remains somewhat vague in this lecture as to the specific nature of these questionings, observing that a similar crisis has dominated particular experimenting aesthetic practices over this same century: 'It then looks as if space and time, the pure forms in which concrete, visual, plastic and musical forms are traditionally synthesized by the faculty of presentation, are in the process of being eliminated, wasted even' (Lyotard, 1988a, p. 18). For Lyotard, such practices have been, and are still being, driven by an anxiety that circles restlessly around what he identifies as the 'sensuous formation of places and moments', where time and space are not 'of givens but of thoughts'. According to Lyotard there is a temporality that is always 'figural' – resistant to the operation of representation and displacing its mechanisms of operation. Bill Readings defines Lyotard's notion of the figural as 'the resistant or irreconcilable trace of a space or time that is radically incommensurable with that of discursive meaning' (Readings, 1991, p. xxxi).

In this article I wish to pursue the implications of Lyotard's thinking on time and space and its relationship to the activity of thinking or, as I shall call it, speculation, with specific reference to his writings on the event. I will juxtapose Lyotard's thinking on the event to my own recollections of two performances by Station House Opera, a highly acclaimed British experimental theatre company which have been touring since 1980. I focus on these works because they appear to be structured through the dynamics of displacement, where the operations of time and space appear to work synergetically: producing an effect greater than their attempted synthesis. The resistance to such a synthesis is important since any representational system requires the ordering of space and time for its untroubled operation. In addition, I experienced these works as a spectator and since the practice of witnessing is central to Lyotard's thinking on the event, my experience (or my retelling of it) as a spectator becomes an integral factor in the writing which follows.

In this article I will argue that the formal structures of these performances can be seen actively to generate various practices of interaction and intervention in the scene/seeing of performance and that (after Derrida) it is the 'temporization' of space and the spatialization of time that permits these acts of speculation.[1] The focus on the event, which for the sake of brevity, will be defined for the moment as *the singularity of an occurrence*, immediately draws attention to the problematic relation of the performer – spectator and the stage – auditorium. The notion of the singularity of an occurrence demands that the complexities of the practice(s) of witnessing and spectating are engaged with. This is because occurrences can only exist as, and through, acts of witnessing, of 'listening', of being before a thing (whether this thing is object, art or text). Lyotard hints at what might define this practice of witnessing indicating that it is 'in the perception of small differences' that the event can be felt. This is a perception which demands a 'floating attention', that puts into suspension the cultural frameworks that create for the self its way(s) of seeing, its way(s) of understanding. These are the modalities of a subjectivity which relies on the arresting of the various temporalities at work in the event and the spatialization, the turning into signification, of everything the eye sees, the ear hears and the body feels. The suspension, the 'floating attention', that Lyotard invokes requires from the reader/spectator/witness a certain exercize in self discipline. He writes:

> In order to take on this attitude you have to impoverish your mind, clean it out as much as possible, so that you make it incapable of anticipating the meaning, the 'What' of the It happens ... The secret of such ascesis lies in the power to be able to endure occurrences as 'directly' as possible without the mediation or protection of a 'pre-text'. Thus, to encounter an event is like bordering on nothingness. No event is at all accessible if the self does not renounce the glamour of its culture, its wealth, its health, knowledge and memory. (Lyotard, 1988a, p.18)

Hence, as Lyotard urges us, we have to become sensitive or open to the 'It happens that' rather than to the 'What happens': we must become open to the event and relinquish the discourse of the pre-/sub-/text. It is a demand that requires the subject to relinquish what it thinks it knows and be open to the 'touch' of an encounter.

Any attempt to write critically of this encounter is made problematic because the specific operation of the event is resistant to an easy definition and translation into the terminology of discourse, since it exists and works in opposition to discourse. What follows is, by necessity, a discourse produced by *my* bearing witness to the events in performance which I attempt to map out and mark by the various moments and instances of my intervention and connection constructed as and through the practice of this writing. These acts of intervention are not necessarily equivalent to the first or real time experience of being in the event itself since I cannot fully recall the complexities of actually bearing witness to the original performance, especially to performances which occurred some time ago. Instead, this writing shadows this process as I attempt to bear witness to the residues and traces left by the original performance, and as such the writing frames this witnessing within the network of a textual encounter. The textual encounter is not equivalent to the encounter precipitated by being (bodily) in the space of the performance. This shadowing is not an imitation of some lost but original notion of being in the event but can be seen as the product or outcome of a new event, a new encounter which, whilst reminding me of the lost moment of performance, demands a parallel but different practice of judgement: a judgement which occurs and re-occurs as (re)reading or reading again. It is a practice of judgement, since it might proceed indefinitely, that Lyotard defines as being indeterminate. This practice of (indeterminate) judgement is different from and works against the processes and tradition of interpretation – which might be defined as the uncovering or discovering of a work's meaning and the location of its representable content – common to the 'pursuit' in the history of literary studies.

Tim Etchells' identification of the creation of meaning in the space and time of performance in the opening quotation to this chapter, cannot be seen as an embodiment or a signifier of a totalizing discourse, since Etchells specifically takes into account the time and place, the instance, of its happening. For Etchells meaning is there not to be 'unearthed'. It is not a known quantity discernible to the theatre practitioner and mysterious to, but discoverable by, an audience. The production or creation of meaning is described in terms evocative of movement, of an encounter and a struggle, as 'falling' and 'tumbling'. This motion does not subscribe to some predetermined direction, it does not operate indexically or teleologically, but rather generates a response which is momentary, 'a feeling' described as being 'on the very edge of accident'. Meaning is positioned as a process of seeing and connecting but also one which resists the formation of a total picture in which all the elements encountered by the subject, can be known and understood either in terms of a hidden intentionality lying within the work or the framing of the work within a wider cultural and/or ideological context. Such metanarrative frameworks are broken down by the possibilities invoked by being present before the work because 'you could've seen something else, heard another line, caught another gesture.' Witnessing, for Etchells, is not static. It is not a singular practice in which meaning is somehow unlocked and summoned forward, but rather becomes the site and time of dispute, where differences can be constantly encountered and negotiated. In this sense the production of meaning, Etchells intimates, is a practice which is both tactical and indeterminate, dependent on being sensitive to the event of witnessing, of being before a work of art which is itself made up out of multiple and constantly shifting events. Such is the delicate activity and practice of 'piecing together'.

## Acts of Invention

In the performance of *Black Works* (1991) by Station House Opera tape-recorded instructions are relayed to the performers via headphones suspended at various points around the playing space. The specific details of these instructions are not heard by the audience since they are denied access to the technology of their communication, although the instructions are occasionally and tantalisingly discernible from the hanging headphones, as a series of repeated and faint metallic voices. The audience are, however, witnesses to the *effect* of these instructions as the performers attempt to execute them as a series of actions. These actions consist of making marks, tracing patterns, and creating imprints in the flour which has fallen like a dense white rain from a huge sieve placed high above the space. This marking is always carried out by the

Figure 1: *Black Works*, Station House Opera
*Photo: Steve Whitson*

performers' body or through the objects the performers encounter in the space such as a chair, sweeping brushes and bottles. Patterns and marks are created before the audience as a series of black or white traces, depending on whether the eye focuses on the floor or the flour, which are then subsequently erased as another performer sweeps the floor clean or sifts flour to construct a new site for marking. This process of marking and erasing, of building upon and adapting the patterns created by one performer and then by another performer, continues for the duration of the performance, which is about an hour. Nobody on stage speaks and the audience is acknowledged only through momentary instances of eye contact. The piece appears to progress without a fictional or narrative frame, although the motif of one of the performers being suspended by wires, combined with his sculptured pose of looking down at the floor below, which is repeated at the opening and then at the end of the performance, seems to allude to a point of departure and return (See Figure 3, p. 233).

Something in my remembering of *Black Works* presses me to consider this performance in relation to Lyotard's thinking on the event. This search for the philosophical referential frame is not simply a result of the demand for a theoretical contextualization, but rather, is instigated by a recognition that these two practices might be working over similar terrain. The audience in the performance of *Black Works* – and within this term I am including the performers who often take up positions to watch the actions of marking undertaken by others – are witnesses to the time and happening (the eventhood) of the creation and erasure of meaning: a creation that occurs with each gesture that results in an impression being left in the flour and with each action of erasure that obliterates the mark and creates a site for a new marking. Meaning is not privileged here as the work's representable content, as what might be *understood* in and by each instance of marking. What we are witness to in the performance space of *Black Works* is the temporality of the mark itself as it appears and disappears before our very eyes. It is a process of marking which, although initiated by an 'authoritative voice' (the tape-recording), is carried through by the performers as a series of repetitions which, in each act of repeating, draws our attention to their differences.

The act of meaning creation in *Black Works* parallels the fragility of meaning (its capacity to 'fall' and 'tumble') which Etchells outlines in the quotation which opened this section. Meaning, in this instance, is not fixed, placed or laid out for the audience to discover or to dissect. It is aleatory and subject to a profound instability in which its components (signs) endlessly shift and rearrange themselves. The operation of meaning is experienced as being dependent on our interaction with and intervention into the representational systems that attempt to order its components. Meaning, here, is not part of a system of progression pointing backwards toward a past or forwards toward a future but is the instance, the moment, of its happening. Meaning thus becomes, as Derrida describes writing, *'inaugural'* and is 'neither before nor after the act' (Derrida, 1978, p. 11). This is echoed in Etchells' emphasis on being there before the work to witness the moment by moment occurrence of signification: 'A sense that comes because *that* happened and *you were there to see it*' (my emphasis); hence, the stress placed on the fragility of this process of signification: 'you always knew you could've seen something else, heard another line, caught another gesture'.

As Etchells intimates, meaning is not absent in this practice of witnessing although meaning always appears in/as a process of disappearance, of a falling off or falling away. This is not to reduce this work to an aesthetic practice which embodies the effacement of meaning, rather it locates within the work practices which interrogate its systems and modalities of representation. The (representational) structures or systems that create meaning are subject to an intense inquiry and are revealed to be fragile and precarious. These structures become landscapes of conflict where the desire for the stability inscribed into the 'promise' of the representational system and the failure or the limit of this promise are explored, enacted and felt as loss. The black floor in *Black Works*, for example, thus becomes the site of dispute in which the practice of marking is worked through both by the performers in their attempt to trace patterns across it and by the audience who engage as witnesses to this activity of marking in their attempt to discern patterns, to feel their effect, as marks appear and disappear before them. If these marks can be seen as being synonymous with units of meaning, as signs, then what I would claim I am witness to is the act of meaning creation in which patterns emerge and recede, in which the process of signification is enacted as a series of gestures which find neither rest nor firm ground. The floor/flour is always shifting. What I look at and engage with are occurrences which appear before me as I attempt, along with the performers, to discern a pattern, a trace, the mark of an inter-action or an invention. I become, like the performers, an arbiter of possibility, a (re)reader of a text never made fully present.

Lyotard's thinking on aesthetics and judgement is littered with references to experimental artistic practices and traditions, especially to those he identifies as occurring in painting and sculpture and in certain types of literature. In his essay 'What is Postmodernism' he suggests that aesthetic experimentation attempts to incorporate the practice of invention rather than subscribe to any rule of truth or to any order of knowledge, since these are based on 'preestablished rules' (Lyotard, 1984). Hence the 'postmodern artist' makes use of and adopts manoeuvres that *dis-place* the representational apparatuses rather than attempting to initiate or establish a new representational system. This distinction forms the basis for Lyotard's differentiation between artistic practices which are identified as being 'inventive' and those which are seen as being 'innovative': 'invention' works *within* the representational system to *displace* its foundational structures; 'innovation' seeks to create new or 'purify' *existing* representational orders (see Readings, 1991, p. 72).

Lyotard's aesthetics of invention, which produce a displacement of the notion of 'the rule of truth' inscribed into any representational system, is not pursued to locate a final truth as it is not a teleological project. The aesthetics of invention produce effects or events which are themselves displaced in turn. The displacement of the rules (of representation) does not result in new rules being firmly established as their replacements. The process of displacement is continuous. As Lyotard puts it:

> The artist and the writer, then, are working without rules in order to formulate the rules of what *will have been done*. Hence the fact that work and text have the characters of an *event*; hence also, they come too late for their author, or, what amounts to the same thing, their being put into work, their realization (*mise en oeuvre*) always begins too soon. (Lyotard, 1984, p. 81)

Lyotard indicates the paradox evident in what he defines as a 'postmodern' aesthetic practice. This practice attempts to operate without rules or conventions in order to permit events to occur, to displace the referential framework within which any particular aesthetic practice is working. This process of displacement is not limited to the spectator or reader. The artist and the writer, since 'they are working without rules in order to formulate the rules of what *will have been done'*, are subject to the same or a similar process of displacement. The artist works 'without rules' to locate new rules and categories but these arrive 'too late' since they occur as a consequence or as an effect of artistic practice and are not predetermined by it. All the author and witness can testify to is the occurrence of an event itself, which is further displaced by another event and so on. Indeed, the making of a piece of work is a product of a network of events, not, of course, necessarily controlled or directed by their maker. As Bill Readings argues, Lyotard's version of 'postmodern art' 'does not seek a truth at all but seeks to testify to an event to which no truth can be assigned, that cannot be made the object of a conceptual representation'(Readings, 1991, p. 74). This inability to assign a truth to the event applies to both the 'author' and the 'reader' of the work. Work is made, whether this be an inventive art practice or the inventive writing of Lyotard's philosophical enquiry, without obedience to the rules of what is being said and how it is saying it. As Lyotard states, 'We write before knowing what to say and how to say it, and in order to find out, if possible'(Lyotard, 1992, p. 119). This does not mean that experimentation, whether it be an art practice or a practice of writing, loses its political or ethical import since Lyotard argues that events or phrases have to be linked by the witness and this process of linking demands judgement. In short, something has to be done with events and this doing, this activity of concatenation, demands a practice of decision making: a practice of judging.

The performance of *Black Works*, as I have outlined, is structured around the multiple events of making marks and tracing patterns in the flour and the continuous displacement of these marks as each performer attempts to translate an instruction into an action of marking. Interestingly, Station House Opera's work, whether it be site-specific or made for theatres, is often structured around rule-based actions and procedures which are broken down and redirected through the performer's interaction with them during the time of the performance. In *The Oracle*, a site-specific piece first performed at The Institute for Contemporary Arts in London in 1992, the instructions for actions are communicated via a network of stainless steel and plastic pipes. In this piece a performer describes her or his actions so that the listener, another performer, can imitate them. This imitation, translated into a physical action, is then described to a different performer who then translates the description into a physical action and passes on the description to yet another performer. This procedure of description and the attempted imitation and translation of description into a physical action occurs throughout the performance. Julian Maynard Smith, the company's Artistic Director, outlines this process in his documentation of the piece. He writes: 'Each performer attempts to describe what they do, and attempts to do what they hear the other describe. If they do not hear the other's voice they are free to instigate action, which they describe as they do it' (Maynard Smith, 1994, p. 63). The process of displacement in *Black Works* is reflected in the multiple and constantly shifting network of marks and traces created on the floor as a consequence of five performers attempting to follow instructions at the same time and in the same space. In *The Oracle* this process is embodied in the mutating physical actions which occur as a result of the (mis)interpretation of the description of physical action. The outcome of this (mis)communication, which occurs as a result of the differences produced for and by the performer in the juxtaposition of description and physical enactment, is a constantly shifting landscape. The body of the performer in *The Oracle*, like the marking in the flour in *Black Works*, becomes the physical site onto/into which the brutal process of displacement is inscribed.

The final section of *The Oracle* enacts the devastating effect that the process of displacement has on the body of the performer. During the build up to this closing moment the soundtrack plays loud music which gradually disintegrates into a 'white noise'. The performers enact highly individualized dances with pieces of the pipe as they go in and out of the gallery. During this activity of what seems like a final dispersal, the complete breakdown of the system, one of the performers (described as performer A in the documentation) carries a bed made out of plastic tubing and places it in the gallery's entrance and lies down on it. A ball, also made out of the plastic pipe is placed beneath the bed. The music subsides and another performer (described as performer B) connects some pipe to the bed, forming a mouthpiece, a line of communication, in order to speak to the figure that is lying upon it. The process of description and imitation is repeated once again as performer B describes the physical actions of the performer on the bed while the performer on the bed attempts to enact them. The body of the figure on the bed becomes increasingly contorted as he attempts to enact the differences inscribed into the descriptions of his original movements.

This difference is an outcome of a temporal and visual intrusion in, and reworking of, the original gesture generated through the activity of describing. The process of description and enactment is articulated as 'feedback' and 'amplification' in Maynard Smith's documentation, drawing parallels with the disintegration of the soundtrack in the previous section and, of course, with the breaking up of the network of pipes which has continued throughout the performance. The outcome of this 'amplification' and 'feedback' is that performer A's body 'is

Figure 2: *The Oracle*, Station House Opera
*Photo: Bob Van Dantzig*

transformed into a twitching and then thrashing mass of unconnected jerks' as he attempts to embody the differences articulated in performer B's description of his (previous or original) action. The gestures produced by performer A are fed back to him through the attempt to reproduce the primary movement. 'Displacement', as Lyotard observes, 'is an energy transfer' and the mechanisms of exchange (from the body to language and then back to the body only to return again to language and so on) are revealed to have a devastating effect (Lyotard, 1976, p. 105). The outcome of this process is the increasing distortion of the performer's body which builds to a frenzy as the piece closes. As a consequence of the increasing frequency of his contortions the 'bed is progressively shaken, twisted and kicked apart' and he falls onto the ball (constructed out of plastic pipes) which had previously been placed under the bed. We witness the final destruction of the system which provided a stability and which promised 'rest': the final displacement of the foundational structures and the rule of continuity (truth) upon which, as Lyotard tells us, the representational system depends. As Maynard Smith writes, 'The bed and ball are both destroyed and A is left thrashing on the floor' (Maynard Smith, 1994, p. 72).

The process of displacement is presented as being continuous, as never achieving a resolution in these two pieces. Rest, the body's inactivity, its escape from the endless exchange of energies, is seemingly only achievable as a consequence of the conventional theatrical act of closure – the fade to blackout: 'The lights fade to blackout, reducing the flow of information to zero, and putting an end to the movement' (Maynard Smith, 1994, p. 72). The artificiality of this gesture, this return to the theatrical apparatus which reduces the 'flow of information to zero', indicates a pause in the fluctuating energies of displacement and its effects rather than pointing to their final exhaustion or disappearance. Likewise the final image in *Black Works* is a caesura rather than a closure (See Figure 3). The closing image in *Black Works* seems to suggest the

Figure 3: *Black Works*, Station House Opera
*Photo: Steve Whitson*

futility inherent in the attempt to resist the energies or the flux of/in displacement. The act of suspension, of a performer attempting to 'fly' above the text (the marks on the floor) appears like a desperate or impossible gesture indicative of a desire for stasis, for control, for knowledge. The attempt to locate a point of view is revealed to be an impossibility, tied as the performer is to the very referential frame or machinery of representation that he wishes to escape from. The figure suspended above the black marks inscribed on/with the white flour witnesses the text's erasure as the flour cascades down from the sieve. Although ghost-like, coated as he is in a fine film of white flour, this moment feels more like a pause in a process rather that its closing action.

On the other hand, the attempt at this control, for this position of autonomy, appears also to be associated with death as the performer hangs and slowly spins above the text and apparatus of representation he seemingly so wished to master.

Both *Black Works* and *The Oracle* are structured around multiple events which depict and create a landscape that is always in motion. Movement, agitation, the 'it happens', as Lyotard puts it, are the event's indices. Stasis is seen to correspond with signification, with the procedures of conceptualization necessary to the rule of the representational apparatus. There is, however, an untroubled symmetry in the interpretation that sees these pieces as being an embodiment of the catastrophic effect of the processes or energies of displacement and the failure of structure(s) to hold representational systems together: the final image in *The Oracle* being the hideously contorted body thrashing on the floor; the closing image in *Black Works*, the crude suspension of one of the performers who witnesses the final erasure of a text (the marks on the floor) he seemingly desires to know by being, quite literally, above it. In short, these works could be read as being indicative of the consequences of the loss both in the value of and belief in the structures which inculcate meaning and which impose a system of order. Read like this, these pieces become works of mourning and dreams of inertia. Of course, the reverse could be equally valid: that the faith in these representational systems or structures is the cause of such catastrophic effects; that the event is the liberating energy or drive which exposes and exceeds the limit of structure (which seeks to reduce events to cause and effects) and embodies the reality of experience or as Lyotard would say 'the question of matter or existence'(Lyotard, 1988a, p. 22); that catastrophe is enfolded in the ecstasy necessary to the transgressive aesthetic practice. This view is expressed by Baudrillard in his essay 'Fatal Strategies'. He writes:

> Perfect is the event or the language that assumes, and is able to stage, its own mode of disappearance, thus acquiring the maximal energy of appearances. The catastrophe is the maximal raw event, here again more event-like than the event – but an event without consequences and which leaves the world *hanging*. (Baudrillard, 1988, p. 192, my emphasis)

In the order of catastrophes, Baudrillard argues, 'events absorb their own meaning, nothing is refracted, nothing is presaged.' Events are catastrophic because, according to Baudrillard, they are without consequence or have too many consequences, which amounts to the same thing: they cannot be conceptualized.

In a statement echoing the two works of Station House Opera analysed above, Baudrillard describes the catastrophe in 'the literal sense' in relation to the effect of light when it is 'harnessed and engulfed by its own source.' The results of this harnessing is 'a brutal involution of *time into the event itself* (my emphasis). The catastrophe is seen as 'an inflection, or curvature that makes *the origin of a thing coincide with its end*, and re-turns the end onto the origin in order to annul it, leaving behind an event without precedent and without consequences – the pure event'(Baudrillard, 1988, 192, my emphasis). These are similar to the dynamics (the coincidences, 'curvatures' and 're-turns') identified as 'feedback', displacement, 'amplification' and disintegration in the work of Station House Opera analyzed above. The outcome of 'the pure event', as Baudrillard observes, is 'the catastrophe of meaning' in that without consequences each event can have every and any cause 'indifferently assigned to it, without being able to choose among them'. As a result of the absence of consequences every event is 'open to all possible interpretations, none of which can fix meaning: the equiprobability of every cause and of every consequence.' The event becomes open to 'a multiple and aleatory ascription'(Baudrillard, 1988, p.193).

Of course, Baudrillard's analysis of the event is open to accusations of nihilism, that it is merely indicative of a theorization of the world and experience which celebrates the nothing (the void or 'black hole') that appears once the foundational structures and systems have been destabilized and removed. Such thinking is seen as the invocation or incarnation of an exponential process of collapse which threatens all the ideological structures which might oppose or provide an alternative to the drive of capitalism or to dominant ideologies. Critics, such as Christopher Norris, view his writings as little more than the re-iteration of the worst excesses of Nietzsche's thinking on meaning and morality which are continually described by Nietzsche himself as being oppressive and in the process of disintegration (Norris, 1990). In *Writing and Difference*, for example, Derrida (after Nietzsche) writes, 'Let us think through this thought in its most terrible form: existence as it is, without meaning or aim, yet recurring inevitably without any finale of nothingness: "the eternal recurrence"' (Derrida, 1978, p. 24). Such a view, however, does not necessarily indicate a passive stance. Derrida and Lyotard, in different ways and clearly in reference to Nietzsche's thinking, locate a perverse opportunity in this vision of the world's nullity. There is an active aesthetic attitude to nihilism which, refusing to draw back from the void, dances upon it. Instead of lamenting the absence of a world suited to our being, one is invented.

## Tracing the Letter

In *Black Works* the material quality of the flour, as it is used to make patterns and take the imprint of a performer's body or a rolled bottle, is reminiscent of the idea of the 'trace' that features in Derrida's writing on language. More specifically, since the flour (at times) takes on the quality of ashes as I look at the imprint of a performer's body left on the black floor (evoking the memory of a photograph that portrays the burnt outline of a human body which stains the pavement as the after image of the nuclear explosion at Hiroshima), I am reminded that Derrida's preferred term for his notion of the trace is 'cinder' (*cendre*). These words such as 'cinders', 'trace', 'track', 'furrow' constantly appear in Derrida's writings as metaphors for what he perceives as being a kind of materiality of and in language, a materiality which is not dependent on language's presence, its being there before me, but rather one that emerges through language's reliance on difference and opposition for its very operation, for its being.[2] Stating a preference for the term that might describe this materiality Derrida writes 'I would prefer *ashes*, as the better paradigm for what I call the trace – something that erases itself totally, radically, while presenting itself' (Derrida, 1987, p. 177).

What does Derrida mean by the trace which disappears as it appears, by the cinder which loses heat as it glows, how might it relate to Lyotard's notion of eventhood and how might it relate to the questions raised in and by these performances? Looking back at the statement made by Lyotard which opened this section, I am drawn to its closing line as a site of comparison and possible suture. He writes, 'to become open to the 'It happens that' rather than to the 'What happens', requires at the very least a high degree of refinement in the *perception of small differences*' (my emphasis). Lyotard's version of differences is intrinsically bound up with the disruption of the machinery of representation which is constantly invoked in his writings. Responding to the harmony created by the two drives of humanism which he observes are its 'well ordered dialectic or hermeneutics' and to the speed in which they create a unified field of knowledge Lyotard writes, 'I do not like this haste. What it hurries, and crushes, is what after the fact I find I have always tried, under diverse headings – work, figural, heterogeneity, dissensus, event, thing – to reserve: the unharmonizable' (Lyotard, 1988b, p. 4). Events are singular happenings made irreconcilable (unharmonizable) because each event is *different* to the next event, hence their singularity. And this encounter with difference may not be at or on a scale where difference(s) can be immediately discernible, hence the need to 'become sensitive to their quality as actual events, to become competent in listening to their sound underneath silence or noise ... ' Events act 'figurally' in that they are the Other to the rule of representation, necessary to it but working against its drive towards homogeneity. The implication of this statement is that while events operate within the order of representation they are unpresentable; they occur only as events; they happen. Although they might be unpresentable and mark the limit of the representational order, as Lyotard indicates, *they can be felt*.

Lyotard draws on the metaphor of the trembling of the earthquake to describe the quality of this figural difference (the event) which might be felt in an encounter between two heterogeneous states (Lyotard, 1977). This trembling, this radical shifting of ground, is the effect of the collision between two different elements or states which are placed in juxtaposition with each other. This is what he means by the term incommensurable: two states or fields placed alongside each other which refuse synthesis into a language (linguistics), into the order of discourse (history), into knowledge (philosophy). In *Discourse, figure*, Lyotard defines the operation of difference and its figural 'nature' in the following manner:

> Difference is neither the flat negation that holds the elements of a system apart (linguistics), nor that profound denigration that opens the referential or representative field in the regard of discourse and if it is the event ... , it's not by chance, it is because in these 'cases', unlike in signification or designation, *the division is not that of two terms* placed on the same level, inscribed on the same support, ultimately reversible given certain operative conditions, but on the contrary *the 'relation' of two heterogeneous 'states' at the same time juxtaposed in irreversible anachronism*. (Lyotard, 1971, p. 137; cited in Readings, 1991, p. 44)

Difference, for Lyotard, is not the network of oppositions which establish and enervate the system of semiology and structuralism but is, rather, the temporality of the event itself which occurs (happens) when 'things' are placed irreconcilably alongside or against each other. It is a temporality which resists sublimation into any terminology defined by time whether it be past, present or the future. As such, difference resists being inscribed into a meaning, reduced to signification, or transformed into a concept. Hence, Lyotard's emphasis on the temporal quality of the event in which he urges us to be 'open' to the 'It happens that' rather than to the 'What happens'. Once we state 'what happens *has happened*', Lyotard argues, 'the temporal system authorizes us to understand: there is an initial trauma, there's an effect of a past event; – and that suffices to repress the event, since a past event is a non-event'. Once the event is conceptualized, made known, it loses the very properties that make it an event. Lyotard describes the temporality of the event as a dizziness, a 'vertigo' which occurs 'when the event doesn't appear in its proper place where everything is ready to receive it, in the future'(Lyotard, 1971, p.137; cited in Readings, 1991, p. 42). This is the caesura, the pause, the opening, 'in space-time' that marks the event as a pure singularity resistant to or, at least, conveniently ignored, by any representational apparatus. Temporality marks the event's occurrence, the 'its happening' and yet it is a temporality, Lyotard argues, that must resist reduction (homogenization) to time's constituents. These constituents or 'sites' of time are analyzed by Lyotard in relation to the American painter Barnett Newman. These sites are identified as 'the time of production' (the time taken for the work's construction), 'the time of consumption (the time taken in looking at the work), 'the time to which the work refers' (the diegetic referent), 'the time of circulation' (the time it takes to reach the viewer) and what Lyotard describes as 'the time the painting is' (Lyotard, 1989, p. 240). While Lyotard is writing about painting the 'sites' of time in performance are not dissimilar. In this analysis of Newman, Lyotard articulates one of his clearest descriptions of the event, positioning the occurrence (the event) against the operation of signification. He writes, 'Occurrence is the instant which 'happens', which 'comes' unexpectedly but which, once it is there, takes its place in the network of what has happened' (Lyotard, 1989, p. 243). Lyotard argues that Newman has somehow embodied temporality within the painting, 'that time is the picture itself'.

Lyotard's description of the instance, which echoes Derrida's notion of 'the becoming-space of time and the becoming-time of space', seems to be reflected in the continuous processes of construction and reconstruction which I have identified as occurring in both *Black Works* and *The Oracle*. Both pieces explore the dynamics in and of communication and enact the energies released by the spatialization of time and the temporalization of space. For, surely both of these inculcate the processes of feedback and amplification which results in the breakdown in the systems (of communication) that seek to control the body and master inscription. This is not to say that these works by Station House Opera can be viewed simply as metaphors for the operation of language, that what these pieces really deal with are the structures and dynamics of writing. A more pertinent observation might be that what these works investigate are *the human interactions with(in) structures*, whether they be the structures (the architecture) of inscription, communication or the specifics of the architectural structures of buildings and the environment.

In my writing on/of *Black Works* and *The Oracle* I inevitably find myself inscribing the events that occurred before me into the order of this discourse. There is, however, something of the event in the juxtaposition of my remembering of the performance and my reading of Lyotard's writing on eventhood and difference. Indeed, this juxtaposition appears to mirror the (dis)connection between the tape-recorded instructions and the marks produced by the performers in *Black Works* as they attempt to put these commands into action; to make sense of them. This juxtaposition also parallels the trauma of/in the encounter between the body and language (description) that occurs in *The Oracle* in which the body refuses, or at least responds traumatically to, the claim language makes for the body's control. These are the traumas, the tremblings and the vertigo that occur as a consequence of the differences that open out between the body and technology; the differences that open out between the presence of the performer and the absence of the author; the differences that open out in the constantly changing network of marks; the differences that open out between the whiteness of the flour and the blackness of the floor; the differences evinced by 'heterogeneous states at the same time juxtaposed in irreversible anachronism'. This difference is also the difference between Lyotard's thinking on the event (in general) and the specific performance events which make up both *Black Works* and *The Oracle*. Just as my writing is irreconcilable with the activity of remembering the performance event, the performers' actions can be seen to be irreconcilable with the instructions they are given. Their repeated attempts, in *Black Works*, at making marks produces a network of traces which obliterate the effect of the (singular) intended action. This, of course, is as a result of the minute differences which occur through the singular interpretations of the instructions felt in and by the body of the performer which are in turn felt in the impress on the flour/floor as instruction is translated into action.

Something similar is occurring as I attempt to write the performance event of *Black Works*. The more marks this writing imprints on my shifting memory of the performance the further the event(s) of the performance recede into the network of this marking. This is not to say that the performance event is completely submerged in the tracery of this marking: utterly transformed into or reconfigured into the representational field of this discourse. Something in the event resists the conceptual operation of remembering and this resistance is an *affect of the attempt to recall*. Lyotard's term for that which cannot be remembered (returned to representation) yet is resistant to forgetting ('consigned to oblivion') is the *immemorial*. The immemorial is a version or adaptation of Freud's *unheimlich* in that it can be defined as 'that which returns, uncannily'.[3] In this sense the performances of *Black Works* and *The Oracle* are past events which are not quite over since they refuse the simple inscription into the historical and theoretical drive of this writing and, at the same time, refuse to be consigned to the silence of the forgotten. There is, if you like, always something more to be said.

This is a problem of and for history since history is a discipline which seeks to represent the past and to reinscribe it into various contexts and ideologies dependent on the idiosyncrasies of authorship. It is clearly a problem for the writing or recording of any event and thus is a problem to and for performance. It is, as Lyotard is at pains to point out, the problem for any philosophy of consciousness 'be it phenomenological, epistemological, or political.' The concern, for Lyotard, is that:

> A past that is not past, that does not haunt the present, in the sense that
> its absence is felt, would signal itself even in the present as a specter, an
> absence, which does not inhabit it in the name of full reality, which is not
> an object of memory like something that might have been forgotten and
> must be remembered (with a view to a 'good end,' to correct knowledge).
> It is thus not even there as a 'blank space,' as absence, as *terra incognita*,
> but it is there nevertheless. (Lyotard, 1990, p. 11)

The immemorial ('a past which is not past') is the figural force which
disrupts the 'full reality' that history seeks to (re)present. The
immemorial is that which cannot be forgotten, which haunts but cannot
be inscribed within representation. As such, something in my
remembering of *Black Works* and *The Oracle* returns, uncannily, to disrupt
the closure implicated in the attempt to inscribe Lyotard's event or
Derrida's trace into its dynamics. Something in or about the (singular)
quality of the events which make up a performance, for a performance is
constructed out of multiple singular events, resists the concatenation
necessary to/for a reading. Indeed, the impossibility of such a reading
might be reflected in the final images of both pieces. At the end of *Black
Works*, as I have described earlier, one of the performers is suspended
from wires with his head bowed towards the floor. The huge sieve above
him is activated by the other performers from the edge of the space and
he is drenched in a cascade of flour as the black marks on the floor are
transformed into a flat white landscape. Coated in a fine dust of flour he
appears in my remembering like a ghost floating above the disappearing
text. Something in the contorted and clumsy attempt *to arrive at a point
where the text might be known in full*, since from his position in the air he
might be able to 'see' and 'map' the complexity and density of the
marks, seems to reflect my own attempt at reading both at the time of
the performance and in my (re)writing of it now. The notion of the
autonomous subject position is rendered an impossibility or the product
of an awkward construction with its wires and machinery exposed. In
the closing image, hovering above his text, tied clumsily to the
referential frame from which he seemingly wishes to escape, the
performer witnesses (reads) the text's final and complete erasure. He
becomes a testament to the incommensurable; to that which has
disappeared and might come again; to that which exists beyond all
measurement; to (im)possibility; to that which can neither be forgotten
nor remembered; to the event.

Once the metaphysical foundations of space and time are unfolded
and revealed to be the 'false' structures of the representational system, as
no longer providing the rigid infrastructure for this system's language(s)
and modalities of operations, then what is left in the place of its
disappearance? One argument would be that 'nothing' (the void) or
'inertia' replaces its exit, that all that remains to play with is the 'tragic'

celebration of catastrophe or the commemoration of the (lost) systems of coherence. These works then become versions of what Baudrillard describes as 'seismic form': 'The form that lacks ground, in the form of fault and of failure, of dehiscence and of fractal objects, where immense plates, entire sections, slide under one another and produce intense surface tremors' (Baudrillard, 1988, p. 195).' Or they may become landscapes that reveal and play out the dynamics of *possibility* and *invention*, where new ways of being might be imagined and acted out.

*Acknowledgements. I would like to thank Adrian Heathfield, Richard Roberts and Jackie Stacey for their advice in the writing of this article.*

## Notes

1. See Derrida's essay *Difference* for his analysis of the trace in relation to what he defines as 'spacing', 'the becoming-space of time or the becoming-time of space (temporization)' (Derrida, 1982, p. 13). See, also, Simon Critchley's *The Ethics of Deconstruction: Derrida and Levinas* for an excellent account of the temporal and spatial operation of the trace which challenges what Derrida defines as the foundational basis of 'metaphysical language' (Critchley, 1992).
2. For an analysis of Derrida's notion of language's materiality see Gasché (1986, pp. 186-94) and Lukacher (Derrida, 1991, pp. 1-18).
3. See Readings (1991, p. xxxii). For a useful definition of Freud's term *unheimlich* see Dianne Chisholm (1992, p. 436): 'Besides having the power to signify antithetical meaning, the uncanny has the power to signify the development of meaning in the direction of ambivalence, from that which was familiar and homely to that which has become unfamiliar, estranging.'

## References

Baudrillard, Jean 1988: *Selected Writings*. Oxford: Blackwell.
Chisholm, Dianne 1992: *Uncanny, the*. In Wright, E. (ed.) *Feminism and Psychoanalysis: A Critical Dictionary*. Oxford: Blackwell.
Critchley, Simon 1992: *The Ethics of Deconstruction: Derrida and Levinas*. Oxford: Blackwell.
Derrida, Jacques 1978: *Writing and Difference*. London: Routledge.
Derrida, Jacques 1982: *Margins of Philosophy*. New York: Harvester Wheatsheaf.
Derrida, Jacques 1987: On Reading Heidegger: An Outline of Remarks to the Essex Colloquium. *Research in Phenomenology*, 17.
Derrida, Jacques 1991: *Cinders*. Lincoln: University of Nebraska Press.
Etchells, Tim 1993: A Few Thoughts about Procedure. Program note for *Club of No Regrets*.
Gasché, Rudolphe 1986: *The Tain of the Mirror: Derrida and the Philosophy of Reflection*. Cambridge: Cambridge University Press.

Lukacher, Ned 1991: Mourning Becomes Telepathy. In Derrida, J. *Cinders*. Lincoln: University of Nebraska Press.

Lyotard, Jean-François 1971: *Discourse, Figure*. Paris: Klincksieck.

Lyotard, Jean-François 1976: The Tooth, the Palm. *Sub-Stance*, 15, pp. 105-10.

Lyotard, Jean-François 1977: *Récits Tremblants*. Paris: Galilée.

Lyotard, Jean-François 1984: *The Postmodern Condition: A Report on Knowledge*. Manchester: Manchester University Press.

Lyotard, Jean-François 1988a: *Peregrinations: Law, Form, Event*. New York: Columbia University Press.

Lyotard, Jean-François 1988b: *The Inhuman: Reflections on Time*. Cambridge: Cambridge University Press.

Lyotard, Jean-François 1989: *The Lyotard Reader*. Oxford: Blackwell.

Lyotard, Jean-François 1990: *Heidegger and "the Jews"*. Minneapolis: University of Minnesota Press.

Lyotard, Jean-François 1992: *The Postmodern Explained to Children: Correspondence 1982-1985*. Minneapolis: University of Minnesota Press.

Maynard Smith, Julian 1994: Station House Opera: The Oracle. *Contemporary Theatre Review* 2 (2), pp. 61-72.

Norris, Christopher 1990: *What's Wrong With Postmodernism: Critical Theory and the Ends of Philosophy*. Hemel Hempstead: Harvester Wheatsheaf.

Readings, Bill. 1991: *Introducing Lyotard: Art and Politics*. London: Routledge.

**Andrew Quick** is a Lecturer in Theatre Studies at Lancaster University. He is co-editor of *Shattered Anatomies: Traces of the Body in Performance* (Arnolfini Live, 1997) and has contributed several articles interrogating place, identity and representation in contemporary performance to the journals *Performance Research* and *Contemporary Theatre Review*. He is currently working on a book entitled *The Event of Art* which examines the political in contemporary experimental art practices.

# The Time of the Real: When Disease is 'Actual'

Monica Greco
Goldsmiths College, University of London

The domain of the normal and the pathological has, in many ways, become both a topical and typical site for questions concerning value. In philosophy, the work of Georges Canguilhem argued for an immanent link between pathology and an activity of evaluation on the part of the living organism, anticipating more recent critiques of the possibility of value-neutrality in medicine (Canguilhem, 1989). In sociology, Talcott Parsons occupies a similar position by having focused on the normativity of medicine as an institution, one step removed from the ontology of disease itself (Parsons, 1951, 1964, 1978). The reflection I begin here does not aim at a truth of the relation between disease and the activity of evaluation – whether by an organism or by 'society' – but, rather, to the socio-epistemological conditions that allow us to relate these terms, disease and value, 'truthfully'.

In *The Birth of the Clinic* Foucault describes the emergence of a positive medicine, 'positive' in the sense of at last working with a notion of disease divorced from the 'metaphysics of evil' (Foucault, 1973, p. 196). This is arguably also the threshold after which the value of somatic disease is no longer seriously questioned as part and parcel of the medical task. Of the disease that we acknowledge as true we do not ask, as a rule: Is it 'good' or 'bad'? What is in it for the patient? To be sure, medical decisions always involve the evaluation of relative benefits and harms in specific situations: it may be 'better' to endure a minor pathological condition if its treatment is likely to produce 'worse' complications (not necessarily only of a medical kind). Indeed, public debate around value in this sense is rife, for example in relation to developments in biotechnology or to the politics of welfare. This type of reasoning, however, might testify not to an opening of the question of value but to a constant attempt at its closure: ideally, *given* the disparity between a condition that is 'better' and one that is 'worse', the better one is chosen. Again, the choice in practice may not be so clear-cut; the variables at play are likely to be many, and perhaps incommensurable. Even so, 'disease' functions as a variable whose generic quality, in principle, is known, and whose specific quantity becomes a consideration only in relation to other competing values: that of another disease, a monetary value, an ethical value, and so on. In and of itself, to establish that something is a 'disease' is also to fix its meaning in the abstract polarity of goods and bads – firmly on the side of the bads. To the extent that this is the case, I suggest that a 'metaphysics of presence' (cf. Derrida, 1976; Heidegger, 1962; Fox, 1993) may have replaced the older 'metaphysics of evil': a logic of presence and absence – the question of whether disease 'is there' – presides over the allocation of values.

Let us pause to ask: when is it today that we stop taking the value of disease for granted – when is it that we contemplate the possibility that disease may signify a form of empowerment?[1] Most conspicuously, and here I shall limit myself to this instance, we do so when disease appears empirically absent, or falsely present. The best example is the whole array of 'somatoform' disorders, ranging from hypochondria to factitious illness, but others – such as chronic pain or ME – may also occasionally illustrate the point. All present symptoms unwarranted by signs and, as a consequence, all constantly brush with the suspicion of malingering.[2] That these examples may appear obscure and untypical underscores, in fact, how typical it is for the negative value of disease to go without saying. As a general background for the material I present in this article, let me then offer this consideration: at the same time as it comes to be taken for granted that true disease represents a negative value, the uncontested signs of the pathological become paradoxically valorized by virtue of their association with truth. This produces many consequences that are of relevance to the present, consequences that not only inflect the social response to suffering but arguably also the ontology of suffering itself (Greco, 1998a). Hence the need to think again: should the question of value, of the meaning and purpose of disease, ever appear self-evident? Is it enough to establish an objective reality of disease for us to know what this reality signifies, in terms of its value? In this article I do not address these questions directly. I limit myself to invoking some arguments that subvert the logic of 'presence' and 'absence' as a way of relating to the problem of illness. The following analysis attempts to contribute to the possibility of articulating new and different questions to match relatively recent developments in medical culture. I particularly have in mind the growing confidence with which the community of medical researchers now appear to address the topic of 'psychosomatic relationships' in health and disease. This positive confidence stems, we are told, from the fact that the objective, material bases for such relationships are beginning to be understood (See Martin, 1997; Sternberg and Gold, 1997). My concern is with this readiness in thinking we now understand, and with the related, modernist presumption, that by adding more and more to what we know and do 'objectively' the negativity that disease represents may, in principle, come to be reversed, eliminated, exorcised.

This concern, in fact, is by no means new in the history of medicine. It is a nodal point in the constitution of psychosomatics as a form of 'problematization' (Greco, 1998b; Foucault, 1984, 1988). Under what circumstances, and for what conditions, is disease interpretable as to its meaning, purpose, and value? And what happens when we open 'disease' to this task of interpretation? These are the questions that earlier this century unsettled a medicine 'that is given and accepted as positive' (Foucault, 1973, p. 196) and that the new medical optimism appears to make irrelevant. I wish here to retrieve them by focusing on two related moments from the genealogy of psychosomatic medicine. The first consists of a set of arguments for regarding the pathological (and psychosomatic relationships in health and disease) as a mode of being-in-time – an account that allows us to question the 'metaphysics of presence' in medicine specifically as to its (medical) value. The second describes a conceptual 'slippage' that occurs in Freud's writings on neurosis, and that illustrates how being-in-time may become discursively fixed to appear as the substantial difference between a disease of the body and an illness of the mind. In an Anglophone context, this can be conveniently described as the slippage between two meanings of the word actual: from 'existing now', to 'existing in fact'. It is with reference to this latter meaning, I argue, that psychoanalysis exempts somatic disease from the task of interpretation.

## Life as 'antilogics': the project of an anthropological psychosomatics

The first moment can be approached by looking at a paper that Viktor Von Weizsäcker delivered to the 55th Wiesbaden conference of the German Society of Internal Medicine, in 1949. Von Weizsäcker, a neurologist and philosopher of medicine, was a prominent figure in the debates surrounding the establishment of psychosomatic research in Germany, where his direct interlocutors on this question included Karl Jaspers and Sigmund Freud.[3] A few words on the more general context of psychosomatic research in 1949 may be helpful to the reader. The psychoanalytic treatment of organic diseases had been performed and written about in German since the beginning of the century by analysts from Freud's Viennese circle such as Sándor Ferenczi and Felix Deutsch, and made controversially popular by Georg Groddeck's oratorical practice in his famed 'Satanarium' at Baden-Baden. Perhaps even more importantly, psychosomatic medicine had been developed to a considerable degree in the United States, where the 1930s saw the first instances of large-scale programmes of psychosomatic research carried out by teams led by Flanders Dunbar and by Berlin-trained Franz Alexander (Powell, 1977; Krasner, 1985; Taylor, 1987). A scientific journal entitled *Psychosomatic Medicine* was founded in 1939 (Jenkins,

1985). In 1949 itself, the first internationally accredited textbook of psychosomatic medicine for general practitioners was in its second edition (Weiss and English, 1949). In the years immediately following, Hans Selye's work on the concept of 'stress' would open the scope for an entire field of research, experimental as well as epidemiological, thereafter becoming closely identified with the endeavours of psychosomatics (Mason, 1975a, 1975b).

Thus, at the time of Von Weizsäcker's address to the German Society for Internal Medicine, a vast number of precedents that were to shape future research and institutional agendas had already been set in place. In that context, Von Weizsäcker's paper raised a difficult but, in his view, inescapable issue. The field of psychosomatics, he declared, was prey to a dangerous self-misunderstanding. This misunderstanding was amply evident from the research agendas of his own contemporaries, both in Germany and perhaps especially in the United States. For this reason it would be of little use to engage directly in the polemics that already structured the field of possible questions and answers: it was necessary, instead, to reexamine 'the nature of the process' of asking questions itself (Von Weizsäcker, 1986a, p. 452).

The search for the 'psychological' in disease, Von Weizsäcker stressed, should be regarded as a symptom: the symptom of a historical conjuncture wherein, as an effect of meeting with certain conditions, medicine was confronted with new tasks and with a new understanding of itself. What was at stake in the project of psychosomatics, was, in fact, a fundamental transformation concerning 'a different conception of man, of diseased man, of disease and of therapy' (Von Weizsäcker, 1986a, p. 451). In the lines that follow, Von Weizsäcker becomes quite explicit and specific as to what psychosomatics would need to look for if it wanted to make a difference: certainly not for an additional set of factors to be included, alongside those already known and ideally with a similar status, in the explanation of what is already understood as 'disease'. This is what we do when we posit a series of variables we attribute to the 'mind', in order to investigate the interaction between the two given research-objects of 'body' and 'mind' in a causal or logical sense. Psychosomatics should begin, rather, by ceasing to consider the event of disease in the manner that we already do: as an 'objective event', an event occurring primarily in, to, or through an object. Hence the formula that Von Weizsäcker uses to express this transformation in a nutshell: the 'introduction of the subject within medicine' (Von Weizsäcker, 1986a [1949]). The questions that can only be asked of a 'subject' cannot be simply added to what we already know, for they will fundamentally transform what we already know; the failure to realize this is what Von Weizsäcker describes as the self-misunderstanding of psychosomatics.

But why the 'subject'? And why does the 'introduction of the subject' alter the cumulative order of knowledge, the possibility of adding the new to the old in a linear sequence of increasing effectivity? Perhaps surprisingly, Von Weizsäcker's insistence on this point stems from his own experimental research in neurology and biology.[4] It reflects his biological realism and the systematic application, rather than the rejection or the bypassing, of orthodox scientific method. Most importantly, it reflects his conclusion that life is not objectively knowable as such (Von Weizsäcker, 1986a[1949], p. 455), a conclusion that might locate his work in a tradition of biological thinking also common to Georges Canguilhem. This tradition may be called 'vitalist', but not in the classical and romantic sense of regarding the living as an exception to the domain of physical causality. It may be called vitalist, rather, in its regarding life as the original context from which to comprehend matter, and from which to comprehend science as an activity of the living. It may be called vitalist also in that it understands the 'vitality of vitalism' itself, in the divided and dialectical history of biological thought, as an expression of life's originality (Canguilhem, 1975, p. 85; see also 1994, pp. 72-4). Von Weizsäcker's emphasis on 'subjectivity' thus stems from his focus on the originality of the living, which we find discussed in a series of reflections entitled *Anonyma Scriptura* (1990). Here he defines 'subjectivity' as the mode of being that must be regarded as proper to all biological acts, and to all that is alive. He also characterizes this mode of being as 'antilogical', in the sense that life, as a form of becoming, is

> ... a significant contradiction ... whereby something neither is nor is not, but rather, more precisely, loses a being and simultaneously receives one. ... An antilogical state of things is ... such that both an assertion and its negation are true ... If for instance I say 'I am becoming', and at the same time I say 'little by little I am dying', both things are true ... *The living is always something permanent that changes.* (Von Weizsäcker, 1990 p. 181)

In these few lines we can hear echoes of the German philosophical tradition, reverberations that become even clearer when Von Weizsäcker brings our attention to language to highlight what is specific about the living. The fact of being alive, he maintains, confers to living beings certain peculiarities that make some questions more relevant than others, both *for* them and *about* them. What is of relevance to life is not so much to say simply that it is, but rather to say that, or whether, it *wants*, it *can*, it *must*. These, in Von Weizsäcker's vocabulary, are 'pathic' assertions that express an antilogical mode of being: if I say I want something, I imply that what is wanted *is not*; if I say 'I can' it remains implicit that what I can *may not* come to be. Thus an 'ontic' mode of being must be distinguished from the 'pathic' mode: 'the first [term] expresses pure and simple being, while the second will indicate existence not so much as it is given, but as it is *undergone* [*erlitten*]' (Von Weizsäcker, 1990, p. 179). Life is such only as contradiction and as permanent oscillation between the possibilities of being and non-being. The self-identity that living beings express and embody is the constant *performance* (hence the reference to biological 'acts' rather than biological 'facts') of a return-to-oneself-in-difference.

Von Weizsäcker gives the name of *Gestaltkreis* ('gestaltic' circle or cycle) to what he calls 'an indication for the experience of the living' (Von Weizsäcker, 1990, p. 184, *my emphasis*). The wording here is important, for the *Gestaltkreis*:

> is by no means a reproduction of the figure of life or of life's movement ... We can represent this circle as a traveller following a certain path (it may be someone who is simply strolling, or someone who has a technical means of transport at his disposal: in this case, the scientist). (Von Weizsäcker, 1990, p. 184)

There is, therefore, no position of externality from whence 'life' or 'life's movement', and hence disease, may be adequately represented. The scientist, like the sick living being, is implicated in the circular trajectory that is proper to all biological activity; their two paths may cross, the two beings may meet but, as each (re)turns to achieve identity with itself, sight of the other is lost. The only difference between them is the availability, to the scientist, of a 'technical means of transport' that might enable him or her metaphorically to rush ahead, but never to look in all directions at once. Every biological act, among which disease and acts of knowledge must be equally included, thus involves an unconscious dimension: a loss-of-sight and a loss-of-effect are produced in the same movement whereby something new is countenanced or achieved. This partial invisibility is a permanent condition, although it always feels provisional; it is not rooted in passing error but in an immanent property of being. Immanent, therefore, is the incompleteness of whatever knowledge of the living we may come to possess: for in acquiring a new perspective we also simultaneously lose one (Von Weizsäcker, 1990, pp. 184-5).

This, finally, explains why, for Von Weizsäcker, it is mistaken to presume that we can add a psychosomatic perspective to what we know-already as 'disease', when by this we refer to that which we identify by (and with) the presence of disease-signs in the body. A properly understood psychosomatics, according to Von Weizsäcker, subverts the self-evidence of disease as we know it, and with it also what is of relevance to the medical task of treatment and cure. I might spell out the implications of this subversion in the following way. We once learned to look for signs rather than trust symptoms as to the truth of disease, and to act on the sign, whenever possible, as the 'real' problem. We must now learn to see the sign itself as not untrue but all the same deceptive: a visibility that is partial, not due to our provisional error but to our immanent lack. We must learn to regard the sign itself as the symptom, in its turn, of something that is always also *other*: if necessary, we must learn to ignore the sign in order to gain access to something equally relevant but different. If this is the case, then the question of 'what is disease' and of whether disease 'is there' cannot be answered by recourse to an unchanging, static formula. It must be posed again and again and differently each time, because the referents for 'disease' constantly shift in value as a result of our own interaction with them.

We have thus looked at 'why the subject', stressing that we should not understand Von Weizsäcker's position on this point in terms of a relativist sociologism or psychologism. We have also looked at why 'introducing the subject' theoretically subverts, or at least suspends, what we already understand as the being of disease. Now I shall move on to considering, still following Von Weizsäcker, what new vantage-point becomes accessible as a result of not following the lead of what we know-already.

To comprehend disease as something proper to what is alive means to regard it as a biological act in life's pathic movement: an indication of something life *wants, can*, or *must* undergo. In other words, it is to search for the meaning of a teleology that always stems from an evaluation of existence – or from the fact that life is never indifferent or neutral with respect to the conditions it meets with (Canguilhem, 1989). For Von Weizsäcker, a correctly understood psychosomatics would have to complement the 'critique of observation' effected by scientific method with a 'critique of motives and ends' that can only be accomplished through hermeneutics (the analysis of meanings and hence of 'significances'). The questions that can only be asked of a 'subject' are questions relating to meaning and value, and they are what a psychosomatic medicine must address in order to make a difference both to the understanding and to the treatment of disease (Von Weizsäcker, 1986a, pp. 453-5).

Von Weizsäcker regarded these questions as especially poignant at the time of his own writing, but indeed, they may be regarded as specifically relevant to the historical conjuncture of modernity as a whole. This is because among the conditions to which 'life is not indifferent' we must now count precisely the fact that the value of disease is not questioned, while its demonstrable presence often is. This is (still) a time when disease is identified with its bodily sign, a bodily sign that is treated as the objective guarantor of illness as a true and unequivocal presence, and hence of the rightful allocation of indemnifications and benefits. The neutrality of objective representations of disease is only apparent (Canguilhem, 1989); yet, a faith in the possibility of neutrality – to which the broader social function of disease-signs bears witness – makes the 'true presence' of disease a condition that is itself, paradoxically, a source of value. By turning disease (signs) into the basis for the legitimacy of a right, Von Weizsäcker writes, 'we bury a most profound experience of every sick person, an experience ... that is probably indispensable for his recovery: namely, the feeling of a condition that should not be there' (Von Weizsäcker, 1986b, p. 42). A medical knowledge oblivious to the question of value as a problem for *research*, unable to approach this question critically, with equal depth and rigour as that with which it approaches the material aspect of disease, can only hope to reinforce, rather than cure, a whole range of pathological mechanisms that are, perhaps, most significant for patients of the present day and age.

It is on the basis of this type of considerations that Von Weizsäcker declares the self-misunderstanding of psychosomatics. The most conspicuous threat to the possibility of a medical reform, in his view, does not stem from the type of medical treatment that is indifferent to the psychological domain, as one might superficially expect. It stems, instead, *from psychosomatic medicine itself*, when it is satisfied to include the psychological on the basis of a superficial understanding of how this changes the task of assessing the presence or absence of signs and symptoms. Psychosomatics has nothing to do with admitting the 'psychological' in the sense of establishing, through experimental research, some further evidence that might be positively added to the aetiological picture of any specific disease. To this research endeavour Von Weizsäcker gives the name of 'naturalistic' psychosomatics, and declares that it has no capacity to effect a reform in medical thinking. Psychosomatics is about admitting the *unconscious* and the relevance of interpretation – which questions anything given as evident in terms of its purpose and value – for all diseases. This Von Weizsäcker describes as 'anthropological' psychosomatics in contrast to the 'naturalistic' approach: the two represent, in his view, two irreconcilable tendencies that are often dangerously mixed for the purpose of research (Von Weizsäcker, 1986a, p. 455).

All this follows from envisaging disease as a biological act (as opposed to a biological 'fact'), and hence as an antilogical mode of being. It follows from considering that the 'body', like the 'mind', is the partial expression of a vitality that, as such, is never completely manifest. Thus, a presence (e.g. of signs or symptoms) is never full or definitive, and an absence is never simply an absence. The pathic (or ontological) being of disease is not exhausted by what is visible in the body, or by what is articulable through the mind. The relationship between 'mind' and 'body' quintessentially expresses the *Gestaltkreis*, the alternation between the possibilities of seeing and not-seeing, of saying and not-saying (Von Weizsäcker, 1990, p. 187). It is, therefore, equally mistaken to assert a substantial difference between 'body' and 'mind' as it is to assert their *in*difference, their equivalence or their identity. The relation between the two, which is socially mediated and, therefore, mutable and inconstant, is simultaneously of the order of 'mutual explication' and 'mutual occultation': 'if we now speak of psychogenesis, we should thereby only mean an historical becoming in the course of which organic changes occur *instead of* [psychic] processes, and vice versa' (Von Weizsäcker, 1986a, pp. 459-60). To this relationship Von Weizsäcker also gives the name of 'principle of the revolving door' (1990, pp. 184-5).

What also follows from the 'principle of the revolving door' is the possibility of understanding all therapeutic activity as an activity of translation, and the activity of translation itself as a form of therapeutics (Chiozza, 1981, 1988). To reiterate, the task facing psychosomatics is not how to demonstrate that the psyche, envisaged as a substance, may produce specific organic effects: a project that has rightly been described as 'aporetic' (Todarello and Porcelli, 1992). Rather, it is 'to decipher organic language ... to translate it into the comprehensible word of the psyche' (Von Weizsäcker, 1986a, p. 458). The practice of interpretation is relevant, in this view, *regardless* of the presence or absence of 'psychological' elements, factors, or symptoms, for even (and perhaps especially) their absence must be regarded as meaningful, as significant. To explicate disease as to its meaning always implies a form of effectivity, since it implies moving along the gestaltic circle on to a different position. This form of effectivity, however, is neither self-evident nor easily attainable. On the contrary, it requires (and deserves) the same amount of rigour and research, and the same dislocation of commonsense concepts, that we normally expect from the purview of science.

Von Weizsäcker argued for the specific pertinence of psychoanalysis for psychosomatics, as opposed for instance to psychophysiology, on grounds that psychoanalysis is 'entirely akin' to organic medicine (1986a, p. 456). This is because both disciplines deal with processes, respectively psychic and organic, that operate from and through a dimension that remains 'unconscious'. Only psychoanalysis, in his view, could therefore match the critical spirit that organic medicine brings to the surface of the visible, on account of its giving central importance to what remains unthought in any mode of thinking. In Foucault's terms, psychoanalysis represents 'a perpetual principle of dissatisfaction, of calling into question, of criticism and contestation of what may seem, in other respects, to be established' (Foucault 1970, p. 373): in this case, what seems to be established is the identity or identification of the reality of disease with what is actually present in the body.

## Freud presenting the unconscious

For the second part of this Chapter I turn to a different episode. It is chronologically anterior to the writings by Von Weizsäcker I have just discussed, but discursively it represents a step in the closure of the questions (re)raised in those writings. Although the argument refers to texts that may appear remote and very narrowly specific, this closure is, in fact, the more familiar horizon of our thinking around disease and the task of interpretation. The texts refer to the moment in the constitution of psychoanalytic concepts when Freud proposes the distinction between 'actual neuroses' and 'psychoneuroses'. In retracing this distinction I shall discuss a meaning for the term 'actual' that reveals 'actual' disease as a specific mode of being-in-time, in agreement with the arguments outlined so far. We shall also see, however, that Freud used this notion to establish, rather than to erode, the impression of a positive difference between 'somatic' and 'psychological' disease. On this basis, Freud confined the relevance of hermeneutics to the psychoneuroses and placed a ban on the application of psychoanalysis to the problem of organic disease. As I have argued elsewhere, this precedent is one of the most significant legacies of Freudian orthodoxy to the projects of psychosomatics (Greco, 1998b).

The term 'actual neurosis' appears for the first time in Freud's work in 1898, to denote anxiety neurosis and neurasthenia. The idea that these conditions should be set apart from psychoneuroses (which include transference neuroses such as hysteria, and narcissistic neuroses) had been developed much earlier (see Freud, 1895). Both nosological categories presented no evidence of organic lesion (or sign, as opposed to symptom) and so were to be considered part of psychopathology by default. While in hysteria the symptom could be, however, a pseudo-lesion, a falsely present lesion, anxiety neurosis presented psychological symptoms such as 'general irritability' or 'anxious expectation' accompanied by 'a disturbance of one or more of the bodily functions – such as respiration, heart action, vaso-motor enervation or glandular activity' (Freud, 1895, p. 94). Freud described these as 'equivalents of anxiety attacks' – examples of which are palpitation, dyspnoea, attacks resembling asthma, sweating, tremor and shivering, vertigo and congestions (Freud, 1895, p. 94). Freud proposed the two groups should be distinguished etiologically on account of the difference between the 'actual' sexual life of the subject and the 'representation' of important sexual events of the past. Here the word 'actual' bears a temporal meaning, to signify what is contemporary or occurring in the present (this is still the meaning of the word *aktuell* in German; the same holds for the French *actuel* and the Italian *attuale*). While 'the cause is definitely sexual in both these types of neurosis, in the former case it must be sought in 'a disorder of (the subject's) contemporary sexual life' and not in 'important events of his past life' (Laplanche and Pontalis, 1988, p. 10). The temporal difference, therefore, implies for Freud a pathogenetic difference. The actual neuroses are precipitated by a disturbance in the sexual economy of the subject that is contingent and contemporary, not already inscribed within a personal history. Such a disturbance produces its pathological effects directly. By contrast, the psychoneuroses have a traumatic origin that is distant in the past. They are precipitated only indirectly through a psychic process of symbolic elaboration. The *actual*, in other words, 'connotes the absence of the mediations which are to be encountered in the symptom-formation of the psychoneuroses (displacement, condensation, etc.)' (Laplanche and Pontalis, 1988, p. 149). Thus, while the hysterical (or psychoneurotic) symptom constitutes the symbolic representation of a conflict to be sought in the past, the actual neurotic symptom is the mere somatic equivalent of contemporary and contingent anxiety, and has no representational value.

The distinction between these two nosological categories hinges on the Freudian notion of 'instinct' (Freud, 1915). As Paul Ricoeur explains, the link between force and meaning makes 'instinct' the limit concept at the frontier between the organic and the psychic (Ricoeur, 1970, p. 151). 'Ideational representatives' of instinct constitute 'a kind of delegate of the soma within the psyche', and it is to these that psychic operations of repression into the unconscious apply (Laplanche and Pontalis, 1988, p. 204). Such 'representatives' are the conditions of possibility for instinct undergoing the 'vicissitudes' that Freud identified as psychic life (and must, therefore, not be confused with the content of 'representations'). Hence, while there *is* a psychological aspect to the actual neuroses (anxiety), this psychological aspect refers only to psychic representatives of instinct that have not (or not yet) undergone any 'vicissitudes' and are, therefore, devoid of the associations and connections typical of psychoneurotic symptoms. In other words, the psychological aspects of actual neuroses are nothing more than a direct and immediate expression of the somatic. This is the reason why a temporal difference becomes a pathogenetic difference: the passing of time is necessary for symbolization to take place, and symbolization in its turn is necessary for the development of symptoms whose manifest content can then be addressed to a latent, hidden, implicit one. When the time for this process to occur is taken out of the picture, we are left with affects that are not represented and therefore immanently unintelligible: affects without an ideational support are inaccessible to consciousness and therefore to analysis (Corsi Piacentini *et al.*, 1983b).

'Abstracting time', and the ambiguity that time implies, is literally what Freud does for the purpose of defining the aetiology of actual neuroses. Let us pause to consider what this means, if we think about it following Von Weizsäcker. In a seemingly inconspicuous move, what Freud does is to assimilate the *immanent unintelligibility* of the 'psychological' to the *irrelevance* of the 'psychological', in favour of a 'somatic' explanation. He does this in a way that easily suggests a substantial difference between the psyche and the soma, or the alternative between an absolute, essential presence, and an absolute, essential absence: 'the difference (between hysteria and anxiety neurosis) is merely that in anxiety neurosis the excitation ... is purely somatic (somatic sexual excitation), whereas in hysteria it is psychical (provoked by conflict) (Freud, 1895, p. 115). Hence, actual neuroses are '*not further reducible by psychological analysis, nor amenable to psychotherapy. The mechanism of substitution* ... does not hold good' (Freud, 1895, p. 97). For Freud, actual neuroses are 'sterile' from a psychological point of view, devoid of any psychic meaning, and, therefore, external to the psychoanalytic endeavour. In order to explain their pathogenesis, Freud relies on the biomedical models of 'reflex arc' and 'phlogistic reaction'. He speaks of the 'toxic' character of actual neuroses, in the sense that they can be accounted for as an effect of 'sexual toxins' originating in the metabolism of the patient (Freud, 1915-1917, p. 387; see Corsi Piacentini *et al.* 1983b).

There are two important effects of this line of reasoning. One effect is to say that psychoanalysis does not apply to 'actual' conditions, not simply on account of a difference named as temporal, but on account of a difference that appears *substantial*, as the difference between what is, despite appearances, 'truly of the body' or 'truly of the mind'. This is reinforced by a second and equally powerful semantic effect. The 'psychological' becomes discernible as a discrete presence, a presence that coincides with the *evidence* of functions of representation and symbolization that characterizes psychoneurotic symptoms (Corsi Piacentini et al, 1983a). In the absence of symptoms *of this kind*, in other words, it is improper to speak psychoanalytically of the unconscious meaning or dimension of a disease. Psychoanalytic interpretation is relevant strictly and only in the presence of 'truly' psychological conditions, that is, conditions presenting symptoms that are 'not actual' or truly somatic. The absence of psychological symptoms appears finite and complete, that is, no longer *significant* as a mode of pathological being: there is nothing to interpret in or about somatic disease.

The pragmatic appeal of such a move, on Freud's part, is undeniable. In this way, a 'psychological' condition can be identified and treated in terms of whether it is ontically present or absent, and psychoanalysis can operate in a manner that is diametrically opposite, but equivalent to, that of somatic medicine. Unlike Von Weizsäcker, who proposed that the logic of the unconscious should be applied to all forms of pathology, Freud appears to have deliberately contained the implications of this logic with respect to the problem of physical illness. Indeed, he repeatedly invited his followers to refrain from trespassing onto the field of the organic. It has been suggested that this prohibition stemmed from reasons of epistemological survival of psychoanalysis as a science accredited within a scientific community, rather than from reasons of internal coherence (Todarello and Porcelli, 1992; see Freud, 1933). This seems eloquently confirmed in Freud's private correspondence with Georg Groddeck and with Von Weizsäcker himself, both of whom saw in psychoanalysis the opportunity for a reform of general medicine:

> In my essay on the *Ucs* which you mention you will find an inconspicuous note: 'We are reserving for a different context the mention of another notable privilege of the *Ucs*'. I will divulge to you what this note refers to: the assertion that the unconscious act exerts on somatic processes an influence of intense plastic power which the conscious act can never do. (Letter to Groddeck of 5.6.1917, in Groddeck, 1977, p. 37)

> I had to keep analysts away from this type of investigation for educational reasons, since innervations, vascular dilatations and nervous pathways would have been exceedingly dangerous temptations for them: they had to learn to limit themselves to a psychological frame of thought. We must be grateful to the internist for the broadening of our knowledge. (Letter to Von Weizsäcker, quoted in Wyss, 1977, p. 210)

Freud constructed the psychoanalytic edifice to be adequate specifically to the problem of (psycho)neurosis. In so doing, he effectively set in place what can be regarded as a flowchart of clinical inferences that would frame the possibility of 'introducing the subject' within medicine, to employ Von Weizsäcker's expression. When and how can bodily disease be considered in terms of a hermeneutical 'critique of motives and ends'? Freud provided relatively clear answers both to the *when* (when the physical symptom is not actual) and to the *how* (through symbolic interpretation in analytical practice). Truly somatic symptoms and hence disease would remain interpretable only in a secondary sense, that is, in terms of the patient's phantasies about them. In this case, the symptom is not different from any other material aspect of the analytic setting, such as the physical appearance of the analyst or the furniture in their study (Codignola, 1977). The early advocacy of psychoanalysis as a foundation for psychosomatics was, therefore, 'aporetic' precisely to the extent that it attempted to conform to the Freudian framework, by proposing alterations minimal in appearance but very important in their epistemological consequences (Todarello and Porcelli, 1992). In some cases this meant extending the psychodynamic models proposed for the psychoneuroses (and especially the model of 'hysterical conversion') to provide an explanatory framework for physical disease, regardless of the materiality of the bodily sign (Deutsch, 1959). In other cases 'actual neuroses' themselves were taken as the model to explain functional disorders, which could be regarded as the non-symbolic consequence of 'chronic emotional states' (Alexander, 1943, 1950). Though still bearing the name of 'psychoanalysis', this approach is probably closer to a form of psychophysiology.

## The Present, the Actual, and the Real: Conclusions

Retrospectively, we may say that Freud's effort to establish psychoanalysis as a legitimate scientific endeavour was in some ways overly successful. Through the distinction between psychoneuroses and actual neuroses, Freud presented the unconscious to the scientific community in terms that were precisely *not* unsettling for medicine as a whole. He described it as something that fulfils ontic criteria of presence; as something evidence of which must be established, before we may legitimately undertake the hermeneutic task of unsettling what is evident. The unconscious dimension of disease, the vital value that any dis-ease immanently expresses, was made secondary and internal to another proposition: namely, that a critique of value applies only in the demonstrable presence of a certain type of symptom – a 'psychological' symptom (Freud, 1926). Although, as we have seen, the 'actual' is a temporal category, this temporal meaning disappears when what is 'actual' comes to coincide semantically with a substantial attribute of being. Actual disease, as disease 'of the body', simply becomes objective disease, the disease that is really present. And by the same token, real disease is no longer intelligible as a mode of being psychologically in time. It appears, instead, as that disease whose being is entirely visible in the body, without residue, without interpretable meaning. The very absence of meaning no longer appears significant.

The purpose of this detour into the history of psychoanalysis and psychosomatics has been to invite reflection on the reality and the actuality of disease. In English, the terms 'actual' and 'real' tend to be used synonymously in the social act of evaluation that discriminates between what is true disease and what is not. But, if we follow Von Weizsäcker and Canguilhem in their description of the logic of the living, the reality of disease always exceeds what is actually visible, actually presentable. It is not that we cannot *yet* demonstrate the presence or absence of certain diseases or causal connections, due to the temporary incompleteness of our knowledge; it is rather that there are aspects of disease that are perfectly real, but not actual. We are accustomed to think of the task of knowledge as one of exhausting what there is to be known. In the same way, we are accustomed to think of psychosomatic, or holistic, approaches as those that address the 'complete picture' of a disease or of a patient. Through the work of Von Weizsäcker, I have suggested that a real alternative to the limits of current medicine may not lie in the capacity for *including more*, in what we take into account, so that we may draw a picture of disease that appears increasingly exhaustive. On the contrary, an alternative would have to pose the problem of how we may *ignore*, or *subtract*, or *suspend* what we already know, without thereby supposing it is being denied. Part of the challenge is to acknowledge that the working assumption that we possess, or are moving towards, a 'complete picture' is itself a pragmatic value, the expression of a preference for mastery and control that is neither inevitable nor unquestionable (cf. Fox, 1993). We should ask whether and how we might work without such an assumption, in our theories but more importantly in our practices, in order to acknowledge the reality of disease that cannot be grasped as actual.

## Notes

1. I ask the reader to imagine that this question is addressed to the subject of medical knowledge, and to the process whereby such a subject constitutes its object, disease; hence not to a layperson who may legitimately seek to modify or contradict a received meaning (see Brody, 1987; Kleinman, 1988).
2. Here and in what follows, disease 'signs' are contrasted with 'symptoms'. The former are taken to refer to the material (and hence objective) lesion and/or physiological alteration that causally explains the 'symptom', i.e. the subjective feeling of illness (e.g. tiredness or pain) reported by the patient. The epistemology of biomedicine involves a 'correspondence postulate' (Fabrega, 1990) whereby it is assumed that disease changes (evident in the 'sign') produce corresponding changes in bodily awareness and function (reported as 'symptoms') through the mediation of cerebral processes and mechanisms. In practice, however, symptoms of illness do not always correspond to ascertainable signs, or 'evidence of disease'; this often generates a conflict of opinions between doctors and patients, which may give rise to dismissive and stigmatizing diagnoses of 'somatization'.
3. To my knowledge, Von Weizsäcker's work is still unavailable in English. His book *Der Gestaltkreis* (1940) was translated into French by Michel Foucault under the title *Le cycle de la structure* (1958). The translations of all extracts are my own. Since writing this paper, my attention has been drawn to a potentially damning involvement of Von Weizsäcker in the activities of National Socialism, on account of having performed and/or facilitated brain research on organs 'harvested' from victims of euthanasia (Friedlander, 1995, pp. 128-9, 155). The exact nature of this involvement is still unclear and currently being researched. I am very grateful to Nikolas Rose for alerting me to this reference.
4. Von Weizsäcker's research in these fields yielded the concept of 'gestaltic cycle' or *Gestaltkreis* (briefly discussed below), whose relevance has been compared to that of Einstein's theory of relativity and to Heisenberg's uncertainty principle (Wyss, 1977). Its relationship to Heidegger's description of the 'hermeneutic circle', and his discussion of the unconcealing, revealing/concealing of Being (Heidegger, 1962; see Stenner, 1998) is also clear.

# References

Alexander, Franz 1943: Fundamental Concepts in Psychosomatic Research. *Psychosomatic Medicine*, 5, pp. 205-10.

Alexander, Franz 1950: *Psychosomatic Medicine*. New York, Norton.

Brody, Howard 1987: *Stories of Sickness*. New Haven CT: Yale University Press.

Canguilhem, Georges 1975: *La Connaissance de la Vie*. 2nd Ed., Paris: Vrin.

Canguilhem, Georges 1989: *The Normal and the Pathological*. New York: Zone Books.

Canguilhem, Georges 1994: *A Vital Rationalist*. New York: Zone Books.

Chiozza, Luis A. 1981: *Corpo, Affetto e Linguaggio*. Turin: Loescher Editore.

Chiozza, Luis A. 1988: *Perché ci Ammaliamo?*. Rome: Borla.

Codignola, Ettore 1977: *Il Vero e il Falso*. Turin: Boringhieri.

Corsi Piacentini, Teresa, Furlan, Pier Maria and Mancini, Antonella 1983a: Mente e Corpo. In Freud, Sigmund, *Alcune Considerazioni: Psicoterapia e Scienze Umane*. 1 pp. 3-21.

Corsi Piacentini, Teresa, Furlan, Pier Maria and Mancini, Antonella 1983b: Mente e Corpo. In Freud, Sigmund, 'Come È' e 'Come Se'. *Psicoterapia e Scienze Umane*. 2, pp. 41-67.

Derrida, Jacques 1976: *Of Grammatology*. Baltimore MD: Johns Hopkins University Press.

Deutsch, Felix 1959: *On the Mysterious Leap from the Mind to the Body*. New York: International Universities Press.

Fabrega, Horacio F. 1990: The Concept of Somatization as a Cultural and Historical Product of Western Medicine. *Psychosomatic Medicine*. 52, pp. 653-72

Foucault, Michel 1970: *The Order of Things*. London: Routledge.

Foucault, Michel 1973: *The Birth of the Clinic*. London: Routledge

Foucault, Michel 1984: Polemics, Politics, and Problemizations. In Paul Rabinow (ed.) *The Foucault Reader*. New York: Pantheon Books.

Foucault, Michel 1988: On Problematization. *History of the Present*. 4 (Spring), pp. 16-7.

Fox, Nicholas J. 1993: *Postmodernism, Sociology and Health*. Buckingham: Open University Press.

Freud, Sigmund 1895: On the Grounds for Detaching a Particular Syndrome from Neurasthenia Under the Description 'Anxiety Neurosis'. In *The Standard Edition of the Complete Psychological Works of Sigmund Freud*. London: The Hogarth Press, Vol. 3.

Freud, Sigmund 1898: Sexuality in the Aetiology of Neuroses. In *The Standard Edition of the Complete Psychological Works of Sigmund Freud*. Vol. 3.

Freud, Sigmund 1915: Instincts and Their Vicissitudes. In *The Standard Edition of the Complete Psychological Works of Sigmund Freud*. Vol. 14.

Freud, Sigmund 1915-17: Introductory Lectures on Psychoanalysis. In *The Standard Edition of the Complete Psychological Works of Sigmund Freud*. Vol. 16.

Freud, Sigmund 1926: The Question of Lay Analysis. In *The Standard Edition of the Complete Psychological Works of Sigmund Freud*. Vol. 20.

Freud, Sigmund 1933: The Question of a Weltanschauung. In *The Standard Edition of the Complete Psychological Works of Sigmund Freud*. Vol. 22.

Friedlander, Henry 1995: *The Origins of Nazi Genocide*. Chapel Hill: University of North Carolina Press.

Greco, Monica 1998a: Between Social and Organic Norms: Reading Canguilhem and 'Somatization'. *Economy and Society*. 27, pp. 234-48.

Greco, Monica 1998b: *Illness as a Work of Thought*. London: Routledge.

Groddeck, Georg 1977: *The Meaning of Illness*. London: Karnac Books.

Heidegger, Martin 1962: *Being and Time*. Oxford: Basil Blackwell.

Jenkins, C. David 1985: New Horizons for Psychosomatic Medicine. *Psychosomatic Medicine*. 47, pp. 3-25.

Kleinman, Arthur 1988: *The Illness Narratives*. New York: Basic Books.

Krasner, David 1985: *Smith Ely Jelliffe and the Development of American Psychosomatic Medicine*. PhD Dissertation (1984, Bryn Mawr College). Ann Arbor: University Microfilms International.

Laplanche, Jean, and Pontalis, J.-B. 1988: *The Language of Psychoanalysis*. London: Karnac Books.

Martin, Paul 1997: *The Sickening Mind*. London: Flamingo.

Mason, John W. 1975a: A Historical View of the Stress Field. Part I. *Journal of Human Stress*. 1, pp. 6-12.

Mason, John W. 1975b: A Historical View of the Stress Field. Part II. *Journal of Human Stress*. 1, pp. 22-36.

Parsons, Talcott 1951: *The Social System*. Glencoe IL: Free Press.

Parsons, Talcott 1964: Definitions of Health and Illness in the Light of American Values and Social Structure. In *Social Structure and Personality*. London: Free Press.

Parsons, Talcott 1978: Health and Disease: A Sociological and Action Perspective. In *Action Theory and the Human Condition*. New York: Free Press.

Powell, Robert A. 1977: Helen Flanders Dunbar (1902-59) and a Holistic Approach to Psychosomatic Problems: The Rise and Fall of a Medical Philosophy. *Psychiatric Quarterly*. 49, pp. 133-52.

Ricoeur, Paul 1970: *Freud and Philosophy: An Essay on Interpretation*. New Haven CT: Yale University Press.

Stenner, Paul H. D. 1998: Heidegger and the Subject. Questioning Concerning Psychology. *Theory and Psychology*. 8, pp. 59-77.

Sternberg, Esther M., and Gold, Philip W. 1997: The Mind-Body Interaction in Disease. *Scientific American*. Special Issue. 7, pp. 8-15.

Taylor, Graeme J. 1987: *Psychosomatic Medicine and Contemporary Psychoanalysis*. Madison WI: International Universities Press.

Todarello, Orlando and Porcelli, Piero 1992: *Psicosomatica come Paradosso*. Turin: Bollati Boringhieri.

Von Weizsäcker, Viktor 1986a [1949]: Psychosomatische Medizin. In *Gesammelte Schriften*. Vol. 6. Frankfurt: Suhrkamp Verlag.

Von Weizsäcker, Viktor 1986b [1930]: Soziale Krankheit und soziale Gesundung. In *Gesammelte Schriften*. Vol. 8. Frankfurt: Suhrkamp Verlag.

Von Weizsäcker, Viktor 1990 [1946]: Anonyma Scriptura. In Thomas Henkelmann (ed.) *Filosofia della Medicina*. Milan: Guerini e Associati.

Weiss, E. and English, O. S. 1949: *Psychosomatic Medicine*. 2nd Ed. Philadelphia PA: W. B. Saunders.

Wyss, D. 1977: *Storia della Psicologia del Profondo*. Rome: Citta Nuova Editrice.

**Monica Greco** is a Lecturer in the Sociology Department at Goldsmiths College, London. She is author of *Illness as a Work of Thought* (Routledge, 1998).

# Presentism – or the Value of the Cycle

Michel Maffesoli
Paris V Sorbonne

The paradox of the tragic, which is tied up in all that is resurgent concerning the *'correspondance'* and the organic nature of things, allows us to remember that all civilization is mortal (Paul Valery), and that it passes through strongly differentiated stages. Although the drama of bourgeois ideology (from the Hegelian dialectic to the theatre of the boulevard, by way of the class struggle) is fundamentally active and dynamic, the distinctive characteristic nature of the tragic is to be somewhat 'non-active', at the very least with regard to what we may call the projective (*pro-jectum*) dimension. It is not, as we would be made to believe, disgust or lassitude that is dominant, it is more the case that a certain relativism tends to establish itself; and it is this which, in having a clearer vision of the 'return of the same,' prompts interest in the present, and the values which are its corollaries (Maffesoli 1979a, cf. Maffesoli 1993).

It is important to insist upon this point, as the understanding we can have of society depends on it. In effect, when we consider the temporal triad (past, present, future), a stress upon one or other of these elements is to be found in the unified whole made up of the acts and representations that structure a given society. The revalorization of the present goes hand in hand with the revalorization of myth which, under different names and in many diverse ways, is beginning to preoccupy modern consciousness. When Proust wished to describe the interlocking of his narrative, he talked of an 'Einsteinized' time, that, as I have often emphasized, is close to the temporality of myth. What is undoubtedly the case, is that the evocative power of past scenes persists so that they allow a better discernment and understanding of the *hic et nunc*, the here and now. It is certainly this power that comes to the forefront in mythic time and, as Gilbert Durand reminds us, it has the ability to makes us 'come out of the one-dimensionality of blind history in order to situate ourselves in a discontinuous universe' (Durand 1979, p.286). There is only a short step between this 'Einsteinization' of time and the cyclical return of the same, just as in the same way there are many points of connection between myth and the present. These are, for example, the small and ritualized instances which clearly demonstrate that tension towards or extension into the future has much less importance than the intensity with which we invest repetition.

It is my view that periods which we call 'decadent' are possessed of the conviction that 'life always starts over again'. We should linger for more than a moment on this cyclical vision, perhaps it would be better to call it the spiralling of things that has so often had a bad press. First of all, it must be noted this vision serves as a bridge between all parts of that great totality concerned with *'correspondance'*, the environment, nature, the local, and so on, besides that other totality which encompasses the various aspects of everyday life, including hedonism and scepticism, in short the valorization of life-experience itself. Naturally the basic presupposition in this involves the recognition of social life as that which is, and not the function of that which 'ought to be'. It is matter of acknowledging that for better of worse there is an acceptance – and even perhaps an affirmation – of existence. This is the *thématique* which Nietzsche the poet declaimed; it is this acceptance which is grudgingly conceded by the 'intellectual' who always intends to decrypt, to decipher, to speak the truth hidden behind the supposedly false appearance. Such figures fear going beyond the attitude of suspicion and thus themselves falling within the compass of banality. Whether the cyclical perspective is attributed to deity or to nature, it is apparent that the grounding principle *'posuit in visceribus hominis sapientiam'* explains the stubborn persistence of life in society.

Of course such a presupposition gives rise to the danger of overvaluing that nebulous entity called 'the people'. But this hypostasis, in so far as it exists, has the advantage of always being able to confront the principle of reality that is life in society, and by virtue of this it can, if need be, be deflated. Such an assumption is not the equivalent of the intellectual pretension that assembles its systems from abstract concepts, and which is able to function perfectly well in a way completely disconnected from straightforward social reality. The first outlook, reminiscent of the Weberian 'ideal type', has the advantage of accentuating a whole series of phenomena that are written into the theatricality of everyday life, and which because of this are generally held in contempt. Western iconoclasm, a cleaver in twain of images and possessed of an obsessive rationalism, is incapable of integrating that which gives itself to be seen and that which is given in life itself. Nevertheless, it is clear that the cyclical scepticism of sociality is best expressed in the play of the imagination, where nothing is uniform, linear, or explicable by an univocal concept. On the contrary, in the imaginary (*imaginaire*) we find abundance, superfluous expression and repetition. In order to be convinced about this it is enough to mention the duplications, the slightly different versions, and the heterogeneous readings through which myth expresses itself. This process implies a veritable technology of cyclicity. It is equally striking when we note the importance that repetition plays in banal description, or in general conversation. Such quasi-obsessional repetition is surely a way of both speaking out and of denying the passage of time.

Now we are able to observe this repetitiveness in mythical duplications, in conversation and in the redundant mockery of comic strips. Perhaps defending themselves or at the very least without explicitly willing it, such minds set out from their implicit dogmatic discourse and thus they create a state of a kind of human invariability in society, of a return of the same. Whether in a ludic manner or even in a more jarring way, these people preserve an agnostic anomie in the academy, a state of mind which allows for no real innovation in histories of the human condition. Although directed against the powers that be, mythic narrative or graffiti effect recall without drawing attention to or attaching much importance to anything beyond the repetitive and self-equivalent present. Such phenomena leave to others the management of religious hell or atomic apocalypse; through their incoherences and repetitions they recall only those things which have significance for *la belle histoire*, or the image they exhaust in the act of recollection. Of course their compilation and presence in collectors albums lend to them the semblance of unity, but they are valued above all for the beautiful moment which they crystallize, the situation which they describe, or the fugitive vision that they sketch. In this sense, they certainly participate in that 'ethic of the moment' which occupies itself obstinately with living in a repetitive monotony, entangled in the *sameness* of the crippling vagaries of life, rather than with their eyes set on celestial paradise or brighter futures. It may well seem futile to linger belatedly on the minor discourses that have some purchase upon an obscure cyclical vision, and it is apparent that these are not the only elements at work in social life. It is nevertheless probable that their contribution will considerably broaden the spectrum of sociological understanding.

One element that allows the importance of cyclical relativism to stand out in the collective consciousness is its bearing upon the political dimension. Once again everyday conversation is richly instructive and we could well dedicate a specific research project to analyse all the nuances of suspicion that target political activity. It would be more precise to say that it is to be considered like an art which has its own conventions. In Mediterranean countries for example, in the image of *bel canto*, political discourse has to know how to excite, to titillate passion, and to solicit emotional affect rather than reason. It is not necessary for it to appeal to conviction. It is particularly amusing to observe these phenomena during the time of elections. In this regard take note of the conversations after a televized political performance, listen to the appreciative comments made when the main personalities come face to face. All this runs counter to those who believe in the importance of rationally-based political programmes. Elsewhere such appeals are becoming more and more rare, and the invasion by public relations specialists of the very heart of all political parties is instructive in this respect. Of course, in Europe electoral campaigns no longer have the allure of American-style spectaculars, but little is made of this. The care lavished by politicians upon their 'brand image' and the importance which publicists lay upon the elaboration of this is not misleading: this is a question of putting on a performance which knows how to strike the emotions rather than challenge the mind.

If politics flaunts itself in the spectacle, then this is because it is because the masses would wish it this way. In effect, beyond electoral programmes and promises, beyond the campaigns of seduction and soliciting, no one deceived themselves about the reality of power and the hard necessities of its exercize.

Of course, in the usual way of thinking sociological inertia makes us vote, and what one votes for in general is this or that political hue, but - except in some rare, historic moments - one does so without great conviction based upon what we might expect to follow from such a vote. Understood from this standpoint the political spectacle is clearly an element of the *'theatrum mundi'* (Balandier, 1980; Maffesoli, 1979b); it inscribes itself in the rules of those good stories (*bonnes histoires*) which serve as interludes, or punctuate the boredom which moulds social life.

One often asks oneself, with more or less seriousness, about this 'voluntary servitude' (La Boétie). The answer is perhaps to investigate it from this side of our insatiable, infantile curiosity: as a doing *'as if'*, to see if something will change. In the absence of being able to 'play at being teacher' or 'play at being mummies and daddies', one plays at having elections. Saying this, I do not intend to invalidate this attitude. What right do we have to pass negative judgement upon an attitude, above all when this belongs to a ludic view of society? This is more a matter of emphasising everything in a social *mentalité* (what could also be called the mass, or the people) that which owes itself to this cyclical conception, and for which 'there is nothing new under the sun'. At the end of the day, the imposition effected by the powers that be stays the same, and this the people know well, albeit in a half-conscious manner. The Princes may change (and it is better that they do so), but their actions always remain abstract; and even when they hear of and act in the name of the most disadvantaged, it is always to ask for submission or conformity to the norm. Could it ever be otherwise? The gulf is far too great between the overhanging standpoint of the political and those things which motivate basic sociality.

These commonsense remarks which one could be able to pursue much as before, and which highlight the 'ambience' in which daily life is immersed, may be compared with more sophisticated considerations. It is always interesting to compare the popular expressions and the learned modulations of the same ideology, in this instance the idea of the return of the same. At the outset, as seen from a Weberian perspective it is plain that the charting and exploration of antinomic value systems as they exist both in different societies and within each individual society (a procedure summed up in the expression the 'war of gods') leads if not to an absolute 'axiological neutrality', then at least to a certain scepticism about the concept of 'Truth' itself as it arises in the human sciences (*les sciences humaines*) (Weber 1965, p. 399*ff*). In a thoroughly paradoxical and dynamic way Max Weber tries simultaneously both to think with rigour and to generalize, whilst also fully taking into account the fickle and ephemeral aspect of human passions. What is apparent, is that a number of his enquiries drive understanding right to the bottom of what I have called popular relativism. The 'antimony of values' can never be fully resolved; in the final analysis this is a function of what allows societies to endure. To sum this up in a rather cavalier manner: 'when the gods make war men are at peace'.

A similar perspective can be discovered in the sociology of Vilfredo Pareto. Just like Lévi-Strauss, who stated that 'man has always thought just as well', the sociologist of Lausanne was convinced that 'man is always the same'. This conviction is to be found in his *Traité de Sociologie générale*. A good many of his investigations are permeated with this scepticism. When one examines Pareto's life and work, it could be thought that such scepticism stemmed from all the disillusionments which marked his career. The ambitious Florentine engineer, the conscientious economist, then the somewhat embittered professor of sociology, each took account of the 'vanity of action', seeing that it is eternal recurrence and repetition which dominates the history of human societies. In this regard (but this is only perhaps a point of detail) I do not use the term 'pessimism' to characterize Pareto, as does his exegete Busino (Busino, 1968, p. 51; Pareto, 1968). It would perhaps be better to say that Pareto is imbued with the tragic sense of life. As an acute observer of the political activity of his time, Pareto knew only too well that any claim of politics to be founded in rational argument was fictitious. Having grasped this, he draws out all the consequences in a way which in the setting of this analysis impels me to regard his perspective as very close to that of popular scepticism. Reason as it purports to invest the political order, but also *a fortiori* as it is seen in all the many human activities which do not purport to derive their authority from a rational source, is but a *'derivation'* (Pareto), a legitimation which conceals the incoherences, digressions and particular interests of emotion. In saying this, one should not forget to think of the Machiavelli of the *Florentine Histories* who brought out so well all the ambiguity and ambivalence of human action. The historical displacements required are of little real consequence; it suffices simply to change the names of the protagonists and parties involved so as to obtain a form of analysis which can be applied to all epochs in which the political dimension has prevailed.

It becomes apparent that the game of politics is a privileged subject matter on the basis of which to observe the cycle of the return of the same. This can be established as a fact in the long term, but it can also be noted in the years, indeed even during the few months which follow an important electoral event. This is, however, the question of a process grounded in many societal attitudes. When the future predominates, the collective consciousness is turned globally towards the future; when the present has the upper hand, a resurgence of the cyclical vision is apparent. Why should this happen? Perhaps it is a function of the mechanism of 'saturation,' well described by Sorokin, in which values like all everything else are used up and wear themselves out. Whatever the answer may be in the absence of a response to the 'why', let us content ourselves by first tackling the 'how' that is by knowing how to draw forth consequences, whilst risking the penalties of not understanding anything about future societal developments. The myth and imaginal function that is staging a powerful return in public entertainment (apparent, for example, in what takes place around such figures as Michael Jackson, Madonna and Eric Cantona) is now affecting the institutions of the republic itself, as seen in a whole range of commemorative celebrations and in a forms of public play, a ludism (*le ludisme public*) enacted in the many festivals organized by local politicians and the public authorities. All this simultaneously explains both the saturation of a conception of linear time, and the desire to retrieve the *'hic et nunc'* which penetrates everyday life. Now, the present is never better grasped and understood than when it is set up in comparison with the great moments of the past. This is well able to clarify the metaphor of an 'Einsteinized' time suggested as a way of understanding Proust. Cyclical life returns us to this time of passion and feeling that overwhelms all rationalized constructions. It is perfectly legitimate to wish to reform or revolutionize this state of affairs, but we must once again recognize that the cyclic rhythm discerned in the different rituals draws us into a renewed epistemology which as yet only exists in its early stages.

It is certain that reflection on the nature of decadence will not be able to develop without reference, however allusive, to the unavoidable consequences that it has for our ways of knowing. From the moment when it is no longer the *'pro-jet'*, the thrust into the future that imposes its dominance upon social life, we are thrown back, at least on the intellectual level, to another manner of appraising social life. This involves a relativist acceptance of *what is*, the affirmation of life in all its contingency, and the recognition that every being or situation is shot through with incompleteness. This is what the logic of the 'it-must-be' (the *'devoir-être'*) is incapable of admitting.

This is the problem: as regards the given of daily life, perfection is a contradiction in the forms of social existence. In this sense and under its diverse forms, 'the dialectic which is dynamized by negation is not metaphorical, nor in the final analysis is it the profane form of theology; both demand a single meaning (a 'terminus *ad quem*' or a 'terminus *a quo*')'. One could also say in terms that metaphorically recapture mystical discourse, that the devil is the spirit which always says 'no', whilst god is always affirmation. The yes to life that corresponds with a decadent world or with a tragic mode of thought is, as it were, a 'divine yes to the all understood as divine, to the social represented as divine' (Maffesoli 1979a, pp.104*ff.*). That is what I have elsewhere called 'immanent transcendence'.

Perhaps this is the logico-experimental method dear to Pareto. Relieved of its positivist clothing, this places its stress upon the fact, upon the present which imposes its demand upon us. This method forces our intelligence to perform ceaselessly what I have called the 'to and fro between formism and empathy'. This is that generosity of spirit which takes us out of our work rooms and studies to trail round pubs, or to stroll in the streets. We may sneer at this, or shrug our shoulders, but it is by these means we come to know how to recognize the amplitude, intensity and variations in the very breath of social life. The object of our study is not a corpse: it may live a monotonous or an irruptive life; it may be truncated or completed, but it lives. It this that the thought eunuchs, the technocrats and knowledge lawyers, will never comprehend. Rather than continue in the perpetual application of the methods that have provided their evidence, but which now have nothing more to say about anything, we should resolutely engage ourselves in what Nicholas of Cusa called the spiral of knowing. In his time medieval dogmatism was running out of breath, a new world was being born; it is not impossible that this is also what we are being presented with today.

Instead of refusing or denying the paradoxes, the antinomies and the antagonisms which present themselves *en masse* in the social reality of everyday life, should we not perhaps tackle these tensions as they are. Naturally our considerations will not have the secure status (or the rigidity) of theoretical or divine Truth, but their shakiness will at least measure up to their labile object. It is perhaps by paying this price that it will be possible, as Edgar Morin has said, to 'transform vicious circles into virtuous cycles'. We have learned from the thinkers of the *Quatrocento* (Machiavelli and Guichardin) that this happens inasmuch as *virtu*' drives us back to the cement which structures the whole of sociality. Such a renewed epistemology has sense only if it sanctions us, outside all conformisms, to think everyday life.

As regards this, it is good to recall the etymology of the term 'encyclopaedia' (*agkuklios paidea*) as an 'apprenticeship that puts knowledge into cyclic action'. It is the latter which comes to the forefront in these remarks: the attention paid to that which is lived, the efficaciousness of the cycle and the renewal of knowledge which are all intimately interconnected. This need not lead to the creation of a closed system or to totalitarian thought in the strict sense, but to an approach that takes into account the discontinuities, the happenings and the small things of daily life. In a word, this gyratory aspect of existence is difficult to reduce to, or be contained within a rigid form of knowledge. Morin (despite his sarcasms) is important here when he characterizes this revolution in thought as, 'a whirling movement that shifts from phenomenal experience to the paradigms that organize experience' (Morin, 1977, pp. 19-20.).[1] This could scarcely be better expressed; the path to knowledge is accompanied by existential wandering, something the intellectual can all too frequently forget. Moreover, we should not think that the kind of existence at stake here is confined to the individual or to subjectivism. I believe that I have already shown under the auspices of the Dionysian paradigm that the existence here in question heads into a communal confusion well characterized by the metaphors of clustered bodies and of the 'territory' that serves to support it. The knowledge cycle underlines the outstripping of individualistic reduction, and it allows us to gain access to the ceaseless movement of the cosmos and to a relationship with the other. In ways opposed to the capitalistic maximization of goods, bodies or theories, this cycle leads us into joyful self-expenditure, a conjunction that we might call incarnate thought.

Contrary to those who confuse the decay of certain values with the death of everything, and with decadence and moroseness or tragedy and melancholy, and also contrary to those who think that the end of *a* world signifies the end of *the* world, it is good to remember the following. Thus, to 'speak of the grey monotony of everyday life, and of the breaks through which it is from time to time illuminated, is also to recognize the orgiastic pleasure of the unbridled senses. All this opens up a vast field of enquiry for us'. Well rooted in this foundation, and with our faces set against the apologists for the future and those nostalgic for the past, we are now in a position to think that decadence allows us to 'envisage the serenity of the Greek *Kairos*: what we might call the temporal opportunities of everyday life' (Maffesoli 1979a, p. 116; and Maffesoli 1996).

## Notes

1. This enterprise may usefully be compared to that in Gilbert Durand's work, *Les Structures anthropologiques de l'imaginaire*, Paris, 1969, deuxième partie, les symboles cycliques, p.321ff.

# References

Balandier, Georges 1980: *Le Pouvoir sur scène*. Paris: Balland.

Busino, G. 1968: *Introduction à une histoire de la sociologie de Pareto*. Geneva: Droz.

Durand, Gilbert 1969: *Les Structures anthropologiques de l'imaginaire*. Paris: Dumod.

Durand, Gilbert 1979: *Figures mythiques et visages de l'oeuvre*. Paris: Berg.

Maffesoli, Michel 1979a: *La Conquête du présent*. Paris: PUF.

Maffesoli, Michel 1979b: *La Violence totalitaire*. Paris: PUF.

Maffesoli, Michel 1993: *The Shadow of Dionysus*. New York: SUNY.

Maffesoli, Michel 1996: *The Contemplation of the World: Figures of Community Style*. Susan Emanuel trans. Minneapolis: University of Minnesota Press.

Morin, Edgar 1977: *La Méthode, 1-la nature de la nature*. Paris: Seuil.

Pareto, Vilfredo 1968: *Traité de sociologie générale*. Geneva: Droz.

Weber, Max 1965: *Essais sur la théorie de la science*. Julien Freund trans. Paris: Plon.

**Michel Maffesoli** is Professor of Sociology at the University of Rene Descartes Paris V and Director of Centre d'Étude sur L'Actuel et le Quotidien. He is the author of many books including most recently *The Time of the Tribes* (Sage 1995), and *Ordinary Knowledge* (Polity Press 1996). Working in the tradition of Gilbert Durand and George Ballandier, Professor Maffesoli has contributed to many areas of global sociology and has published widely in international journals.

# Time, Virtuality and the Goddess

Richard Roberts
Lancaster University

Today the future has caught up with the present, but time, individually and collectively, has remained limited. New resources of time are in demand. They are opening up through the extension of time in the present and through the availability at all times which technologies make possible. But the latter in their turn demand the temporal availability of human beings. So where is the time to be found? (Nowotny, 1994, p. 15)[1]

This chapter's focus will be especially on change affecting gender identity and more generally constitutive human self-identifications. Our focus in particular will be on transformations grounded in assertions of ultimacy and in reconceptions of the sublime. In this context, we shall see, perhaps surprisingly to many, theological traditions in Western thought find new relevance. We shall explore such relevance in relation both to contemporary social theory and to notions of virtual reality. We shall see that ancient sources, such as the time and eternity axis exploited in systematic theology, can be brought into connection with the cultural practices, discourse and theory of spatio-temporal transmutation. And this in turn can be used to explore and interrogate the religious field in innovative ways.

The *champ religieux* now exhibits a new dynamism and salience; moreover, this field now comprises a set of strange junctures. It comprises an ever more complex refraction between globalizing integration and localized intensifications, virtual reality and cybernetic enhancement. These post-millennial movements clash with potent drives towards an earth-centred chthonic identification this identification is very often gendered, very often female. As such it is frequently designated as 'the Goddess'. These contrasting developments may be regarded simply as integral factors in cycles of cultural production in so-called advanced capitalist societies (Beckford, 1989, ch. 2). Such limiting and even reductive strategies, however, should not be allowed to submerge perception of a gender-suffused recomposition of the religious field in which decayed patriarchy and resurgent matriarchy furnish fascinating and important analogues with other areas of cultural change. The present paper sets out to chart some areas of this complexity with a view to providing an explanation of the increasing salience of the religious and quasi-religious factors in contemporary culture.

The positive representation of postmodernity as socio-ethical critique by such writers as Zygmunt Bauman (1992, chs. 4 and 9), and the theoretical stretching of the imaginative possibilities prefigured in strands of science fiction have great purchase on welfare and religion today. Thus in the *imaginaire* of cybernetic culture and virtual reality, time, space, self, body, gender, community, and modes of 'transcendence' (that is, focal points of sublime identification) are all subject to visionary and revisionary treatment. These recompositions do not simply repel or distance premodern religion or contemporary religiosity grounded in the 'turn to the self' (Heelas 1996), but subject it to an unparalleled creative destruction. Thus, in more general terms, the virtual as vehicle of the religious (or quasi-religious) does not simply function as a psychological or quasi-religious compensator for disappointed and displaced aspirations (Stark and Bainbridge, 1987). It instead becomes the dynamic and problematic 'third nature' that succeeds a primal raw 'first' nature, and the industrially and technologically transformed 'second' nature. And at the same time virtuality undermines the reality and significance of *both* the former modes of nature.[2]

In this setting, 'postmodern religion', whether understood as 'shadow of spirit' (Berry and Wernick, 1992) or the 'after-life of religion' (Steiner, 1977), is seemingly outrun by temporal possibilities which loosen ties with traditions and their transformations. The new temporal possibilities also distance human experience from the ritual cycles that underpin viable cultures, and devalue everyday practices. Indeed, the forced universalization that stems from a virtual simultaneity may, as will be argued below, be understood as promoting yet further trivialization of the cultural universals of myth, ritual and symbol that inform the religious experience of humankind. In this chapter we examine the decomposition and recomposition of the cultural field. Here we examine the coalescence of reality and religiosity within the 'transcendence' afforded by virtual worlds and the transformations enabled by cybernetic empowerment. These changes advert us to an end of the human, a posthuman poised on the brink of escape from history and the human condition (Lyotard, 1991). There is a parallel between the present time-based analysis of the role of virtuality and the apparent abolition of the time-order, and Francis Fukuyama's (1992) depiction of the 'end of history' after the triumph of capitalism. Both the temporal and the historico-cyclic analyses assume the inescapable totalizing power of the globalized world system. But the virtualist or aspirant cyborg and the global trans-national manager part company as regards the solutions they propose for the problems of the posthuman and post-historical conditions.

The scenario sketched above has serious consequences for contemporary understandings of 'the religious'. Whilst there is a growing awareness of the increasing salience of the religious (or quasi-religious) factor in contemporary social and cultural change, and thus also in the human and social sciences that have addressed and represented such change, the expert reaction has so far been unimpressive. Responses have for the most part been confined to lengthy discussions and critiques of secularization.[3] Closely related have been the lengthy controversies concerning the categories of 'religion' and the 'sacred'. Here we have witnessed a split between functional reductionists and empathetic substantivists. The former see themselves as 'scientific', and true to Enlightenment principles. The latter, influenced by Mircea Eliade and Ninian Smart, see religion as possessing a fundamental and irreducible significance for human beings (Roberts, 1992b).

The functional reductionists self-consciously perform a series of final acts in the demolitionary explanation of the religious category. The substantivists, comprising historians of religion and phenomenologists, for their part retain a fundamental and unchanged religious empathy. There are, however, I shall argue, more dramatic re-assimilations that are taking take place. This re-assimilation features the confrontation of residual religious traditions and emergent spiritualities, on the one hand, with the 'quasi-religion' integral to crucial dimensions of socio-cultural change.[4] Not least, such developments may be traced through patterns of spiritual commodification. The confrontation activates the *self-critical* discourse of religion, in other words its function as *theological reflection*. In this sense, this paper may also be understood as an exercize in postmodern theological reflection.

In the main body of this chapter, the following issues are briefly investigated, each of which bears its own legitimate complexity. First, we briefly outline the use of the category of time in twentieth-century Western theology and religious thought and interpret this as a partial and distorted assimilation of modernity. Second, we develop and apply Helga Nowotny's notion of temporal simultaneity so as to broaden the framework of interpretation. This opens up a frame in which the religious implications of the assimilative power of contemporary cultural change may be understood. Third, central to such change is the growing polarity between two alternative ultimate points of resolution of the human condition. Both of these can be understood in terms of the sublime. The first sublime, that we shall explore, is the informatically sustained virtual reality and the prosthetic enhancement of the cyborg. This affords, in particular gendered ways of escape from the limitations of both first (raw) and second (industrial) nature. The second sublime can be detected in the recomposition of the religious field which increasingly reveals gendered tendencies that condense from highly involuted cycles of de-traditionalization and re-traditionalization. Here the celebration of the resurgent matriarchy takes place in the rediscovery of the Goddess in chthonic, earth-related sublime identifications. In conclusion, we will consider this polarity of the alternative *noetic* and *chthonic* sublimes focused in expanded (virtual) mind, and earth-centredness, respectively. This transformatory *imaginaire*, in both empirical religion and theoretical critique, may hopefully facilitate creative co-habitation between increasingly reflexive mainline religious traditions and the new array of innovative religiosities.

## Theology: The Temporal Matrix

In historical terms, the socio-scientific study of religion is traceable to such texts as David Hume's *Dialogues on the Natural History of Religion* where it originally distinguished itself from theology understood as the normative exposition of revealed truth expressed in sacred narrative. From the Enlightenment onwards, notably following Wilhelm von Humboldt's separation of theology from the *Geisteswissenschaften* (as the correlate of the institutional organization of the University of Berlin into separate faculties for theology and the humanities), the study of theology and of religion have come to occupy largely unrelated disciplinary fields. Interpreted from the stand-point of time, the evolution of modern Christian (and indeed Jewish) theology was obliged to respond to German idealist philosophy and to the challenge of historicism. The religious alternative thus stood between the idealising (for our purposes the noetic) tendency to resolve history into absolute mind or its surrogates, and a reductive historicist critique which eliminated absolute (originally revealed) truths in favour of an infinitely complex, but in the final analysis closed system of contingency and historical causality, a position expounded *par excellence* by Ernst Troeltsch.

The Swiss-German Reformed theologian Karl Barth (1886-1968), attempted to overcome the dilemma between this idealist loss of time and the exclusion of absolute truths from the contingent realm. He did this first of all by the adoption of a radicalized eschatology, and then, after a prolonged intellectual crisis he rebuilt his theology around the axis of eternity and time (Roberts, 1992a, ch. 1). Barth thus moved from the theological equivalent of the Hegelian *Momente*, dialectical 'moments' of eschatological intrusion which occupied interstitial 'breaks' in the seamless causality of historical time, to the re-functionalization within a grandiose systematic theology of the ancestral theological *totum simul*, the idea of divine simultaneity which originates in its classic form in Boethius' *Consolations of Philosophy*. Thus Barth recapitulates the whole Western tradition within a reasserted zone of revealed truth, reminiscent of the way that Proust researched and re-presented the 'lost time' of his own experience. Barth's representation of an eternity as 'God's time' for which the succession of past, present and future is not an insuperable obstacle, presages and parallels the contemporary rebirth of, we shall see, the patriarchal time of ancestral Western thought.

Yet twentieth century Protestant Christian theology, and in particular its representation of time and space, may be understood as manoeuvres played out in a long-standing strategy of retreat in the face of an aggressive modernity. It is possible to subsume both the internal development and the external relations of Christian theology into a secularization model in which the categories of time and space provide an effective means of mapping the disjunction of the theological sphere from other representations of reality. Now, however, the 'market' of theological and religious possibilities is far more differentiated and equitable than the orthodox secularization model might suggest, both within theological traditions and as found in new or revived forms of religiosity. Main-line Abrahamic religions are in persisting crisis and part of their difficulty is to be seen in the disintegration of patriarchy, both in theology and in religious cultural practices. A peculiarly well-focused aspect of this process is what, following Nowotny's analysis, can be now represented as the fragmentation and reconstitution of patriarchal time.

## Modernism as postmodernity: the time/space matrix

At the end of the twentieth century we are faced with neo-apocalyptic consciousness, postmodern panic thinking and an 'ecological eschaton'. At the same time a resurgence of religious activity is taking place against the background of a much contested 'End of History' in which invasive capitalism seemingly knows no bounds. This array of factors, all contestable, forms part of complex processes of reconfiguration of society and cultures. In the setting of resurgent modernism perceived as postmodern, Nowotny has argued in *Time: The Modern and Postmodern Experience* for the centrality of the concept of time, or rather of *times*, for:

> [I]t is we human beings who make time. The more complex the society, the more stratified the courses of time also become which overlap, form temporal connections with and alongside one another ... Time has become a fundamental issue for all sciences, since it raises problems central to the understanding of the phenomena under investigation. (Nowotny 1994, p. 7)

The differentiation of 'times' out of unified time, and what Nowotny depicts as the 'disappearance of the category of the future and its replacement by ... an extended present' (Nowotny, 1994, p. 8) are central features of modernity and technological modernization. The world-wide drive for simultaneity now confronts a variety of cultural 'times' in the temporal manifestation of the global/local matrix. The capacity for and attainment of simultaneity within global markets is what differentiates the rich from the poor who are strictly localized in time. Attempts to attain simultaneity are (according to a law of diminishing returns) progressively more difficult, and are also associated with qualitative changes in the perception and utilization of time. We might say (when permitted a neologism) that we inhabit a 'nanocracy' in which the capacity to compress and accelerate temporal processes is a prime index of wealth and power. Thus distinctions between the premodern (characterized by a unified temporal order), the modern (exhibiting quantified and commodified time) and the postmodern (that manifests accelerated time tending to simultaneity) can be located in a differentiated continuum that tends towards a point of culmination in the abolition of both temporal succession and future reference:

> Whilst in the phase of industrialization it was above all the equation of time and money which resulted from the industrial capitalist logic of production and made time a scarce commodity, time is [now, in the information society] becoming accelerated innovation. (Nowotny, 1994, pp. 10-11)

The latter equation of time with accelerated innovation is commensurate with Lyotard's classic definition of the 'postmodern condition' as dynamic, yet persisting transition:

> A work can only become modern only if it is first postmodern. Postmodernism thus understood is not modernism at its end but in the nascent state and this state is constant. (Lyotard, 1984, p. 79)

Nowotny's two basic contentions concerning the disappearing future and the extension of the present are complemented by a further third axiom, the assertion that the boundaries between past, present and future are not universally valid. Thus as in Karl Barth's account of theological temporality so with Nowotny, simultaneity threatens to overturn time as mere succession. This radical suggestion is grounded in difference of temporal judgement that is in turn correlatable with changing cultural conditions:

> With the end of an age in which, by means of the time-structure of industrial production, both linearity and the belief in progress were sustained, the category of the future is losing much of its attractiveness. A present geared to accelerated innovation is beginning to devour the future. Problems which could formerly be deferred into the future reach into the present for their part, press for solutions which admittedly may

not be on the agenda until tomorrow but demand to be dealt with today. (Nowotny, 1994, p. 11)

If, as Nowotny suggests, linear time has 'died' then what might have replaced it? Is it plausible to hope that time will be stopped, or that the continuum will be replaced by the technological and temporal equivalent of the Kondratiev business cycle. The relation between and content of time and value has changed - and is changing. Further exploration and explanation of the cultural consequences of this change could well begin with a consideration of the temporal implications of Lyotard's declaration that, *'Postmodern* would have to be understood according to the paradox of the future *(post)* anterior *(modo)'* (Lyotard, 1984, p. 81). Nowotny crystallizes her argument around the notion of 'one's own time' *(Eigenzeit)* which she associates with the emergence of women from the private (as opposed to male-dominated) public temporal sphere of bourgeois society. Time and its disposal thus become a matter of rights and of the differentiated political sphere, rather than the *imperium* of a patriarchal universal. As we shall see, technological developments permit the virtual and cybernetic extension and enabling what is exposed in the recent history of time. As a hard-headed materialist and feminist social scientist, Nowotny pursues a pragmatic line and avoids the excess of the hyper-stimulated *imaginaire* of the *prosthesophiliac* (Lury, 1997). Nonetheless, she does propagate the conceptual neologism of competing 'uchronias' in modernity/post-modernity. Yet such is the intensity of the rational, maximising demands imposed upon the reserve of time, that in practical terms a countervailing strategy is required:

> Learning to handle one's own reserves of time better in the face of a limited term of life, resiting the pressure of time, presupposes an appreciative openness towards the strategically playful aspect in time. Some things may be learnable in seminars on time management, but there are innumerable playful approaches and strategies. (Nowotny, 1994, p. 14)

The *ludic* treatment of time, and what we might call the re-learning of a considered slowness, is similar in some respects to the reappropriation of time through ritual in the context of deep ecology and chthonic spirituality to which we turn later (see Pearson, Roberts and Samuel, 1998). Nowotny nonetheless regards the successful exploration and management of temporal transition (Hassard, 1996) as a central human pre-occupation of late or advanced modernity. Nowotny's work incorporates what is for her an implicit cultural tension within women's existence between the managerial self-maximization enacted in enhanced, competitive performance, as opposed to primal biological identification grounded in 'slowness'. This tension between the exploitation of simultaneity as the arena of performance and efficiency and 'slow' biological time will recur in the innovative religiosities of New Age and Neo-Paganism to be examined later in the present paper.

Nowotny's interest is concentrated upon the transformation of time-consciousness from early modernity onwards; she is pointedly uninterested in pre-modernity. The change from pre-modernity begins, so she implies, at the turn of the thirteenth century. Repeating the French historian LeGoff's assertion that it was at this juncture that God's time gave way to the time of the traders, Nowotny links social change to material causes. Reflecting the influence of Schumpeter's (rather than Marx's) account of the rise of the entrepreneur, she argues it is the risking of assets that becomes the touchpoint of development and nascent modernity. Curiously, it is only with the eighteenth century that the horizon of the future is activated: 'The idea of progress entered the history of the human race' (Nowotny, 1994, p. 16). Now there also emerged a pervasive disjunction between measured time difference and lived time, that is between 'world time' (*Weltzeit*) and 'life time' (*Lebenszeit*) (Blumenberg, 1986). Nowotny's subsequent analysis largely ignores the ongoing cultural impact of an active historic residue of ideas of time and the perspectives latent in the religious and eschatological dimensions of Western history explored, for example, in the historical works of Ernst Bloch[5]. Thus if Nowotny were to have included the conceptual pre-history of the scenario of modernity/postmodernity, this would have provided the basic analogue to the loss of future and growth of simultaneity that she regards as typical of the chaotic proliferation of 'times' characteristic of postmodernity. Again, it is theological conceptuality which provides the apposite analogue of spatio-temporal compression and over-arching simultaneity.

There is, indeed, a marked deficit in Nowotny's work, which recalls that of Marx: the religious past of the West is either virtually ignored, or it appears in derisory, even parodic forms. Thus the imposition of standardized time on a global scale associated with economic and political integration, transportation, informatization, and so on, approaches world-wide simultaneity in response to which people '*want to have more time for themselves*' (Nowotny 1994, p. 18, author's emphasis). However brilliant Nowotny's mapping of the social and cultural change that leads to this juxtaposition of globalized and localized temporal economy may be, her account is circumscribed. Nowotny has set to one side the question of God. By contrast, the 'history of God' in Western culture can be rendered concrete through the mapping of time change and the role of simultaneity in relation to economic and societal factors (Blumenberg, 1983). As Marx hints in percipient passages of the *Grundrisse*, the 'jealous God' of capitalist accumulation, in short, ontologized money, is the 'God' that once mediated Western culture. Recent technological developments turn the omniscience, omnipotence, omnipresence and simultaneity of 'God'/capital expressed by Marx in conceptual terms (See Morris, 1995, pp. 88-120) into 'realities' accessible to a mass culture. Thus rather than God 'giving way' to the time of the traders, God's time becomes the temporal empowerment incarnated in capital itself.

As both Nowotny and David Harvey (1980) argue, the 'first postmodernity' of rampant cultural modernism in the early decades of the twentieth century had two interrelated aspects, speed and simultaneity. But it is a second, more intense, intoxication, what Nowotny calls 'the illusion of simultaneity', that affects - even afflicts - our own era, the 'second postmodernity', by way of permanent oversatiation (Roberts, 1992b, p. 30). This situation is not value-free, for 'simultaneity has everyone under control' (Nowotny, 1994, p. 30). We can now see how Nowotny's position exhibits parallels to the refunctioning of the ancient philosophical and theological notion of the *totum simul* to be found in twentieth century theology as indicated earlier. To this may be added the relevance of theological explorations of the distinction between significant and mere chronological or narrative faciticity (i.e. the contrast of *kairos* and *chronos*), and the parallel juxtaposition as significant and mere history (i.e *Geschichte* as opposed to *Historie*) in twentieth century religious thought (Fastenrath, 1982). Given the modernist perspective which Nowotny and Harvey substantially share, it is the expressionist, apocalyptic and eschatological dimensions which they both neglect. Examination of the parallel histories and textualities of twentieth century theology and religious thought expands and deepens our understanding of the temporal narrative presented by Nowotny.

## Virtual *Noesis*: Cyber-space and Redemptions of the 'Flesh'

What might be the temporal effects of a 'third nature' proliferates in virtual reality and cyborg culture? Klaus Eder focuses upon the consequences of this expansion in an undramatic, but nonetheless pointed way:

> The nature question decides whether in modern society it is possible to take a path of social evolution of practical reason which will allow us to block off practical unreason in interacting with nature. The nature issue is predestined to start a renewed ideologization of modern practical reason. For the social state of nature that has been achieved in modernity offers a concept of practical rationality that can do without morality. The 'cybernetic state of nature' looming on the horizon is based on a concept

of practical rationality that reduces morality to the reproducibility of this state of nature. (Eder, 1996, p. 57)

The 'reproducibility' of the state of nature may indeed have rather more dramatic implications than Eder would seem prepared to allow for. For William Gibson cyberspace is 'a consensual hallucination ... [People are] creating a world. It's not really a place. It's not really space. It's notional space' (See Kramarae, 1995). More generally 'virtual reality' is an expanding sphere open for appropriation realized (in both noetic AI and physical prosthetic terms) on the technical foundation of cybernetics. Cybernetics itself was originally defined as the scientific theory of control and communication in the animal or machine. Cybernetics is generally assumed to have begun (in terms of its own myth of origin) with Norbert Wiener's neologism derived from the Greek *kubernetes* (steersman). The cyborg is an adjunct of virtual reality and has been represented as 'postbiological humanity' (Featherstone and Burrows, 1995, p. 4). The ethical and political implications are considerable: relatively painless re-allocation and *Lebensraum* in virtuality are regarded as possibilities.

Paradoxically this discussion is not driven simply by the actual experience of cybernetically-induced virtuality but also by certain texts which have attained the status of a formative 'Word' in networked communities dedicated to its representation. Thus, for example, 'Gibsonian space' is a construct derived from William Gibson's science-fiction novel *Neuromancer*. This derivation has some similarity with Nowotny's treatment of 'times' as opportunity for the expansion of women's potential. In a rather remarkable way the socio-cultural theorization of cybernetic possibilities is in the first instance a text-governed, rather an experience-following, empirically-induced community activity. Here it is possible to speak of a quasi-sectarian or quasi-cultic activity that prefigures the 'real' as it is deconstructed and virtualized through technology. Gibson's (1984) foundational text *Neuromancer* (Gibson 1984) prefigured contemporary cultural transmutations and has served as a conceptual bank upon which theory has subsequently drawn.

Remarkably, a close reading of key passages of *Neuromancer* reveals a theological *Doppelgänger* in which a redemptive drama of the flesh is played out. Gibson provides us with a virtual theatre in which the re-enactment of some of the primal myths of the West is staged. In *Neuromancer*, the nightmarish, gender-specific narcissisms of mind (a malleable, contested, identity-bearing commodity) and 'meat' (a Frankenstein-like corporeality) are countered by a dream-like regression, a partial decoding of lost memory, a recapitulatory *kenosis* of human pretension. In Gibson's work, this is not so much part of an overt quasi-political agenda as the expression of a complex nostalgia implicit in a retelling of the drama of fall and redemption. In one of the most resonant and suggestive passages in *Neuromancer*, Gibson unfolds the life narrative of his hero:

> Case was twenty-four. At twenty-two, he'd been a cowboy, a hustler, one of the best in the Sprawl. He'd been trained by the best ... He'd operated on an almost permanent adrenaline high, a by-product of youth and proficiency, jacked into a custom cyberspace deck that projected his disembodied consciousness into the consensual hallucination that was the matrix.
>
> He stole from his employers ... they were going to make sure he never worked again.
>
> They damaged his system with a wartime Russian mycotoxin.
>
> Strapped to a bed in a Memphis hotel, his talent burning out micron by micron, he hallucinated for thirty hours.
>
> The damage was minute, subtle, and utterly effective.
>
> For Case, who'd lived for the bodiless exaltation of cyberspace, it was the Fall. In the bars he'd frequented as a cowboy hotshot, the elite stance involved a certain relaxed contempt for the flesh. The body was meat. Case fell into the prison of his own flesh. (Gibson, 1984, pp. 11-12)

On a superficial level, with its allusions to a fall into the 'prison of the flesh' (and hints of Samson and Prometheus) this passage could be accorded a 'gnostic' reading, but this would be misleading. For imprisonment in the flesh does not lack irony; Case's recovery of humanity, the challenge to his hubris, begins with his 'Fall' into the limitations of the body. Likewise, his (residually female) partner struggles with feline cyborgic enhancement; yet in sexual communion the union of bodies constitutes a moment of reclamation:

> It was a place he'd known before; not everyone could take him there, and somehow he always managed to forget it. Something he'd found and lost so many times. It belonged, he knew – he remembered – as she pulled him down, to the meat, the flesh the cowboys mocked. It was a vast thing, beyond knowing, a sea of information coded in spiral and pheromone, infinite intricacy that only the body, in its strong blind way, could ever read. (Gibson, 1984, pp. 284-5)

This is redemption through the recovery of the fleshly body and its limitations. It challenges the unending demands for both physical and mental performance in the Gibsonian world of virtuality and cyborgic enhancement, in which 'human nature' no longer exists other than as the point of departure for accretion and processes of 'self'-improvement determined by low cunning and enacted in the predatory economy of body parts and cybernetic implants. 'Mind' and 'Body' have capacities for permanent cyborgic transformation, a potential limited in principle only by the capacity of each subject to access his/her advancement through economic resources and crime. In Gibson's trans-temporal Panopticon, the struggle against total transparency is a battlefield for the privacy that secures identity. *Neuromancer* is, at least in part, a narrative of redemption from the spiral of dehumanising self and corporeal-enhancement conjoined with the endless opportunities of virtuality and cyber-space. The truth lies in the flesh; the transcendence of self-appropriation involves a retreat (at first enforced as punishment) from the illusory grandeur of the mental and bodily realms of the prosthesis to the banality of an original, limited embodiment. Significantly, the recapturing of the body, even its limitations, is paralleled by similar developments in the recomposition of the religious field.

In Gibson's textual space, the past and present, original and artefact, coexist in a haunting duplicity. The leading characters not only co-exist in each others' consciousness and ceaselessly strive to expand their limitations, but they also strain to decipher each face for signs of real youth in the endless rebuilds of their 'meat'. Vat-cultivated and real flesh, cybernetic, narcotic and genetic implants and the warring mutual invasion of consciousness constitute an *imaginaire* that Gibson extrapolated from a then (1984) relatively limited technological actuality. *Neuromancer* helped launch a cloned culture of cybernetic and virtual expansion enacted in a series of films and in a corpus of socio-cultural theory. Mutually so engorged, media and theory have exercized significant social agency as they help drive forward cultural change in a labile popular consciousness. Thus the destruction/reconstruction of the post-human in *The Terminator*, Donna Haraway's 'femancipatory' agenda, and the self-experimental elite of 'prosthesophiliacs' (Stone, 1995 pp. 393-406) instantiate a Gibson-like drive towards emancipation from biological and socially-constructed.

As Haraway has maintained, cyborg potential releases body and consciousness from all limitations, including any limitations imposed by gender identity. Like the feminist theologian Judith Plaskow (1980, p. 3), who has argued (against Reinhold Niebuhr) that for women, sin is 'the failure to take responsibility for self-actualization,' Haraway (Haraway, 1991, p. 181) is free to exercize mythopoetic imagination in the creation of a regime of uncluttered female potentiation. Race, gender, and capital require a cyborg theory of wholes and parts. There is no drive in cyborgs to produce total theory, but there is an intimate experience of boundaries, their construction and deconstruction. There is a myth system waiting to become a political language to ground one way of looking at science and technology and challenging the informatics of domination - in order to act potently. The ecstatic reappropriation of body-transcending self-potentiation (as opposed to divinization) is expressed in Haraway's (1991, p. 181) utterance 'I'd rather be a cyborg than a goddess'. This issues in the vision of the female emancipate, cyborgically enhanced and freed from biological identity-determination. Without embarrassment, or the neurotic depotentiation generated by Feuerbach or Freud, Haraway's *Cyborg Manifesto* proclaims an increasingly pervasive image of the *Überweib*, a gender-transcending Superwoman emergent as the cyborgic ideal.

Unlike Gibson's tormented male hero Case, the equally tested and increasingly androgynous heroic warrior character Ripley, created by Sigourney Weaver in successive *Alien* films, provides a powerful and contrasting image of struggle. Looked at in terms of elective affinities within the vocabulary of images provided by the cultural inheritance upon which the creators of both sagas draw, Case enacts (as a male at the end of patriarchy) a *kenotic* (self-emptying) quasi-christological descent from transpersonal potency into the vulnerability of the worn, limited body. By contrast and in inverse correspondence, Haraway's cyborg 'femancipate' climbs out of the body in a *plerotic* (self-filling) ascent to power. Weaver's character Ripley acts out something akin to a warrior Christology in the performance of a representative role reminiscent of a *Christus Victor*, a battler against insidious, nameless, relentless evil that resists all (male) efforts at its exclusion.

Haraway's sympathies lie within a continuing materialism, a this-worldly political agenda in which women exploit all means available to enhance their potency freed from the social and biological cultural construction that is projected upon them as 'nature'. But recently Sherman and Jundkins (1992, p. 134) have argued that virtual reality 'affords glimpses of heaven' in the next century. Here virtual reality is seen to provide a specifically male refuge from ecological degradation and the involuntary *kenosis* of patriarchy through a scheme disempowerment imposed by women. This is evidence of a more alarming flight from responsibility. Yet the incipient polarity between 'femancipation' and what we might call 'demancipation' has, as we shall shortly see, intriguing points of correlation with current developments in the changing religious field.

## Gendered Ultimacies and the Religious Field: The Chthonic Goddess

The ideas of informational time as simultaneity and discussion of cyborg culture have underscored the reconfiguration of the religious field as a noetic, quasi-gnostic resolution of human identity into an inner individuality (Heelas 1996). This field is at the same time undergoing restructuring by a drive towards chthonic identification. This chthonic imperative is stated with uncompromising clarity by prominent Neo-Pagans like, for example, Monica Sjöö and Barbara Mohr who derive all human social life culture from the hearth around which the primeval women gathered (Sjöö and Mohr 1987, p. 11). For them, 'Human survival does indeed depend on a sacramental relation to nature' (Sjöö and Mohr, 1987, p. 80). Original human identity was female, women were the bearers of culture until the 'fall' occasioned by the discovery and aggressive deployment of metal (above all iron) by men. With a mythopoetic intensity Sjöö and Mohr elaborate a vision of primal female identity which, like that generated by Haraway, reflects all too readily contemporary gender politics. Thus woman as embodiment of the Goddess emerges, a figure endowed with perfect politically correct attributes,

> The original witch was undoubtedly black, bisexual, a warrior, a wise and strong woman, also a midwife, also a leader of her tribe ... The nature of the Goddess was in no way the pale, meek, and solely maternal one that has been associated with 'feminity' in patriarchal culture. (Sjöö and Mohr, 1987, p. 216)

As a female activist and Pagan,[6] Monica Sjöö is prepared to make challenging discriminations between different strands of contemporary spirituality and religiosity. Indeed, in her passionate and sometimes eccentric cultural artefact, *New Age and Armageddon*, Sjöö condemns certain tendencies out of hand as world-injurious, even pernicious and to cut across the plethora of diversity in New Age beliefs and practices (Sjöö, 1992, ch. 1). She erects a basic distinction between what we here designate as the *chthonic* and *noetic* alternatives, which, in preliminary analytic terms separate Paganism from New Age. The broad elective affinities of the two categories are extremely important. The association of some main forms of Paganism (or Neo-Paganism) with earth-centred spiritual practices, ecological activism and the mythic and practical celebration of the pre-modern and (ultimately the matriarchal) prehistoric human condition is indicative. The predominant stress upon cyclic time within an aeonic conception of the evolution of the human condition conceived as having fallen from pre-metallic, matriarchal origins involves a conscious primitivism but (as we have seen from Nowotny's analysis of the 'recovery of slowness') is but one side of an emergent recomposition of the religious field.

The manifest assimilation, indeed the striking mutual empowerment of New Age practices and contemporary globalized (and thus simul-taneity-seeking) capitalism in a cult of performativity (inseparable from time-acceleration) also fall within the parameters of Nowotny's account of the recent history of time and (post)modernity. Regarding the slowing of time in order to gain possession of it, the Pagan might break with the practice of hyperperformativity through ritual intervention, while Nowotny would advocate a review of time-management. Both the neoprimitivists and the postmodern theorist seek to recapture time, and thus value, from the invasive *totum simul* of a virtual reality empowered by global capitalism and realized by information technology in an interlinked constellation of possibilities largely controlled and exploited mainly by men.

## Conclusion: Recompositions and Mutualities?

From the standpoint of mainline religious traditions the quasi-theologization of virtual reality and cyborg discourse presents itself as an illicit expropriation of conceptual territory. In this transcendence and the sublime become adjuncts of technology and the market. Today's Neo-paganism, for its part, proposes a re-enchantment of the earth, re-investing nature with intrinsic meaning. Such a re-peopling of the cosmos with divinities is doubtless problematic, not least for those bred on the uncompromising purities of either rationalism or monotheism. Yet infused through the interlinked recompositions of the religious and the cultural fields an epochal transition is taking place on the level of gender. In consequence, the whole evolving compact of secularized theism with patriarchal modernity comprised under the modes of rationality and instrumental reason associated with male hegemony is also called into question. These developments may now, we venture to suggest, be coming to assume the proportions of a paradigm shift from a masculinist and patriarchal to a feminist and matriarchal sensibility. Both paradigms exist in parallel, comprising an increasing area of contested space within the religious field.

Thus main-line religion and the Abrahamic traditions are faced with two major alternative possibilities. The first is the continued decline of the patriarchal universalism of the 'grand narratives' (and correlative 'grand times') of the Jewish and Christian traditions. The second is an aggressive and particularistic alienation into the 'time' of the radical conservatism of the fundamentalisms. The apocalypticism and the latent or actual violence and ecological catastrophism often characteristic of such forms of religious resurgence is evidence of deep alienation from a common time analogous with a global 'common good'. This resurgence exists alongside the dispersed option of a globalized, superficially differentiated market in spiritualities of the 'New Age movement' (Heelas, 1996). There are affinities between New Age and the paradigm of simultaneity described above in Nowotny's work and in cyberculture.

Standing in opposition to this are of course the regressive tendencies of the Pagan emergence.

In the face of a dichotomy in the religious field between the world alienative resurgent patriarchal 'times' of patriarchy religion and global fundamentalisms and the quasi-theological *nunc stans* of New Age self-religion and its compact with capitalism (and equal ecological indifference) what possibility might there be for a more benign configuration in a recomposing religious field? As *tertium quid*, an alternative third path might be the democratic and reflexive re-appropriation of myth and ritual in the service of humankind and of a re-conceptualization of the divine in terms which incorporate female attributes. Here time might be remade, revalued through liminality and grace-acknowledging embodiment. This would be a religiosity of individual risk and communal enterprise, a distinctive response to the routinized, bureaucratized and faded charisma of much mainline religion. Such a vision cannot simply flow from fiction-driven theory, nor can it be confined to the dialectics of lone masculinity and the counter-natural of the virtual or the cyborg. It is quite literally on the ground where the incarnational *kenosis* of the linear time of male God and the cyclic temporal *plerosis* of the Goddess suggest the possibility of mutual gendered reconciliation; but this meeting of *animus* and *anima* calls for many-layered transvaluations, the beginnings of which are scarcely known, far less the endings. The 'times' of the God and the Goddess diverge: whose time is now to come?

## Notes

1. Helga Nowotny (1994). Originally published in 1984 under the title *Eigenzeit Entstehung und Strukturierung eines Zeitgefühls* this work has attained wide recognition.
2. The ritual suicide of the Heaven's Gate collective and the affective mass cultural dynamics of the death of the Princess of Wales would be obvious starting-points for explorations of the interaction of the virtual and the 'real' and the transmutations of quasi-religion with explicit and normative mainline religiosity.
3. Notable exceptions are Beyer 1995 and Robertson 1992.
4. I explore this more fully in my forthcoming book *Religion and the Postmodern Condition: A Sociological Study*, London: Sage.
5. For anyone sensitive to what might be termed the 'eschatological criticism' applied to Western thought by Bloch, Nowotny's work has interesting limitations. See R. H. Roberts (1990).
6. North American readers may be more familiar with the term 'Neo-Pagan'. European and British Pagans tend to assert (not uncontentiously) a historical continuity of indigenous practice and thus prefer the designation without

prefix. See Ronald Hutton's contribution to Pearson, Roberts and Samuel (1998 forthcoming).

# References

Bauman, Zygmunt 1992: *Intimations of Postmodernity*. London: Routledge.
Beckford, James 1989: *Religion in Advanced Industrial Society*. London: Unwin Hyman.
Berry, Philippa and Wernick, Andrew (eds.) 1992: *Shadow of Spirit: Postmodernism and Religion*. London: Routledge.
Beyer, Peter 1995: *Religion and Globalization*, London, Sage.
Blumenberg, Hans 1983: *The Legitimacy of the Modern Age*. Cambridge, Mass.: MIT.
Blumenberg, Hans 1986: *Lebenszeit und Weltzeit*. Frankfurt: Suhrkamp.
Eder, Klaus 1996: *The Social Construction of Nature: A Sociology of Ecological Enlightenment*. London: Sage.
Fastenrath, Elmer 1982: *'In Vitam Aeternam': Grundzüge christlicher Eschatologie in der ersten Hälfte des 20. Jahrhunderts*. Erzabtei St. Ottilien: Eos Verlag.
Featherstone, Mike and Burrows, Roger (eds.) 1995: *Cyberspace/Cyberbodies/Cyberpunk: Cultures of Technological Embodiment*. London: Sage.
Fukuyama, Francis 1992: *The End of History and the Last Man*. London: Hamish Hamilton.
Gibson, William 1984: *Neuromancer*. London: Victor Gollancz.
Haraway, Donna Jeanne 1991: A Cyborg Manifesto: Science, Technology, and Socialist Feminism in the Late Twentieth Century. In *Simians, Cyborgs, and Women The Reinvention of Nature*. London: Free Association Books, pp. 149-81.
Harvey, David 1989: *The Condition of Postmodernity: An Enquiry into the Origins of Cultural Change*. Oxford: Blackwell.
Hassard, John 1996: Images of Time in Work and Organisation. In *Handbook of Organisation Studies*. Clegg, Stewart R., Hardy, Cynthia and Nord, Walter R. (eds.). London: Sage, pp. 581-98.
Heelas, Paul 1996: *The New Age Movement: The Celebration of the Self and the Sacralization of Modernity*. Oxford: Blackwell.
Kramarae, Chris 1995: A Backstage Critique of Virtual Reality. In *CyberSociety: Computer-Mediated Communication and Community*. Steven G. Jones (ed.), London, pp. 10-35.
Lasch, Christopher 1980: *The Culture of Narcissism*. London: Abacus.
Lury, Celia 1997: *Prosthetic Culture*. London: Routledge.
Lyotard, Jean-Francois 1979/84: *The Postmodern Condition*. Manchester: Manchester University Press.
Lyotard, Jean-Francois 1991: *The Inhuman: Reflections on Time*. Cambridge: Polity.
Morris, Paul 1995: Judaism and Capitalism. In *Religion and the Transformations of Capitalism: Comparative Approaches*. Roberts, Richard H. (ed.), pp. 88-120. London: Routledge.
Nowotny, Helga 1994: *Time: The Modern and Postmodern Experience*. Cambridge: Polity Press.

Pearson, Joanne, Roberts, Richard H. and Samuel, Geoffrey (eds) 1998: *Nature Religion Today: Paganism in the Modern World*. Edinburgh: Edinburgh University Press.

Plaskow, Judith 1980: *Sin, Sex and Grace: Women's Experience and the Theologies of Reinhold Niebuhr and Paul Tillich*. Washington, DC: University Press of America.

Roberts, Richard H. 1990: *Hope and its Hieroglyph: A Critical Decipherment of Ernst Bloch's 'Principle of Hope'*. Atlanta: Scholars Press.

Roberts, Richard H. 1992a: *A Theology on Its Way: Essays on Karl Barth*. Edinburgh: T. and T. Clark.

Roberts, Richard H. 1992b: Religion and the 'Enterprise Culture': the British Experience in the Thatcher Era (1979-1990). *Social Compass*, 39(1), pp.15-33.

Robertson, Roland 1992: *Globalization: Social Theory and Global Culture*. London: Sage.

Sherman, Barrie and Jundkins, Phil 1992: *Glimpses of Heaven, Visions of Hell: Virtual Reality and its Implications*. London: Hodder and Stoughton.

Sjöö, Monica and Mohr, Barbara 1987: *The Great Cosmic Mother: Rediscovering the Religion of the Earth*. San Francisco: Harper.

Sjöö, Monica 1992: *New Age and Armageddon: The Goddess or the Gurus? Towards a Feminist Vision of the Future*. London: Women's Press.

Stark, Rodney and Bainbridge, William Sims 1987: *A Theory of Religion*. New York: Peter Lang.

Steiner, George 1977: *In Bluebeard's Castle*. London: Faber and Faber.

Stone, Sandy 1995: Split Subjects, Not Atoms; or, How I fell in Love with My Prosthesis. In *The Cyborg Handbook*. Chris Hables Gray (ed.), London: Routledge, pp. 393-406.

**Richard Roberts** holds a Chair in Religious Studies at Lancaster University. Prior to that he held the Chair of Divinity at the University of St. Andrews. Professor Roberts has published books on Ernst Bloch and Karl Barth, and edited collections on *The Recovery of Rhetoric: Persuasive Discourse and Disciplinarity in the Human Sciences* (1993), *Religion and the Transformations of Capitalism* (1995) and *Nature Religion Today: Paganism in the Modern World* (1998).

# Staging the Self by Performing the Other: Global Fantasies and the Migration of the Projective Imagination[1]

Luiz E. Soares

IUPERJ – Graduate Institute for Social Research of Rio de Janeiro
and UERJ – State University of Rio de Janeiro

Let me begin with two simple tales – simple but telling. Each brings up a set of provocative questions on the social dynamics of global scenes. The main focus of these ethnographic narratives is the limits and paradoxes of reflexivity and the complex politics of imagination. Each drama or comedy was staged in a different national arena, though both crossed national boundaries and referred to transnational relations, values and meanings. I intend to show how the playing of identity in the global ecumene, as Ulf Hannerz would say, or in the world taken as a single place, as Roland Robertson would say,[2] operates through a mechanism of displacement and projection. In this process, I shall suggest, the construction of the self becomes a residual derivative of the process of imagining the other, of performing imaginary otherness.

## Tropical Wildness Through the Looking Glass

During a stay in Sweden, trying to understand better the achievements of the social democratic welfare state, so deeply admired by Brazilian socialists, I had the opportunity of getting acquainted with some colleagues, who were nice enough to invite me to dinners and parties. I realized quickly that images of austerity, seriousness, self-control, and introspection, conveyed worldwide by Ingmar Bergman, were not at all easily falsefiable. Dinners were frequently followed by singing: each one would receive a booklet of lyrics so that the songs could be sung collectively. My hosts took pleasure in improvising a choir. But most striking was the immobility of the bodies and the homogeneity of the slow rhythm. Everybody sang seated around the table, as if the scene of the meal were being staged again, the ritual of eating replaced by the choir; or the ritual of eating unfolding as a choir. I could not avoid Durkheimian musing on the power of society over individuality, on the religious dimension of collective life. I recalled Marcel Mauss's interpretation of the rhythm of parades as a performative metaphor of order, regulation of time, exorcism of death, taming of chance, and a tool for the shaping of sociability. I confess I could not refrain from projecting Apollonian virtues onto my Swedish friends' celebrations.

Recollecting my brief Swedish adventure would dare to suggest that drinking can also be understood as a social metaphor, as a realm of practices, rules, values, and language games deeply rooted in a society's way of dealing with themes of order, death, uncertainty, identity, change, permanence, time, repetition, obsessions, cravings, pleasure, imagination, bodily drives, meaning and power. In Sweden, it seems to me, drinking must be strictly regulated and disciplined, largely because its cultural framework stimulates a dualistic pattern of behavior: either abstinence or overdrinking, either refusal or excess. Introspection and self-control come together with transgression and absence of control. My Brazilian eyes saw the Swedish experience under the sign of Apollo. Yet within the Apollonian context, transgression is the other side of order, its implied necessary other, its immanent, constitutive domain.

The following year, my Swedish friends came to Brazil, reciprocating my visit. It was my turn to invite them to my apartment for beers and chatting. My wife and I had in mind a nice, friendly, happy, yet quiet evening. The lack of intimacy between us and the introspection I attributed to the guests made me worry a bit about the success of the meeting. Nonsense. After all, we were in Brazil and my foreign friends had their own strong feelings and expectations about a tropical party. Besides, Rio de Janeiro was the city of carnival, the wonderland of sin and pleasure, a warm, colourful and sensual paradise. The symmetrical opposite of Apollo's cold continent. My party was supposed to stage the spectacle of full and radical otherness. My Swedish friends arrived in time for the accomplishment of a dream. Welcoming my guests and anticipating Apollo, I was not ready for Dionysus.

I was not, but they were. My friends never hesitated, did not feel ashamed, embarrassed or in need of feedback on their convictions, which were clear and precise indeed: they were about to experience a typical wild Brazilian party. It did not matter if what was 'typically' Brazilian was completely alien to Brazilians' experience of themselves. I noticed from the outset that I was no longer in charge. My Swedish friends made me feel at home but began to stage, at my home, what they supposed was a Brazilian party. Actually it was a Brazilian party from the point of view of the Swedish imagination, through which they were trying to experience their own identity from a distance, from an inversion of it, turning it upside down.

There is surely no such thing as a Swedish stable identity as a uniform reified essence. The movement of distancing oneself from one's own usual way of doing what comes naturally, or in other words, the movement of performing imaginary otherness created a very interesting displacement, meaningful in itself. Displacement was the act of moving away from oneself by *staging* a difference. This movement generated a space or a symbolic field of force, a realm for new intensities, practices, powers, feelings, emotions, interpretations of invented roles. Moving away from oneself opened up a realm for the *performance* of new dramatic personae as well as new relationships. Identity was reduced to the intangible condition of possibility for the experience of difference as such – an experience targeted at imaginary figures, targets constructed and interchanged throughout the global *ecumene*. Being the intangible condition of possibility does not reduce social identity to a Kantian transcendental. I think of it as the symbolic negative reference of the meanings elaborated by and through the experience of being different, of being the imaginary other. It is the virtual pole (only describable from a distance, within a movement of staging otherness) of the performative displacement towards collective migrant fantasies.[3]

Back to earth, to the Swedish Brazilian party. My friends took charge of the CD player, chose what they thought could work as the sound track for such a special evening, invaded bedrooms, dancing all over the place, rehearsing some Portuguese words and a couple of samba steps. I can testify they had a wonderful time. They were twelve. The only Brazilians were my wife and myself. After the first hour, we were almost forgotten. My friends were sharing the Brazilian party among themselves. I experienced the invisibility of empirical 'reality' while 'Brazilianness' was being invented and staged, according to global fantasies. They did not need Brazilian characters to stage their Brazilian dream. My friends were extremely happy and grateful at the moment of farewell. Each one of them could not have been more emphatic in thanking us for that unique opportunity. My wife and I provided my Swedish friends what they considered an unforgettable exquisite experience, a touch of 'Brazilianness'.

Another way of describing the scene would be that the celebration of an imaginary Brazil realized a fantasy of not being Swedish for a while. But not being Swedish is different from not being English, American, French, Greek, Italian, or Brazilian. I would dare to suggest that in the Swedish Apollonian context the other has to be staged as transgression and inversion. Therefore, the images of wildness associated to Brazilian life were incorporated into the Swedish imagination as the domain of Dionysus. Brazilianization could have many meanings. The fact that the Swedish reading of Brazilian global mythology stresses the Dionysian semantic spectrum is itself telling about the Swedish style of playing this global identity game.

The other side of this coin was my own reading of the Swedish mythology as Apollonian, as well as my own reaction to the interpretation of Brazil staged by my Swedish friends in my apartment in Rio de Janeiro. My wife and I tried spontaneously to adapt ourselves to the invisible position assigned to us. Actually, we acted as if we were invisible, so as not to spoil the dream of a Brazilian party. By hiding beneath the shadow of Dionysus, we were to a certain extent moving away from ourselves, operating a displacement analogous to the one performed by my Swedish friends. We were moving towards invisibility, which implied at that specific moment, given the features of that particular situation, complete adaptation to the Swedish staging of the imaginary tropical feast. In other words, we accepted the myth and contributed, through our passivity, to its full realization. Of course, being gentle requires a great amount of tolerance and adaptability, from hosts, wherever they are, whoever they might be. Nevertheless, at that point, the obligations of a host did not explain every dimension of our behaviour. We were smoothly undergoing a transition, through adaptive invisibility and accommodation, from a casual if not formal attitude to an informal if not playful posture. Staging a joyful and happy spontaneity seemed to be a Dionysian performance to my Swedish friends, which in itself could be understood as a displacement compatible with an Apollonian cultural framework. Correspondingly, I could describe the smoothness of my wife's and my adaptation to the Swedish Brazilian party as revealing of features of Brazilian identity. Here, instead of dualistic polarities, such as order and transgression, Apollo and Dionysus, the language game and imaginary figures through which identity is played out may rather be based on continuity, hybridization, metonym, and metamorphosis.

Let me stress again I do not intend to capture essential reified identities as 'national cultures'. On the contrary, by describing the Swedish invention of tropical wildness, as well as my own perception of Swedish parties and my reaction to the Swedish staging of an imaginary Brazilian feast, I intend to focus on the displacements from identities towards imaginary topoi, and the migration of global fantasies. A further step would take us to a higher level of complexity and abstraction. Let me summarize it in a brief statement: globalization could impose a shift from a structural logic displayed by the dialectics of identity and reflexivity to a dynamic continuum of displacements targeting imaginary figures, whose movement refers to a missing point of departure, an absent origin. Therefore, in my ethnographic example, Swedish identity could be thought of as Apollonian only when and while it is being denied and referred to as a missing original source. In direct and simple words, adopting a pragmatic approach: being Swedish, in my ethnographic snapshot, was imagining, staging, and performing the typical Brazilian party as Dionysian.

## Staging Modernity by Local Means: Misunderstandings and Misleading Tips

In Pasto, a beautiful small town in Colombia, there is a hotel under Galeras, a majestic volcano. It was the arena of two revealing misunderstandings. In my first evening there, I went to the front desk and asked to be awakened the next morning at a certain time. A polite and attentive gentleman wrote down my request, making sure he had got my name, my room number and the time correctly. However, the next morning I was not awakened. Disappointed, I complained before breakfast. To my perplexity, I was told that the hotel did not provide this kind of service. I could not figure out who was telling the truth and why someone lied to me. Later, at the hotel's restaurant, two colleagues and I ordered from the lunch menu. The waiter listened carefully, politely, and took notes. After half an hour he brought our dishes. None of them coincided with our order. He had got it all wrong, in spite of our efforts to speak the best Spanish we could. We regretted the mistake very patiently and insisted on our order. The waiter, surprisingly enough, did not seem to be surprised. He did not apologize but again was polite, fully understanding our complaint. Half an hour later, he returned with new dishes, which again had nothing to do with what we had ordered. It was too late for a second refusal. So, we accepted what had been served.

Later that day, an American colleague resident in Colombia for fifteen years, listened to my narrative of both episodes and pacified my perplexity with an explanation: the rules of courtesy had been more relevant than the codes of efficiency or functionality. It would be rude to refuse a request of a guest, even if the guest would later have to face the frustrating reality. The hotel did not offer a wake-up service. The dishes we insisted on ordering were not available on that day of the week. The waiter did his best to avoid frustrating us directly, telling us personally that our wishes could not be granted. This would be impolite, according to local rules of hospitality. We should be more careful, doing our part in the common effort of building the best possible relationship. We should understand the gestures of writing down name, room number, time, or of taking note of our lunch order, not as functional, but as dramatic moves driven by the best intentions and values, as cordiality. These were moves that implicitly required our acknowledgment, our sensitive and quiet acceptance. Moves that worked as passwords authorizing our access to higher levels of mutual respect and understanding. Underlying the words and gestures on the surface, there was a silent subtext of a welcoming disposition unfolded by our hosts.

Both episodes staged the same plot: the collision between the modern code of efficiency and the traditional code of hospitality; between the universal practice of professionally receiving guests and the cosmopolitan practice of welcoming foreigners, performed through local means, by local actors, according to local languages. The significance of this collision cannot be described as a local, parochial refusal of a global modern code. It cannot be described as a conflict of cultures, meanings, and interpretations, but only as the interweaving of two codes or patterns of behavior, both oriented towards complementary ends, not only commensurable but convergent. The collision cannot be described as a local appropriation of a global code either. There is an interweaving of codes, not a functional solution through 'localization' of the global code, which would very much please the anthropological common sense. There is neither parochial refusal nor assimilation (through passive full acceptance or local reinterpretation and adaptation), but an interweaving of different codes and procedures, producing unanticipated effects and dysfunctional consequences.

There are different ways of being modern, as we know. But in this case something else is at stake: modernity is being staged by means of a native, local, traditional performance. The gestures and words play the expected game of modernity. Nonetheless, gestures and words contrive a fake reality. Under the fake modernity, the old pattern of hospitality is kept through the creative theatrical performance of the local agents. *Modern efficiency is the other to be staged.* In contrast with the Swedish staging the other, staging modern efficiency in Pasto did not imply departing or taking a distance from oneself. On the contrary, it implied resuming local meanings, values, and practices. Performing oneself in a fake, theatrical context, made possible a movement towards modernity, staged on the surface. Getting close to the other, to modernity, meant the reproduction of the traditional identity, was performed through the staging of modern gestures.

## Increasing Differences by Copying

It is now time to retrace our trajectory. The first scene was staged by the Swedish Apollonian reading of Brazilian global image, which implied a Dionysian performance and a displacement of identity. The dominant force at work was projection of an image that migrates, crosses boundaries, and realizes Brazil in the global arena long before any actual direct experience with the Brazilian society takes place. The second scene was staged as a traditional appropriation of imaginary modernity, in which identity was acted out through foreign codes of behavior. It was an Andean plot where hospitality triumphed over practical functionality. Modernity was celebrated as a new set of clothes, a fake suit, for old values and practices. Modernity was cannibalized. The force at work was the engagement with oneself, with one's own identity as tradition.

What could we learn from these two simple scenes? Different approaches could focus different levels of each scene. One possibility is that they displayed strategies of reassurance, economies of confirmation, processes of moral reproduction. The first one produced the satisfying, reassuring confirmation of some Swedish beliefs about Brazilian wildness, a case of self-fulfilling prophecy. Projection was the dynamic by which confirmation was produced. Its condition of possibility was the availability of images of Brazil at the global level. This points us towards a political economy of transnational flows of images, available for projections and construction of a repertoire of imaginary archetypes. The second scene reinforced a Colombian tradition threatened by modern functionality. It reassured as well their way of being modern. The price to be paid was the acknowledgment of the falsity of their modern functionality.

Another angle would read the first scene as a playful deficit of reflexivity. The transnational imagined archetype was taken at face value, the commonsensical images about Brazilian society accepted without any doubt whatsoever. In the second scene, face value was established as the relevant ground for communication. The fake nature of the modern roles and functions at work was not to be hidden. Proper behavior would be acting as if it were natural. Saying no to a guest would be impolite, just as denouncing the theatrical responses and gestures would be insulting. At this point we come across the symmetrical opposite of a reflexive position. We are not facing a deficit of reflexivity, a lack of criticism. Much more than that what happened here is the radical inversion of the reflexive attitude. Instead of the Enlightenment, there is a latent invitation for Romantic participation in the collective performance of modernity. Instead of unveiling, unmasking, revealing, throwing light, criticizing, the guests are invited to take part in the collective game. The main rule of the game is act as if you were doing something else. Here you are not falsifying reality or lying. It is a matter of good manners and mutual respect, of following a moral tradition. Falsehood is meaningful only from the point of view of a rational investigation about truth. At issue are two ways of playing out reflexivity: by absence or deficit and by radical negation. At issue are two experiences of performing identity: departing from one's own identity and staging the fantasy about the other; and resuming one's own identity through faking otherness.

Could these two examples contribute to our study of identity formation and reflexivity on the global level? I think they could bring to the discussion some suggestions: (1) There are many different ways of playing with modernity, incorporating it while resisting its overwhelming pressure (Canclini, 1995; Velho, 1997, Carvalho, 1997, DaMatta 1997). (2) Dealing with identity is staging the fantasy about the other. By performing otherness it is possible to experience one's own image from a distance, displaced through a movement of inversion. This could suggest the following hypothesis: when colonized people copy something from their dominating agents, they might be staging the other, through imaginary games, so that they could experience their own identity within a process of displacement. Copying could mean becoming different and distant from one's own identity as dominated. Therefore, copying would not necessarily imply identification with the other – in this case, with the aggressor. Copying could be the available experience of change. More than that, the possibility of copying could be experienced as proof that identities change and positions can be transformed. Mimicry can be a weapon against the political reification of identities.

This idea of copy or cultural mimicry is different from though not incompatible with Roland Robertson's conception of 'selective emulatio", or with Lacan's and Homi Bhabha's concept of elusive 'camouflage'.[4] Robertson's thesis,[5] is that globalization can generate more differences and deeper heterogeneity. My proposition could be stated as follows: globalization increases the opportunities for copying, for staging the other by performing one's own fantasies about the other or even by mimicry. These fantasies are more easily available, since migration of the imagination is a result of the development of cross-national relations. On the other hand, copying can mean moving away from oneself, or experiencing oneself through displacement, through becoming different. The experience of being something else challenges reified identities and brings the possibility of circulating, shifting, and changing to the forefront of social and cultural life. Copying increases differences by the performance of fake similarities. Copying denaturalizes the reproduction of collective selves. Playing fake opens up the experience of being in society among others to the uncertainty of not being any longer what one was before. If capitalism was destined to perform a progressive historical role by destroying traditional domination, perhaps cultural mimicry, stimulated by globalization (even by imperialism), could similarly deconstruct the naturalization of identities, one of the main bases of conservative values and beliefs.

## Some Theoretical Implications: Risk, Hesitation, Tragedy, and Irony

Until now focus has been on the observed, the 'objects' of interpretation. Now we turn the narrative upside down and focus on the observing stance: the observer as author in the global intellectual field. Who speaks knowingly of Brazil as it is fantasized by Swedes? Of identity as a virtually denied reference in the imaginary adventure of performative displacement? Of tradition imposing its temporality on the rhythm of modernized life in Pasto, generating something different from the hybrid, the *bricolage*, the syncretic form that aestheticizes cultural resistance and appeases it by means of rational explanation? Who speaks of producing dissyntony and arrhythmia but nonetheless exercising friendly sociability? Who suggests a rereading of the copy as attempted displacement? Who dares to celebrate the copy – standing for defeat and co-optation – as a move that encourages self-distancing, criticism, and change? Who dares to redescribe the tawdry, vulgar cultural copy as the poor, massified version of reflexivity typical of the risk society? Who redescribes the passivity of the copy as an activity, as the establishment of an imaginary camp that allows self-redescription, self-aestheticization, the reinvention of the subject? Who speaks? And from where? What is the source of power and legitimacy that allows such boldness? To answer these questions, I will address authorship, dialogue, and intellectual labour as forms of life; aestheticization as political action; political action as an ethical experiment.

Theoretical discourses are networks of texts, voices, cosmologies, disseminations. They are hypertexts, with overt and covert links, virtual tensions, silences, hiatuses, knots, polyphonies, contradictions, intensities. The author here is no longer the point of unification for the multiplicity of semantic flows, the index of a common virtual origin, the subjectivity that commands and expresses its essence. Masks, personae, are generated by discourses in the process by means of which they are stated and engender themselves. Further, those who dare sketch an ontology of co-presence question the conditions of dialogue, of communication. The language we inhabit, Gadamer observes, allows us to play a certain number of games in which we are agents only in part, since the horizon of tradition and of assumptions, however open and dynamic, circumscribes our movements and limits ascription of meaning, intelligibility, and understanding. We are comprehended by the language we call our own, just as we take part in a community. To comprehend – the goal of hermeneutic practice – is to make the space that comprehends us turn around itself once more, displacing it creatively. We are authors of the mediation by means of which tradition is extended and renewed. In this sense, belongingness to a group (a culture) is what distinguishes and defines us, as Herder said, synthesizing the Romantic refusal of the rationalist universalism of the Enlightenment.

To save hermeneutic dialogism from Romantic relativism, Habermas, *contra* Heidegger, constructs his own version of the Kantian schematism. Here the governing concept is that rational is all that derives from reason. This is not a tautology, since this derivation implies mediations, so that pure reason is contaminated by the all-too-human flaws of sensibility. Intersubjectivity, ruled solely by the deducible principles of discursive reason, will generate consensus. If to Gadamer – echoing Herder – understanding is a product of co-belonging, to Habermas, whose dream is to save Kantian universalism from its idealistic traps, co-belonging may be the object of decision of autonomous individual agents. Here the individual as rational agent is independent of his belongingness (Habermas rejects also the sociological and anthropological turns of Simmel, Durkheim,[6] and Mauss). Here decision is grounded in the universality of an ethics based on (intersubjective) reason. All well-meaning interlocutors will believe and opt for a purified Western modernity, reduced to its fundamental values of liberty, equality, and fraternity.

Rawls found a more ingenious vocabulary to propose the same argument: if we forget who we are (by submitting to the experimental veil of ignorance) but preserve our knowledge about collective life and its history, and if it is up to us to choose the social order under which we wish to live, all would make the same choice. According to Rawls, everyone would opt for the specific kind of social organization that was least harmful to any type of individual. The ideal society, the object of the rational choice of each and every individual, thinking from the standpoint of the general will, (Rawls, 1971, p. 587) would be liberal and socially balanced. It would encourage the maximization of two ruling principles: freedom and equality, with the first overruling the second whenever the two should clash.

Habermas promises consensus, and Rawls only anticipates its actual content. Intersubjectivity is postponed. In both cases the dialogue is idealized and controlled, *ex ante*, so as not to be experienced as risk, uncertainty, irreducible polyphony. Conversation remains an impossibility. There can be no dialogical confrontation conceived as an unpredictable adventure of two or more subjects, which potentially implies the agonistic affirmation of alterities. However interesting and persuasive Rawls's experiment, and however generous Habermas's democratic intentions, for both authors the dialogue is replaced by its simulacrum: the subject comes face to face with itself, reason refers to itself, prefiguring, on the intelligible plane, unanimity on the sensible or historical plane. Paul De Man was quick to perceive the reductionist character of this theoretical conception in criticizing readings of Bakhtin that ultimately negated differences and reduced dialogue to a 'substitutive transitivity' or permutations of the same (De Man, 1986). The same criticism applies to Habermas's and Rawls's dialogical models. Certainty of consensus is the reduction of the plurality of voices to the univocity of transcendental reason: the viewpoint sub specie aeternitatis. If Rawls's Neo-Kantian stand is explicit, Habermas's is disguised by the effort to combine the foundational rationalism of Kantianism with the contingent limits of the sublunary: history, the body, society, culture, language (Habermas, 1984). Thus can be understood Habermas's concepts 'intersubjective reason' and 'discursive ethics'. This compromise solution, according to Habermas's critics like Rorty (1979, 1989, 1991a, 1991b), results in the metaphysical deadlocks of every foundationalist philosophy. Gadamer's solution runs into its own problems. His Neo-Romanticism may preclude the construal of difference. Here the multiplicity of voices, gestures, and reasons is subordinated to the continuity of tradition. Here the challenge of conflicting traditions is forgotten.

To Habermas, the subject is independent of his/her belonging to a specific society, tradition, or culture. That is why the issue of identities is so uncomfortable for him. For him identity tends to be reduced to identification with an abstract grouping, say class, gender or a political grouping. Identity corresponds to association, and association is ultimately seen as the object of a decision, a matter of choice or judgment, potentially rational, depending on the intersubjective procedure that generated it. Hence the wishful thinking of David Hollinger (1995) and Rorty (1997), who hope for the decline of multiculturalism and the end of the hypertrophy of so-called identity politics in the U.S., which tend to subvert priorities in democratic struggles. They see these phenomena as mistakes that can be corrected if only everyone will opt for the supremacy of their identities as citizens, relegating all other individual choices to the background. Though I share their political fears and their utopian democratic goals, I believe that the field in which identities are produced is not ruled by rational control and choice. Underneath self-formative movements of subjectivity, we have, not rational subjects or individuals, but mere possibilities of actualization of self-poietic attempts. That is, the individual is an historically constructed and spatio-temporally limited category.[7] Identities are not choices made by individuals. Rather, they prescribe and delimit spheres of the exercize of individuality and self-perception as such. To begin with, one may live and be socialized in, for example, a highly racialized society, and it is only at a later stage that one makes political decisions, including those having to do with how much weight one is to attribute to the racial dimension of one's own choices and stands.[8] It is perfectly possible to step back from one's own life history, colour, and primary loyalties in order to tackle common problems with an open mind and a heightened rationality. But such a distancing is not miraculous: it cannot enable the subject of the decision to pull him or herself up by his or her own hair. This distancing cannot make the subject conscious of all the assumptions arising from complete immersion in a racialized society. Moreover this distancing remains the move of a racialized subject – an engendered and racialized subject.[9]

Rorty criticizes Habermas, but he too seems to attribute to the agent the power of an idealized subject. Rorty's pragmatic themes of action as experimentation, risky wager, openness to error (which Dewey took over from John Stuart Mill) rhyme philosophically with freedom and contingency, creativity, transgression, rupture and change. Pragmatism, however, replaces the dismal nightmare of disenchanted reproduction by the dissolution of the social as a limiting and formative condition of actors. Society is apparently seen as the aggregate result of individual decisions, of the actions of those who are individuals before associating – precisely the position defended by liberal economists and political scientists who follow the reductionist models of rational choice theory.[10]

I am deliberately following a pendular path in my argument. Now it is time to break the circle that cannot escape the background dilemmas – dialogue, alterity, difference, subject, belongingness, and action – and so to come closer to the answers to the questions with which I opened the last section of this essay. Even as I break the circle, I will preserve the pendular motion and the circularity of the dilemmas. I return to the description of identity as a virtual source of displacement, denied and referred to indirectly by negation: I refer to the tacit staging of 'Swedishness' through the performance of imaginary 'Brazilianness'. Thus Judith Butler observes:

> ... difference is that which both conditions and contests the postulation of identity in thoroughgoing ways. Identity is only constituted through the foreclosure of a field of possibilities, a field that nevertheless conditions that identity in absentia. To the extent that that field is constitutive (there can be no constitution of identity without the foreclosure of that field), every identity is implicitly or potentially contested by that field. (Butler, 1995, p. 441)

At issue is an absent field, constituted not as a condition of possibility and a potential chain of destabilizing challenges, but rather as the reference of a performance. In this allusive field of semantic reverberations meaning is actualized by dramatized inversion. Thus the performance of Brazilianness carnivalizes Swedishness and invests it with Apollonian overtones by tacitly staging it as the reverse of Dionysus. But there is more than just the field of polar opposition, silent and present, which at any moment, depending on the context and the powers aroused, disturbs identity, exposing its vulnerability. Depending on the context and on the drama being staged, there may be virtual fields alluded to and evoked as virtualities that are constitutive of the multidimensional constellations mobilized by the performative attempts of identities.

Let us bring together ethnographies and theorists. Let us look at the opposition of fields not just for the Swedes and Brazilians, but for theorists too. In Habermas's virtual horizon (virtuality here having the meaning I gave it in the interpretation of the Brazilian party) are the atavistic, the Nazi ghosts generated by the Romantic concern with belongingness: the being-in-the-world read in the light of Heidegger's dangerous liaisons. In the virtual field of Habermas's public persona, of his political and cultural identity, there is perhaps a refusal of the unpredictable dialogue and of the uncontrollable indiscipline of the other, and a fear of uncertainty. Authorial rhetorics are also literary performances.

Works are as porous and vulnerable as authors, figures suggested by the works and the performances by means of which they stage contingent possibilities of themselves, in variable settings. Discourses are speech acts – with the emphasis on 'acts'. What Butler (1997) calls 'excitable speech' produces effects. At issue is the process of self-aestheticization? Self-aestheticization involves transmuting the persona and its atmosphere, its ambiance, its ethos. Mutations succeed one another. Reversibilities are not entirely possible, just as permanence and continuity are posed as projects of reproduction of the same. This brings together the vertigo of difference and the self-identity that characterizes the same: being as repeating, reiterating oneself. Iteration is a risk – and inexorable project – to any identity unit, and to any appeasing and idealistic theory of dialogue, interaction, or sociability. When philosophers and linguists discuss dialogue, they are resorting to other *tropoi* to face the root problem of the social sciences: sociability.[11]

Self-aestheticization and thus performativity interrupt the pendular motion between the conceptual fields of the Enlightenment and Romanticism. They make it possible to redefine this same motion as an ethico-political position. Instead of looking at it as a logico-conceptual zigzag, made up of comings and goings determined by deadlocks and animated by anticipated solutions, one may redescribe it as the expression of an ethico-political choice. This pendular motion may be understood as the synthetic expression of a hesitation, an ambivalence. Hesitation and ambivalence can mean the adoption of defined evaluative position, in a given politico-cultural context.[12]

As seen from Brazil from the periphery of capitalism, the winding, circular trajectory opposes and brings together authors and traditions, discourses and values, vocabularies and issues, performances and rhetorics. The narrator of this trajectory constructs an evanescent persona that is present in the tempo, the rhythm, the very breathing of the evocation and displacement of works and horizons. As seen from Brazil, with its huge contrasts – traditional and modern, hierarchical and individualistic, globalized and parochial, the world's ninth largest economy and a land of extreme poverty – the winding pendular motion seems perfectly compatible with the most laudable ethico-political reasons. Here hesitation and ambiguity celebrate the tragedy, the openness to fortune and undecidability with irony. Thus the global conversation is shifted from the agonistic and aporetic plane to that of pragmatic tolerance, to a tense coexistence with no possibility of a dialectical synthesis.[13] Brazil, a world between worlds, is an interesting vantage point from which to describe clashes and dialogues, retreats and advances, without the eschatological expectation of universal enlightenment and everlasting peace. This is possible without necessarily surrendering to interpretations that detect the syncretic *bricolage* and depoliticize it, to redescriptions that disfigure the agonistic tension that makes hesitation ethical. In Brazil the ambiguity returns. The vantage point of a Brazilian thinker gives him/her an opportunity for self-stagings that are hesitating but nonetheless politically active, ambivalent but critical. These self-stagings evoke the tragic but modulate it through irony. They point out the agonistic dimension of globalized culture but preserve the humility that comes from awareness of the precarious and finite nature of the identity it dramatizes. The self-aesthetic possible in the periphery is the invention of what, in the formation of subjectivity, eludes the copy and its opposite: the fetishistic and dogmatic idealization of authenticity.

This self-constitutive aesthetic evokes a political ethic: an experimentation of sociability that relies less on law, obligation, and exchange than on the care for the other (Baier, 1994; Levinas, 1980). This is the 'gratuitousness' Michel De Certeau (1987) speaks of. Wager and risk, hesitation: the language is closer to Pascal than to Carl Schmitt. The ungrounded leap-wager is not just an anticipation of the tragedy and collapse of the dialectic of Enlightenment. The tropics have learned to live with uncertainty. Audacity is the single virtue of the periphery. In a certain sense, hesitation is a sign of weakness. But what about perseverance in hesitation, redescribing the dialogue about dialogue in a pendular motion? In circles, I return to the strategy of ambivalence: a rhetorical performance to exhaust prudence and legitimate the wager?

This pendular motion I am addressing is at once performed and grounded in the place of belonging. It is in this sense similar to what Scott Lash (1994, p. 168) has called a 'groundless community', a 'being in the world which is simultaneously radically contingent'. Let me suggest an additional twist: these groundless communities may not have all the same legitimacy and the same power. There may be a certain particularity in partaking of a groundless community whose language is Portuguese, and whose land is Brazil. From the vantage point of the peripheral tropics, perhaps the opening to ambivalence must be experienced as a rigorous requirement of commitment to politics as the public virtue that domesticates the effects of fortune. Perhaps this necessarily implies further ambiguity. Perhaps it entails hesitation as a point of view. Perhaps it entails acknowledgment of the tragic that must be, like a pendulum, established and neglected, so that hope will emerge only to be immediately eclipsed.

1. This essay is dedicated to Kathleen White and Roland Robertson. An earlier version of this paper was presented at the Conference Time and Value (10 - 13 April, 1997). I am indebted to Bjorn Ramberg, for his suggestions, and to Paulo Henriques Britto, who translated the last section of this essay. I am also indebted to three Brazilian institutions: CNPq, UERJ and FAPERJ.
2. See Robertson (1992), Hannerz (1996)
3. This way of describing identity is different from the two main theoretical models: (1) the structural-functional tradition conceives identity from the point of view of differences (Evans-Pritchard, 1937, 1956). Later Lévi-Strauss was to work on the similarity among this perspective, Saussurean linguistics, and Trubetzkoy's phonology (Lévi-Strauss, 1962, 1977). The formalism of dual opposition came to be replaced by triangular dialectics, but the theoretical model has been preserved. (2) Deleuze and Guattari (1972, 1980) developed the concept of a dynamics of identity, which is described as a coming to be (*'le devenir'*). Viveiros de Castro (1986), a Brazilian ethnologist, employed this approach in the study of the Arawete, a Guarany society in Brazil. According to their culture, through cannibalism the social actors experienced an ontological transformation which would make them turn into the Gods, by a process of symbiosis. In the case I am describing, the Swedish do not become Brazilians: they act in the way they think Brazilians do. By doing that they move away from their identity, which only then, while displaced and virtually referred to through the movement of staging the other, comes into being. It is neither a dialectic surpassing not a formal static opposition..
4. See Robertson (1992)and Bhabha's (1994, p. 90) 'Of Mimicry and Man'.
5. See Hannerz (1996) and Appadurai (1996).
6. See Lash (1994, p. 149).
7. See Rorty (1989).
8. It is only at this rather specific level that I disagree with Hollinger (1995) and Rorty.
9. See Morrison (1992).
10. See Lash (1994, pp. 143, 144).
11. See Mouffe (1993, 1997) and Laclau (1997), who treat insurmountable undecidability as the elementary condition of politics (and, I would add, of ethics), and who develop the implications of this tragedy that is built into the humblest everyday dilemmas. Mouffe elaborates an agonistic democratic theory that distinguishes her from the liberal tradition. I find this same sensibility to the tragic in Rorty's refusal to equate dialogue with mutual argumentative persuasion. Rorty has much to say about conversation, the conversation of humanity, but unlike Habermas, Apel, and the Neo-Kantians, he does not describe conversation as a rational game in which concepts and arguments are submitted to the judgement of each interlocutor, anticipating consensus, which would derive from the supposed common and universal capacity for the use of reason. In this respect Rorty is radically sceptical, and does not assume that arguments are the coin in a game of exchanges tending toward equilibrium, a game homologous to the market, which would correspond to the idealized conversation. The coin in question is counterfeit, and there is no equilibrium (which again reminds us of Derrida 1991). Rorty describes the conversation tacitly (or so I read him, at

least) as a field for the circulation of metaphors, images, affects, powers, loyalties, antagonisms, projections, expectations, prejudices, and so on. That is: he brings conversation, which Habermas had elevated to the sphere of arguments exchanged by rational beings, down to the ground of the empirical, of history, of contingency. And he derives political consequences from this redescription that is sensible to the tragic and agonistic dimension of dialogical meetings, without idealization. That is why he values art, journalism, and ethnographic accounts: all of these mobilize powerful resources of identification that touch the feelings. I propose that undecidability – the counterpart of the refusal of foundational rationalistic idealism – be understood as the equivalent of relative argumentative incommunicability, of the relative solipsism with which Rorty, as I read him, describes dialogue. Rorty's sceptical view of argumentative communicability is followed by a moderate optimism as to affective and imagistic, sensible and esthetic communicability. Perhaps 'optimism' is not quite the term; let us instead speak of a tentative belief (perhaps similar to Pascal's wager?) in the possibility of communication.

12. See Bauman (1991).
13. I do not think of the tragic as the void arising from the refusal of metaphysical foundationalism, but rather as the space open to contingency, human action, the wager, belief, chance: 'Rather than filling a space voided by the dissolution of Christian or metaphysical faith, however, the tragic ... is openness to fortune ... ' (Dillon, 1996, p. 137).

# References

Appadurai, Arjun 1996: *Modernity at Large*. Minneapolis, MN: University of Minnesota Press.

Baier, Annette 1994: *Moral Prejudices*. Cambridge, MA: Harvard University Press.

Bauman, Zygmunt 1991: *Modernity and Ambivalence*. Ithaca, NY: Cornell University Press.

Bhabha, Homi 1994: *The Location of Culture*. London: Routledge.

Butler, Judith 1995: Collected and Fractured. In K. Appiah and H. Gates (eds.) *Identities*. Chicago, IL: The University of Chicago Press.

Butler, Judith 1997: *Excitable Speech*. New York: Routledge.

Canclini, Néstor 1995: *Hybrid Cultures*. Minneapolis, MN: University of Minnesota Press.

Carvalho, José 1997: 'Globalization, Traditions and Simultaneity of Presences', in L. Soares (ed.) *Cultural Pluralism, Identity, and Globalization*, Rio de Janeiro: UNESCO.

DaMatta, Roberto 1997: Globalization and National Identity: Considerations based on the Brazilian Experience. In L. Soares (ed.) *Cultural Pluralism*. Rio de Janeiro: UNESCO.

De Certeau, Michel 1987: *La faiblesse de croire*. Paris: Seuil.

Deleuze, Gilles & Guattari, Félix 1972: *L 'Anti-Oedipe*. Paris: Minuit.

Deleuze, Gilles & Guattari, Félix 1980: *Mille Plateaux*. Paris: Minuit.

De Man, Paul 1986: Dialogue and Dialogisme. In *The Resistance to Theory*. Minneapolis: University of Minnesota Press.

Derrida, Jacques 1991: *Donner le Temps*. Paris: Galilée.

Dillon, Michael 1996: *Politics of Security*. London: Routledge.

Evans-Pritchard, E. 1937: *The Nuer*. Oxford: Clarendon.

Evans-Pritchard, E. 1956: *Nuer Religion*. Oxford: Oxford University Press.

Gadamer, Hans-Georg 1982: *Truth and Method*. New York: Crossroad.

Gadamer, Hans-Georg 1986: *The Relevance of the Beautiful*. Cambridge: Cambridge University Press.

Habermas, Jurgen 1984: *The Theory of Communicative Action, Volume I*. Boston, MA: Beacon Press.

Hannerz, Ulf 1996: *Transnational Connections*. London: Routledge.

Hollinger, David 1995: *Post-Ethnic America*. New York: Basic Books.

Laclau, Ernesto 1997: Universalism, Particularism, and the Question of Identity. In L. Soares (ed.) *Cultural Pluralism*. Rio de Janeiro: UNESCO.

Lash, Scott 1994: Reflexivity and its Doubles. In U. Beck, A. Giddens and S. Lash *Reflexive Modernization*. Palo Alto, CA: Stanford University Press.

Levinas, Emmanuel 1980: *Totalité et Infini*. Paris: Martinus Nijhoff Publishers.

Lévi-Strauss, Claude 1962: *Le totémisme aujourd'hui*. Paris: PUF.

Lévi-Strauss, Claude (ed.) 1977: *L'Identité*. Paris: Grasset.

Morrison, Toni 1992: *Playing in the Dark, Whiteness and the Literary Imagination*. New York: Vintage.

Mouffe, Chantal 1993: *The Return of the Political*. London: Verso.

Mouffe, Chantal 1997: Democratic Identity and Pluralist Politics. In L. Soares (ed.) *Cultural Pluralism*. Rio de Janeiro: UNESCO.

Rawls, John 1971: *A Theory of Justice*. Cambridge: The Belknap Press.

Robertson, Roland 1992: *Globalization*. London: Sage.

Rorty, Richard 1979: *Philosophy and the Mirror of Nature*. Princeton, NJ: Princeton University Press.

Rorty, Richard 1989: *Contingency, Irony, and Solidarity*. Cambridge: Cambridge University Press.

Rorty, Richard 1991a: *Objectivity, Relativism, and Truth*. Cambridge: Cambridge University Press.

Rorty, Richard 1991b: *Essays on Heidegger and Others*. Cambridge: Cambridge University Press.

Rorty, Richard 1997: Global Utopias, History and Philosophy. In L. Soares (ed.) *Cultural Pluralism*. Rio de Janeiro: UNESCO.

Velho, Otavio 1997: Globalization: Object, Perspective; Horizon. In *Cultural Pluralism*. Rio de Janeiro: UNESCO.

Viveiros de Castro, Eduardo 1986: *Araweté; Os Deuses Canibais*. Rio de Janeiro: Jorge Zahar Editor and ANPOCS.

**Luiz E. Soares** is an anthropologist, political theorist and novelist. He has published seven books, the last as editor, *Cultural Pluralism, Identity and Globalization* (UNESCO, 1997). He is the coordinator of the Graduate Program in Social Sciences of the State University of Rio de Janeiro (IUPERJ).

# Being After Time:
# Towards a Politics of Melancholy

Scott Lash
Lancaster University

Heidegger claims in *Being and Time* that time is the horizon upon which we are to come to encounter and understand the meaning of beings: the horizon on which beings have meaning for us. Time is the horizon on which that very specific being, *Dasein* – or our singularity as human beings – comes to have meaning for us. Heidegger was, of course, a philosopher and philosophers tend to think in terms of the transcendental. In this chapter I suggest that much can be gained in grasping Heidegger's thesis, not in terms of transcendentals, but rather in terms of socio-cultural change. I suggest that we think our identification of beings and the self on the horizon of time as something specific to modernity. I suggest that we ask on what temporal horizon did we constitute the meaning of beings and ourselves before we did so on the modern horizon of time. I want especially to consider whether we still are encountering beings and ourselves on the horizon of time. I want to think about the possibility of an epoch of temporal experience prior to that of time, which can be understood as tradition or better yet 'history'. And I want to speculate about an epoch posterior to that of time, what might be called a temporal experience, not of time, but of 'speed'. In other words, I suggest that we might think about what being may be like *after* time. I propose to interrogate how we might encounter beings and the self in this new epoch of temporal experience. I want to raise the question of where we might locate the political, or politics, in not only the temporal experience of time but also in the era before that of time and the one after the time-era. I want to examine what sort of politics are possible in an era of speed, in an era of 'being after time'. I want finally to argue that in an era of being after time there should be a politics, not of difference, but of *melancholy*.

Some words of warning before I begin.[1] First let me underscore that I am using the locution 'time' in a very restricted sense: i.e. to understand a mode of temporality that is characteristically modern. May I ask the reader to bear with me and suspend his/her propensity to think about the notion of time generically? The term that I am using to cover all the generic modes of time in this essay is 'temporality'. I want to use 'time' only in the sense of time in modernity, because it is in modernity that the idea of time has been lifted out and abstracted from ongoing social relations in a way that it is not typically in traditional social orders. Second, when I speak about 'we' I am referring to people living in the era that is emerging subsequent to the age of 'time'. I am referring, in particular, to people who have access to the information and communication flows of contemporary information societies. But I am also referring to those who are more or less excluded by these flows. The experience of the excluded is also radically reconfigured in speed's temporality. And they, too, are perhaps fated to a politics of mourning, a politics of melancholy.

As a guide for these modes of temporal experience I want to use the work of Walter Benjamin in general and 'The Storyteller' in particular. This essay by Benjamin is the best I have seen in evoking crucial dimensions of temporal experience prior to the age of time, whether the latter is conceived as history, tradition or memory.

## Stories and Novels

If time is the horizon on which the meaning of being is constituted in modernity, then this surely was not the case for the storyteller. *Being and Time* is mostly about Time and *Dasein*, mostly about time and the self. For Heidegger (1986, pp. 142-7) a future oriented notion of 'becoming' is essential to the way we perceive the meaning of beings and ourselves, if there is to be authentic existence on the horizon of time. Even more important for Heidegger is that we come to know and experience ourselves in terms of the temporality of death, of our own singular death. He means that we are a death bound subjectivity, and that we can best know just what sort of subjectivity we are through grasping our existence towards our own singular (i.e. not universal and not particular) death.

Walter Benjamin's 'The Storyteller' is an essay consisting of a set of fragments which are, at the same time, a series of proverbs that principally juxtapose two types of text; the storyteller and his story on the one hand and the novel on the other. The story, or more precisely the tale, (the storyteller is *Der Erzähler*) corresponds to a mode of temporal experience that precedes time. It is integral to a temporality not of time but of history. The novel for Benjamin – who draws heavily on Lukacs's theory of the novel – is very similar to the Heideggerian temporality of the modern. The novel, 'warms the reader's shivering life with a death he reads about' (Benjamin, 1977, p. 457). The novel like *Dasein* is concerned, indeed derives its structure, its 'inside', its meaning, from a being towards a single and singular death: the death of the protagonist, that of the novelist and that of the reader, and as importantly, the death or closure of that singular novel, that singular narrative itself (Benjamin, 1977, p. 449). The storyteller's tale for its part deals not with one singular death but instead with lots of deaths: indeed death circulated within the gift-economy of the community of storytellers and story-hearers (Benjamin, 1977, p. 450). Whereas Lukacs contrasted the novel with the epic poem and epic poet, Benjamin places the novel in juxtaposition to the craftsman, the artisan, the travelling journeyman of the gothic city (Benjamin, 1977, p. 447). Now, if the reader of the novel warms his shivering life with a death he reads about, the life of the artisan is not shivering. It is sturdy. It is embedded in a set of values, in forms of life, in collective memory, that are alien to the reader of the novel.

The novel, unlike the tale, is a narrative: a single narrative with beginning, middle and end. The tale of the storyteller is not a single disembedded narrative but is tangled up with what Benjamin calls a 'web' of tales, a web constituting a ladder that spans space and time, the profane and the sacred (Benjamin, 1977, p. 457). The novelist's narrative is a work of art. It is disembedded and finds its meaning as such. The storyteller's tale is, like the artisan's product, not art but artefact. It is inextricably intertwined in a set of practices (Benjamin, 1977, p. 448). Told slowly, the story, unlike the novel, is not written against death but has plenty of time (Foucault, 1977). The temporal experience of the tale is *Erfahrung*, of the novel *Erlebnis*. Paradigmatic for the storyteller was the experience, the '*Erfahrung*', of the '*erfahrende Geselle*', the journeyman, the master artisan who was exper*ienced*. Here experience was not separated from the grain of forms of life, from practices linked to forms of the good life. Tale telling was from the teller's to the hearer's experience. Tale telling took place at work, ingrained in the experience of work, according to the rhythms of work (Benjamin, 1977, p. 441). The chrono-experience of the novel and the era of time is clearly *Erlebnis*, or subjective experience, disembedded from forms of life. *Erfahrung* is grounded in a temporality where values inhere in forms of life, in *Erlebnis* we create our own subjective values. The 'novel', writes Benjamin, 'gives evidence to the profound perplexity of the living' (Benjamin, 1977, p. 455). The novelist is 'isolated'. The novelist does not speak from his experience, from his situation. He is isolated. The storyteller works from his experience to the listener's situated experience. The novelist and reader are do not communicate experience, nor are situated in their own experience. Both reader and writer are lifted out from their experience.

If the story gives counsel through the communication of experience, the novel centres around 'the meaning of life' (Benjamin, 1977, p. 455). The story-hearer, grounded in experience, is not concerned about the meaning of life. The story-hearer cannot get, and surely does not want, that sort of distance on life. Death, in the novel, lets the reader intuitively grasp that the meaning of life in that death is the end of temporality. In its closure (as in classic narrative) death imparts to the reader the meaning of life when the novel ends or character dies. Thus the novel imparts meaning through death as closure, while the story imparts meaning through death as continuity. The novel imparts meaning through death as 'finis', as irreversible time (Benjamin, 1977, p. 455). The story imparts meaning through death as reversible time: indeed, through the reversible time of history (Baudrillard, 1976 p. 207).

The story works from a number of deaths, the novel from a single death. In the story memory is 'reminiscence' and in the novel 'remembrance'. Remembrance is 'dedicated to one hero, one odyssey', while reminiscence is too 'many diffuse occurrences' (Benjamin, 1977, p. 453-4). Through reminiscence the story-hearer receives counsel in the 'moral of the story'. The single remembrance in the novel imparts to the reader, not the moral of the story, but the meaning of life. This becomes available only through remembrance, i.e. when, 'the subject' ... has 'insight' into the ... ' unity of his entire life ... out of the past life-stream which is compressed in memory' (Benjamin, 1977, p. 455). This unity of remembrance is the experience of death (as irreversible finality). The reader must read the novel in terms of the already known death of the protagonist. Only then can the reader grasp the meaning of life from the novel.

The novel, Lukacs said, is the form 'of transcendental homelessness', and 'time' can only be 'constitutive' in this context (Benjamin, 1977, p. 454). Only in a situation of transcendental homelessness can time – in the sense of death as finality – become constitutive of the meaning of life. Heidegger's notion of time and death thus becomes no longer a philosophical transcendental, but a sociological characteristic of modernity. That is time is the transcendental horizon of subjectivity, and of being, only in modernity. Time is integral to an quintessentially modern *episteme*. Time as irreversible, as abstracted from practices, as abstracted from history and tradition, would be only thinkable as a topic in modernity's *aporia*, in modernity's perplexity. In this sense Newton's homogenous space-time partakes of the same temporality as the novelistic time – in which death constitutes duration – of Bergson, Proust and Heidegger.

Being, for the storytelling and hearing artisans, would appear not on the horizon of an 'outside' of time or death, but in the very unapocalyptic rhythms of *history*. Being would appear in tradition. The storyteller and the craftsman work to slow rhythms. The storyteller works, not through the strong intentionality of the novelist, but through the *habitus* and through habit. To listen to a story requires not the vigilant monitoring of late-modern self-identity, but 'a state of relaxation'. It requires, not the alertness of the novel reader, but 'a state of boredom as the apogee of mental relaxation'. Such relaxation is only possible in 'the listener's self-forgetfulness' that arises 'when the 'rhythm of work has seized him'. Only then 'does the gift of retelling come to him all by itself' (Benjamin, 1977, p. 446). This is the 'web' (*Netz*), the web –

'now becoming unravelled at all its ends' – connecting listener-tellers in which 'the gift of storytelling is cradled' (Benjamin, 1977, p. 447). This is the slow and repetitive temporality of the story. It works only through being repeated. *Der Erzähler* works, not creatively, but as a natural being imitating other things of nature. He does not create but lets things of nature achieve their own perfection. He works in an eternal time, so he has plenty of time. He does not share the novelist's worries about closure, but instead partakes in 'a patient process' in 'which a series of thin, transparent layers are placed one on top of the others' – 'a patient process of nature', a 'product of sustained, sacrificing effort' typical of an age 'when time did not matter' (Benjamin, 1977, p. 448).

The storyteller initiates the web, of not just the retelling (*erzählen* shares similar roots with 'the tale' and 'to tell') of the one story, but of all the stories. 'One ties to the next', in an endless time, perhaps best known in the great Oriental storytellers. 'In each there is a *Scheherazade* who thinks of a fresh story whenever her tale comes to a stop' (Benjamin, 1977, p. 453). For the historian (and in historiography as distinct from history, time is already lifted out and problematized) and the novelist, the heavens and the earth 'have grown indifferent to the fates of the sons of men and no voice speaks to them from anywhere'. Now stones, for example, 'are measured and weighed and examined for their specific gravity and density, but they no longer proclaim anything to us. Their time for speaking with men is past'. But the storyteller keeps faith with the 'naive poetry' of things. His is not just a temporal web from teller to hearer, from master to journeyman to apprentice. It is also a spatial web, a vertical webbed ladder. A 'web' that is both the 'golden fabric of the religious view of the course of things' and the 'multicoloured fabric of a worldly view' (Benjamin, 1977, p. 452). A web that is a 'ladder extending downward to the interior of the earth and disappearing into the clouds' which is 'the image for a collective experience to which the deepest shock of every individual experience, death, constitutes no impediment' (Benjamin, 1977, p. 457).

## Politics of Difference

The age of the storyteller was the age of what Hannah Arendt called 'the political': politics and the meaning of being – and human beings – were subordinated to the logic of the good life (Benhabib, 1996), to practices, internal goods, virtues and *values* woven into the fabric of forms of life. Time, in this sense, was woven into the grain of a set of embedded values. Whereas political constitutions of modern states are based on a set of procedural rules within which individuals can pursue their own value-choices, these substantive values were the ground principles of ancient political constitutions. The logic of these pre-modern values, as carried in the stories of the storytellers, centred around a substantive goal that was the good life of the political community, of the *polis*.

Now in the age of time, the age of the Proustian perplexity, the undecidability of the novel, the political takes on vastly different contours. The political and the meaning of beings and human beings comes to appear in the space of undecidability known as the space of 'difference' (see Grosz, in this volume). Derrida thus pronounces in *Given Time*, *'es gibt Zeit'* and *'es gibt Sein'*, i.e. 'it gives time and it gives being' (Derrida, 1991, pp. 201-2). Here Derrida is criticising implicitly, and going a step beyond, Heidegger's temporal constitution of the meaning of being. For Heidegger, time is the horizon in which the meaning of beings is unveiled. For Derrida, talking of the gift in terms of *'es gibt'* (it gives), this *'es'*, this *'it'*, which should be understood in the German as the 'es' (i.e. the id, the real), is what gives, is the horizon for the understanding of both beings and time. What is this *es*, this it? It is surely the space of difference.

For Heidegger 'the same' or meaning of beings is constituted via the other, i.e. death or time; the inside is constituted by the outside, presence by absence. Difference, instead, is the space *between* presence and absence, the 'third space' between the same and the other, the space of undecidability, of ambivalence of the *aporia*, of perplexity. The space of difference is a margin, a border, the tain of a mirror, a fold, that is the border between the inside (beings) and the outside (time or death). It is a semi-permeable fold that is the 'invaginated' surface separating the restricted economy of the same and the general economy of the other. This is the place of difference, more primordial than either being or time. The space of difference is the space of the political, it is a space of antagonisms, of perplexities of *aporias*, unresolvable and unavoidable tensions between freedom and necessity, same and other, being and time. It is Bauman's (1991) space of 'ambivalence', of the unclassifiable, Bhabha's (1990) 'third space' of 'performativity'. This space is significantly referred to by Derrida as the 'es' of the *'es gibt'*. This *es* is, of course, in contrast to the *Ich* and *Uber-ich* is what we know in English as Freud's *id*, it is Lacan's real. It is not the papered over 'same' of the symbolic, nor the complete otherness of melancholy and schizophrenia. It is, instead, the place of political antagonisms – the unresolvable 'friend vs. foe' logic of the political.

## Speed, Indifference, Apocalypse

In 'The Storyteller' there are, not two but three modes of cultural inscription, each of which opens out onto its own characteristic temporality. The first is the story which connects to history (tradition). The second is the novel whose characteristic temporality is 'time'. The third type of inscription is *information*. In 'The Storyteller' Benjamin hinted vaguely towards an age of information, based on discussion of the newspapers, in which narratives of the novelistic became fragmented into the brutality of the fact. No longer either an artefact or a work of art, no longer concerned with death, these newspapers were of no use tomorrow, fully located in a temporality of 'the now'. For Benjamin information is facts which carry their own explanation in them (Benjamin, 1977, pp. 444-5). Indeed, the logic of Benjaminian history is one of the unravelling of a web; the ever extending and never ending web of stories of the storyteller, connecting cultural spaces and the generations in time, fragments into the individual narratives, which now are limited to the individual's subjective cultural space and to one generation of time. This is, of course, the closure of classical narrative: as the web of stories fragments into a large number of short *durée* narratives. As we move to the postnarrative age of information there is a further fragmenting of the web. The web fragments further into a number of events, as individuals and objects now no longer are stories or even subjectivities but only points or nodes in a network. In this age of brute information the time of events and the society of the network are part and parcel of the new post-time temporal experience of *speed*.

The chrono-experience of history, tradition and the storyteller, as I discussed above, is the embedded time of *Erfahrung*. The subjective time of the novel implies *Erlebnis*. In this context, the immediate time of information connotes a third experiential mode of '*Chokerlebnis*' (Benjamin, 1974d, p. 729). *Chokerlebnis* is the time of the assembly line which is neither a tale nor a narrative but a succession of jolts as 'nows'. The *flâneur*, and more generally Benjamin's melancholic, also live in an ambience of *Chokerlebnis*, overwhelmed by the violence of the rush of images, of events, of commodities in the city. Chokerlebnis takes place in a temporality not of difference or perplexity of ambivalence, but, instead, in a temporality of *indifference*. This temporal experience, no longer that of 'time', but, instead, of 'speed', is one which speaks volumes to the contemporary cultural sensibility – in films, pop music. If the era of time is the era of difference, as the boundary, the fold between same and other, the era of speed heralds a time of *in*difference, a time of the explosion of the boundary, of the margin, the invaginated fold of difference, of ambivalence. The temporality of speed involves an indifference between inside and outside, it is the explosion of any limit between restricted and general economies. Now, no longer does 'technology' constitute the space of the same, of presence, and death the space of the other or absence. Desire is no longer in the space of lack, hence undecideability – thus constituting the ego's same and superego's other. But technology death and desire – as in J.G Ballard's and David Cronenberg's *Crash* ñ themselves become signals. Technology, death and desire themselves become bits, become units of information on the horizon of speed's electro-magnetic field. Here they take their place alongside other informational units, alongside the humans and non humans, alongside microbes and units of genetic information caught up in the swirling vortex of speed.

Now, no longer is it a question of *es gibt* but of *es denkt*, that is, it thinks, in an age of the inhuman, the post-human and non human, of biotechnology and nanotechnology. If the symbolic was collective in the age of history, and individual (psychoanalysis) in the age of time, then the age of speed and information explodes the symbolic, breaking it into fragments: into fragments of the objects we track in cities (Benjamin), or track in life on the screen (Turkle, 1995). The imaginary, too, is fragmented, leaving only the *es*, the real, and the real no longer is a desiring, but now itself a *thinking* 'substance'. *Es denkt*, it thinks, the era of speed is the era of thinking, calculating, information rich and design-intensive non humans.

If difference is exploded, then so is the political. The space of antagonisms is not resolved but exploded, as if antagonisms no longer matter: as if antagonisms and undecideability itself are nothing more than the baroque and meaningless ruins surrounding the melancholic of *Trauerspiel* (and *Trauer* is mourning: the mourning of, among other things, difference), of the *flâneur* (Benjamin, 1974a). The age of time was also the age, not of tradition, but of the human, the very end of the age of the human. *Dasein* is a being, though while mortal, is of fully different status than other beings: even Derrida's difference circumscribes a clearly human subjectivity. In the age of time and difference, things make a difference for *subjectivity*, meaning is deferred for *subjectivity*. But when things and animals and the unconscious also think, the human, in its singularity, is no longer privileged. The perplexity, the undecideabilty of human subjectivity is no longer decisive. *Aporias* recede into relative insignificance, undecideability no longer matters. There is nothing more at stake.

The age of the novel, that is of time and difference, gives us also the risk society. There is, surely, a shift of important dimensions as we move from the risk society to the network society (Castells, 1996). Risk takes place in that same space of difference, the partial determinacy, the *'riskante Freiheit'*, the need to cobble together what is a partly indeterminate life history (Beck, 1986). Reflexivity, in the sense of Kant's (1952) reflective judgement, is the epistemological basis both of risk society and of difference. In each case we are talking about a judgement in which the rule is not pre-given – as it was in the age of history – but where we must find the rule and even then that rule can never cover, never finally explain, that particular case we are judging, that particular decision we are making about our lives or in politics. Hence the centrality of not just knowledge, but also non-knowledge in both notions of difference and risk. But what happens when that space of difference explodes, when that margin, that third space vanishes into air? When all the fears and dangers of the risk society become realized in apocalypse, in disaster, in catastrophe? What happens when difference turns into indifference, when risk turns into apocalypse or disaster? What happens when the greatest fears of the politics of insecurity are realized: when we are living in the vortex of disaster?

The chrono-experience of the age of speed is a temporality of the apocalypse, not of risk. Benjamin's *flâneur* for his part is, at the same time, apocalyptic and post-apocalyptic. In post-apocalyptic time, perplexity is not at issue because what really counts has already happened and there is nothing to do but stroll, or better stagger, among the ruins of dead landscapes, cityscapes and 'culture-scapes'. Apocalyptic or catastrophic time, is the chronology of a series an uncontrolled rhythm of shocks, a vortex of overstimulation. The *flâneur* is both overwhelmed by the *Rausch* of commodities, of images, yet his attitude is not one of perplexity, but indifference, it is blasé (Benjamin, 1974b, pp. 560 ff.). Since meaning and the possibility of the good has been removed from the world, he is at the same time underwhelmed. The temporality of speed is apocalyptic and post-apocalyptic. The reaction, again, is that of the neurasthenic to sensory overload. It is Simmel's (1971) blasé attitude. What was at stake in the age of difference (time) and undecideability preceded the apocalypse. Apocalyptic time thus is not at all the time of perplexity. At issue is not a sort of existential temporality of *Dasein*, of difference or of risk. In the age of the history, predominant, in the continuity of the generations was the past, the given-ness of the past. In the age of difference and risk, predominant is the future, the undecideablity of the future. In the age of apocalyptic and post-apocalyptic time, the age of indifference and speed, there is nothing more at stake, there is no future. In an important sense the melancholic is already dead; or at least lives amongst death – as just another signal, yet another sensation – in a sense quite foreign to the age of history.

The new temporality is neither reversible as in history, nor irreversible as in the novel. The reversibility-irreversibility of pre-modern and modern time only makes sense if chronological experience is of past, present and future. But whereas the storyteller operates in reversible time and the novelist in irreversible time, the allegorist, the *flâneur*, operates in a now without past or future. This is the time of hypersurveillance, in which the past, digitized and stored, is available all of the time and the future – that is techno-capitalism's future – is omnisciently and algorithmically and more or less probabilistically predictable, as humans approximates God's omniscience and begins to be stationed outside of time (Lyotard, 1991). The now time's chronology is the speed of light: the instantaneous time in which – as the increment between departure and arrival incessantly shrinks – there is the simultaneous arrival of everything without there ever being a departure

(Virilio, 1990). In an experience of generalized simultaneity, the experience of simultaneity – so central to the temporality of the novel – itself vanishes. Without a temporal horizon of narrative, simultaneity loses significance.

The age of speed is, for Virilio (1986), an era in which there is no longer an opposition between culture and technology. No longer is culture a property of the 'I' and the eye of the transcendental subject, occupying a space still metaphorically of the sacred and standing counterposed to the world of objects, to the profane world of technology. In the age of speed technology and 'the machinic' invade the space of culture and the subject. This emerges first in World War I with the appearance of the 'war machine'. The principle of technology and the machinic displace the principle of the subject in war once the weapon is no longer an extension of the eye. Now the eye and subjectivity is disrupted by the lightening of air attacks, and the more rapid and disruptive movements of machines (tanks), of troop dispositions and blitzkrieg. The war machine, like recently emergent cinema, is also a 'vision machine'. In cinema, as distinct from the novel, we view the narrative through the eyes of not the protagonist, but of technology, of the camera (Poster, 1995). We no longer identify with the unified and coherent field of vision of the protagonist, but with the machine and thus a plurality of perceptual fields. Yet in these early days only the margins of social life were affected by the encroaching logic of speed. Subsequently, however, the culture-machines have come to invade the home. Now the brown goods, information and image machines like television, video, computers, computer game consoles, satellite consoles, set top boxes and telephone answering machines come to invade the household. With the encroachment into the space of the private the age of speed also becomes the age of the most crippling and static inertia.

What happens to the meaning of being, of both things and human beings, in the age of speed? Where do we find the political? For the storyteller, the temporal horizon for the meaning of being was history. In the age of the novel, the horizon for the meaning of being has been time, or, as we saw, difference. But when the tale and the narrative are de-legitimated, neither history (collective memory) nor time, (individual – conscious or unconscious – memory) can function as the temporal horizon. Not even difference can be such an horizon for the (deferred) meaning of beings and the self. What is emergent now is being after time. In being after time, the meaning of beings and the self take place against the background of a 'negative horizon' (Virilio, 1984). The horizon, whether as history or time, as tale or narrative, comprises an imaginary and a symbolic. The imaginary is staged on the level of perception, it works through resemblance. It is learned and it consists selectively of the images, icons, indices that are significant to a society, though not yet in any systemic way. The symbolic works through the systematization of these icons into a system so that classifications and law are possible. The imaginary works, more or less, analogically, the symbolic, more or less, logically. In the age of history – of collective memory, of reminiscence and reversible time – the symbolic as in and the imaginary were collective (Durkheim and Mauss, 1963). Both symbolic and imaginary were in the *habitus*. Now, with the shift from collective to individual memory, to Proustian remembrance, there is an individualization of the symbolic and the imaginary, as well as a repression into the unconscious. The images and symbols are still learnt, but now they are no longer merely unreflected as they were in the age of the storyteller. They are now unavailable to consciousness because repressed.

But what happens to symbolic and imaginary in the age of speed, the age of the negative horizon, in our apocalyptic and post-apocalyptic culture? Both symbolic and imaginary are exploded into fragments and disseminated outside of the subject into the space of indifference in which they attach to a set of human and non humans, to objects of consumer culture, to images, to thinking machines, to machines that design. All that is left is a body without organs, a body that thinks, a machinic body that thinks, that symbolizes, that imagines. The individual, the human along with the symbolic, does not implode, but like the heads in David Cronenberg's *Scanners* explodes, spewing microbes, non humans, information, units of desire, death, images, symbols, semen and the like out into what is now the pace of indifference. The sex drive and the death drive mix and mingle with the hard drive.

What about value? The embedded values and virtues and good life of the era of history (i.e. where values are attached to virtue and the good life) ceded to an age of time in which values are either no longer attached to the good life but to *goods* (homogenous labour *time* as capital) or to the subjective time and *Erlebnis* and the subjective do-it-yourself values of the individual. What happens in the age of speed in which the individual, the human dissolves in the vortex of catastrophe? Perhaps the only thing possible, then, are neither traditional values, not human values, but also non human values in which not just are values inhering in non humans or real worth, but also where non humans are doing the evaluating, where non humans are doing the judging (Latour, 1992).

## Politics of Melancholy

Where do we look, then, for the meaning of being, of beings and of the self when the political has been exploded? We might ask who is the subjectivity of such an age? Who is *Dasein* in a problematics of being and speed? What might political subjectivity be like? The answer may be that the existential hero of the age of time as political subject would need to be replaced by the melancholic. At stake in the age of difference is an existential politics of undecideablity. At stake in the age of indifference, the age of speed, is a politics of melancholy.

I would conceive of melancholy in the sense of the baroque melancholic that Benjamin discusses in *The Origins of German Tragic Drama*. This is the early modern melancholic. This is literally a melancholic in the sense of the doctrine of the humours: of the melancholic, the choleric and the phlegmatic. The melancholic is always mournful of a dying epoch. In the Reformation the melancholic is engaged in mourning of the sociality of the traditional *Gemeinchaft* and the ritual of the Catholic Church as these are threatened by transcendental God, Protestant ethic and absolutist ruler of emergent modernity. The melancholic appears again in a much later modernity as mournful of the ruins of the commodity in Baudelaire's and Benjamin's Paris. This is an initial and precocious appearance of speed's melancholic, in both cases mourning an earlier memory.

The politics of melancholy is first of all a politics of limits. *Dasein* is supposedly a finite being, a finite human being, a mortal, Heidegger insists. Yet there is something Faustian, something heroic, something activist, a pronounced intentionality, and especially a fully different ontological status from other beings which suggests the nearly unlimited powers of *Dasein* or the existential hero. He makes his own decisions. She puts meaning into her own life. The politics of speed, of indifference, is a politics of much more radical finitude and limits. In the age of indifference rights, for example, are granted to non humans – thus Latour (1992, pp. 144-5) speaks of a parliament of things, of non humans including animals and nature. In these post-human politics, non humans are recognized as having powers of judging (Latour), gazing (Benjamin), thinking (Deleuze, see Zourabichvili, 1994, pp. 7-8), procreating (Haraway, 1992). In post-human politics the microbe, the virus, the gene which attain an enhanced ontological status. At issue is not only post-humanist time but also post-human values granting rights to non humans. The age of speed is also an age of inhuman rights.

Unlike *Dasein*, unlike existential subjectivity or the subjectivity of difference, the melancholic is basically passive. In the age of history, in the pre-modern age of the *polis*, politics was embedded in the good life: this was largely an aristocratic politics, a noble politics, one had to be a man of substance to be a citizen. But melancholy is the basest of the humours. The melancholic, unlike Aristotle's virtuous and noble man, is a man not of the mean but of the extremes (Benjamin, 1974a, pp. 318-9). Melancholics – the figures of the city, the prostitute the rag picker, opium eater and the thief – are not virtuous but vicious (Menninghaus, 1980). They are inactive. They do not use time, they – like prisoners – 'kill time'. They are the outcasts, occupying the wild zones, the dead zones of the city (Lash and Urry, 1994, Luke, 1996). The politics of speed, of melancholy, of indifference is a politics of the outcasts, of the wild zones. The melancholic leads, not the good life, but the bad life. These outcasts, for Benjamin, are most likely to be allegorists, most likely to glimpse the meaning of being and the self through the disused objects and the ruins of the city. This is not a politics of difference, not one of those living in the margins as undecidables or unclassifiables, but of people living on the other side of the margins, ab-jected or extruded into the wild zones.

It is a politics of innovation. Another group massively increasing in the age of speed, of indifference, are the legions of techno-scientists and techno-designers, of techno-artists, coming to populate the advanced sectors – biotechnology, software, communications technology, but also for example, printing and multimedia in general (International Labor Office 1996). These workers in the vastly expanding techno-culture sectors are producing life: they make thinking substance, they manufacture reflecting and reflective objects. They form communities with non humans – with biotechnological and info-technological objects. They work less often in organizations or institutions than in unstable rhizomatic networks that dissolve and once again reform – operating in disorganizations. These techno-scientists and designers can run counter-current to the 'now' temporality of capital – of omniscience and surveillance of a determinate or probabilistically determinate past and future. They create indeterminacy in the future and resist its colonization. But for all the exhilarating innovation opened in the lines of flight of these technoculture workers, their's will be an impoverished politics of irresponsibility in the absence of melancholy's memory and work of mourning.

Walter Benjamin's *angelus novus*, we remember, was dragged into the future. He was dragged into the accelerated now-time of speed, while always looking back at the past. Cast off and onto the junk heap by the utilitarian time of capital accumulation, the melancholic directs his gaze to past objects, to disused things, to the ruins of the city. The melancholic, as allegorist, has not forgotten the storyteller. Dragged into the future he looks back on not just the *Erlebnis* of individual memory, but onto and through the retrieval of collective memory, into the *Erfahrung* of the collective symbolic and imaginary. The melancholic looks back on tradition. She invents tradition. The melancholic, looking backwards, is a practitioner of a hermeneutics not of suspicion (as is the perplexed critical theorist) but a hermeneutics of retrieval . Indeed one of the archetypal memories that this politics of melancholy is straining to retrieve is the memory, the ghost, of difference itself. The politics of the melancholic reunites in another register dimensions of both time and value. For the storyteller, values (virtues) were part and parcel of the grain of everyday temporality. Similar to the modern sociologist's (see

Adam, ch. 8, this volume) separation of fact from value, the world of the novel prepares the diremption of time and value. Value in modernity may well be the condition of possibility of time. But, as between the realms of necessity and freedom, there is a gulf, an *aporia* between the realms of time, on the one hand and value, on the other. The indifference of global information culture for its part involves the explosion of the *aporia*: the disintegration of both time and value into the immanent and planar space of speed. A space from which it seems that there is no way out, no time out. Yet the melancholic may still inhabit the edges, the margins, of the space without margins of these global and digital forms of life. Through his work of mourning, through his chronic inability to forget, the melancholic may be our best hope of retrieval of any sort of politics of value.

## Notes

1. I would like to thanks the referees of this article for their comments on a previous draft. I have drawn especially on the suggestions of Scott Wilson to make improvements on that draft.

## References

Baudrillard, Jean 1976: *L'échange symbolique et la mort*. Paris: Gallimard.
Bauman, Zygmunt 1991: *Modernity and Ambivalence*. Cambridge: Polity.
Beck, Ulrich 1986: *Risikogesellschaft*. Frankfurt: Suhrkamp.
Benhabib, Seyla 1996: *The Reluctant Modernism of Hannah Arendt*. Thousand Oaks, CA: Sage.
Benjamin, Walter 1974a: Ursprung des deutschen Trauerspiels. In *Abhandlungen, Gesammelte Schriften, Band I-1*. Frankfurt: Suhrkamp. pp. 203-430.
Benjamin, Walter 1974b: Charles Baudelaire. Ein Lyriker um Zeitalter des Hochkapitalismus. In *Abhandlungen, Gesammelte Schriften, Band I-2*. Frankfurt: Suhrkamp, pp. 431-690.
Benjamin, Walter 1974c: Uber den Begriff der Geschichte. In Idem., *Abhandlungen, Gesammelte Schriften, Band I-2*. Frankfurt: Suhrkamp, pp. 693-703.
Benjamin, Walter 1974d: L'oeuvre d'art a l'époque de sa réproduction mécanisée, *Abhandlungen, Gesammelte Schriften, Band I-2*. Frankfurt: Suhrkamp, pp. 709-39.
Benjamin, Walter 1977: Der Erzähler, Betrachtungen zum Werk Nikolai Leskows. In *Aufsätze, Essays, Vorträge, Gesammelte Schriften, Band II-2*, Frankfurt: Suhrkamp, pp. 438-465.
Bhabha, Homi 1990: The Third Space. In J. Rutherford (ed.) *Identity, Culture, Difference*. London: Lawrence and Wishart, pp. 207-21.
Castells, Manuel 1996: *The Information Age: Economy, Society and Culture, Volume I, The Rise of the Network Society*. Oxford: Blackwell.

Derrida, Jacques 1991: *Donner le temps, 1. La fausse monnaie.* Paris: Galilée.
Durkheim, Emile and Mauss, Marcel 1963: *Primitive Classification.* London: Cohen and West.
Foucault, Michel 1977: 'A Preface to Transgression', in Idem, *Language, Counter-Memory, Practice,* (ed.) David Bouchard. Oxford: Blackwell. pp. 29-52.
Haraway, Donna 1992: *Primate Visions.* London: Verso.
Heidegger, Martin 1986: *Sein und Zeit.* Tübingen: Max Niemeyer Verlag.
International Labor Office 1996: Multimedia Convergence and Labor Relations. Geneva: International Labor Office.
Kant. Immanuel 1952: *The Critique of Judgement.* Oxford: Oxford University Press.
Lash, Scott and Urry, John 1994: *Economies of Signs and Space.* London: Sage.
Latour, Bruno 1992: *We Have Never Been Modern.* Hemel Hempstead: Harvester Wheatsheaf.
Luke, Tim 1996: Identity, Meaning and Globalization: Detraditionalization in Postmodern Space-time Compression. In P. Heelas, S. Lash and P, Morris (eds.) *Detraditionalization.* Oxford: Basil Blackwell, pp. 109-33.
Lyotard, Jean François 1991: *The Inhuman, Reflections on Time.* Cambridge: Polity.
Menninghaus, Winfried 1980: *Walter Benjamins Theorie der Sprachmagie.* Frankfurt: Suhrkamp.
Nancy, Jean-Luc 1990: *Une pensée finie.* Paris: Galilée.
Poster, Mark 1995: *The Second Media Age.* Cambridge: Polity Press.
Simmel, Georg 1971: The Metropolis and Mental Life. In *Georg Simmel on Individuality and Social Forms.* D. Levine (ed.) Chicago, IL: University of Chicago Press, pp. 324-40.
Thompson, John 1981: *Critical Hermeneutics.* Cambridge: Cambridge University Press.
Turkle, Sherry 1995: *Life on the Screen.* New York: Simon and Schuster.
Virilio, Paul 1984: *L'horizon negatif.* Paris: Galilée.
Virilio, Paul 1986: *Speed and Politics.* New York: Semiotexte.
Virilio, Paul 1990: *L'inertie polaire.* Paris: Christian Bourgois.
Zourabichvili, François 1994: *Deleuze, Une philosophe de l'événement.* Paris: Presses Universitaires de France.

**Scott Lash** is Professor of Sociology and Director of the Centre for Cultural Studies at Goldsmiths College, London. He is author or co-author of *The End of Organised Capitalism, Sociology of Postmodernism* and the forthcoming *Another Modernity, A Different Rationality.*

# 'Moving at the Speed of Life?'
# A Cultural Kinematics of Telematic Times and Corporate Values

Timothy W. Luke
Virginia Polytechnic Institute

## An Opening

In 1998, a consortium of large aerospace, electronics, and telematic firms led by the Motorola Corporation intends to open a high-capacity, large-bandwidth digital communications system carried by a network of 66 satellites in low earth orbit. Named Iridium, this new global infrastructure will pull an essentially seamless, telematic canopy of audio, video, and data transmission over the entire planet, making it possible for someone with a cell phone in Kenya to order flowers back home in Germany or anyone with a wireless laptop to have a business meeting in Toronto from the beach in Bora Bora all for $3 a minute.[1] Time and space will be compressed into instantaneous uplink/downlink connections as Iridium's virtual circuits of communication efface duration and erase distance. These 66 satellites will operate as a paraplanetary reality in which, as long as users have the cash or credit to purchase network access, electronic telecommunication will sublate their temporal and spatial locations in compressed streams of data. Iridium's many boosters, of course, prophesize that its telematic traffic will totally revolutionize life as we know it, but these expansive claims are a bit overblown. Iridium at best only makes manifestly obvious in one corporate system, what has been latently true around the world for quite some time, namely, the increasing compression of time and value by the transnational firms supporting today's informationalized global economy.

This brief study reconsiders the cultural characteristics of compressed time and value in this 'omnipolitan' economy and society. Omnipolitanization flows from the hyperconcentration of commercialized values and economic practices in a 'world-city, the city to end all cities', and, in these basically eccentric or, if you like, *omnipolitan* conditions, the various social and cultural realities that still constitute a nation's wealth will soon give way to a sort of 'political' *stereo-reality* in which the interaction of exchanges will no longer look any different from the – automatic – interconnection of financial markets today (Virilio 1997, p. 75).

In keeping with Fredric Jameson's explorations of postmodernity, omnipolitanization 'is what you have when the modernization process is complete and nature is gone for good' (Jameson, 1991, p. ix). Economy and society, culture and politics, science and technology all acquire the qualities of a second or even third nature with their own time within/over/beyond the now lost verities of first nature's time and space now long suppressed by multiple modernizing projects. As the Iridium satellite telcom system indicates, at this conjuncture time and value are increasingly unhinged from fixed social formations defined by multiple canons of natural tempo and local worth. The latter are set within delimited geographic locations in many shared, stable, and structured solar time-zones as these are redenominated by flexible technoeconomic flows. There, one finds human time and value reset in shared interfaces and timed access between more univocal just-in-time, real time, or machine time operations. This preliminary overview will be incomplete, imperfect, and unfinished; but, in view of the impermanent nature of time and value in globalized omnipolitan space, it cannot be otherwise.

Time and value in a world under Iridium's footprint are much more than merely in motion--they are 'on speed'. Whether one labels it 'McWorld', 'time-space compression', or 'fast capitalism' (see Barber 1996, Harvey 1989, Agger 1989),[2] the current situation, as Paul Virilio suggests, is increasingly one of 'chrono-politics' in which the sense of temporal chronologies, spatial geographies, and moral axiologies shared by many human beings is reshaped by speed. While Virilio's overall project is not without faults, his sense of speed is quite useful. In this chronopolis, speed rules over many more aspects of everyday life as it experiences 'the dromocratic revolution' (Virilio and Lotringer, 1983). These effects are global in their scope and impact, even though their disparate influences in any single locality are not yet entirely understood.

Consequently, this analysis develops a cultural kinematics, for time and value, or a study of how conventional understandings are being reshaped by technological, social, and economic motions in themselves, to disclose how power now is coevolving with speed in the rushing ephemeralities of global flows. 'Since movement creates the event', as Virilio argues, 'the real is *kinedramatic*' (Virilio, 1995, p. 23). A critical appreciation of such kinedramatics suggests that global events often flow in cohesive structures of movement on a global scale, or perhaps 'kineformations', which are serving as an unstable new mode of cultural organization, or, perhaps more accurately, new social 'flowmations'. The actually existing new social structures of the fast capitalist McWorld are held together in the compressed time-space of flowmational discourses and practices. Whether it is McWorld or MacWorld, Planet Reebok or The Nature Company, Microsoft or Leading Edge, the cultural values and time scales of such new corporate, social and technological flowmations contain the kinedramatic outlines of globalization as the dominant operating system of this New World Order (for additional discussion see Greider, 1997, pp. 11-53).

These new social flowmations exist as just-in-time assemblies; their communities, uniformities, collectivities happen in flight as unstable but cohesive serializations of subjectivity and organizations in objectification. Just-in-time unities, therefore, often are occluded otherwise-in-space as purely local phenomena or essentially stable tendencies. New values, in turn, emerge just in time. Without too much irony, Shell Oil claims that getting there 'at the speed of life' is what most now value, while 'moving at the speed of business', according to United Parcel Service, articulates the valorizing pay-off of business itself in the many businesses of speed. As speed acquires value for its own sake, slow folks are separated from the fast class, steady savers slip away from fast money, and slow growth falls behind fast pay-outs. Speed rules that fellow travelling in time may soon eclipse common residence in space as a key nexus of personal and social identity. The volatilization of once solid communal states by global trade, media, traffic, and data flows has compressed many fixed values from once traditional sedentary cultures into today's more flexible, shape shifting ephemeralities, embedding the industrial ecologies of corporate engineered technoregions in the reproduction of everyday life amid hitherto autochthonous bioregions (Luke, 1992).

In a world where digital scanners are coupled with networks of computers to verify human identities from somatic scans, sweeping their sightless perceptual arrays across a person's eyeballs to authenticate corporeal subjectivity from variations in retinal structures against stored cyberprofiles, this project is quite significant. Virilio's analysis of speed, then, follow from 'the philosophical question of the *splitting of viewpoint*, the sharing of perception of the environment between the animate (the living subject) and the inanimate (the object, the seeing machine)', which leads, in turn, to value (con)fusions between 'the factual (or operational, if you prefer) and the virtual; the ascendancy of the 'reality effect' over a reality principle already largely contested elsewhere' (Virilio, 1994, p. 60).

Splitting sight also paradoxically can split sites, creating parallel reality effects of new kineformative times and spaces, like the flowmations of globalization, beyond, behind, between or beneath fixed social locations ordinarily accorded to geophysical/ethnocultural spaces constructed within any living subject's personal reality. As the Iridium system's time and space distorting capabilities show, motorization and computerization – by accelerating physical bodies and virtualizing mental perceptions – are generating their own hyperchronic or hypertopic properties, which transfer many human activities 'from the actual to the virtual' (Virilio, 1994, p.67). Images of the real spaces of objects, data about the real properties of subjects, and telemetry on the real time behaviors of objects interacting with subjects now often (dis)place/(re)place actual observables with virtual nonobservables. Their reality effects on a machinic time-line become more real than the actual events experienced by any other living subjects left out of the flowmational chronologies generated in data streams or image flows.

Such synthetic illusions cannot be easily dismissed, because the time and space of these virtual environments increasingly are where motorized and computerized subjectivities now dwell. For example, in the Persian Gulf during 1988, the air space of an Iranian Airbus was neutral, the real properties of its passengers were peaceful, the basic qualities of the flight plan were nonthreatening, and the actual time of take-off was perfectly normal. Even so, the digital battle command center aboard the Aegis-class *U.S.S. Vincennes* sensed some nonobservable menace in its battle management datascapes whose virtual effects snapped awake the ship's defensive countermeasures, leading to the tragic shootdown of the Airbus. On one level, this event perhaps was merely a string of screw-ups that culminated in this lethal accident, but on another level it marks a bizarre collision of the actual and the virtual in the acceleration lane of digital bits. Speed rules, but speed also kills inasmuch as the action of any event is fused immediately with event reactions. Digitalization destroys duration, or that somatic space for human volition and analysis that falls between the act perceived and the act interpreted, as human physical processes are displaced by fuzzy logic chips in telematic timelines on digital datascapes.

Hypermotorization in actual space and/or hypermediatization in virtual space put reality effects on speed. Speed perverts 'the illusory order of normal perception, the order of arrival of information. What could have seemed simultaneous is diversified and decomposes ... it is this intervention that destroys the world as we know it' (Virilio, 1991a, pp. 100-101). Speed, then, recreates the world as humans have not known it, because kineformative effects now 'are preparing the way for the *automation of perceptions*, for the innovation of artificial vision, delegating the analysis of objective reality to a machine' (Virilio, 1995, p. 59). These diverse decomposed dimensions must be explored to understand how time and value can be reworked in the fast capitalist world being remade by Iridium and other technoscientific kineformations.

## Environmentalized Kineformations: Biosphere 2

The fast, flexible, and fluid social flowmations of the New World Order clearly bring unprecedented disorder to the old world of naturalized regularity, organic continuity, and earthly stability. The primal statics of 'being' in Nature as such resonate heavily with deep ecological ontologies of veritable changelessness, which many have mapped conventionally in social discourses through the figures of 'geological time' and 'physical geography'. Humanity's existential grounding in 'first nature' amidst the natural biosphere during human prehistory and antiquity has anchored all foundational narratives, marking some point of origin, scale of social time, and certain field of action for human communities, which they share with all organic life. First nature, then, gives and takes identity from the natural bioscape/ecoscape/geoscape of terrestriality. Earth, water, sun, and wind provide the geophysical elements of the biosphere/geosphere that, in turn, influence human life with natural forces in a solar time-line on a geological time scale. In representing Nature as first nature, as Smith suggests, 'nature is generally seen as precisely that which cannot be produced; it is the antithesis of human productive activity ... the natural landscape presents itself to us as the material substratum of daily life, the realm of use-values rather than exchange values' (Smith, 1984, p. 32).

Against this chronological current, human actions in a 'second nature' of artificial technospheres become more concentrated during the modern/capitalist/industrial era. The scales of power, space, order, time, value, and community now considered 'normal' by many, in turn, are much more artificial as humans build their communities and states within the second nature thrown forth by the inorganic energies and materials of modern science, capitalist exchange, and industrial technology. In the manufactured expanses of second nature, 'this material sub-stratum is more and more the product of social production, and the dominant axes of differentiation are increasingly social in origin ... the development of the material landscape presents itself as a process of the production of nature' (Smith, 1984, p. 32). The nation-state, mass society, corporate markets, and global geopolitics all are historical artifacts whose time-lines are measured in constructing, and then conquering, the built environments and social spaces of this second nature. Second nature often finds its highest expression in the artificial ethnoscape/metroscape/socioscape of territoriality. A vast phantom objectivity of inorganic mechanical apparatuses now coexists with organic human beings as both coevolve in second nature's time and space.

Many prevailing notions of power, subjectivity, and community, however, cannot cope completely with the complex changes in the industrial technosphere of second nature and ecological biosphere of first nature as they are happening now, because things are speeding up, yet again. Elaborate human constructions of Nature's identity are being overlaid, interpenetrated, and reconstituted by the 'third nature' of an informational cybersphere/datasphere/telesphere. As Vattimo asserts, 'the society in which we live is a society of generalized communication. It is a society of the mass media' (Vattimo, 1990, p. 1). Their compression routines clearly matter: speed overcomes space, time moves standards, values change denomination. Third nature, at this juncture, assumes the virtual forms of the cyberscape/telescape/mediascape in informatic telemetricality. Capitalist performativity now drives most values on a worldwide scale, and third nature extrudes new times and spaces in exchange-value forms in unprecedented ways from the use-values of the electromagnetic spectrum, the industrial era's telecommunication infrastructures, and the contemporary restructuring of everyday life around more accelerated modes of labor and leisure.

Such pluralized spaces capture the iterated registers of omnipolitan performativity at 'the end of Nature'. Here is where flowmational associations of humans and nonhumans move back and forth between first and second nature in the frontier spaces of third nature. Time is a social construct, and omnipolitan time is time constructed out of the recombinant rhythms of highly technified terrestriality/terri-toriality/telemetricality mixed and matched in technoscientific registers: televisual air time, supersonic flight time, cybernetic real time, bioengineered reaction time, commodified show time. 'As a social product', the spatiality of third nature remains 'simultaneously the medium and outcome, presupposition and embodiment, of social action and relationship (Soja, 1989, p. 129). Faced with such fractalized (con)fusions of fragments from first/second/third Nature in the completed modernization project, humans retreat to stabilized terms of unity, like 'the environment'. This conceptualization could prove quite powerful, because the 'environment' as a concept is a term related to forms of strategic action. An environment is the state of being produced by a verb: 'to environ'. Environing implies to encircle, encompass, envelope or enclose. It marks the physical activity of surrounding, circumscribing, or ringing around something. Its semantic derivations even indicate stationing guards around, thronging with hostile intent, or standing watch over some person or place. To environ a place or a person is to beset, beleaguer or besiege it.

Given this spin on 'the environment', the kinedramatic space-time of contemporary new social flowmations can be rethought in a far more suggestive manner. An environmental act is already, in a sense, an instrumentally rational maneuver, aiming to construct or delimit some expanse in nature – a locale, a biome, a planet as biospherical space or some city, any region, the global economy in technospherical territory – in some policing envelope of denaturing control. Suddenly discovering 'the environment' amidst a long gone Nature makes it possible to ignore or, at least, evade the cultural inconsistencies of traditional Nature philosophies with all of their misconstrued naturalisms, and recognize how 'the environment' also is now increasingly a kineformation: a bounded space encircled by fast flows of time, energy, information, matter, and beings. Centering discourse and practice upon the environment also endows first/second/third natures with a new historical *a priori*, or 'a series of complex operations that introduce the possibility of a constant order into the totality of representations. It constitutes a whole domain of empiricity as at the same time *describable* and *orderable*' (Foucault, 1970, p. 158).

The multimedia environments of informational society – in which the kineforms of third nature now impose their own dynamics upon second and first nature – permit us a glimpse of new time-space conditions where the mode of being, totality of experience, and field of knowledge is shifting. The 'environmentalization' of first/second/third nature indicates a fresh historical *a priori* coming into play. By accepting the realities of globalizing flowmational collectives of humans and nonhumans, a chronopolitical critique could begin to address the human and nonhuman things speeding along in the kineformations of such technogenic environments. Kinedramatics, then, draw our attention to the most profound and pervasive rupture of/in our time: the environmental crisis. Fast capitalism's tendency to divide Nature – as first nature by third nature to resource second nature – in order to exploit its many environments attains its fullest expression in the just-in-time kineformations of transnational commodity chains. The speed and scale of exchange begin to attain a temporal-spatial momentum hitherto confined to the dreams of science fiction, namely, the 'terraformation' of an entire planet. Quite ironically, however, the planet being terraformed here is Terra itself – the Earth. By reimagining the entire world, or what once was 'Nature', as a vast buildable environment for what still is named 'Society', the command and control centers of transnational business as well as the worldwatch dogs among the planet's domesticated green resistance end up dividing the world's long gone Nature into the built, the yet-to-be-built, the once-built, and the never-to-be-built environments.

Remainders of first nature may survive in dispersed ecotopias amidst the yet-to-be and never-to-be-built environments, but second nature, as the domain of built environments, now grounds the productive activities of global businesses intent upon creating greater and greater built expanses from out of the yet-to-be-built environment. Third nature, on the other hand, is still a heterotopian site where the built/yet-to-be-built/once-built environments, coexist in code systems and wired/wireless networks inside and outside of first and second nature. Here, the kineformations begin endocolonizing the physiological domains of first nature – xenotransplant-ridden bodies, DNA engineering, bionic organs, designer chemical consciousness – as well as the physiomechanical spheres of second nature – smart houses, nanotechnologies, intelligent materials, industrial metabolisms – by locking third nature's cybernetic informational networks into an emergent mode of world governmentality – GIS surveillance, artificial lifeforms, imagineered meteorologies, informatic ecologies – to materialize the new social flowmations all the way down to the molecular levels of life (Luke, 1997). Transnational terraformation, then, involves getting the owners and users of corporate-owned-and-operated technosciences to recognize how 'we no longer need to send technology to other planets, we can land it in our own bodies' (Virilio, 1991b, p. 113). The most successful terraformation projects will not be off-world exocolonization campaigns; they will instead operate as at-home endocolonization maneuvers, like Iridium's global telecom system, which will reboot human time consciousness in its own quickened registers of 7x24 informationalized awareness to the extent that such technoscientific kineformations can become their own time zone.

These dynamics are not easy to detect, but a recent technoscience project, namely, the Biosphere 2 experiment, crystallized many of them in a very unique consolidation of space/time, theory/practice, statics/dynamics. For nearly three years, a handful of Biospherian human and nonhuman inhabitants were locked down in this artificial world under glass to see if they could survive on the world product of its self-sustaining ecological outputs. Due to financial and scientific difficulties, the experiments were suspended in 1994. Nonetheless, the Biosphere 2 experiment remains a very suggestive experience. Biosphere 2 now is a biotic retort managed by Columbia University whose present experiments are tracking the ecosystemic effects of developing omnipolitan trends on the planet (See Rabinovitz, 1995 and Wheeler, 1993). In posing as an engineered emulation of first nature, or Biosphere 1, Biosphere 2 conflated second (industrial) nature/third (informational) nature in a built environment which only simulated the organic ecologies of first nature in its selectively sampled systems of the environments made by late industrial kineformations. What took millenia to produce 'naturally' on Earth to serve life, Biosphere 2 concocted in a few months through a hyperchronic acceleration of engineered food chains. Vast mechanical systems generated its atmospheres, watered its soils, cleansed its air, captured its energies inside of a commodity-chain bound vision of using an artificial planet to feed humans at the pinnacle of their little terraformed ecologies (Luke, 1995).

Within the design assumptions of Biosphere 2, one can witness the fast capitalist flowmations, which now are ravaging the macrocosm of Biosphere 1, coming into ecological play inside this little simulated microcosm. Indeed, one can observe in Biosphere 2 how biophysical and sociohistorical processes on the Earth within 'the territorial body' of entire communities are now rigorously reconfigured in the manner of the 'animal' body of the runner or athlete such that it is 'wholly reconstituted by speed ... instead of escaping our natural biosphere, we will colonize an infinitely more accessible planet – as to often in the past – that of a body-without-a-soul, a profane body, on behalf of a science-without-a-conscience that has never ceased to profane the space of a body of animals and slaves, the colonized of former empires. We have never, in fact, dominated geophysical expanse without controlling, increasingly tightly, the substance, the microphysical core of the subject being: from the domestication of other species to the rhythmic training of the soldier or servant, the alienation of the production worker, force-feeding sports champions anabolic steroids' (Virilio, 1995, pp.104, 113-4). On these simulated terrains, one sees the just-in-time simultaneity of third nature colonizing the Earth as speed totally reworks our senses of place and experiences of time by accelerating ecology itself to serve today's fast capitalism.

The Biosphere 2 experiment concentrated all of the contradictions in that controlled chaos remaking the Earth's environment with its just-in-time biomass deliveries and continuously improved processes of ecological service generation to sustain the Biospherian inhabits. As Virilio suggests, the ruining of Nature's relatively stationary equilibria 'merely revealed *that tendency to chaos,* which, according to Schlegel, *is hidden in all ordered creation'* (Virilio, 1995, pp.71-2). The purposive construction of chaos clearly advances the interests of transnational enterprise inasmuch as the new strange attractors of personal desires and collective goods seem to spontaneously order the chaotic flow of needs and satisfactions in its global markets. Liberating these flows to go anywhere anytime anyway has extraordinary kinedramatic effects, because it means

> ... not only annihilating the duration of information – of the image and its path – but with these all that endures or persists. What the mass media attack in other institutions (democracy, justice, science, the arts, religion, morality, culture) is not the institutions themselves but the instinct of self-preservation that lies behind them. That is, what they still retain of by gone civilizations for whom everything was a material and spiritual preparation directed against disappearance and death, and in which communicating meant to survive, to remain. (Virilio, 1995, p.53)

Volatilizing old ecosystems and their social formations can generate turbulent chaos in today's New World Order, and out of which new kineformations emerge around the vortices of various strange attractors and shapeshifting ecosystems.

## 'Real Time' in New Social Flowmations

'Real time' represents the kineformation's technoeconomic abolition of space in which the polychronies of various heres and theres are linked in the isochrony of immediate teleactivity, telepresence, or teletopia. Biosphere 2 illustrates how, as Virilio suggests, 'real space' infrastructures are being eclipsed by 'real time' infostructures that eradicate traditional forms of temporal duration by sublating spatial extension. Mass transportation networks from the nineteenth century and electronic communication systems emerging in the twentieth century now interact as 'a mutation and commutation that affect both public and domestic space at the same time, to the point where we are left in some uncertainty as to their very reality, since the urbanization of *real space* is currently giving way to a preliminary urbanization of *real time*, with teleaction technologies coming on top of the technology of mere conventional television' (Virilio, 1997, p. 9). In 'real time', televisual or telematic mediations can (con)fuse the near and far, here and there, then and now in a complicated machinic isochrony. Consequently, 'real time', as Virilio argues, 'is not the opposite of 'delayed time,' as electronics engineers claim, but only of the 'present' ... this is what the teletechnologies of real time are doing: they are killing 'present' time by isolating it from its here and now, in favour of a commutative elsewhere that no longer has anything to do with our 'concrete presence' in the world, but is the elsewhere of a 'discreet telepresence' that remains a complete mystery' (Virilio, 1997, pp. 10-11).

The time regimes of organic life for the most part are those of comparatively slow somatic motion. Walking, swimming, running, sleeping, eating at a normal human rate usually mark the gait set by solar time in some limited terrestrial space. Capturing the equally terrestrial energies of animals, plants, wind, or water might slightly augment ordinary human rates of living, but temporal discontinuities as well as the destabilization of values which accompanies them, do not become problematic until steam power and electricity begin warping such terrestrial time and value with the 'unnatural acts' of rapid transportation and communication. At that point, space becomes a secondary function of speed, and embedded values from this 'here' quickly collide with disembedded values from that 'there' as time regimes driven by inorganic energies and materials increase the frame rate of everyday life.

In 1875, the transcontinental railroads in the United States overthrew localized solar time awareness and imposed a standard time system regulated by the rhythms of their train traffic traveling from coast to coast. A decade later, a world remade by transoceanic telegraphy, fast steamships, and electro-mechanical telephony convened a global conference on time standards and divided the world into its current twenty-four hour zones pegged to Greenwich Mean Time (Landes, 1983, pp. 285-7). Motorized transportation and electrified communication tunnel through these standardized time-zones, compressing space in a machine-made time marked in measures of transit by the millisecond, second, minute, hour, day, or week. As Lewis Mumford observes:

> Human pregnancies still lasted nine months, but the tempo of almost everything else in life was speeded, the span was contracted, and the limits were arbitrarily clipped ... The acceleration of the tempo became a new imperative for industry and 'progress'. To reduce the time on a given job, whether the work was a source of pleasure, or pain, or to quicken movement through space, whether the traveler journeyed for enjoyment or profit, was looked upon as a sufficient end in itself ... Apart from the primitive physical delight in motion for its own sake, this acceleration of the tempo could not be justified except in terms of pecuniary rewards ... The increase of power and the acceleration of movement became ends in themselves: ends that justified themselves apart from their human consequences. (Mumford, 1963)

Thus, acceleration evolves into a new gold standard of value: a rare element's durable fixity is displaced by a common practice's evanescent fluidity in measuring power, profit, and progress.

Compressing time's duration in machinic systems of acceleration revalorizes time saving rather than saving through time. Going faster equals getting better; accelerating becomes improving; quickening cashes out as value adding. Time no longer remains a solar day's durational passage. Time is marked by machinic operations, transmission events, or transport engagements in machine-time, system-time, travel-time, production-time, payoff-time, and reception-time. Value, then, flows out of compressing more time and labor out of production, while impressing more energy and information into work. 'And as time was accumulated and put by', Mumford notes, 'it was reinvested, like money capital, in new forms of exploitation ... Time, in short, was a commodity in the sense that money had become a commodity ... Time divorced from mechanical operations, was treated as a heinous waste' (Mumford, 1963, pp. 197-9).

Those who collaborate in the collective construction of actual transnationality out of capitalist kineformations, in turn, no longer necessarily hold as dear their nominal nationality within territorial space. Instead, they increasingly slip into other registers of time and space working and living as co-accelerant, com-motive, or con-chronous agents of fast capitalist firms. In moving from the spatio-temporal perspectives of territoriality to the acceleration effects of instant communication and rapid transportation,

...all of Earth's inhabitants may well wind up thinking of themselves more as *contemporaries* than as *citizens*; they may in the process slip out of the contiguous space, distributed by quota, of the old Nation-State (or City-State), which harbored the *demos*, and into the atopic community of a 'Planet-State' that unfolds as 'a sort of *omnipolitan* periphery whose *centre will be nowhere and circumference everywhere*'. (Virilio, 1995, p.36 and 1997, p. 74)

The omnipolitanization of the planet is articulated in many 'real time' events: the greenhouse effect, new national diasporas, holes in the ozone layer, the global demographic explosion, twenty-four hour a day currency markets, narcocapitalist agrarian economies, the environmental movement, and 7x24 TV news channels. Time and space are tightly compressed, like the hyperchronic geological time of Biosphere 2, which repositions 'real time' observation/participation in the collective value consciousness of the everyday lifeworld.

Embedding time and value so deeply in many various national contexts, however, captures them both dangerously in operational bands with very narrow degrees of freedom. Shifting currency markets, secular consumption trends, or slippery civic arrangements all lead to lost time and value. Globalization struggles to work around the specificities of national locality, while at the same time gaining the flexibilities of transnational generality. Transnationalized kineformations generate their own intra-firm economies of time and value, hollowing themselves out to maintain adequate profitability at fairly low levels of capacity utilization by in/out-sourcing anything from anywhere to sell to anybody. The time horizon is the firm's daily production deadlines, and the value standards of its quarterly reports guide the enterprise's survival. Omnipolitanization advances further with every downsizing, value-adding, or restructuring maneuver by transnational capitalism. Omnipolitan time and value expand, because, as William Greider notes, to succeed:

> ... firms must become globalized, not American or German or Japanese, but flexible hydras with feet planted in many different markets, making so-called world products that are adaptable across different cultures. Multinationals are already from nation to nation, continent to continent, maximizing profit by continually adjusting the sources of output to capitalize on the numerous shifting variables: demand, price, currency values, politics. To function on the global plane, managers must be prepared to sacrifice parts of the enterprise, even the home base, at least temporarily, to protect themselves against the transient tides that undermine profit margins. (Greider, 1997, pp. 50-51)

Sacrificing home base, however, often means forsaking its grounded values and leaving its time zones to accelerate along the 'real time' lines of capital's transnational valorizing flight. Marginal profits made in seconds, as calculated in cross-national currency matrices, now rezone time economies and value expectations. This is omnipolitan time: the transnational rush of financial, monetary, and capital telemetry on the bottom of 7x24 TV news channels or front and center in major market intranet monitors (see Kennedy, 1993, pp. 47-64). The kineformation is kinedramatic, and kinedramas control events as they make financial times and set monetary values.

The stable serialization of such kinedramatic moments shapes the contours of kineformations, or organized social formations whose members are unified by shared movements, matched rates of speed, or common trajectories. On one level, one sees the discursive traditions and common values of omnipolitan society becoming more kinedramatic as shared movements through televisual reality or collective interactions in telematic connectivity coalesce in common emotions, i.e., shock from images out of Bosnia, repulsion at news feed from Rwanda, fear in contemplating Chernobyl, pathos from the wreck of *Exxon Valdez*, loss on the passing of Mother Teresa, grief in Princess Di's car crash. On another level, however, the kinedramaturgies of global cultures also are sustainably developed by global commerce's kineformations of production, consumption, accumulation, exchange.

Robert Reich captures the kineformative qualities of capital in contradictions between nominal nationality and actual transnationality in the corporate world. Old territorialized containments of national, high-volume enterprise with the values of top-down control and time sense centralized executive ownership are being displaced by new telemetrical webs of transnational, high-value enterprises unified by their rapid reactions to problem-solving, problem-identifying, solution-creating, solution-brokering challenges. In this mode of valorization, efficient capital becomes new type of kineformation whose variable informational and industrial geometries operate:

> ... in many places around the globe other than the United States. As the world shrinks through efficiencies in telecommunications and transportation, such groups in one nation are able to combine their skills with those of people located in other nations in order to provide the greatest value to customers located almost anywhere. The threads of the global web are computer, facsimile machines, satellites, high-resolution monitors, and modems – all of them linking designers, engineers, contractors, licensees, and dealers worldwide. (Reich, 1991, p. 111)

Transnational kineformations completely bypass nominal nationality and territorial spatiality, centering their own kinedramatic movements of capital, labor, technology, and goods within their own 'real time' interactions. In 1990, for example, 'more than half of America's exports and imports, by value, were simply the transfers of such goods and services *within* global corporations' (Reich, 1991, p. 114), which suggests much of America's, and many other nations', GNP is simply the gross corporate product of transnational flowmations operating inside their increasingly irrelevant national borders.

Within the global webs of capitalist kineformations, value arises from continuously improving the rate and scope of any firm's quick, flexible, and thorough response to market forces. Using just-in-time outsourcing techniques, as Reich notes, goods and services 'can be produced efficiently in many different locations, to be combined in all sorts of ways to serve customer needs in many places. Intellectual and financial capital can come from anywhere, and be added instantly' (Reich, 1991, p. 112). Within global webs of commerce, 'products are international composites' (Reich, 1991, p.113), and so too, then, are values and time frames. By the same token, producers/consumers/accumulators/exchangers are internationalized compositors, moving in shared channels of mobilization at common rates of speed in the same timeframes. International trade less often produces finished products and now more frequently forms fast capitalist kinedramatic happenings, like 'specialized problem-solving (research, product design, fabrication), problem-identifying (marketing, advertising, custom consulting) and brokerage (financing, searching, contracting) services, as well as routine components and services, all of which are combined to create value' (Reich, 1991, p.113). Echoing the effects of 'real time', capitalist kineformations efface space, distance, and complexity, which once were the organizational norm in top-down, pyramidal corporate behemoths, in a machinic (con)fusion of near and far, here and there, center and periphery within 'an enterprise web ... There is no 'inside' or 'outside' the corporation, but only different distances from its strategic center' (Reich, 1991, p. 96).

## Commotive Communities, Coaccelerant Collectives

Now there are many valued centers of timely biopower generation intent upon fixing their own timely equilibria of energy and motion in 'the right disposition of things, arranged so as to lead to a convenient end' (Foucault, 1991, p. 93). Many managers of global businesses no longer pace their sense of right disposition, convenient ends or even useful things as such in narrow national terms. The Gillette Corporation's chair, Alfred M. Zeien, claims, for example, that his firm does not 'find foreign countries foreign', and, as a result, it plans not 'to tailor products to any marketplace, but to treat all marketplaces the same' (Uchitelle, 1994, p. C3). This tailoring of marketplaces to products as fast as tastes change, or can be changed, is the fast acting dromocracy of new social flowmations. Transnational businesses, media groups, crime syndicates, and ideological blocs all are feeding these tendencies in a globalized flexible regime of fluid governmentality as each advances their own polyglot imaginations of convenience in seeking nonstatal ends out of the right disposition of things.

The kineformation of commodities merge as part and parcel with major dromocratic shifts which no longer 'isolate the economy as a specific sector of reality' (Foucault, 1991, p.102), but rather generalize economics as the universal totality of the real. And, once these flowmationalizing disruptions get launched, the world's populations, like Biosphere 2's plants and animals, get deported from their Hometowns, Homelands, Homeworlds to the selectively sampled kineformations of Nike Towns, Disneylands, and MacWorlds. Once there, deterritorialized fast capitalist agencies, and not territorialized nation-states, increasingly generate the disciplines and/or delights needed 'to manage a population' not only as a 'collective mass of phenomena, the level of its aggregate effects', but also 'the management of population in its depths and details' (Foucault, 1991, p. 102). So fast capitalist lifestyles articulate various highly stylized modes of living to serve as high standards of model living and then cash out as living up to high standards in the flows. Individuals, in turn, judge their personal success more often by the goods and services shared by the other 'successful fifth' of global coaccelerants than by the state of the 'failed four-fifths', who while they might still be perhaps fellow citizens, they are no longer commotive contemporaries riding on the same fast capitalist tracks in polyglot global flowmations (Reich, 1991, pp. 268-300).

This borderless world, however, constitutes a standing invitation for all to become even more orderless as technoeconomic flowmations and collective choices displace once heavily emplaced social formations and individual activities. Flowmationalization is the melting of all that was once locally solid into air, so that its displaced particles might mix and match with all of the other fluidized particularities speeding along in the global flows. Eroding in-stated places away into un-stated spaces now guides the neoliberal agendas of globalizing enterprises. As one key architect of these changes asserts, the most rational form of global order will be one of completely un-stated (b)orderlessness. That is, the state apparatus should do nothing to retard global flows; it should instead serve as an active accelerant, changing 'so as to: allow individuals access to the best and cheapest goods and services from anywhere in the world; help corporations provide stable and rewarding jobs anywhere in the world regardless of the corporation's national identity; coordinate activities with other governments to minimize conflicts arising from narrow interest; avoid abrupt changes in economic and social fundamental (Ohmae, 1990, appendix). Here, again, value as the ease of access by people to things and time as the speed of things getting to people drives the imagineering of kineformative development.

Flowmational spaces are social sites with material location, cultural content, and social sensibility, even though they often are politically displaced or un-stated. The quick cinematic pace of life creates a timely cinematicism with its own brand loyalties or corporate sensibilities as popular tastes are suitably adapted to each particular corporate connection with focus(ed) groups of production and consumption. A heavily emplaced statal point of view from territorialized/centered regimes dematerializes into lightly located corporate viewpoints from flowmationalized/decentered enterprises. Without much remorse, Frank Biondi, the CEO of the Viacom media conglomerate, believes after running Viacom's MTV corporate operations that transnational firms must be total institutions: 'There will be MTV movies, MTV products. Why not? You see Disney going into the cruise business. Maybe there will be MTV cruises and MTV special events. MTV's mission is connecting with the global audience, to the MTV Generation ...We want to provide a point of view for the MTV Generation. Why do you read the *Times* when you can get almost all the same information on-line? Because you want a point of view, a sensibility. That is what we are selling' (cited in Seabrook, 1994). While Biondi's admission by itself is not enough, it indicates how connecting with such global audiences often means disconnecting from national publics, and why global enterprises are selling a kineformative sensibility with their own globalized points of view.

Flowmationalization is purposive decentering, intentional unbounding, planned deterritorialization. Flowmational structures never come to rest anywhere save perhaps only in their trajectories of flight to and from any discrete point of source and reception. Like the subsidiary components of finished goods kept permanently within just-in-time flight as fixed subunits of unfixed superunits, like as the proto-parts and sub-pieces of whole Toyotas prior to their final and full 'Toyotafication' at assembly plants tying together totalities through the pieces of innumerable disassembly lines, flowmations are shaped and steered by fast telemetries with their own in flight regulations as well as the strangely organized attractions of chaos. Modernization always has suggested implicitly something like these ever rushing flight paths of mobilization/acceleration/intensification as the biorhythms of ageless customs become infused with kineformative forces. Today's time-space compression, however, is a radical xenotransplantation of energies and motions from fast zones to slow zones, fulfilling *in toto* Marinetti's notions of Futurism: *'with us begins the reign of uprooted man,* of multiple man who gets tangled up in iron and feeds on electricity. *Let's make way for the eminent and inevitable identification of man with the motor'* (Virilio, 1995, p. 129).

## A Closing

The speed-bodies of omnipolitan living can be tracked and scanned to disclose how their tangles of kinedramatic events shape the spaces in which building, dwelling, thinking happen. The means of acceleration – material and symbolic – produce differential outcomes for the fast and slow classes whose power, status, wealth, labor, and information vary with their relations of access to, use of, and possession by accelerative forces. Coacceleration – at fast, slow or stalled rates – generate shared consciousness or brake against mismatched awarenesses as those outside of shared time warps or spatial distortions soon prove either not to be like us or to simply not like us. Indeed, kinedramatic realities are the thought and action of kinematic social formations engaged constantly in acts of kineformative conflict or cooperation. Such speed-bodies express the solidarities, identities, communities of commotive agents as well as the divisions, deceptions, disunities of conchronous structures. When Reich asks 'who is *us*?', the answer obviously is simple: everyone 'on the go' transnationally, not anyone 'stuck in place' nationally. Coaccelerants in virtual realities are time-sharing, compression routinizing, and parallel processing in common kineformational sites, while dropping out, breaking away, slowing down disconnects human consciousness from the kinedramatic. Today, for anyone 'to disconnect is to disinform oneself' (Virilio, 1995, p. 95). Shared speed forms new agents in accelerated states, because these movements in-form the events of informationalized consciousness. Nonmovement represents dis-information, un-eventuality, and kine-nonformation for all those are either codecelerating or simply remaining at rest.

'Speed is less useful in terms of getting around than in terms of seeing and conceiving more or less clearly' (Virilio, 1994, p. 71), which now must include time and value consciousness. The split viewpoint of actual materiality and real virtuality turns all of lived/embodied space-time into evasive maneuvers or decoy effects, causing the principle of relative illumination (biophysical sight in optical range or radioelectric images looking over horizons/through matter/back in time) to shift. Consequently, '*the time frequency of light* has become a determining factor in the apperception of phenomena, leaving *the spatial frequency of matter* for dead ... today 'extensive' time, which worked at deepening the wholeness of infinitely great time, has given why to 'intensive' time ... this *relative difference* between them reconstitutes a new real generation, a degenerate reality in which speed prevails over time and space, just as light already prevails over matter, or energy over the inanimate' (Virilio, 1994, p.71-2).

Many existing visions of extensive time and value must be revised with the coming of the dromocratic revolution. The 'vision machine' is needed to apprehend intensive time effects, whose characteristics surpass the sighting of observables or nonobservables by sweeping through kinedramatic space-time with a sightless vision that tracks speed as stealthier image energies or digital effects in specialized instrument cites. Such active machinic optics 'will become the latest and last form of industrialization: *the industrialization of the non-gaze*' (Virilio, 1994, p. 73). as the cites of machinic sensors generate all definitive perceptual feeds of observed energy, image space or figurative matter to represent ever increasing levels of acceleration as fleeting sights in time or as fluid sites in space. In worlds made of fast capital, 'we urgently need to evaluate light signals of perceptual reality in terms of intensity, that is 'speed,' rather than in terms of 'light and dark' or reflection or any of the other now dated shorthand (Virilio, 1989, p. 74).

Time warps and space distorts, leaving zones of machinic sensor processing, making duration a new figure of absolute zero. In the omnipolitan chronopolis of informational kineformations, 'photographs', or light writing, now must describe/enscribe 'geographs', or space writing – an image affirmed by every computer graphic animation of Iridium relaying one's digitized discussions around the planet through its net of satellites. To Virilio, 'if the path of light is absolute, as its zero sign indicates, this is because the principle of instantaneous emission and reception *change-over* has already superseded the principle of *communication* which still required a certain delay', and so these new forms of communicative light energy 'help modify the very definition of the real and the figurative, since the question of REALITY would become the PATH of the light interval, rather than a matter of the OBJECT and space-time intervals' (Virilio, 1994, p. 74). At this juncture, a 'chrono-politics' exerted in the flow of accelerated time and apprehended as speed effects does sublate 'geo-politics' in the compressed expanses of space, not unlike Biosphere 2's sampled and accelerated ecosystems under glass. Spatial extension folds into an all-enveloping kineformative chronopolis as it emerges out of the omnipolitanization of dromological effects. As fast capitalism builds speed shops and stop-in markets, fast capitalists rush toward improving their just-in-time performance. New technosystems, like Iridium's environmentalized telephony, just enables many of them to reach out from second nature into compressed times and spaces, and 'touch someone' located in first nature through the telematic constructs of third nature. While 'moving at the speed of life', the kinematic culture of globalization is fabricated by big businesses seeking even bigger business.

## Notes

1. *Businessweek*, March 17, 1997, pp. 103, 105.

2. These tendencies also have been described as 'space of flows.' See Castells, 1989.

# References

Agger, Ben 1989: *Fast Capitalism: A Critical Theory of Significance*. Urbana, IL: Universityof Illinios Press.

Barber, Benjamin 1996: *Jihad vs. McWorld*. New York: Ballantine.

Castells, Manuel 1989:*The Informational City*. Oxford: Blackwell.

Jameson, Fredric 1991: *Postmodernism, or, The Cultural Logic of Late Capitalism*. Durham: Duke University Press.

Foucault, Michel 1970: *The Order of Things*. New York: Vintage.

Foucault, Michel 1991: Governmentality. In Graham Burchell, Colin Gordon and Peter Miller (eds) *The Foucault Effect: Studies in Governmentality*. Chicago: University of Chicago Press, pp. 87-104.

Greider, William 1997: *One World, Ready or Not: The Manic Logic of Global Capitalism*. New York: Simon and Schuster.

Harvey, David 1989: *The Condition of Postmodernity*. Oxford: Blackwell.

Kennedy, Paul 1993: *Preparing for the Twenty-First Century*. New York: Random House.

Landes, David S. 1983: *Revolution in Time: Clocks and the Making of the Modern World*. Cambridge, MA: Harvard University Press.

Luke, Timothy W. 1992: From Commodity Aesthetics to Ecology Aesthetics: Art and the Environmental Crisis. *Art Journal*, 51 (2), pp. 72-76.

Luke, Timothy W. 1995: Reproducing Planet Earth? The Hubris of Biosphere 2. *The Ecologist*, 25 (4), pp. 157-62.

Luke, Timothy W. 1997: At the End of Nature: Cyborgs, 'Humachines', and Environments in Postmodernity. *Environment and Planning*, A (29), pp. 1367-80.

Mumford, Lewis 1963: *Technics and Civilization*. New York: Harcourt, Brace and World.

Ohmae, Kenichi 1990: *The Borderless World: Power and Strategy in the Interlinked Economy* New York: Harper and Row.

Rabinovitz, Jonathon 1995: Columbia to Take Over Biosphere 2 as Earth Lab. *The New York Times*, November 13, 1995, B2.

Reich, Robert 1991: *The Work of Nations: Preparing Ourselves for 21st-Century Capitalism*. New York: Knopf.

Seabrook, John 1994: Rocking in Shangri-La. *The New York Times*, October 10, pp. 64-78.

Smith, Neil 1984: *Uneven Development*. Oxford: Blackwell.

Soja, Edward 1989: *Postmodern Geographies*. London: Verso.

Uchitelle, Louis 1994: Gillette's World View: One Blade Fits All. *The New York Times* January 3, p. C3.

Vattimo, Gianni 1992: *The Transparent Society*. Baltimore: Johns Hopkins University Press.

Virilio, Paul and Lotringer, Sylvere 1983: *Pure War*. New York: Semiotext(e), pp. 43-51.

Virilio, Paul 1989: *War and Cinema: The Logistics of Perception*. London: Verso.

Virilio, Paul 1991a: *The Aesthetics of Disappearance*. New York: Semiotext(e).
Virilio, Paul 1991b: *The Lost Dimension*. New York: Semiotext(e).
Virilio, Paul 1994: *The Vision Machine*. Bloomington: Indiana University Press.
Virilio, Paul 1995: *The Art of the Motor*. Minneapolis: University of Minnesota Press.
Virilio, Paul 1997: *Open Sky*. London: Verso.
Wheeler, David L. 1993: New Lease for Biosphere 2. *Chronicle for Higher Education*, 41 (2), p. A12, p. A27.

**Timothy W. Luke** teaches political science at Virginia Polytechnic Institute and State University in Blacksburg, Virginia. His most recent book is *Ecocritique: Contesting the Politics of Nature, Economy and Culture* (University of Minnesota Press, 1997).

# *Fugit Hora*: Fashion and the Ethics of Style

Hilary Radner
Notre Dame University

## Femininity, Aesthetics and Ethics

Fashion bears the brunt of a significant strand of feminist scholarship that dismisses it largely as a means of reproducing a social hierarchy, grounded in gender, that constructs 'woman' through 'subordination'. Susan Bordo comments:

> Through the pursuit of an ever-changing, homogenising, elusive ideal of femininity, a pursuit without a terminus, requiring that women constantly attend to minute and often whimsical changes in fashion, female bodies become docile bodies, bodies whose forces and energies are habituated to external regulation, subjection, transformation, 'improvement'. (1993, p. 166)

Other scholars such as Elizabeth Wilson (1985), and Angela McRobbie (1991) argue that fashion supplies women with a locus of pleasure that is only more or less regulated by their positions as 'docile bodies'. Yet another important approach to feminine culture, perhaps best exemplified by the work of Nancy Armstrong on the construction of the bourgeoisie in the nineteenth century, discusses how women manipulated the codes of fashion in order to advance their interests as members of a specific class.

Focusing on Michel Foucault's concept of the ethical system adumbrated in his later work,[1] and on contemporary popular articulations of the role of fashion for women, offers an alternative to the above approaches, which situate fashion within a largely social context. This adjustment of emphasis offers a more complete understanding of how 'fashion' acquires value within feminine culture as the cultivation of a feminine self. The 'value' of fashion is not, then, fully realized within a social framework, as implied in the above approaches. The three constructions of fashion above, as a function of social control, as a function of libidinal expenditure that resists social discipline, as a function of the acquisition and maintenance of social status (which I would argue are not necessarily mutually exclusive) fail to completely account for the 'value' of fashion as a means of regulating the relationship of the self to the self.

Locating 'fashion' in the context of Foucault's notion of 'ethics' grounded in 'aesthetics', highlights the manner in which this notion of 'ethics' poses certain problems for the feminist scholar. In choosing to discuss fashion in terms of Foucault's conceptualization of the role and function of ethics, I deliberately focus on a seemingly obviously inappropriate object; however, it is precisely in the inappropriateness of the object as an example that lies its usefulness, its ability to underline a certain difficulty inherent in the concept of an ethics grounded in the aesthetic self.

Certainly, Michel Foucault's work on ethics points to the necessity of developing a different way of thinking about politics in which the relationship of the self to the self as an aesthetic project is a critical element. This politics grounded in practice parallels an earlier rewriting of politics by feminists of the 1960s such as Betty Freidan who emphasized the importance of the private as a political arena; however, this move from aesthetics to feminist politics is not an easy one. The problem for the feminist scholar lies in defining this move within the social reality of the feminine, a political terrain already fraught with difficulty in which the value of woman as the feminine (one of the instruments of her oppression) has been, more often than not, her construction as an aesthetic object. I do not propose to resolve this particular issue; however I argue that an elucidation of the value of fashion within feminine culture suggests why this particular problem, the reconciliation of ethics and politics, has remained such a pressing concern across a number of disciplines for feminist scholars.

# Harper's Bazaar[2]

A concern for the self as the territory upon which certain kinds of battles might be fought is not the exclusive prerogative of academic feminism. We cannot by surprized by the fact that women's magazines interrogate the role that fashion might or might not play in the construction of feminine identity. However the terms in which an article in *Harper's Bazaar*, a high fashion magazine, couches and elaborates these questions are somewhat unexpected. 'Why doesn't fashion work on TV?' the author queries. In the course of the article, the writer's question becomes a complaint about television's inability to instruct and advise women in the same manner as do women's magazines: television does not respond to women's needs and even more drastically its programming on fashion runs counter to women's interests (Szabo, 1996, pp. 214-15, 262). Inherent in this complaint is the somewhat unusual assumption that fashion is 'work'. Television fails because it does not work for women (and may even work against women) in this important area. *Harper's* chastises television's representation of fashion in the following terms:

... these shows are alienating. They confirm preconceptions that fashion is nothing more than an idle pastime for the rich and famous, that it plays no part in their (*women's*) seriously busy lives, that it's ridiculous and hardly merits their (*women's*) attention, and that it's beyond their (*women's*) means, anyway, and therefore not worth aspiring to. (Szabo, 1996, p. 214)

As scholars we may indeed be somewhat astounded by the conclusion that television is, in fact, hard at work promoting a philosophy that would meet with the approval of feminists critics such as Susan Bordo. Not unsurprisingly, *Harper's* ultimately does not agree with a feminist anti-fashion stance: 'Fashion is a potent medium of self-expression and self-empowerment ... And it's something we all can participate in, on every budget'(Szabo, 1996, p. 214). Apparently, women television producers concur with *Harper's*. Jeanne Beker host of *Fashion Television* claims: 'If the mandate of our show were to be really consumer-driven, that would be quite another story. But we're entertainment first and foremost' (Szabo. 1996, p. 215). Implicitly, then, both *Harper's* and television producers recognize that consumption is serious labour indeed, a point frequently made by cultural critics. In this context, the work of the 'fashion' industry is to assist a woman in making sense of 'this insane maze' (Szabo, 1996, p. 215) of consumer culture in a manner that facilitates expression and empowerment. We might say that the work of fashion, according to *Harper's*, is the work of 'constructing' a self, of providing, in the now familiar terms of Michel Foucault, 'technologies of the self' to its practitioners (Foucault, 1997, pp. 223-51) within the context of consumer culture.[3]

*Harper's* query leads to further questions: what is a practice that might be thought as an appropriate cultivation of the self for contemporary women; where is that practice articulated; what is the role of television? Is television mere entertainment, a waste of time but somehow fun. *Fugit hora*, time flies, when you're having fun. Is fashion work, and television fun? Is this 'almost a misuse of the medium' in the words of Lynne Seid, president of Partners and Shevack, a New York ad agency (Szabo, 1996, p. 214)? Or, is television quietly instructing women even as it pleases many, and displeases some? Perhaps the work of fashion on television is, in the words of Angela Partington, to create 'a site for the active production of class specific values and means' (Partington, 1993, p. 149). When *Harper's* claims that fashion does not work on television, underlying this complaint is the observation that on television 'fashion' works against the hegemony of taste in which an elite group of regionally specific industries are the final arbitrators of style.

*Harper's Bazaar* fails to recognize that television 'authorizes' categories of style that are paradoxically not 'high fashion' but nonetheless 'stylish', that femininity itself is articulated and defined in terms of class markers. Femininity, as feminists such as bell hooks (1984) have noted repeatedly, is not a monolithic° homogeneous category. Television testifies to this heterogeneity, underlining the issue of class and its inflections of gender in the production of 'style' as a discourse of authority. Not inconsequentially, *Harper's* ignores programs such as *America's Store* as an alternative to shows such as *Fashion Television* (cited above) that serve to ridicule the fashionable while offering it as spectacle.

*America's Store*, and other consumer oriented networks and programming, are by their very nature 'consumer-oriented', in contrast with the programming discussed above that positions fashion as a spectacle offered for the viewer's entertainment. In fact, *America's Store* (directly offering objects for purchase by the viewer) invites an intimate relationship between consumer and image that is 'between women' in which women are minutely instructed in the use and warned against the misuse of the objects, in particular clothing and jewelry, that they are encouraged to buy.[4] From *Harper's* perspective, this form of instruction misleads women by encouraging them to purchase unwisely. That is to say, this instruction is not formulated within a discourse of self-expression and self-empowerment. Again *Harper's* appears to align itself with the harshest of feminists in its condemnation of mass consumption. Yet it also seems clear that television does 'instruct' its viewers, if not perhaps in a manner in keeping with *Harper's* goals of self-expression and self-empowerment.

In failing to recognize television's role as 'a fashion magazine show that does actually instruct as it entertains' (Szabo, 1996, p. 262), *Harper's* fails to recognize the heterogeneity of the production of power within television discourse. 'Television style' contests the class and the regional hegemony that posits New York as the fashion capital of the country, a nodal point from which a set of elements are generated that can be variously reconstructed as 'style'. In this conversation, *America's Store* is only one 'voice'. In its capacity as a visual and oral catalogue this programming constitutes a departure from television's emphasis on narrative. Narrative rather than the enumeration of injunctions and their implications dominates television programming on style.

## MTV and CNN[5]

Programs such as 'MTV's *House of Style*' and CNN's *Style With Elsa Klensch* generate stories about style rather than focusing on the formal attributes that constitute a given look. These programs do not offer a single aestheticized object or set of objects, time flies to tell a story about how and where to shop, producing an 'attitude' rather than a specific 'look'. 'House of Style', for example, tends to position the viewer against 'high' fashion as something that takes itself too seriously. Represented by 'youth icons' such as the Spice Girls, femininity as to-be-looked-at-ness is negotiated in a playful even ironic manner, in which the 'story' evolves around the notion that girls and shopping equals 'fun'. Fashion is not threatening but a playful tale that any girl could tell, in which 'girl power' consists of rewriting style in terms that are above all economically feasible. MTV fashion corresponds to 'a consumer milieu' that Colin Campbell defines in terms of 'the gratification of wants and desires' (Campbell, 1997, p. 175). In the somewhat cynical words of *Vogue* (another high fashion magazine), 'The Spice Girls prove not that everybody, but that anybody can be a star' (Meter, 1998, p. 135), that is to say that fashion, in this context, provides the means (or at least the fantasy) of gratifying desires on the basis of desire alone, rather than on the basis of need or of merit. Nothing is required of the subject except desire itself in the form of youth and energy.

Klensch as the voice of authority in CNN's *Style with Elsa Klensch* articulates 'not-fashion' in a manner that contrasts with the unpretentious 'flash' of Daisy Fuentes, current host of *House of Style*. Klensch is clearly set in contrast to the almost catatonic models in the runway segments, which document actual 'shows'. The morbid pallor of the models, often emphasized by the black clothing, highlights Klensch's reassuring smile, attractive bright lipstick, and her calm, evenly inflected, friendly descriptions of the sequences. Klensch represents visual authority and cultural competence, a pristine newscaster, distinct from the disasters, crimes, and catastrophes that she reports to a concerned audience (echoing the general CNN mandate). Often symmetrically framed by the camera, set in a minimalist undefined environment, she is formally inscribed as separate from both the viewer and the scenes upon which she comments. Her discussion, though it recounts the catastrophes of consumer insanity among those privileged with wealth, fame, and youth, is, visually positioned as objective, and impersonal, free from the bias of intimacy. She formulates style as 'serious business indeed', a shoring up of 'value' against the undisciplined onslaught of fashion disasters. Far from playful or seductive, her clothes are sensible and timeless (words that come up again and again in her own book), 'quality' in contrast with the frivolity of the fashion/art world (Klensch, 1995).

Klensch represents the 'real life' style of the upper middle class and upper class woman, the most visible example of which is Hillary Clinton, as an exemplar of mature yet vital femininity in which business, responsibility and self-restraint take precedence over fun, celebration and self-expression. This maturity seems to take the attitude represented by 'House of Style' to task for its 'Lolita' qualities, which prolong a girlishness associated with pre-adolescence while promoting fashion as a source of pleasure and expression. Klensch and her cohort might say that MTV style undermines its bid for feminine authority through its deliberate construction of the woman as 'immature'. Rebellion is a playground promoting childish hysteria, an excess of expression, pure libidinal expenditure.

Klensch's support of an austere but pronounced femininity might be seen as 'empowering' if leaving little room for 'expression'. The photographs and drawings in Klensch's manual of fashion published in 1995 are staid and conventional, seeming 'out-dated' (even at the moment of initial publication), emphasizing continuity rather than change. The goal of the volume is the production of a set of 'normative' relatively limited choices for the ambitious woman. This impetus towards the production of norms and standards contrasts vividly both with MTV and with the arty images affected by high fashion; however, it is in keeping with the manner in which Klensch associates 'style' with professional accomplishment.

'I always wanted a successful career. And I built my style with that in mind' claims Klensch in *Style by Elsa Klensch* (1995). According to Klensch 'the value of well-designed clothes' consists in the fact that: 'They can create an illusion of power which can help you get whatever it is you want'. This emphasis on the relationship between 'style' and 'status' points to *Harper's* implicit assumption, contradicting Klensch's position, that 'style' ought to be its own reward; fundamentally fashion is about 'the kind of relationship that you ought to have with yourself' in the words of Michel Foucault (1997, p. 262). Here then Klensch 'preoccupies' herself 'without shame in acquiring wealth and reputation and honors' the terms with which Socrates admonishes his judges (cited in Foucault, 1997, p. 226).[6] In claiming that fashion 'can change our mood and raise our self-esteem', *Harper's* tells us that we should concern ourselves with ourselves, the proper focus of the ethical individual according to Socrates (Foucault, 1997, p. 226). In this sense, one might say that fashion ought to offer (from *Harper's* perspective) an 'ethics', a set of technologies of the self that 'permit individuals to effect by their own means, or with the help of others a certain number of operations on their own bodies and souls, thoughts, conduct, and way of being, so as to transform themselves in order to attain a certain state of happiness, purity, wisdom, perfection or immortality'(Foucault, 1997, p. 225). The *Harper's* article gives voice to the desire for an ethics that, like that of the Greeks, according to Foucault, was based on 'the will to live a beautiful life, and to leave to others memories of a beautiful existence'(1997, p. 254).[7]

Klensch has quite a different project, a career, social status, in which her identity and position in relation to the external social world is at stake. MTV is similarly externally oriented. Its promotion of youth culture is tied precisely to the 'mass consumerism', 'the insane maze' that *Harper's* explicitly critics. MTV embraces the maze as a source of frenetic pleasure and as a feature of rebellion against the austerity of figures such as those represented by Klensch. MTV, thus, also constructs a social position by default, as it were, the identity of which consists in its defiance of authority (or at least its icons). MTV and Klensch have in common, then, an emphasis on social position and identity. The failure of television fashion, according to *Harper's*, ultimately consists in its unwillingness to assist women in a project that is not about a relationship to the external world but to the 'self' as distinct from the social.

MTV as the *enfant terrible* of television that takes as its maxim '*épater le bourgeois*' is defiantly anti-fashion. It can come as no surprize that it falls under *Harper's* disapproving eye. Yet Klensch's position is equally antithetical to the principles evoked by *Harper's;* however, she also constitutes a more serious challenge to these principles in that she does indeed offer 'guidance and service' (Szabo, 1996, p. 262), a crucial principle of fashion within *Harper's* discourse. The techniques of style elaborated by Klensch in her position as commentator, fashion survivor rather than fashion victim, are explained in detail through her eponymous book. Klensch's '*telos*' in Foucault's terms, is 'authority', mastery over others rather than mastery of the self. If self-discipline is necessary it is in the pursuit of another further goal. *Harper's* through its evocation of the goals of 'self-expression' and 'self-empowerment' posits internally articulated affect, feelings, as its '*telos*'.

## Fashion, ethics, and the self as art: *Cheap Chic*

According to Foucault an ethical system can be understood in terms of four axes, 1)ethical substance, 2)subjectivation, 3)technologies 4)*telos* (1997, pp. 253-80). Fashion as a practice within consumer culture can be described in terms of the first three categories. Embedded practices of dress, clothing and appearance can be seen as circumscribing a specific ethical substance. The larger rules governing choices about clothing and appearance implied by a given economic and social organization, including the assignment of a gendered identity underscores the process of subjectivation. Technologies such as shopping, working out, dieting, cosmetic surgery, etc. stress relations to things as the consumer object. These are givens that neither *Harper's* nor Klensch contest. The schism here depends upon the category of *telos*, in which Klensch's dicta, in so far as she is concerned with an external order, social position and relations of power, revolve around the *telos* of advancement within a social and economic hierarchy. *Harper's* evokes a more properly ethical system in Foucault's terms because it posits style as a pursuit in which 'the self is not given' but created 'as a work of art'.

An ethical system is defined by its elements; however, it is clear that Foucault implicitly posits certain ethical systems as more ethical. These encourage 'care' or 'concern' for the self, as that which is the proper terrain upon which to enact the relationship of the self to the self and thus move the self towards a position that might eventually produce a new politics. Traditional Christian ethics errs in that it draws the attention of the self away from the self (Foucault, 1997, pp. 285, 289). Klensch invests heavily in the object, well-designed clothing as something that can be purchased. Certainly underlying the purchase is a principle of selection and determination, but this principle is a principle of acquisition. In this sense we might say that this distinction in *telos* affects other categories, though I would argue that the set of possibilities within each category remains the same. For Klensch, the woman who cannot afford the well-designed suit is out of luck. *Harper's* underlines the way in which a system of style cannot be reduced to the acquisition of a set of appropriate objects because it should be available to every women, on 'any budget'. Style as the expression of the self, the work of art, is in itself its own justification, its own *telos*. For *Harper's*, style 'is not clothing, tools, or possessions; it is to be found in the principle that uses these tools' (Foucault, 1997, p. 230).

The principles of style invoked by *Harper's* were perhaps most clearly available in a volume entitled *Cheap Chic* published in 1975, as part of a general Second Wave Feminist sensibility. These principles were expressed in the work of number of designers such as Betsey Johnson, Donna Karan, Agnès B., etc. This group later enjoyed a significant success through the production and distribution of ready-to-wear clothing that corresponded to a specific ethics of style closely related to that found in *Cheap Chic*. These lines were deliberately not 'high fashion', (thus, not inspired by *haute couture*) were designed to be 'seasonless', and encouraged a consumer *bricolage* of past and present, expensive and cheap, European and non-European, formal and informal, etc. I am not proposing that this book provided the manual that came to generate a subsequent history; on the contrary, certain designers, such as Betsey Johnson, were actually interviewed by the authors. Rather, the book expresses a discursive system prevalent, though far from dominant, in the 1970s, that continues to inform a certain discourse within women's fashion today in which the self is created through a process of subjectivation that is largely aesthetic in its nature. This process of subjectivation is not dependent upon external aesthetic norms, but upon the injunction to know oneself, to the extent that this self is a self constructed through style. This ethics emancipates the woman from a normative code of correct dress while guiding her towards a knowledge that will enable her to create a personal aesthetic. Though theoretically this 'aesthetic' is available across class, ethnic, and regional boundaries, the very fact that the material must be read points to a readership similar to that which purchases *Harper's* (as distinct from the more general viewership of television itself). Yet the models, the women who represent the ideal in *Cheap Chic*, are extremely varied, from a student to a divorced women making it on her own (Milinaire and Troy, 1975, pp. 102, 120). Men are included; however, they are usually implicitly coded as 'gay' (1997, p. 179) and rarely seen in the company of a woman. In this sense, the self is represented on its own, for itself, so to speak, only marginally defined by the social hierarchy so significant to Klensch's practice.

*Cheap Chic* begins with a statement that posits fashion as emancipating, non-normative, and non-hierarchical: 'Personal style is what this book is all about. Fashion as a dictatorship of the elite is dead' (Milinaire and Troy, 1975, p. 9). Thus, the volume promotes the idea that to use fashion in a bid for authority is to misunderstand its fundamental nature in contemporary culture. It cautions against the dangers of consumer culture: 'Surrounded by mass manufacturing and mass marketing, we stuff our closets with masses of mistakes' (Milinaire and Troy, 1975, p. 9). Against the superfluous excesses of consumerism, the volume invokes a regime, a principle of asceticism in which the 'wardrobe' stands for a way of life. 'Paring down your wardrobe is going to simplify your life' (Milinaire and Troy, 1975, p. 9). This way of life evolves around the precept that 'Looking good makes you feel good'(Milinaire and Troy, 1975, p. 9). Creating a 'self' as an aesthetic project (subjectivation) through a form of discriminating consumer asceticism (*techne*) achieves the goal of 'feeling good' (*telos*). Though *Cheap Chic* ultimately advocates 'gratification of wants and desires' in Campbell's terms quoted above, it does so by advocating a regime of restraint, a minimalist consumerism that emphasizes the aesthetic as discipline rather than as pleasure. Indeed, here, fashion is 'an act of self-formation' associated with 'shopping' (Falk, Campbell, 1997, p. 4); however, we should not conclude that it is necessarily best understood as 'a process located in the imaginary' as do Falk and Campbell (1997, p. 4).[8] *Cheap Chic* (which is not in fact 'cheap' at all in the sense of restricting women's investment in fashion) locates fashion as a socially defined set of 'practices' (technologies) in which 'desires and wants' are submitted to a certain discipline.

It would be misleading, however, to posit clothing as the substance of this practice. 'The most basic element of *Cheap Chic* is the body you have your clothes on. Building a healthy, lively body is far cheaper than buying a lot of clothes to distract from it' (Milinaire and Troy, 1975, p. 10). 'There are no secret recipes for keeping your body together, but learning to take a certain pleasure in self-discipline is a first step'(Milinaire and Troy, 1975, p. 11). Though this body is constructed through discipline, a discipline prior to which the body appears to be without ontological status (a body that is not 'together', that must be built), this body is not the body of the ascetic. Rather, it is one that finds its full expression in its sensuality, its ability to feel. 'Once you have a body programme set up, start having fun with your clothes. Perhaps the best place to start thinking about the evocative nature of fabric, colour, and clothes is with the senses: Touch ... Smell ... Sound ... Sight ... ' (Milinaire and Troy, 1975, p. 11). Style functions as an extension of the body as a perceptual apparatus, one which perceives first and foremost itself, but which does not exist prior to the discipline that constructs as such, as 'body'.

Variations on this particular system have fuelled the publication of a seemingly endless series of popular books: *Living a Beautiful Life* (Stoddard, 1986), *Simplify Your Life* (St. James, 1994) and the Chic Simple series (*Chic Simple Clothes, Chic Simple Home, Chic Simple Face, Chic Simple Body*, etc.) with its own web site: http://www.chicsimple.com. and the motto 'The more you know, the less you need' (Gross and Stone, 1995 p. 6). *Chic Simple Clothes* rehearses its genealogy, locating its origins in the 1960s during which period according to its mythology 'Clothes retreated to the garden of hippiedom and became body art, manifestations of the soul. Fashion's mandate was forever subverted' (Gross, Stone, 1993, p. 20). Perhaps more accurately, for a certain readership at least, fashion's mandate was transformed; its principles were redefined in terms of a new consumerism in which less functioned as more, of which the underlying dictum was 'To live well' (Gross, Stone, 1993, p. 23). The commercial success of the Simple Chic venture indicates that an 'ethical' consumerism nonetheless fully participates in its culture, a culture of consumption. This proliferation of literature in a number of arenas beginning in the 1970s that purport to assist the reader in the construction of the self as aesthetic project, demonstrates the extent to which as a historian Foucault was very much in touch with his own culture.

At the same time, the very proliferation and success of these technologies of the self raise a set of crucial questions about the nature and role of ethics within the context of contemporary feminine culture. To what extent can we say that this formulation of the nature of ethics as that which is concerned with the relation of the self to the self provides a framework that resolves the dilemmas of a feminist practice within the context of a consumer culture? Feminist philosopher, Lois McNay comments:

> Foucault claims that contemporary society has reached such a degree of scepticism with regard to large-scale systems of belief that any form of contemporary ethics must arise from a more individual or localized basis. (1994, p. 141)

She then concludes: 'The freedom of the individual from oppressive aspects of modern society is not contingent, therefore, on any metanarrative of justice or morality grounded in an idea of transcendental rationality' (1994, p. 143). If we accept this logic, then we must accept the system proposed by *Cheap Chic* as an appropriate and ethical response to the dilemmas of consumer culture. McNay would express concern: 'The problem that arises from Foucault's work for feminists is the clash between positing a politics of engagement without providing normative guidelines for action' (1992, p. 197). Without 'normative guidelines', an 'engagement' runs the danger of losing sight of its goal within a social and economic arena. Yet from a Foucauldian perspective, it is only to the extent that technologies of the self counter the normative technologies of the social and the economic that the self can said to provide a terrain for the exercize of resistance.

The feminist project is a social project by definition; one of it primary concerns is the construction of gender and its literal embodiment as the feminine. Not unsurprising then, the feminist rejection of what I will call ethical consumerism for want of a better term derives from debates and convictions about the materiality of the body. In so far as the grounds of style as an ethical practice are constituted by a body (constructed as such through this same practice), this body, these bodies are also the principle terrain on which women are 'exploited' by consumer culture. We might claim that feminist theory[9] and consumer culture have sought to reconfigure the body as part of the project of modernity; however, these discourses appear to have operated in radically different directions. Feminist theory has moved towards an increasing sense of the indecipherability of the body as an expression of the individual; popular culture, towards the consolidation of market segments as the expression of the social through the assertion of individual agency. From another perspective, one might say, however, that feminist theory and feminine consumer culture have in common that each throws into question the essential nature of the feminine body. Feminist theory underlines the 'deconstructability', of the body. Popular culture emphasizes the 'reconstructability' of this body as a space that is defined by consumerism. A body as a market, a group, that in economic and symbolic terms can be said to have a cohesive identity, this body is defined by the fact that woman consumes for her 'self' rather than the family. These shifts have altered the task of feminist scholarship in which feminism must assess the ethical dimensions of the consumer's gesture to take repossession of her body as the territories upon which are written the relations of the self to the self.

# The Paradox of Femininity

From Foucault's perspective the privileged terrain of the relations of the self to the self in which one might presuppose an 'active' subject is legislated by a limited set of systems available at a given moment. Foucault comments that if he is:

> ... interested in how the subject constitutes itself in an active fashion through practices of the self, these practices are nevertheless not something invented by the individual himself. They are models that he finds in his culture and are proposed, suggested, imposed upon him by his culture, his society, and his social group. (Foucault, 1997, p. 291)

Bordo asks us, quite legitimately, if as feminists we can accept as 'ethical' a system of ethics that is predicated upon creating a 'self' as a work of art in a culture in which the excesses of consumer culture define the 'models' available to 'woman' in contemporary consumer society. If, ethical action, as resistance, is inevitably undertaken from a position of general epistemological uncertainty, as Bordo claims (1997, p. 191), then ethical action never 'be' ethical from the perspective of a given subject as agent of that action. Ethical actions (as opposed to ethical systems) are foolhardy enterprises condemned to the failure of uncertainty. The continual reconstruction of the body, within the limited social space accorded it, might be read as a glorious if inevitably flawed exercize of the faculty of agency in the face of other technologies that work towards its atrophy, even its erasure. Such a position would imply that feminists accept both philosophy and popular culture as practices that struggle with the difficult project of maintaining possibilities, in particular the possibility of ethical action (however improbable).

To articulate possibilities, to maintain possibility, of identities, of mastery, and of selves, are perhaps the most urgent tasks of contemporary feminist theory. These are feminist tasks in so far as feminism has always been about the social constructions of the body *qua* body and the ethical stakes of these constructions. In the pursuit of this precarious project, we cannot disregard any potential allies or enemies. We cannot afford either to ignore the ethical gestures of popular culture or to accept these gestures at face value.

Joan Scott's claims that: 'The ambiguities of the republican notion of the individual (its universal definition and masculine embodiment) were ... carried into and exposed by feminist arguments' (Scott, 1996, p. 11). This republican notion of the individual clearly remains necessary to feminist conceptualizations of political agency. From Scott's perspective, then, 'agency' within a feminist political framework is grounded in paradox (Scott, 1996, p. 11). Certainly we have not resolved the paradox that Scott underlines as crucial to the genesis of a feminist politics, that feminism depends upon a 'discourse of individual rights that represses sexual difference' (1996, p. 175). Yet it seems worthy of our notice that women, many of whom would not dare to consider themselves feminists, continue to carve out arenas in which they might play out these paradoxes with an eye to their own interest, with a sense that in the last instance they enjoy the obligation and the right to care for themselves as women. As women they will decide when they are wasting time.

# Notes

1. Much of Foucault's later work, including numerous lectures and interviews (1994) focuses on the issue of ethics; however, this concept or rather set of concepts are most concretely documented in the three volumes of *The History of Sexuality* (1990).
2. Simmons (1994, pp. 3, 15, 75) reported that *Harper's Bazaar* was read by 1.2 percent of their sample. The readership is predominantly women (91.4 %), and white (87.4 %). Almost half the readers (49.5 %) are between 25 and 44 years of age. (1994, p. 3, 75, 15). *Harper's Bazaar* has a total circulation of 705,027 (*SRDS.*, 1994, p. 340). I owe a special debt to Allan Campbell for providing the data used in this chapter.
3. Foucault discusses these concepts in a number of volumes; however, I choose to reference the brief essay 'Technologies of the Self' (Foucault, 1997, pp. 223-52) because it offers a succinct and clear overview of the concepts written by Foucault himself. Throughout this piece I will refer to the essays in the volume *Ethics, Subjectivity and Truth* for similar reasons. For a more extensive discussion of these issues, their appearance in Foucault's work, and their significance to feminist scholarship see McNay, 1992; McNay, 1994.
4. Infomercials, and other extended forms of paid programming that sell products directly to consumers directly work similarly if less coherently.
5. SRDS (1998) reported that the CNN cable network ranked second among U.S. networks with 71.2 million viewers; MTV was thirteenth with 66.5 million viewers (1253). Simmons (1994) reported that CNN is watched by 32.5 percent of total surveyed, of which 47.9 % are women, 89.1 percent are white, and 42 % are aged 25-44. MTV is watched by 9.3 percent of the total surveyed of which 45.9 % are women, 82.4 percent are white, and 71.2 % are aged 18-34 years. (Simmons, 1994, pp. 6, 78, 18). Neither *House of Style* nor *Style with Elsa Klensch* are typically aired during prime-time (times vary according to market).
6. This essay does not address the issue of whether or not Foucault is accurate in his characterisation of the Greeks. At stake here is the definition of ethical principles offered by Foucault and the degree to which these last can be said to describe certain tendencies in contemporary feminine culture.
7. In practice, there is an overlap in these various systems; however, I argue that the difference in emphasis is significant.
8. There is a certain justification for discussing 'fashion' in terms of this 'imaginary', which Falk relates to a Lacanian notion of the subject (Falk,

Campbell, 1997, p. 12 note 3) when approaching the photographic image. I discuss the relationship between the feminine subject and the image at greater length elsewhere (Radner, 1995, pp. 55-65).
9. Here I am specifically referring to the tradition of inquiry that has culminated in, for example, Judith Butler's discussion of the body (1993).

# References

Armstrong, Nancy 1987: *Desire and Domestic Fiction : a Political History of the Novel*. New York: Oxford University Press.
Bordo, Susan 1993: *Unbearable Weight: Feminism, Western Culture, and the Body*. Berkeley: University of California Press.
Bordo, Susan 1997: *Twilight Zones: the Hidden Life of Cultural Images from Plato to O.J.* Berkeley: University of California Press.
Butler, Judith 1993: *Bodies That Matter : on the Discursive Limits of 'Sex.'* New York: Routledge, 1993.
Campbell, Colin 1997: Shopping, Pleasure, and the Sex War. In P. Falk and C. Campbell (eds.)*The Shopping Experience*. London: Sage, pp. 166-76.
Falk, Pasi, Campbell, Colin 1997: Introduction. In P. Falk and C. Campbell. (eds.)*The Shopping Experience*. London: Sage, pp.1-14.
Freidan, Betty 1963: *The Feminine Mystique*. New York: Dell.
Foucault, Michel 1990: *The History of Sexuality* . Hurley, trans., New York : Vintage Books.
Foucault, Michel 1994: *Dits et écrits : 1954-1988*. Paris : Editions Gallimard.
Foucault, Michel 1997: *Ethics: Subjectivity and Truth*, Rabinow, ed. New York: the New Press.
Gross, Kim Johnson and Stone, Jeff 1993: *Chic Simple Clothes*. New York: Knopf.
Gross, Kim Johnson and Stone, Jeff 1995: *Chic Simple Women's Wardrobe*. New York: Knopf.
hooks, bell 1984: *Feminist Theory from Margin to Center*. Boston: South End Press.
Klensch, Elsa 1995: *Style by Elsa Klensch*. New York: Perigee.
McNay, Lois 1992: *Feminism and Foucault*. Boston: Northeastern University Press.
McNay, Lois 1994: *Foucault: A Critical Introduction*. New York: Continuum.
McRobbie, Angela 1991: *Feminism and Youth Culture : from 'Jackie' to 'Just Seventeen'*. Boston : Unwin Hyman.
Meter, Jonathan Van 1998: *All Spice*. Vogue, January, pp. 132-6, 185.
Milinaire, Caterine and Troy, Carol 1975: *Cheap Chic*. New York: Harmony Books.
Partington, Angela 1993: Popular Fashion and Working-Class Affluence. In Ash and Wilson (eds.) *Chic Thrills*. Berkeley. Los Angeles: University of California Press, pp.143-61.
Radner, Hilary 1995: *Shopping Around: Feminine Culture and the Pursuit of Pleasure*. New York: Routledge.
St. James, Elaine 1994: *Simplify Your Life*. New York: Hyperion.
Scott, Joan 1996: *Only Paradoxes to Offer: French Feminists and the Rights of Man*. Cambridge, MA: Harvard University Press.
Simmons Study of Media and Markets 1994: *M4: Multi-Media Audiences*.

*SRDS Consumer Magazine Advertising Source 1997*: 79: 12 (December).
*SRDS TV & Cable Source 1998*: 80:1 (First Quarter).
Stoddard, Alexandra 1986: *Living a Beautiful Life*. New York: Avon.
Szabo, Julia 1996: 'Why Doesn't Fashion Work on TV?' *Harper's Bazaar*. November, pp. 214-15, 262.
Wilson Elizabeth 1985: *Adorned in Dreams: Fashion and Modernity*. London: Virago.

**Hilary Radner** is Associate Professor in the Department of Communication and Theatre at the University of Notre Dame. She is the author of *Shopping Around: Consumer Culture and the Pursuit of Pleasure* (Routledge, 1995), a co-editor of *Film Theory Goes to the Movies* (Routledge, 1993), and *Constructing the New Consumer Society* (Macmillan, 1997).

# Time and Neutrality:
## Media of Modernity in a Postmodern World

Elizabeth Ermarth
University of Edinburgh

The political dangers of postmodernity have spurred some commentators into expressions of anxiety unaccompanied by much analysis. And such anxiety is well enough founded because postmodernity represents seismic shifts in the foundations of European humanist culture: a culture that still sustains so much of personal, political, social, and academic life in the Atlantic countries. At the extremes this anxiety is expressed either in shallow and uninformed ways, as for example almost uniformly in the *Times Literary Supplement*, but also in certain wilful incomprehensions among political activists who are intent on bringing previously marginal groups into the political mainstream and who see postmodernity as a threat to that modern project. The former indulge in Podsnapian dismissals; the latter seem to fear that identity politics is dissolving just as former marginals reach the point of participating in it; some activists even suggest that postmodernism is just another patriarchal ploy in the shell games of a power system primarily intent on keeping out marginals at all costs. This position seems to rest on the belief that once marginals have discovered the levers of power, some patriarchal Star Chamber exists that will shift power elsewhere rather than share it. Such a conclusion would not only be silly, it would entail serious mistakes about postmodernity and about its political possibilities. While these positions do not represent the best and most productive work being done on the central critique of modernity, they have become significant obstacles to its progress.

The persistent lack of common terminology in discussions of postmodernity obviously reflects a cultural will. It certainly keeps conversation alive. But terminological confusion over the definition of postmodernity obscures its cultural challenges and political consequences, especially for democratic societies. At the risk of introducing too much clarity, then, I want to offer some definitions that will hold the terminological confusion at bay long enough to glimpse what is at stake in postmodern formulations of time.

These definitions concern especially two troubled terms: first, 'postmodern', and second, 'time'. No general agreement exists about the meaning of the term 'postmodern' and in fact in its singularity it covers completely incompatible cultural interpretations. This lack of agreement exists in part because similar lack of agreement exists concerning the term 'modern'. It is relatively obvious that the term 'postmodern' indicates whatever it is that comes after modernity; but what is 'modern'? To some the term gets conflated with 'modern*ism*' and indicates a fairly local event around the turn of the twentieth century; to others it indicates the era since the late eighteenth-century Enlightenment; still others use the term as historians do, to mark the Modern as something distinct from and subsequent to the Medieval. According to the last view, which I share, postmodernity involves a crisis of a humanist rationality as it was constructed by Renaissance and Reformation Europe, which is to say, by something older and more profoundly disseminated than the Enlightenment rationality that developed from it several centuries later.

The second troubled term to be stabilized is 'Time': a term used uncritically in ways that universalize what is only a particular construction of temporality, one which humanist culture has naturalized and thus universalized but which, nevertheless, belongs only to a certain phase of culture. I want to unpack the relation between that particular humanist construction of time on the one hand, and on the other hand, a postmodernity which denies it validity.

Time is a term we take for granted. We treat time as something quantifiable, as something almost material which can be bought and sold. For example, I continually feel plagued by time-scarcity. To 'have no time', to be 'out of time', to lack 'free time', or 'quality time'; to feel pressured to 'make time'. I am all-too-familiar with these phrases. If time is money, I am definitely caught in negative equity; I will never have enough time to break even. A colleague said to me recently that he had only two kinds of time: sacred, and booked. I must say, I know the feeling, and I expect that I am by no means alone.

During the past few years, time has become a topic for discussion and for theorizing, and the problem has been, that the theorizing generally stops far short of a thorough analysis of the conventions by which we maintain this 'time' that is so quantifiable and scarce. Looked at historically in terms of the invention and development of cultural grammars, 'time' in the sense we assume it – as a neutral, homogeneous medium extending infinitely and 'in' which mutual relevance can be measured – belongs to a fairly unique phase of Western culture: one in which European humanism underwrote empirical science and its technologies, just as it underwrote representation in politics and in art.

Even philosophical discussions of 'time' (sometimes it is used interchangeably with 'history') tend to take those terms for granted. Let me mention only a very few examples. Jean-François Lyotard, in essays like 'Time Today', or 'The Sign of History', as well as in other writings uses phrases like 'gaining time' or 'the time of exchange' where the term 'time' is not itself challenged; 'time' is just, well, time. J. T. Fraser, Julia

Kristeva and others consider *supposedly* different *kinds* of time – linear time, cyclic time, ritual time, women's time – but again, without significantly challenging the term 'time'. Especially in Anglo-American traditions, the word 'time' functions insistently in its humanist construction only – time as a common denominator, a neutral, homogeneous medium, a basis for linkage and mediation. The mind slips, inevitably it seems and not always uncreatively, into complicity with the discourse supposedly being analyzed.

You would never know from these discussions that time-construction differs historically and culturally, and that 'time' for Homer or Euripedes or even Augustine was not anything like the same thing it is for us. One particular construction of time, and its entail of values and prohibitions, keeps reasserting and reinscribing itself. This construction of time has been foundational in the West, and has had profound implications for the entire cultural enterprise of Western democratic society.

This commonly held assumption about time presents it as a medium, like space, 'in' which objects and events exist; in fact it can be argued that 'objects' and events *only* exist in such a medium: crucially a *neutral* medium – one that does not disturb what is contained 'in' it, and one that can therefore act as a kind of infinite common denominator for every object and event – a sort of metaphysical ether. This is the time of Newton and Kant, the time of history and project. It is the time that makes possible the mutually informative measurements that have been essential to the development of empirical science, representational politics and art, certain forms of music and mathematics, and even the plaguing sense of time-scarcity that I mentioned as I began. 'In' this time of history and project – this neutral time – we pursue our plans and develop our personalities, we compare forms and measure distances. This historical time is open-ended, homogeneous, universal and, above all, neutral.

But this neutral medium is achieved, not found; there is nothing natural about it. It was constructed according to principles established at least six centuries ago, and first expressed in spatial forms like architecture and painting and especially in the art of the Quattrocento. Those principles involves a certain grammar of perspective, one that also underwrites realist art, democratic politics, and empirical methodology. Elsewhere I have discussed this complex cultural phenomenon in some detail (Ermarth 1998, Chapters 1-3), so for the purposes of this argument I will only summarize briefly the key point. Because it involves a concise rendering of cultural inscriptions to be found in geometry, painting, narrative, and theo-politics, it necessarily engages us at a certain level of abstraction.

The single-point perspective system in visual arts offers the most synchronic representation of the cultural grammar that enabled

Renaissance artists and others literally to objectify the world by mapping it according to a common grid. This common grid creates the illusion of a spatial medium that is neutral, homogeneous, and infinite. The objects that materialize 'in' this medium act mainly to specify and carry the generalization about the oneness of the world maintained by the perspective grammar. Neutral space is what single-point perspective systems primarily represent; they produce it; it is their most important achievement. The immense possibilities of that neutrality, and of the common horizon it sustains, became brilliantly evident in Renaissance painting and architecture, in cartography and exploration, and in many subsequent cultural specifications including advances in geometry and new forms of politics (Ermarth, 1998, Chapter 2). This perspective system produced and disseminated for the first time in European culture, and perhaps for the first time ever, the value of neutrality.

The temporal counterpart of this spatial common-denominator system is 'history'. By coordinating past, present, and future into a single system of measurement, the historical convention organizes – one could say rationalizes – the faculty of consciousness in much the same way that realist painting, with its commanding structures of single-point perspective, organizes (or rationalizes) the faculty of sight (Ivins, 1973). According to this perspective system, whether in space or in time, all perspectives regardless of variety converge in one horizon, one common medium, one and the 'same' world. Historical cultural narratives exploit more prominently the serial potential of this perspective system (even in painting it implies a serial collection of viewpoints, a power to 'walk around' objects that had not been seen in that light previously). And historical narrative developed the grammar of single-point perspective much later than its spatial inventors did. Nevertheless historical narratives provide for readers a similar sense of the profound neutrality of time and thus of the oneness of the world contained 'in' it. And not only painters and historians but, over several centuries, mathematicians, philosophers, politicians, and architects explored the potential of this new paradigm that erased the fissures between worlds and recognized this world as One: unified by the presence of common denominator media 'in' which mutually informative measurement becomes possible. By means of this powerful grammar of perspective they replaced the typological world of medieval iconography with the neutral media of modernity and their objectified world of verisimilitude.

Under ideal circumstances I could introduce here some colour plates showing various Renaissance paintings which exploit in varying degrees the grammar of single point perspective: Giovanni di Paolo's *St. John the Baptist Retiring to the Desert*, Raphael's *School at Athens*, from the Pope's study in the Vatican; Leonardo's *Last Supper* on the refectory wall of Santa Maria della Grazie in Milan; or one of the many church interiors by Pieter Saenredam (e.g. *The Buukerk at Utrecht*) all of which would help to demonstrate the ways in which, from the fourteenth to the seventeenth century, this particular grammar of perspective produces a common medium running to infinity and containing all the world without boundary or contradiction. In these works the main event is not, as it must have seemed to early viewers and may still seems to many, the faithful reproduction of objects; the main event is the production of conditions in which such reproduction becomes possible. The objects so realistically rendered are only the carriers of a larger, more powerful generalization about the world: specifiers of an abstract and powerful system that invites comparison among particulars, that renders them mutually informative, and that provides an infinite horizon.

One especially paradoxical feature of this perspective grammar is that it masks the abstraction upon which it depends. It seeks to erase the evidence of its constructedness and to engage us in the admiration of verisimilitude by pretending to be a 'mere' reproduction of spectator awareness. It may be difficult for us to recover the éclat of that particular gesture for a world in which few artists anywhere had ever made such concessions so systematically. Even sophisticated viewers can go badly wrong, as Roland Barthes does (1972, p.3) in this denunciation of the Dutch painter, Pieter Saenredam:

> Saenredam painted neither faces nor objects, but chiefly vacant church interiors, reduced to the beige and innocuous unction of butterscotch ice cream. These churches, where there is nothing to be seen but expanses of wood and whitewashed plaster, are irremediably unpeopled, and this negation goes much further than the destruction of idols. Never has nothingness been so confident ... He articulates by antithesis the nature of classical Dutch painting, which has washed away religion only to replace it with man and his empire of things. . . . Behold him, then, at the pinnacle of history, knowing no other fate than a gradual appropriation of matter.

Here the voice of Barthes the moralist reveals itself. But unfortunately Barthes entirely misses the point of Dutch realism. Such pictures have very little to do with material objects they putatively represent, and what they chiefly represent is something quite different from the expanses of plaster and wood, the 'objects' that Barthes mainly notices. What such pictures represent is precisely space, and Saenredam's atmospheric interior spaces perhaps more than most. They make visible that neutral, common denominator medium that, above all else, is so fundamental to modernity and all its projects. It is *precisely* the emptiness of Saenredam's interiors that calls attention to the existence of that space, that common atmosphere 'in' which the world is One: perceptible in terms of a single system of measurement. Of *course* such pictures show empty space; that is their whole point. The material 'in' that space merely acts as a support or carrier for the powerful, overarching generalization about space and relationship that the realist painter chiefly presents. How powerful, and how easy to miss, are these media of modernity, neutral space and neutral time.

So in sum, what Renaissance painters do for space and what later historians do for time is to construct a neutral medium by coordinating perspectives into a single system of observation and measurement: spatial perspectives most famously in painting and architecture; and the newly aligned temporal perspectives of past, present, and future which increasingly appear in narrative. This system thus provides the common-denominators that objectify the world and make it One. Such common-denominators can be found across humanist culture, from Isaac Newton's temporal constant – what he called 'God's time' to the 'commonweal' of emergent Parliamentary democracy.

Beginning around 1800, this view of time as history becomes very powerfully disseminated, not least in the writings of novelists intent on considering the new social agendas created by revolution or the threat of it. Three things particularly interest me about this construction of neutral, historical time:

- first, the fact (despite its still-current claims to universality) that it, like neutral space, is the construct of a particular era of European humanism and thus relatively unique in world culture and history;

- second, the fact that we have naturalized this particular construction to such a degree that we take it for granted – like space, time is somehow like a medium we move 'in' and

- third, that like neutral space, this construction of time has almost totally disappeared in the art, and to a considerable degree in the science of the twentieth century. Picasso, Braque, the surrealists and others have very largely done away with the kind of spatial medium that the Renaissance realist painters bequeathed to Europe; similarly many of the best novelists and filmmakers have done away with the kind of temporal medium of history bequeathed to us by the nineteenth century. Even in important branches of physics, time is no longer the imperturbable duration that Newton made it for more than two hundred years (Mook and Vargish, 1987).

To take the first and second points together: we have constructed time and naturalized our construction. This thought takes some getting used to, and that is not as easy as it may at first seem. Most citizens of Western democratic societies, and most theorists who write on 'time', take for granted that time is a universal, constant, common denominator. But, to repeat, this time has only been widely disseminated since around 1800; it is not Homer's time, which is fractured by directives from the gods, or fate (moira); nor is it Augustine's essentially phantasmal time. No, our time, like our space, is a neutral medium 'in' which causalities unfold, entities subsist, and our faculties are rationalized.

Because of the abstractness of this massively deployed and disseminated perspective convention it may seem that the neutrality of time is a 'natural' condition and that it makes collective agreements possible. What I am arguing is that the reverse is at least as true: that through a particular perspective grammar, collective agreement makes possible neutral time and space (Ermarth, 1998, p. 54). The unsettling implication of this is that a collective agreement might well produce entirely different results, including a different kind of time which would have no interest in objectifying the world.

The abstractness of our 'time' constant is very difficult to keep in view, so accustomed have we become to this construction of temporality and to what depends upon it. Seeing its historical limits and relative uniqueness almost seems counter-intuitive. Looking backwards from the late twentieth century it is easy to create what the historian, Herbert Butterfield called a 'gigantic optical illusion' of 'history' (Butterfield, 1963, pp. 5, 23-4) running its neutral course from the origin of the world to the present day, including in it everything from Homer to holographs; from the Big Bang to the Final Twitter; a kind of cosmic motorway in fact.

But there are political dangers in such an optical illusion, as Butterfield once reminded his fellow historians. It can act as blinder or filter: not only influencing our interpretations of the past but, more potently, masking the function of those interpretations in the present. For example, 'it is astonishing to what an extent the historian has been Protestant, progressive ... and the very model of the 19th (sic) century gentleman', and to what extent since about 1800 the historian has contributed to the development of European nationalism, even 'romantic nationalism'. Such unexamined practices can have ominous implications: 'It is possible (Butterfield concludes) for historians to mislead a nation in respect of what it might regard as its historic mission' (1969, p. 30). The construction of temporality, he implies, is context bound, value laden, and politically consequential.

So much has depended upon the possibilities established by these neutral media of modernity. It is precisely the lack of a grammar of perspective that accounts for 'much of the failure of classical and medieval science' (Ivins, 1973, p. 9). And it is precisely the presence of that grammar, from the *Quattrocento* onward that makes possible the projections and rationalizations that have supported cartography, exploration, a new astronomy, eventually empirical science, and even representational government which itself is a perspective system *par excellence*.

At the risk of being repetitive, and partly as a consequence of experience concerning reception of these concepts, I want to insist that the key feature of this temporal construction is neutrality, and only neutrality: our humanist, historical 'time' is not uniquely characterized by linearity, nor by chronology, nor even by causality, all of which appear in other kinds of sequence and accompanying other constructions of temporality, and none of which particularly characterize the time of representation and historical project.

This point is worth emphasizing because contemporary discussions of time routinely invoke 'linearity', or 'chronology', or 'sequence', or 'causality'. But all kinds of cultural narratives can accommodate the linear, the sequential, the chronological, even the causal, and can still lack the neutrality characterizing the time of modernity. For example, medieval chronicles of miracles and magic have chronology; so do and Garcia Marquez's stories; even the most ahistorical narratives have sequence; causalities that have nothing to do with history operate in all sorts of narratives – Aristotelian causality, for example, which cheerfully operates in the most *a*historical medieval philosophy and theology and, for that matter, even in some twentieth century literary criticism. 'Linearity' is an especially common description of time that does nothing whatever to distinguish between any of these widely varying temporal modes. Even circular epics can be considered 'linear' because one thing follows another, even though that sequence is not evolutionary. It is true that linearity develops particular value in neutral time – 'in' a neutral medium, the linear trajectory is identifiable and has interest because it is productive – but in itself linearity does not produce the temporality we call 'history'.

*Neutrality* alone distinguishes the time of modernity, or in other words, historical time. Neutrality in the medium is what the grammar of a single-point perspective system distinctively produces. History is exactly *not* end-stopped or riven by divine agency but open and infinite; it is not the time of heroes, but the time common to all.

Because the characteristic neutrality of modern time has importance well beyond master narratives, its virtual disappearance in contemporary writing and in the greatest narrative art of the twentieth century, is a cultural event of considerable magnitude. This mutation indicates change in the basic cultural codes which for several centuries have witnessed and validated the existence of a common world, a world of common denominators.

Now I turn briefly to the contemporary abandonment of this long-standing and still powerful construction of time. Among the most powerful revisionary acts of postmodernism has been its treatment of time as finite. And this most powerful act has been perpetrated and disseminated, it bears repeating, by philosophers and scientists and especially by artists: by the writers, painters, filmmakers and others interested in experimenting with and renewing or reshaping the foundations of cultural codes. The most original and creative narratives produced after modernity or in postmodernity, beginning with Joyce and Kafka, revise out of existence that neutral medium 'in' which so much has been possible. Instead of the unproblematic medium of 'time' produced by the grammar of perspective, a time whose neutrality permits transparent communication and comparison across temporal and spatial distances; instead of a common time 'in' which we all live in more or less mutually relevant: these postmodern narratives inscribe a time that has only local definition, a time that is a dimension of events not a medium for them, a time consistent with a new physics and its new description of nature. It is no mere coincidence that Einstein arrived at the Special Theory of Relativity only when, he said, 'at last I realized that time was suspect' (Clark, p. 84). It is no coincidence, because both new narrative and new physics belong to a set of cultural codes that have changed the foundations of perception and knowledge from the durable neutralities of empiricism and representation, to something new and different. The neutralities of humanist culture look positively quaint in an era where media are electronic, can be switched on and off, can be bought and sold, and manipulated.

The writers and filmmakers who have provided us with really new uses of language and new kinds of sequence requiring new acts of attention – Borges and Garcia Marquez, Duras and Robbe-Grillet, Hawkes and Nabokov, Kundera and Calvino, Buñuel, Resnais, Jost and a host of others – these also treat that neutral, Newtonian medium as suspect. Time in their work, as in special relativity, becomes a finite dimension of an event. The inconvenient fact in such writing is that no common denominator exists between one time frame and another: no agreement (that is, no formal consensus), about the fundamental terms for describing and operating in the world precisely because a singular world no longer exists. In such constructs each arrangement has its own time, but there is no common time 'in' which common objectives can be reached by means of common causalities.

All writing taken up in these conditions necessarily addresses new problems of subjectivity and project. And in postmodernity, as Cortázar said, 'everything is writing, that is to say a fable' (1963, ch. 73). Where no neutral media of modernity are present, no world of events and objects can materialize, including that ultimate object, 'the subject'. Whatever takes place does so, not in a finite segment of neutral, infinite time, but instead takes place in such a way that temporality itself is finite, a dimension of events, an element confined to certain rhythmic intervals or 'rhythmic time' (Ermarth, 1992, pp. 45-71). When such a temporal sequence is over its time, like the time of a musical improvization, also is over; no potential extension appears to naturalize and universalize its meanings: no neutral temporal medium guarantees its larger application or retains any residue. Postmodern time is bonded to the phrase, to the unrepeatable phase, to the expression that, like language and like all discourse, is both finite and unbounded. Paradoxical though that Einsteinian formulation may sound, it makes practical sense fairly easily in terms of the kind of differential linguistic value first theorized by Saussure and subsequently developed by post-structuralist philosophy and cultural criticism. Another term for this finite, postmodern temporality is 'Ph(r)ase time' (Ermarth, 1995), a term that invokes the deeply *philological* quality of the postmodern critique of modernity, and its insistence that all cultural systems and codes operate like language, indeed, *are* language.

Familiar problems emerge from this absence in postmodernity of the neutrality familiar from modernity's temporal and spatial common denominators: problems of linkage, problems of mutual effort, problems of pluralized or fragmented identity, problems of agency. Postmodernity entails political dangers to the systems European societies have taken for granted for several centuries because, first among other things, it challenges the very existence of the common world invented by a cultural grammar now demonstrably faded. What becomes of individuality ('the subject', the *cogito*)? What becomes of responsibility and ethical choice, when the stable subject of European humanism loses its discreteness, its Cartesian durability and becomes instead what the linguistic turn has essentially made of it: a function in a differential system, a questionable-subject-in-process? Similar questions can be asked about objectivity, empiricism, history, and representation, and in politics as well as in art. Conceived as discourse, that is, as functions defined differentially and systemically, these familiar furnishings of humanist discourse become problematic as they threaten to disappear into systemic functions.

These issues certainly are not new but discussion of them has not progressed far and remains in a chaotic state. On the one hand, those attempting to explore the positive possibilities of this now broadly held critique of modernity often do so in a hit-and-run style that many find unengaging. On the other hand, those impressed only by the negative implications of postmodernity often associate it with one or another traditional villainy, such as for example the Marxist critic identifying it as a symptom of 'late phase industrial capitalism' (i.e., as something already predicted and already interpreted in advance). Both approaches occlude, among other things, the contemporary mutation that has taken place in the codes maintaining the neutral media of modernity, and that has rendered them partially, if not hopelessly inadequate. This incompleteness of discussion is not surprising given the incremental magnitude of the change involved. The value of neutrality – as the blue berets in former Yugoslavia testify – remains culturally central, and it is always difficult to analyze functional assumptions, especially deeply rooted ones; discussion becomes hampered by cognitive dissonance. The neutral media of modernity have functioned for at least 600 years and very largely function still in our politics and education; we continually construct them through a sustained and near-miraculous collective act of faith.

If these media have been foundational for democratic, identity politics, what happens to the politics without them? Does this postmodern mutation in the media of modernity threaten the destruction of all we hold dear? These important questions remain, and should remain, open questions. In support of such openness, I want to end with two related points concerning individuality and concerning values: first, that the disappearance of neutrality and of the objectified, common world it supported, and even the associated disappearance of objects like 'the subject', does not mean the destruction of all values; and second, that personal responsibility by no means disappears with the so-called 'autonomous individual' of fable and rhyme. If Derrida is right and language speaks us; if, in other words, language is a habitation, not an instrument: this in no way reduces personal responsibility. Far from it. In fact, the opposite may be truer: that personal responsibility begins where the autonomous 'natural' individual ends. In fact, the very idea of 'individual' autonomy, as it is understood late in the twentieth century, was only invented in the seventeenth century (at the earliest) and remains culturally a relatively recent and unique invention. Foucault correctly said of this 'individual' that it is a fundamentally religious idea, which is to say, an idea that suggests and confirms values that have standing as absolutes. Is this 'individual' necessary for guiding conduct? I think not.

Of course I function in and am shaped by codes, by discourses, by languages that I have not created. This fact was not invented by postmodernists; they have merely recovered it from the occlusion that rationalism has imposed on the multiplied contradictions that overflow and deny singularity to 'the' world. To speak of myself only, I was born into a gender, with everything that has implied for me whether I liked it or not, and whether I knew it or not; I was born into the English language, with everything that implies for my psychic definition, like it or not. I was born into a nationality, and into cultural and family and community agendas about which I had nothing to say whatever. But being constructed by these languages is not a limitation; only having no language would be that. On the contrary, the multiple codes at my disposal constitute my only means for developing, if I can, my individual *parole*. Dispersed as I am in semiological functions of so many kinds, am I not still here, as opposed to there, and speaking, not silent? Does not this particularity by definition make a difference, though not by 'choice' in the sense that the monadic individual subject came, trailing clouds of glory, to deliberate and choose in its 'freedom'. The question is not whether I speak, but how; the question is not *whether* I make a difference – 'we are difference' as Foucault puts it (1972, p. 131). The postmodern question is only, what difference is it that I *do* make and, perhaps even, is it the one I want to make? If, as Borges suggests, language is social memory, then language by definition maintains that memory in basically irrational (unrationalizeable) ways: on the one hand, languages or codes provide the set potential that we call grammar or *langue*; on the other hand, the speech act, or *parole*, remains unique, unpredictable, distinct and finite. In-between this powerful potential and this precise inscription lies the arena of freedom, an arena full of circumscribed and multiplied potentials, to be sure, but one where every detail counts.

My second and briefer thought carries on from the first, in the form of the assertion of a personal uniqueness far more complex and creative than that once asserted by Cartesian philosophy: a personal uniqueness not given, but constructed; a uniqueness I create as I go from day to day, specifying in particular ways my multiple shared potentials. Politics, and gender, and family, and speech, and nationality, and profession, and pleasure – let us not forget pleasure – all belong to the grammars, the *langues* which I specify, more or less uniquely, in various and continuous *paroles*. Combining them half aware, using inadvertent repetitions, half-baked memories, conscious choice and trained instinct, I make more or less creative use of the various grammars available to me, positioned by them but always specifying them as I go. The true definition of deprivation is being deprived of this varied range of available grammars: a definition that social scientists certainly should understand better. From this aura of potentialities, then, and with all my limitations upon me, I construct, just as you construct, he and she construct, the unique and unrepeatable poetry of an individual life. It is not the basis for a Mission statement; it is not a World Historical vision of identity and action; in short, it is not the vision available in the infinite neutralities of modernity. It is smaller, humbler; but for all that, no less creative.

# References

Barthes, Roland 1972: The World as Object. *Critical Essays*. Richard Howard trans Evanston, IL: Northwestern University Press, pp. 3-12.

Butterfield, Herbert 1963: *The Whig Interpretation of History*. London: G. Bell and Sons.

Butterfield, Herbert 1969: *Man on His Past*. Cambridge: Cambridge University Press.

Clark, Ronald 1971:*Einstein: The Life and Times*. New York: World Publishing Co.

Cortázar, Julio 1966: *Hopscotch*. Gregory Rabassa trans. New York: New American Library Plume Book.

Ermarth, Elizabeth Deeds 1992: *Sequel to History: Postmodernism and the Crisis of Representational Time*. Princeton, NJ: Princeton University Press.

Ermarth, Elizabeth Deeds 1995: Ph(r)ase Time: Chaos Theory and Postmodern Reports on Knowledge. *Social Time* 4.1 (February), pp. 91-110.

Ermarth, Elizabeth Deeds 1998: *Realism and Consensus in the English Novel: Time, Space and Narrative*. Edinburgh: Edinburgh Univ. Press.

Foucault, Michel 1972: *The Archaeology of Knowledge*. A. M. Sheridan-Smith, trans. New York: Pantheon.

Fraser, J. T.(ed.) 1966: *The Voices of Time: A Cooperative Survey of Man's View of Time as Expressed by the Sciences and by the Humanities*. New York: George Braziller.

Ivins Jr., William J. 1973: *On the Rationalization of Sight, with an Examination of Three Renaissance Texts on Perspective*, Paper No. 8. New York: Metropolitan Museum of Art.

Lyotard, Jean-François 1984: *The Postmodern Condition: A Report on Knowledge*. Geoff Bennington and Brian Massumi trans. Theory and History of Literature, Vol. 10. Minneapolis, MN: University of Minnesota Press.

Kristeva, Julia 1981: Women's Time (Les temps des femmes 1979). Alice Jardine and Harry Blake trans. *Signs* 7.1 (Autumn 1981), pp. 5-35.

Mook, Delo and Vargish, Thomas 1987: *Inside Relativity*. Princeton, NJ: Princeton University Press.

**Elizabeth Deeds Ermarth** writes on the construction and eventual deconstruction of the humanist culture of representation in Europe, from the Renaissance to the present. She has published four books: *Realism and Consensus: Time Space and Narrative* (1983; with new preface and bibliography, 1998); *George Eliot* (1985); *Sequel to History: Postmodernism and the Crisis of Representational Time* (1992); *The Novel in History, 1840-1895*. She currently is Saintsbury Professor of English, and Director of the Postgraduate School at the University of Edinburgh.

# The New Global History: History in a Global Age

Roland Robertson
University of Pittsburgh

I deal in this chapter with the increasing interest in world – or, as I would prefer to say, global – history. The issue as to whether we should best speak of either world or global history is one which is currently being disputed, but I will leave this matter for a later stage of my discussion. Some historians are now speaking of the revival of the interest in world history and addressing the ways in and the degree to which this should be reconstituted in relation to the type of world history that was in vogue in much of the Western world in the early years of the twentieth century (Costello, 1993). That type of world history was undoubtedly Eurocentric (Gran, 1996), and, moreover, a great deal of it was written within the genre of universal history. It was within the latter tradition that the most important of the well-known German contributions were made, the names of Hegel, Marx, and Max Weber – with Kant (1963) in the background – being particularly conspicuous. The specificity of universal history as a brand of world history (Kossok, 1993) is a matter that I will weave into my deliberations.

The world history that was in vogue about one hundred years ago was largely centered on the problem of the 'superiority' of the West, more particularly of Western – and, to a degree, Central – Europe, as well as of the relatively young United States; although, of course, the theme of the Decline of the West (Spengler, 1926, 1928) was a significant variation on that tendency. The Orientalism that is to be seen in different forms in the very influential writings of Hegel, Marx, Weber and others was in fact a pivotal element in their projects of writing universal history (Robertson, 1985). For in each of these three men's writings, whatever the differences among them, the view that the Orient was off the path of world history was central to their respective oeuvres. Talk of the *decline* of the West should in this perspective be seen as a reaction, in particular, to the increasingly strong presence in the world as a whole of East Asian societies, most notably Japan.

Even though 'Western' attempts to work in the vein of world, or universal, history, certainly did not disappear after World War I (Costello, 1993), it was certainly a much less conspicuous and respectable genre after that period. The long war from 1914 until 1945, and beyond, and then the eruption of the focus on the Third World, particularly from the early 1960s onward, clearly made old-style world history an unpromising subject. And yet, on the other hand, the focus on the Third World came to constitute a pivotal aspect in the making of a new type of world, or global, history. The massive critique of conventional modernization theory launched by Wallerstein around 1970 – following the rise of dependency theory in particular reference to Latin America – was based on the proposition that it was entirely wrong to study individual Third World societies as 'islands' on their problematic way to becoming 'Western,' without comprehensive attention to a history of the world that would account for the very existence of Third World societies in a heavily stratified 'world system (Wallerstein, 1979; cf. Nettl and Robertson, 1968; Robertson, 1992, pp. 8-31). The point was not to talk – as, for example, Weber had done – about the insignificant contributions to universal, world history of 'Southern' societies or what are now called indigenous peoples, but rather to address directly the issue as to the ways in which their peripherality had come about at all. Not that Wallerstein et al. set out to redo world history as such, but Wallerstein's project has stood firmly in the tradition of the kind of world history that Marx developed in revision of Hegel, as well as of Kant; even though it cannot easily be described as universal history.

## Historical Sociology or Sociological History?

A main concern in this chapter is to consider the global circumstances that facilitate interest in world history. As I have said, I prefer the term global history, not least because, I will argue, there is an intimate link between the fates of brands of history of the world and empirical processes of globalization (in its comprehensive, multidimensional – as opposed to its economic-reductionist – sense). But a few words on what has become widely known as historical sociology are necessary at this point. Writing quite recently, Dennis Smith (1991, p.1) observed that 'fifty years ago historical sociology was on the verge of extinction.' Arguing that Fascism and Stalinism were very hostile to what Smith calls 'its critical perspective,' historical sociology as such was not widely practiced again until the second half of the 1960s. But since that period, Smith (1991, p.1) has argued, 'it has emerged from the ashes like a phoenix. By the 1970s and 1980s it was soaring high.'

Why did historical sociology gain such momentum, notably in Western Europe and the USA, during this period? The resurgence of historical sociology in the late 1960s had much to do with a leftward turn in sociology. The late 1960s was a period in which there was an increasing theorization of the Third World, accompanied by an accentuation of interest in social history, more specifically 'popular' history – the history of those who had previously not had much of, if any, recognized history. This was epitomized in Britain by the wide discussion of E.P. Thompson's *The Making of the English Working Class* (Thompson, 1968). This concern with a 'national' proletariat (Gilroy, 1993, pp. 5ff.) was paralleled (also in Britain) by a rapidly developing concern with the Third World as a global proletariat (Worsley, 1964; cf. Lagos, 1963). I am not, it should be made clear, attributing to British scholars a privileged position in the reinvigoration of historical sociology – particularly in the light of major contributions that have been made since the beginning of the twentieth century by French scholars. But it should be emphasized that the work of British historians and sociologists has been very consequential in the relatively recent rise of historical sociology, not least because of the connections between historical sociology in Britain and the rise of neo-Marxian cultural studies in the same country. This cannot be the place for an exploration of the links between historical sociology – or sociologically informed history – and the remarkably influential form of neo-Marxist cultural studies that largely originated in Britain and has blossomed in various parts of the English-speaking parts of the world and beyond since the early 1970s. In spite of the strong presence of materialist Marxism in the modern resurgence of historical sociology, there can be no doubting the considerable impact of Gramscian cultural Marxism – which has been at the center of much of the British form of cultural studies (Harris, 1992) – in accounting for the present concern with world history.

Much of recent historical sociology has, however, been undertaken in the USA, notwithstanding the impact of the work of such British writers as Thompson, Hobsbawm, Benedict and Perry Anderson, and Mann. In 1985, the American sociologist, Skocpol edited a book entitled *Vision and Method in Historical Sociology* (1984). This volume consisted primarily of essays on Marc Bloch, Karl Polyani, Eisenstadt, Bendix, Perry Anderson, Thompson, Charles Tilly, Wallerstein, and Barrington Moore, Jr. In the volume published six years later by Smith (1991) – himself a contributor to the Skocpol collection – the perceived scope of historical sociology was considerably widened, with the inclusion of writers such as Braudel, Collins, Elias, Gellner, Giddens, T.H. Marshall, Lenski, Parsons, Runciman, Skocpol, and Smelser. Other books on historical sociology with different foci have appeared during the period in question, including those by Burke (1992), Lloyd (1986), Stinchcombe (1978), Tilly (1981) and Abrams (1982).

Two points should be made about the lists of historical sociologists produced in such books. First, 'official' historical sociology – which has been institutionalized in various journals and academic organizations, particularly in the USA – is, in the terms of these compendia or surveys – very much a 'North Atlantic' enterprise. Second, one sees, particularly when one compares the edited book of Skocpol with the survey of Smith a clearly discernible enlargement of the category, historical sociology, most conspicuously in the form of a shift from those with a concern with historical detail and contingency to a view of historical sociology as a sociology that is deeply informed by history and temporality.

A word or two is in order at this point about the very concept of historical sociology. Here I have in mind the choice that we have in talking about historical sociology or *sociological history* (Therborn, 1995a, p. 1). Therborn's classification of his own recent work on European modernity – *but one of a number of different* 'routes to/through' modernity (Therborn, 1995b) – as an exercise in sociological history, rather than historical sociology, is interesting because he seems to be saying that sociological history is the more appropriate term for works that are concerned with contemporary history, rather than with 'long,' or 'deep,' history. I would, however, tend to make the distinction between historical sociology and sociological history more significant and consequential than that. Are 'we' doing a qualified history or a qualified sociology? Does history or sociology have the pivotal, nounal status? Is sociology or history to become our real focal point? It is, I think, not the nomenclature that really matters: rather it is the spirit and thrust of our endeavors. If I had to choose I would opt for sociological history, in large part because the contemporary discussion of global issues in historical perspective demonstrates, in my view, that it is the discipline of history that is most in need at this time of sociology. I doubt very much if the historical ingredient of sociology will whither away in the foreseeable future. On the other hand, contemporary historical concern with globality and related themes is very much in need of the new sociological ideas that have emerged in recent decades in specific reference to world society.

## The New World History in a Global Age

I consider particularly a recently published article in *The American Historical Review*, by Geyer and Bright (1995). I use this item as a counterpoint for the display of my own argument. In their paper Geyer and Bright address the theme of 'World History in a Global Age.' In so doing they raise critical and exciting issues. On the other hand, I believe their work to be significantly flawed.

We are in a crucial phase when the relationships between history, as an orientation, history as a discipline (academic or otherwise), history as a profession, historiography, the philosophy of history, and so on, are almost impossibly confusing. It is upon this site of confusion that 'historical sociology' has, so to say, landed. On the other hand, historical sociology has certainly added to the confusion, not least because the historicization of sociology, relative to the theorization of globalization, has helped to precipitate a 'crisis' within sociology. My perception is that many people aspiring to the status of historical sociologist have thought of themselves as surrogate historians and/or as academics feeling a kind of awe for colleagues who 'really know' about the world in temporal terms; although I am sure that there are quite a few people discussed in the books of Skocpol and Smith (among others) that I have previously mentioned who do not in fact have this highly deferential attitude toward 'history' and historians. There is, to be precise, considerable variation from society to society or from civilization to civilization, as to the pecking order of historians and sociologists. I do want, however, to remark that on the more-or-less sociological side of the fence some prominent practitioners appear to be claiming legitimacy via temporal length. In other words, among historically inclined sociologists there is a not inconspicuous tendency to claim, at least implicitly, that the further back we go in historical time the greater the legitimacy and explanatory power of the relevant thesis. One sees this kind of contest occurring currently in the sphere of world-system studies (e.g. Sanderson, 1995).

In any case, claims as to which discipline or sub-discipline is the most foundational are in dispute. Here again, there is variation from global region to global region, from country to country, and so on. Additionally, the relationships among cultural studies, sociology, comparative literature, philosophy, communication studies, history – and yet other disciplines – vary greatly across the contemporary global field (Robertson, 1992). My fear is that we will get caught-up in a contest between disciplines, rather than a concern with (1) what is in the best interests of humanity and (2) what most advances comprehensive knowledge of the human condition (relative to its variously conceived animate and inanimate environments). In other words, disciplinary distinctions ought to be, and to some extent are currently being, transcended. On the other hand, there are very powerful academic-organizational and professional forces at work that constitute a brake on the move toward what I call transdisciplinarity.

In their 'World History in a Global Age,' Geyer and Bright start by remarking that in the USA, world history has for long been regarded as 'an illegitimate, unprofessional, and therefore foolish enterprise' (Geyer and Bright, 1995, p. 1034). Although they speak of dilettantish exceptions, they convincingly argue that world history 'fell victim to ... relentless professionalization' and to the 'specialization and the objectivity it promised' (Geyer and Bright, 1995 p. 1034). They conclude their 1995 piece by speaking of 'the challenge of the twentieth century as an age of world historical transformation' (Geyer and Bright, 1995, p. 1060; cf., Bright and Geyer, 1987). This is a circumstance in which 'humanity' has become a pragmatic reality with a common destiny' (Geyer and Bright, 1995, p. 1060).

I agree with this general claim (although the argument as a whole demands much closer scrutiny than that which can be supplied here).

The considerable amount of recent talk among historians of the new possibilities – indeed the need – for either a revival of world history or a new kind of history of a global kind also calls for a new kind of historical sociology, or sociological history. To put it more sharply, contemporary arguments for a new world or global history lead inexorably to considerations of a definitely sociological nature. In previously considering selected aspects of historical sociology I dwelled upon the historical turn in sociology. Now, at this point, we need to emphasize the sociological turn in history. I believe that the sociological turn in history, which has been growing rapidly since the early 1960s, has largely been occasioned by the challenge of and to – more important, the increasing need for – comparative history in the circumstance of accelerating globalization and the seemingly unavoidable concern with what are sometimes called transnational, as well as inter-continental, issues (cf. Tilly, 1995; J. Goodwin, 1995).

World history has become one of the most rapidly growing and contested areas of teaching during the past twenty years or so. Geyer and Bright argue:

> World history at the end of the twentieth century must ... begin with new imaginings. It cannot continue to announce principles of universality, as if the processes shaping the globe into a materially integrated totality have yet to happen. Global integration is a fact, now part of the historical record; but, because it has little to do with the normative universalism of Enlightenment intellectuals or with the principled particularisms *tiermondists*, nothing is gained by spinning out ideas about westernization of the world or the authenticity of non-Western cultures. The effects of globalization are perplexing, but the world before us has a history to be explained. (Geyer and Bright, 1995, p. 1037)

They further contend that:

> The central challenge of a renewed world history at the end of the twentieth century is to narrate the world's pasts in an age of globality. It is this condition of globality that facilitates the revival of world history and establishes its point of departure in the 'actually existing' world of the late twentieth century. (Geyer and Bright, 1995, p. 1041)

Another provocative point made by Geyer and Bright is that the big narratives produced in the Enlightenment vision of universal history and then in the nineteenth-century tradition of comparative civilizations 'ceased to produce explanations at precisely the moment that a global history became possible ...' (Geyer and Bright, 1995, p. 1041). 'The project of universal history that sought to narrate the grand civilizations comparatively was always an implicit meditation on Western exceptionalism and, as the West moved (comparatively) 'ahead,' a justification for Western domination' (Geyer and Bright, 1995, p. 1041). But, it is emphasized, the destabilization of world historical narratives cannot 'be remedied by a more all-in, encyclopedic approach, as if equal time for all the world's histories will make history whole' (Geyer and Bright, 1995, p. 1042).

What, then, do Geyer and Bright propose? In advocating that we now need to concentrate on the world's pasts, they insist that this is not primarily for reasons concerning the desirability of more comprehensive coverage but 'because, in a global age, the world's pasts are all simultaneously present, colliding, interacting, intermixing – producing a collage of present histories that is surely not the history of a homogeneous global civilization (Geyer and Bright, 1995, p. 1042). In attempting to clinch this particular point they speak of 'the rupture between the present condition of globality and its many possible pasts ... (Geyer and Bright, 1995, p. 1042). Indeed, it is according to these authors that it is this *rupture* that 'gives the new world history its distinctive ground ... ' (Geyer and Bright, 1995, p. 1042).

When, then, do Geyer and Bright see this 'rupture' as having occurred? Their answer: in the mid-nineteenth century. This response is embedded in the perspective of a 'long' twentieth century, involving increasing global heterogeneity – in contrast to the more fashionable stress on increasing global homogeneity. Although I have written at length in opposition to the latter thesis (e.g., Robertson 1992, 1994, and 1995), I do not find Geyer and Bright to be convincing in terms of their own perspective on heterogeneity. They do not appreciate the importance and salience of the complex relationship between universalizing tendencies, on the one hand, and particularizing tendencies, on the other. For them particularizing, difference-making thrusts appeared *first*. These thrusts constituted 'the rupture.' *Then* universalizing, 'global age' trends made their appearance. This is implausible.

Geyer and Bright emphasize heterogeneity because they think that conceiving of globalization as a relatively recent phenomenon of the 'real' twentieth century tends to restrict our vision to homogenizing tendencies. I have, on the other hand, insisted that *even if* one were to think of globalization as a recent phenomenon (which I certainly do not), it would still be more than appropriate to consider the pivotal aspect of globalization to be the ongoing *interpenetration of universalizing and particularizing tendencies*. This interpenetration I have specified, in summary conceptual form, in the concept of glocalization (Robertson, 1992, 1994, 1995a, 1995b; Roudometof and Robertson, 1995).

Before coming to the relevant details of my own thesis let us consider the basis of the proposition of Geyer and Bright that until the middle decades of the nineteenth century 'global development rested on a series of overlapping, interacting, but basically autonomous regions, each engaged in processes of self-organization and self-reproduction' (Geyer and Bright, 1995, p. 1044). Here, rather ironically, Geyer and Bright invoke two genres that otherwise they oppose *in support of* their thesis: Prior to the mid-nineteenth century rupture, when the global age is said to have begun, the pre-global circumstance was 'a reality represented very successfully in the narrative and analytic conventions of comparative civilizations and empire studies' (Geyer and Bright, 1995, p. 1045). They see the mid-nineteenth century as of caesural significance largely because it was then that there was a series of revolutionary disturbances and counter-revolutionary reactions. The nineteenth century ended with 'the world being drawn together as never before but with peoples asserting difference and rejecting sameness on an unprecedented global scale' (Geyer and Bright, 1995, p. 1044).

This is not at all an adequate account of an historical rupture. For no serious attention is paid to the process of globalization per se. *Nor is any attempt made to explain why the events of the mid-nineteenth century that they indicate should themselves have led to global compression on an 'unprecedented scale.'* In this connection they overlook the ways in which 'world society' was being formed in relative independence from the circumstances to which Geyer and Bright draw attention. The word globalization, as well as the highly problematic notion of 'global integration,' make frequent appearances in their paper, but neither concept is in fact defined. The 'global age' is conceived as following directly from the *simultaneous* eruptions of the middle decades of the nineteenth century. When they use the phrase 'global scale' Geyer and Bright are employing – or so it seems – the adjective 'global' simply to mean worldwide, or nearly worldwide. This is not at all unusual these days, but one has nonetheless to distinguish carefully between global as denoting wide geographical scope and global as referring to features of the world as a whole. It is in this, second sense that Geyer and Bright appear to use the adjective 'global' when they employ uncritically the concept of 'global integration'.

Geyer and Bright see what they call 'global development' as being grounded in 'a series of overlapping, interacting, but basically autonomous regions, each engaged in processes of self-organization and self-reproduction' (Geyer and Bright, 1995, p. 1045) until the mid-nineteenth century. Up to that period this regional autonomy was reproduced by 'spatial distantiation.' The 'regions' were linked by 'specialized mediators and interlopers' until at least the middle decades of the nineteenth century. This argument, which depends a lot on the idea of 'a series of parallel, simultaneous crises in the organization of power, production and culture ... of virtually every region of the world' (Geyer and Bright, 1995, p. 1045), brings sharply into focus a number of things which we should regard as highly problematic. Perhaps the most basic of these are the very ideas of 'region' or 'civilization.' Geyer and

Bright veer toward a kind of geographical, or spatial, essentialism. They appear to subscribe to a view that 'the map' of the world is essentially 'true,' reflecting a reality in-itself. They do not acknowledge that, like history, geography is 'Kantian'. Specifically, the regionality and spatiality of the world have, like history, been intersubjectively constructed.

Part of the problem here is the scepticism of Geyer and Bright (1995, p. 1044) concerning my own notion of global consciousness. They object to my considering global consciousness as a corollary to globalization, whereas I have in fact *defined* globalization as partly *consisting* of the extension of 'global consciousness.' It is materialistic and positivistic to deny ideas, beliefs, values, symbols, and so on (generally, 'culture') a place in the globalization process. I have been attempting to theorize the analytical-interpretive idea of people-in-the-world-as-a-whole becoming directly or indirectly aware and, positively *or* negatively, oriented to the global circumstance (Robertson, 1992, pp. 61-84). How this can be denied or marginalized is puzzling. When Geyer and Bright speak of historians having to comprehend the conditions of their own interest in world or global history they undermine their own thesis by dismissing 'global consciousness' as a relevant factor. Open engagement with what I would call the cultural factor (Robertson, 1992, pp. 32-48; Hunt, 1989; Mah, 1992) is, it seems, still something of a problem for contemporary historians; although 'culture' is rapidly becoming problematic for all disciplines, partly because of its inflationary deployment and partly also because of the tenacity with which many analysts still cling to the idea of culture as binding 'homogenized' individuals into relatively cohesive communities.

Given that they emphasize the 'ever-renewing contestations over the terms of global integration' (Geyer and Bright, 1995, p. 1045), it is difficult to see how Geyer and Bright can at the same time speak so much of the increasing integration of the world as a whole. Their dismissal of my own emphasis on global consciousness, in the sense of awareness of the world as a whole, as an ingredient of globalization is in fact contradicted by their own concern with 'contestations over the terms of global integration'. If the terms of such integration are indeed contested and disputed – as is to be seen, to take but one example, in the contemporary inter-civilizational disputes over human rights – then how could they not take place in terms of what I would call (Robertson and Khondker, 1998) the *discourse(s)* of globalization?

When Geyer and Bright (1995, p. 1046) talk of 'new global imaginings' at the very point that they say (wrongly) that I conceive of 'a global consciousness as a corollary to globalization' (I see it as *intrinsic* to globalization), one cannot see what kind of distinctions between consciousness and imaginings they have in mind. Geyer and Bright stress that the nascent global imagination, while seeing the world as an interconnected whole, 'saw these connections differently from every vantage point (Geyer and Bright, 1995, p. 1046). This 'particularistic universalism' is indeed something that I have stressed time and time again; although the concept of particularistic universalism is alien, it should be stressed, to the Geyer-Bright lexicon – or so it seems. The very process of globalization is itself pivotally defined by the relationship between universalism and particularism, and between processes of homogenization and processes of heterogenization.

Geyer and Bright themselves contend that 'Western exertions produced ... a disorderly world of proliferating differences, a world in which the very production of difference was lodged in the processes of globalization that the West had presumed to control' (Geyer and Bright, 1995, p. 1052). Here Geyer and Bright fully divulge their subscription to the widely held – but, I believe, very misleading – view that globalization has been, or at least originally was, a Western product. Here they are insufficiently subtle in recognizing the difference between the Western *form* of globalization and the *project* of Westernization. While they try to distance themselves from what they rightly call 'the obsessive fear of homogeneity that has lately become a specialty of French intellectuals in their campaign against Americanization' (Geyer and Bright, 1995, p. 1056), much of the argument of Bright and Geyer nevertheless sits very easily with the predominant French-intellectual perspective. In France the idea of American homogenization has acquired a hegemonic, ideological status, from Right to Left. This is a phenomenon that has to be explained – not merely noted. French – or, better, French-*intellectual* – conflation of 'Americanization' and 'globalization' is a crucial and very interesting *feature* of globalization, in a sociologically sophisticated rendering of the latter concept. World/global history has to theorize an issue such as this – not merely record it, as if it were just another intellectual and/or ideological stance.

It is the 'new condition of globality' that deprives us of the 'capacity for narrating our histories in conventional ways, outward from one region ... ' (Geyer and Bright, 1995, p. 1058). Now, they contend, we are 'gaining the ability to think world history, pragmatically and realistically, at the interstices of integrating circuits of globalizing networks of power and proliferating sites of localizing politics' (Geyer and Bright, 1995, p. 1058). The difficulty with this stance is that Geyer and Bright *provide no convincing reason as to why we should now have fewer, rather than more, local, national and civilizational narratives.* Surely globalization *encourages* the proliferation of these non- or even anti-global narratives. This is in fact one of the central features of the heterogeneity and difference-producing of the overall globalization process (Robertson, 1995a). It is also another perspective on the complex relationship between universality and particularity.

The promise of world history now coming to comprehend the conditions of its own existence is not fulfilled. Geyer and Bright remain victims of the very form of world history that they have sought to discredit. This is particularly apparent in two respects. First, their unreflexive opposition to old-style universal world history leads to them becoming obsessed with the universalizing and homogenizing thrusts of the Kantian dream (Kant, 1963), so much so that they have looked for the earliest possible time after the European Enlightenment project had crystallized for clear signs of particularistic resistance to that project (which they claim to discover in the mid-nineteenth century). Had they, on the other hand, been less obsessed with the Enlightenment project, they might well have been able to see that the relationship between universalism and particularism should not simply be seen as a temporal one of 'thesis and antithesis,' but rather that it has crucial synchronic (as opposed to diachronic) aspects. The interplay between universalism and particularism is many centuries older than the European Enlightenment. It is, to use Durkheim's phrase, the 'elementary form' of globalization.

Second, Geyer and Bright do not even vaguely attempt to consider the historical details of the globalization process. For them that ill-defined process apparently has no interesting history and, in spite of a few general nods toward the long history of globalization, they tend to see globalization as a relatively modern phenomenon. But surely the least that should be attempted in trying to grasp the conditions of our interest in world, or global, history is to study the ways in which relatively recent globalization is inextricably linked to different genres of world/global history. Indeed it is supremely ironic that Geyer and Bright should at one and the same time deny the significance of global consciousness, on the one hand, and speak of the condition of globality that is currently facilitating our historical consciousness about the making of the contemporary world, on the other. In any case, I maintain that different kinds of world history are to be found in different phases of globalization (Robertson, 1992, pp. 57-60 and generally). Geyer and Bright are fond of talking about *the terms* of 'global integration,' but they never indicate what they mean by the phrase 'the terms.' Were they to do that they would probably find that the disputed terms of relatively recent globalization were in fact primarily European in origin, *but* that the spread and/or imposition of these terms has led considerably to their modification.

## Global History in a Global Age?

I now turn, much more briefly, to a different critique of universal-world history. Specifically I refer to the work of Mazlish and his colleagues (Mazlish and Buultjens, 1993). In their volume *Conceptualizing Global*

*History* the presentism that worries Geyer and Bright to some degree is not seen as a problem; presentation being the term commonly used to indicate the way I which present circumstances shape conceptions of the past. In his own contributions, Mazlish (1993a, 1993b) draws attention specifically to the way in which global history has to be developed and conceptualized as a new perspective in the context of recent changes and trends: 'Perhaps the single most distinguishing feature is that of perspective, awareness, or consciousness (to use a number of overlapping terms), as combined with the lived reality of globalization' (Mazlish, 1993a, p. 6). Mazlish (1993a, p. 1) maintains that 'the conceptualization and practice of global history must start from our *present* position, where new factors building on the old have given a different intensity and synchronicity to the process of globalization' (emphasis added).

This insistence on starting with the process of globalization is welcome, notwithstanding that – like Geyer and Bright – Mazlish and his colleagues never explicitly define globalization. Like many people in numerous disciplines and across a number of global regions Mazlish frequently invokes the term 'globalization' but never really conceptualizes it. He does not theorize it so as to make it amenable to historical, or sociological-historical, study or application. In other words, in spite of some significant differences between the work of Mazlish, Schäfer (1993, 1996) and other contributors to *Conceptualizing Global History*, on the one hand, and Bright and Geyer, on the other, there is a common failure to tackle directly globalization as a long-term historical process.

In proposing that global history should be cast as *contemporary* history, Mazlish makes this argument:

> One might ... argue that, whether acknowledged or not, all history is contemporary history in the sense that the perspective brought to bear on past events is necessarily rooted in the present. In this light, global history may simply be more conscious of its perspective and interested in focusing it more directly on contemporary happenings, as well as on the past. Serious problems of selectivity or documentation then remain, as they do with any history. (Mazlish, 1993, p. 3)

Mazlish here raises some important historiographical considerations, in which connection it is relevant to point out that precisely such issues were directly addressed during the period of birth of modern sociology, notably by Georg Simmel (1977) and Max Weber (1958, pp. 13-31). In his epistemological essay, *The Problems of the Philosophy of History*, first published in 1892 and then revised for republication in 1905, Simmel indeed argued that all history is contemporary history in the sense that 'the perspective brought to bear on past events is necessarily rooted in the present' (Mazlish, 1993, p. 3), but Simmel did not argue that it followed that consciousness of the present should necessarily lead to a more direct concern with what Mazlish calls 'contemporary happenings.'

Simmel, in spite of working within the general tradition of German universal history, was critical of both Hegel and Marx. In part this might well be accounted for by the fact that Simmel was one of the major founders of 'the sociological perspective' and was well aware of the crucial ramifications of the historian being conscious of and reflexive about the sociological circumstances of doing history as an intellectual project. Thus for Simmel 'history' was in the first instance a cognitive orientation and (only) secondarily a form of study of the 'real past.' Simmel's overall argument in this respect is most certainly not without its problems, but even though he did operate within the broad genre of German universal history, he brought what might be called a sociological-Kantian perspective to bear on the idealist history of Hegel and the materialist history of Marx.

Although they differed on a wide range of issues, Weber's position with respect to universal history has some resemblance to that of Simmel. In his much read 'Author's Introduction' (written in 1920) to *The Protestant Ethic and the Spirit of Capitalism*, which had in fact been written approximately fifteen years earlier, Weber starts in the following way:

> A product of modern European civilization, studying any problem of universal history, is bound to ask ... to what combination of circumstances the fact should be attributed that in Western civilization, and in Western civilization only, cultural phenomena have appeared which (*as we like to think*) lie in a line of development having *universal* significance and value. (Weber, 1958, p. 13; first emphasis added)

It should be specially noted that I have highlighted the words that Weber himself placed in parenthesis: 'as we like to think'. This phrase is crucial in that it clearly shows that Weber was registering a significant caveat with respect to the nineteenth century tradition of universal history. He was saying that what appeared to his German contemporaries to 'lie in a line of development' that had universal significance was just that. It was an appearance, one which Weber felt bound to think and write in terms of. He was thus acknowledging, in a way that parallels Simmel's ideas, that we are sociologically constrained by and that we should openly declare that our historical vision is structured by contemporary trends and consciousness. Very few historians would deny that our historical interests are thus framed, but there is a big difference between mere recognition of this, on the one hand, and treating it is a matter for reflexive-sociological emphasis, on the other. However, no matter what the virtues of the Simmel-Weber orientation was in this respect, they did not explicitly recognize in their respective works the significance of the rapidly accelerating processes of globalization that were occurring in the very period that they wrote (Robertson, 1992, 1993). That period is what I call the take-off period of modern globalization, lasting from the 1870s until the mid-1920s.

It was precisely the take-off period of recent globalization when modern world-historical study began, with the writings of Wells, Spengler and Toynbee – to name but three of the most prominent figures. In his very helpful survey of these and more recent writers – notably Sorokin, Dawson, Mumford and McNeill – Costello (1993, p. ix) argues that 'the writings of the world historians of our century have sought to articulate and answer the crisis of their own civilization by putting it into the context of a universal history'. Moreover, Costello sees the kind of world history that has been produced in the West during the present century largely as what he calls 'an interrupted dialogue with providence.' Specifically, he regards most of the 'metahistorians' with whom he deals in the perspective of exploring 'the way in which these paradigms have evolved to digest Spengler's cyclical view to save a progressive movement in history' (Costello, 1993, p. ix).

I think that Costello is correct to emphasize the efforts on the part of the world historians discussed by him to 'save a progressive movement in history'. But when we consider the type of global history that is being debated at the end of the twentieth century it is possible to discern a new and more sociological turn, one that is not driven by the idea of saving a progressive movement, nor certainly guided directly by teleological concerns. What is different now is that we are becoming much more conscious of the circumstances that produce world history. At this historical juncture our much more developed sense of what has come to be called – however diffusely or vaguely – globalization makes it less likely, although certainly not impossible, that we will return precisely to the providential outlook of earlier generations of Western world historians. This is indeed one good reason why we should change nomenclature and speak now of global history.

# References

Abrams, Philip 1982: *Historical Sociology*. New York: Open Books.
Bright, Charles and Geyer, Michael 1987: For a Unified History of the World in the Twentieth Century. *Radical History Review*, (39), pp. 69-91.
Burke, Peter 1992: *History and Social Theory*. Ithaca, NY: Cornell University Press.
Calhoun, Craig 1995: *Critical Social Theory: Culture, History, and the Challenge of Difference*. Oxford: Blackwell.
Costello, Patrick 1993: *World Historians and Their Goals*. DeKalb, IL: Northern Illinois University Press.

Dusserl, Edmund 1995: Eurocentrism and Modernity (Introduction to the Frankfurt Lectures). In *The Pôstmodernism Debate in Latin America*, John Beverley, José Oviedo, and Michael Aronna (eds). Durham, NC: Duke University Press, pp. 65-76.

Geyer, Michael and Bright, Charles 1995: World History in a Global Age. *American Historical Review*, 100 (4), pp. 1034-60.

Gilroy, Paul 1993: *Black Atlantic: Modernity and Double Consciousness*. Cambridge, MA: Harvard University Press.

Goodwin, John 1995: 'A Case for Big Comparison,' *Newsletter of the Comparative and Historical Sociology Section of the American Sociological Association* 8 (1 and 2), pp. 1 and 6.

Gran, Peter 1996: *Beyond Eurocentricism*. Syracuse, NY: Syracuse University Press.

Harris, David 1992: *From Class Struggle to the Politics of Pleasure: The Effects of Gramscianism on Cultural Studies*. London: Routledge.

Hunt, Lynn (ed.). 1989: *The New Cultural History*. Berkeley, CA: University of California Press.

Ianni, Octavio 1992: *A Sociedade Global*. Rio de Janeiro: Editoria Civilizacão Brasileira S/A.

Johnson, Paul 1991: *The Birth of the Modern: World Society 1815-30*. New York: Harper-Collins.

Kant, Immanuel 1963 (1784): Ideas towards a Universal History from a Cosmopolitan Point of View. In *On History*, L.W. Beck (ed.). Indianapolis: Bobbs-Merrill, pp. 11-27.

Kossock, Manfred 1993: From Universal History to Global History. In *Conceptualizing Global History*. Bruce Mazlish and Ralph Buultjens (eds). Boulder, CO: Westview Press, pp. 93-112. .

Lagos, Guastavo 1963: *International Stratification and Underdeveloped Countries*. Chapel Hill, NC: University of North Carolina Press.

Lloyd, Peter 1986: *Explanation in Social History*. Oxford: Basil Blackwell.

Mah, Harold 1992: Undoing Culture. In *Theory, Method, and Practice in Social and Cultural History*. Peter Karsten and John Modell (eds). New York: New York University Press, pp. 115-24.

Markoff, John and Veronica Montecinos 1993: The Ubiquitous Rise of Economists. *Journal of Public Policy* 13 (1), pp. 37-68.

Mazlish, Bruce 1993a: An Introduction to Global History. In *Conceptualizing Global History*. Bruce Mazlish and Ralph Buultjens (eds). Boulder, CO: Westview Press, pp. 1-24.

Mazlish, Bruce 1993b: Global History in a Postmodernist Era? In *Conceptualizing Global History*, Bruce Mazlish and Ralph Buultjens (eds). Boulder, CO: Westview Press, pp. 113-27.

Mazlish, Bruce and Buultjens, Ralph 1993: *Conceptualizing Global History*. Boulder, CO: Westview Press.

Nettl, J. P. and Robertson, Roland 1968: *International Systems and the Modernization of Societies*. New York: Basic Books.

Robertson, Roland 1985: Max Weber and German Sociology of Religion. In *Nineteenth Century Religious Thought in the West*. Ninian Smart et al. (eds). Cambridge: Cambridge University Press, Vol. III, pp. 263-304.

Robertson, Roland 1992: *Globalization: Social Theory and Global Culture*. London: Sage.

Robertson, Roland 1993: Globalization and Sociological Theory. In *Knowledge and Passion: Essays in Honour of John Rex*. Hermnio Martins (ed.). London: I.B. Tauris & Copp, pp. 174-96.

Robertson, Roland 1994: Globalisation or Glocalisation? *Journal of International Communication*, 1 (1), pp. 33-52.

Robertson, Roland 1995a: Glocalization: Time-Space and Homogeneity-Heterogeneity. In *Global Modernities*. Mike Featherstone, Scott Lash and Roland Robertson (eds). London: Sage, pp. 25-44.

Robertson, Roland 1995b: Theory, Specificity, Change: Emulation, Selective Incorporation and Modernization. In *Social Change and Modernization: Lessons from Eastern Europe*. Bruno Grancelli (ed.). Berlin: Walter de Gruyter, pp. 213-31.

Robertson, Roland and Khondker, Habib Haque 1998: Discourses of Globalization: Preliminary Considerations. *International Sociology*, 13 (1), pp. 25-40.

Roudometof, Victor and Roland Robertson 1995: Globalization, World-system Theory and the Comparative Study of Civilizations. In *Civilizations and World Systems: Studying World-Historical Change*. Stephen K. Sanderson (ed.). Walnut Creek, CA: Altamira Press, pp. 273-300.

Sanderson, Stephen K. (ed.) 1995: *Civilizations and World Systems: Studying World-Historical Change*. Walnut Creek, CA: Altamira Press.

Schäfer, Wolf 1993: Global History: Historiographical Feasibility and Environmental Reality. In *Conceptualizing Global History*. Bruce Mazlish and Ralph Buultjens (eds). Boulder, CO: Westview Press, pp. 47-70.

Schäfer, Wolf 1996: The Frame and the Picture: Civilizational Singularity and Cultural Pluralism in Global History. Draft paper presented at the Annual Meetings of the American Historical Association, Atlanta, Georgia, USA.

Simmel, Georg 1977 (1905): *The Problems of the Philosophy of History: An Epistemological Essay*. Guy Oakes, trans., ed. and introd. New York: Free Press.

Skocpol, Theda (ed.) 1984: *Vision and Method in Historical Sociology*. Cambridge, UK: Cambridge University Press.

Smith, Dennis 1991: *The Rise of Historical Sociology*. Oxford: Polity Press.

Spengler, Oswald 1926, 1928: *The Decline of the West*. 2 volumes. New York: Knopf.

Stinchcombe, Arthur 1978: *Theoretical Methods in Social History*. New York: Academic Press.

Therborn, Goran 1995a. *European Modernity and Beyond*. London: Sage.

Therborn, Goran 1995b: Routes to/through Modernity. In *Global Modernities*. Mike Featherstone, Scott Lash and Roland Robertson (eds) London: Sage, pp. 124-39.

Thompson, E.P. 1968: *The Making of the English Working Class* (originally published in 1963). Harmondsworth, UK: Penguin.

Tilly, Charles 1981: *As Sociology Meets History*. New York: Academic Press.

Tilly, Charles 1995: Macrosociology, Past and Future. *Newsletter of the Comparative and Historical Section of the American Sociological Association*, (8/1 and 2), pp. 1 and 3-4.

Wallerstein, Immanuel 1979: *The Capitalist World-Economy*. New York: Cambridge University Press, pp. 132-7.

Weber, Max 1958 (1904-5): *The Protestant Ethic and the Spirit of Capitalism*. New York: Charles Scribner's Sons.

Wells, H.G. 1965: *A Short History of the World* (revised edition). New York: Penguin.

Worsley, Peter 1964: *The Third World*. London: Routledge.

**Roland Robertson** is Professor of Sociology at the University of Pittsburgh. Following an early interest in the intersection of modernization theory and the discipline of international relations, he became involved in debates within the sociology of religion, but with strong reservations as to the status of the sub-discipline as a relatively sequestered enterprize. Robertson has become a key and innovative participant in the development, interpretation and application of globalization theory. His major recent book *Globalization: Social Theory and Global Culture* (London: Sage, 1992) contains a comparative analysis of the cultural impact of globalization and forms the theoretical point of departure for his contribution to *Time and Value*.

# Values in the Cultural Timescapes of Science

Barbara Adam
Cardiff University

## Introduction

For industrial and industrializing societies, science is a cultural value. It is the knowledge system that is called upon by the globally powerful to establish the truth, provide proof and guide public as well as private action. Although culturally valorized, scientific knowledge is expected to be value neutral: objective, true, and basis for globally valid action. As such, scientific knowledge is admissible as evidence in courts of law, promoted in the media and utilized in political debates at the national and international level. Whether we are dealing with litigation, with pollution, European-wide political action over BSE (Bovine Spongiform Encephalopathy) or justifications for research in biotechnology and the genetic manipulation of organisms, science as provider of objective truth is relied upon to arbitrate between the claims of competing socio-political positions.

From the Latin *scientia*, science is knowledge acquired by study. What this 'knowledge acquired by study' meant, however, differed fundamentally throughout the ages. In today's context where science is a valorized and globally utilized 'public good', the meaning of science is associated with a very specific kind of study that takes place within a clearly defined institutional context. The valorization, in other words, is tied to a distinct epistemology and methodology as well as a cluster of institutionally fortified antinomies such as nature and culture, space and time, fact and value, means and end. Since the 1970s much academic energy has been expended on deconstructing those dualisms and dismantling the icon. So far, however, these efforts have had little effect on the valorization of science in the public sphere where it serves as a convenient tool for maintaining the *status quo*, where for example, scientific proof is required as pre-condition for political action in situations where such proof is unobtainable. The bracketing of all things temporal is crucial to this maintenance of *the status quo*.

In this paper I use the explicit focus on time to provide a novel interpretation to this widely debated area of study. Time tends to be taken for granted in social scientific analyses of values. When time is taken to the centre of the analysis it alters what we can see and understand. In what follows I will suggest a theoretical re-alignment of traditionally separate spheres – that is, of science, values, nature, culture, time and space – that arises with an explicit focus on time. In this I will need to examine how and why these spheres have become disconnected. I will explore the reasons for bringing them into such close proximity today, and consider the implications of such a re-vision for cultural praxis. Towards this end, I re-examine from a temporal perspective Weber's classical statements on science and values in the contemporary context of socio-environmental hazards. To appreciate the cultural depth of the distinctions, I begin by noting some of the roots of the pervasive separation of culture from nature and argue the temporal case for its transcendence as a pre-condition to a responsible engagement with the long-term future.

## Time and the Flight from Nature and the Body

Throughout history, humans have sought to transcend their earth-bound conditions and the limits set by nature: shelter and clothing, aided transport and the taming of fire as well as the institutionally located relationship to death and finitude being some of the earliest modes of such transcendence. The strategies employed towards this general aim have been numerous and varied. Technology, the separation of mind from body and the relationship to time have played particularly pertinent roles. Technologies from the axe to nuclear power can be seen as expressions of the human effort to extend by artificial means the boundaries of the senses and the `natural' powers of the body: wheels and later machines to speed up movement across space; telescopes and x-rays to extend vision; computers to expand the capability of the brain. Today, geno-technology is to facilitate the human capacity to redesign evolutionary processes and control nature at source, that is, at its ability to create life. Equally central to the effort to transcend nature and thereby gain some control over human destiny has been the strict separation of mind from body, with the relegation of the latter to a lower level of existence. Whilst their bodies remind humans of the inescapability of death and the earthly dimension of being, cultural activities facilitate the belief in human distinctiveness and a distancing from all things natural. Consequently it is through mind-based culture that humans have sought to overcome their earth and body-bound conditions of existence. Art and writing, ritual and religion, exchange based on money and social regulation based on abstract time have all been means designed to overcome human finitude and the physical boundaries of existence. With perspective in art and the scientific production of knowledge this separation of mind from body has found its most coherent expression. The embodied person is displaced by the head and the mind's eye, the body left behind, rendered irrelevant to knowledge. Disembodied, de-temporalized and stripped of feelings and emotions, the living, interactive self is transformed into an eye of distance whose fixed, singular, a-temporal viewpoint and neutral, impartial gaze are assumed to leave its subject matter untouched.[1] When reality is understood scientifically today, it is likewise perceived from a position outside the earth by a being that is capable, as Ingold (1993, p. 155) suggests, of 'being everywhere at once and nowhere in particular ... a consciousness at once immobile and omnipresent'.

Collectively, these developments have contributed to an ever-increasing power differential between natural processes and cultural activity, that is, culture over nature, mind over body. In the light of this history, it is not surprising that the genesis of (Western) industrial societies is accompanied by an effort to put on ever firmer footings the difference between human culture and nature, mental activity and the physicality of being. These separations, moreover, are deeply entrenched in the disciplines associated with the understanding of human cultural existence: philosophers and social scientists engage with cultural phenomena and processes whilst natural scientists explore and deliberate on the workings of nature and the cosmos. Not only are the academic disciplines divided along the nature-culture divide but their respective subject matters are distinguished by specific temporal characteristics and different means for transcending finitude, death and transience. Thus living nature may be transcended through birth, regeneration and reproduction. Culture fixes time in artefacts, creating permanence through art, writing, all forms of record keeping and the formation of institutions. Culture achieves control over time itself through the creation of a social time in artefactual form.[2]

The conceptual dualism of nature and culture, we need to appreciate further, is deeply embedded in and fortified by the industrial way of life. That is to say, it is not only implicated in its knowledge systems but also in the public and private sphere of that way of life: in the relation to nature and the socio-physical environment as well as in responses to environmental degradation, pollution and hazards. It is integral to the belief in an external, objective reality that is under human control, to the preoccupation with nature's visibility, materiality and spatial extension, and to the notion that facts and values belong to different knowledge spheres. As such, it is buttressed by the rationalization of time and the role of decontextualized time in the industrial way of life.[3]

## The Industrial Timescape

Time, as it crystallized in highly industrialized societies, is a synergy of aspects, a mixture of contradictory, yet mutually supportive, characteristics that have their roots in the developments of calendars and mechanical clocks and constitute an essential precondition to Newtonian science and neo/classical economics. This is a taken-for-granted time that is conceived simultaneously as a vector from past to future, a parameter and external framework within which life is organized, a quantitative resource, a measure of motion, and a commodity that is sold and used as an abstract exchange value in the socio-economic relations of labour and production. Yet, despite the diversity and incongruence of these conceptualizations, there is something that unites them: in all of them, time has an abstract, decontextualized and external quality. In all of them the link of time to specific places, spaces and contexts has been severed: one hour is one hour irrespective of whether it is summer or winter, in Iceland or Italy; whether it is morning or evening, at home or at the place of work. Calendar time provides an external and objective framework within which to locate historical events and establish their sequence and causality. Clock time provides a similar framework, if on a smaller scale, for structuring daily activities and institutional routines: hours of work, education and play, opening and closing times. In the case of both calendar time and clock time, external criteria and not the temporality of phenomena establish sequence and temporal definition. Their rationality and invariability create a sense of stability, certainty and predictability. The clock time's abstraction from seasonal variation and the rhythms of day and night, moreover, facilitates transferability from one context to another. When time and space become separated, then de-contextualization, abstraction, objectivity and transferability can arise as social values

As such, the a-temporal, rationalized and de-contextualized time of the clock is an essential pre-condition to scientific measurement and economic exchange. Thus, when scientists measure motion, time is not only de-contextualized but understood to be symmetrical with respect to the past and future. This means on the one hand that both past and future are conceived without value and, on the other, that time is viewed as reversible,[4] which in turn has significant implications for scientific action. When past and future are conceived to be reversible then the underlying assumption is that it is in principle possible to undo action, reverse processes, de-toxify the earth, repair the ozone hole, revoke global warming, recall previously released genetically modified organisms. Although not explicated, the scientific assumption of reversible time has been absorbed into industrial societies' every-day public understanding of socio-environmental processes. That is to say, reversibility is an unquestioned presupposition even though un-living, un-dying, or growing younger would be recognised as impossible nonsense. As implicit assumption, the belief in reversibility has implications for the relation to environmental degradation and hazard production: when reversibility is presupposed, there seems little need to act with caution especially when the assumption is coupled with the belief in progress and faith that science has an infinite capacity to find new means to undo the damage wrought by previous innovations, policies and actions.

In economic exchange too, time as abstract exchange value is utilized as a quantity without reference to context, past or future. In work relations, this de-contextualized commodified time is imposed on the social relations and activities of embodied, temporal, contextual, past-and-future extended beings for whom their specific timescape matters. For people it clearly makes a difference whether they are working at night or during the day, at home or in a public place. It matters for how long and how fast they are working. Time as abstract exchange value, however, is traded as if one hour were the same irrespective of how old, how skilled or how tired the people are whose labour time is being exchanged for money. In contrast to the non-directional time of economic exchange, a strong present orientation is demonstrated by the way time enters financial markets in the form of discounting the future. Discounting entails evaluation of future products or services in terms of their present economic value and the quantification of this specific time preference: how much better it is to have those products or services now rather than at some future date. In this pervasive economic practice, directional time and value stand in an inverse relation to each other. When economists discount the future, value goes down as time proceeds.[5] As a package, this scientific and economic approach to time prioritizes abstraction, de-contextualization and detachment. At the same time, it detracts from transience, contingence, indeterminacy and the importance of place, context and the future. As such, it devalues temporal becoming, embodied being and contextual difference and it encourages the belief that we can control the future in the present through financial and technological means. In other words, it strengthens the illusion of stability and fosters the delusion of control.

The flight from nature and the body in conjunction with the externalization, de-contextualization and de-temporalization of time have dominated industrial societies' science and technology-driven way of life and their associated knowledge systems. The legitimacy of these traditional knowledge bases is being questioned today. Particularly in the light of ceaseless production of environmental hazards by the very knowledge systems called upon to alleviate them, the taken-for-granted assumptions and distinctions are beginning to be questioned and, in the ensuing conceptual turmoil, science and values, time and space, nature and culture reconfigured.[6] This shifting ground of conception and knowledge confronts us with the scientific realm of values and presents an opening for seeking fresh answers to the question 'How shall we live?'[7] and 'What future presents are we to create for our successors?'.[8]

## Max Weber on Objective Science and the Realm of Values

There is a need to seek new answers since the ground upon which this value sphere is emerging today differs significantly from the one that has been established at the turn of the century when Max Weber, for example, was considering the role of values in and for the socio-cultural sciences. Since much of the social sciences' contemporary debates about values continue to circle around the issues set out by Max Weber and since today's public perception of science shares some of the implicit assumptions that underlie Weber's work on this topic, it seems pertinent to outline his position as a base from which to develop points of departure grounded in a more time-sensitive analysis. This seems particularly relevant given that the assumptions associated with the contemporary public valorization of science no longer hold, even constitute in part the source of environmental hazards creation associated with the industrial way of life.

In Max Weber's seminal work, and particularly in his methodological writings,[9] values were tied not to economic principles but to questions about how we should live our lives.[10] On the basis of this work, the issue of values continues to be associated in the social sciences with three central distinctions which cover facts and values, the is-ought dimension and the means-ends dualism. Whilst far more complex and sophisticated than the every-day understanding embedded in the public valorization of science, Weber's distinctions and his delineation of science, as I have already mentioned, do not differ significantly from the implicit assumptions associated with the contemporary public perception of what science is and ought to be about, a perception that is demonstrated on a daily basis by media portrayals of the role of science and media representations of political debate. Equally compatible is the implicit temporal orientation arising from the dualistic conceptions in which facts pertain to the empirically available present whilst values belong to the projective, normative realm of politics and interests, beliefs and ideals. Similarly, the 'is' dimension is thought to be delimited by the factual present and the 'ought' to cover the future realm of norms. In the means-end distinction, finally, means are considered to constitute the technical way to a pregiven goal or end.

These three antinomies, in turn, were central to Weber's delineation of a number of academic disciplines: the difference between the natural and socio-cultural sciences on the one hand and the distinction between social science and social policy on the other. The logic of scientific knowledge, Weber suggested, is tied to and delimited by a phenomenal, empirically accessible world. It is factual, rational and objective. This means science is investigating a world that is in principle and ultimately knowable: the achievement of full knowledge, 'enlightenment' and 'truth', so the implicit assumption, is merely a question of time and further investigation and study. The value sphere, in contrast, is thought to be beyond the reach of an empirical science. Science therefore cannot give answers to the question `how shall we live?' It has no basis from which to comment and adjudicate between competing values. 'An empirical science', Weber therefore argued, 'cannot tell anyone what he should do but rather what he can do (and under certain circumstances what he wishes to do)' (Weber, 1904/1949, p. 54). This means that science can tell us how to achieve pregiven ends/goals/values but it cannot pronounce on the values themselves. 'It can never be the task of an empirical science', Weber (1904/1949, p. 52) argued, 'to provide binding norms and ideals from which directives for immediate practical activity can be derived'. It means further that certain value-laden presuppositions of science are not scientifically provable. Thus, science can establish neither that the logic and methods of science are valid nor that the results of science are worth knowing or important since such pronouncements would depend not on scientific, factual proof but on values.

Weber's insights about the logic of science and its value-based limits are today so widely accepted that they have been naturalized in the public understanding of science. Science can tell us what is healthy but the choice between alternatives is one of values, preference or need: whether or not we should become vegetarians, whether or not we should give up the car in favour of the bicycle, whether or not we should take a holiday abroad. How we should live our lives, so the perceived wisdom, is a question of values and beliefs, not science.

Science as a non-evaluative, rational means to specified ends, Weber insisted further, had to be differentiated from politics which provides norms from which directives for practical action can be derived. In the world of social policy, values are needed for making selections, for setting priorities and for definitions of significance, importance and meaning. Matters concerning social policy, he argued, cannot be resolved on the basis of purely technical considerations which already assume ends. In distinction to science, social policy is inescapably value driven. The values entailed in policy decisions, moreover, can and must be objects of dispute not merely because of class interest but because of people's varying views on life and cosmologies (*Weltanschauungen*): the value spheres of the world are incompatible and stand in irreconcilable conflict with each other (Weber, 1904/1949, p. 56). He further suggested that the more general and generalized the problem – in contemporary terms, the more globalized the problem – the more culturally significant it becomes. Increased generalization and globalization are tied to rising levels of ambiguity and an increased reliance on values. This, he insisted, is the opposite relation from the one that pertains in the natural sciences where the increased level of generality provides a decreased problem of ambiguity and values.

The spheres of science and values stand in a highly complex relation to each other since, Weber pointed out, all cultural knowledge is subjective and meaningful. '*All* knowledge of cultural reality', he wrote, 'is always knowledge from particular points of view (Weber, 1904/1949, p. 81)'. This means that any cultural science necessarily has to engage with subjective presuppositions of what is valuable, significant and important which in turn is contextual and historical. Consequently, Weber (1904/1949, p. 84) suggested, 'A *systematic* science of culture .... would be senseless in itself'. Culture, to Weber, is a finite segment of an infinite and meaningless universe upon which we confer significance and meaning:

> The fate of an epoch which has eaten from the tree of knowledge is that it must know that we cannot learn the *meaning* of the world from the results of its analysis, be it ever so perfect; it must rather be in a position to create this meaning itself. It must recognize that general views of life and the universe can never be the products of increasing empirical knowledge, and that the highest ideals, which move us most forcefully, are always formed only in the struggle with other ideals which are just as sacred to others as ours are to us. (Weber, 1904/49, p. 57)

That is to say, all cultural actions and inactions imply values in their consequences. Looking back to approaches that preceded his work, he wrote, `Forty years ago there existed ... the belief that of the various possible points of view in the domain of practical political preferences, ultimately only one was the correct one... Today this is no longer the case' (Weber, 1917/1949, p. 3). Instead of an ethical imperative he insisted on the acceptance of relativity and acknowledgement of a 'patchwork of cultural values' (Weber, 1917/1949, p. 4).

Collectively, these features make the social and cultural sciences inherently value-laden and thus moral enterprises. And yet, as a *science* the socio-cultural sciences are tied to the logic of science. As such, Weber argued, they need to differentiate meticulously between the empirical realm of facts and the ideational sphere of norms and values, interests and motives, irreconcilable commitments and beliefs. They need to distinguish between factual observation and value judgements. Approval or pardoning of certain actions is not for them to give.

Whilst Weber acknowledged that the natural sciences too are located in cultures and therefore dependent on selection, setting of priorities, signification and interpretation, he suggested that these evaluative processes belonged to the ante-chamber of science and that as long as these choices and considerations were openly acknowledged they would not interfere with the deliberation of facts. At the same time, however, he insisted that scientists as culturally located beings cannot escape moral responsibility. 'An *attitude of moral indifference*', he wrote (1904/49, p. 60), 'has no connection with *scientific objectivity*'. Scientists were required instead to make explicit where their factual statements ended and their evaluations began. In simplified form this requirement has survived in the public perception that sees science as the source of factual, objective, value-neutral knowledge and insists that 'scientific truth' be differentiated from personal or political, motivated, biased opinion. It is the assumptions which underpin these distinctions that I want to scrutinize here from a time-sensitive perspective.[11]

## Absolute Distinctions Revisited

Aware of the tensions that arose from his analysis, Weber pushed the classical dualist perspective to its limits without, however, following through the implications of his insights. By retaining the fact-value, is-ought, science-policy dualisms on logical grounds, he also held on to the assumptions that underpin the separations: that facts are empirically accessible sense data; that there are absolute distinctions between present and future, observer and observed; that there is an external reality to be discovered and known. It is these presuppositions which find their contemporary expression in the public valorization of science that are at issue and scrutinized here from a temporal perspective.

When these distinctions are revisited and subjected to a time-sensitive analysis, we begin to realize that facts can be facts only after they have been de-temporalized, that is, abstracted from the ongoing temporality of being-becoming. Facts, we appreciate, are tied to a specific way of knowing that is, to object-thinking and an emphasis on the spatial and material. Object-thinking brackets, and thus conceals, the temporal and invisible, the immaterial and unbounded in the subject matter. Since temporal becoming and ongoing transformation in the context of an interactive relationship with others and openness to the environment are the mark of life and social activity, an approach that negates these key characteristics of life can only deal with (real and conceptual) *dead* things.

Time may be used as a measure but it is not an empirical sense datum. Time tends to be invisible and thus has to be *inferred* from phenomena and processes. It can be deduced only by conceptual or technically aided comparisons of earlier and later 'states' that indicate a difference between before and after. In this comparative form, object-thinking allows 'observers' to see only time slices, that is, facts as freeze-frames, moments frozen in time and space. This means, facts are not isolated in and of themselves: we make them so in order to render the temporality of reality accessible and manageable, that is, to infuse the infinite, transient and contingent complexity of life with clarity and simplicity. As such, this a-temporal stance on temporality facilitates not only counting, measurement and classification but also the illusion of objectivity and ethical neutrality. Under the pretence of objectivity, responsibility for personal choice and action can be abandoned; ethics can become an add-on, after-the-event issue.

When we turn our attention to contemporary socio-environmental hazards – such as nuclear radiation, chemical pollution, global warming, genetically modified organisms or BSE, for example – we can see how the assumption that science produces factual truth becomes unstuck. These hazards are time-space distantiated and marked by indeterminacy, contingency. They are characterized by extensive periods of latency before symptoms arise sometime, somewhere. Anything resembling a factual truth statement, however, requires that phenomena be linked and bounded in time and space. When this link is broken and effects are open-ended, the establishment of 'facts' in the conventional sense ceases to be possible. Equally, when the unknown present and future far outweigh that which can be known, then certainty and truth are no longer available and the personal-political context becomes the basis for differences in 'scientific opinion' and interpretation. The very public scientific debates and disagreements over global warming, BSE, the release of genetically modified organisms or safe levels of pollution are prime illustrations for this point.

Equally unsettled by a time-based analysis is the assumption that facts belong to the empirical realm of matter whilst values pertain to the conceptual sphere of ideas. The technology-impregnated, irreversible, time-space distantiated action and immanent formation of socio-environmental hazards, for example, is neither material in the traditional sense nor evaluative and thus conceptual/ideational in the Weberian sense. That is to say, with such contemporary manufactured perils, the material cannot be separated from the non-material in such a clear and unambiguous way. Neither conceptually constituted simulacra nor empirically accessible sense data in the conventional sense, these culturally produced threats need to be conceived as dynamic process-phenomena whose im/material consequences arise from globally and historically interconnected socio-physical in/action.[12] From this perspective, the physical world is inescapably permeated and constituted by the cultural realm of ideas, norms and values. The enacted cultural world of ideas, in turn, has socio-physical consequences. This acculturated *physis* and natured culture needs to be recognized as both material reality and latent process-world of an encoded invisible reality, a realm beyond the reach of the senses, beyond the world of linear causal connections. To recentre the temporal, therefore, is to emphasise not merely the symptoms but equally stress the importance of the immanent *Wirkwelt*, the constitutive invisible reality *between* the flapping of a butterfly wing and a storm in another time and place.

When viewed from a position that takes time seriously, the traditional is-ought distinction too is shown to be inappropriate. On the basis of the traditional schema, facts, the dimension of the 'is', are in the present and thus open to discovery by the senses whilst values, the 'ought' dimension, belong to the ideational realm of the future. In their futurity, values encompass our goals and aspirations, our beliefs about what is right and wrong, our hopes and utopias, fears and terrors. They are our future-based sources for action in the present – the stuff that underpins wars and demonstrations, supports our choice of religion, politics and voluntary activities. A similar conception of the present and future is entailed in Weber's means-end schema: the 'end' or 'goal' as the equivalent of the 'ought' dimension and clearly located in the future beyond the reach of the senses. The 'means', in contrast, are viewed as scientific/technical ways to help us achieve those pregiven ends, goals and visions. They are the definable paths by which we reach into the future. Knowing the goal, we can apply the counterfactual schema if ... then. Thus, for example, if we want to get rid of greenflies then science can list for us the 'means' available in the present to achieve the desired future state of no greenflies. Science can tell us nothing, however, about the merits or value of this goal – it can merely tell us in a factual, non-evaluative way what needs to be done if we want to get rid of greenflies.

Whilst I have no problem with Weber's assertion that science has no *logical* base from which to establish values, I have grave reservations about the conception of the relation between past, present and future which underlies these schema. This particular understanding becomes inappropriate once we recognise the interpenetration of past, present and future. The goal to eradicate greenflies can once more serve as a useful example to illustrate the point. Let us assume that we have chosen to use an insecticide as the means to our pre-defined goal. First, the effectiveness of the insecticide is inescapably tied to past uses and the reflexivity within the eco-system (in which I include humans and the industrial way of life). The past therefore is ineradicably implicated not only in the present but also in the means to achieving a given end. Secondly, the use of an insecticide creates an open-ended future that affects the eco-sphere for an in(de)finite time. As such, the future features in the present as an encoded reality. Past, present and future interpenetrate and mutually implicate each other. Boundaries and distinctions between them are perforated.

From a temporal perspective, therefore, the world of the 'is', the realm of the present, is not neatly definable, not temporally bounded, not the exclusive province of the senses (not that it ever was, of course). Equally, the realm of goals, values and beliefs about how we think the world ought to be, is not a separate future state, not abstractable from the present and our constitutive actions. Moreover, as contemporary natural scientists are only too willing to concede, it is also not predictable on the basis of past knowledge – so the means to some future goal which is based on knowledge of the past may very well not achieve that desired end. Instead, it is likely that the unintended consequences match and even surpass the achievements of the industrial way of life.[13] The apparent control tends to stand in an inverse relation to the created indeterminacies and the loss of control over time-space distantiated impacts. Equally, there is a need to appreciate that such dualistic schema are static, that they fix and generalize into an atemporal, decontextualized form processes and relationships that are contingent, transient, specific, embodied and embedded.

From the vantage point of a timescape analysis, values and contextually rooted interpretation become recognisable as inescapable structural components of 'factual' scientific investigation, deeply implicated long before the issue of scientific funding enters as an additional complicating factor, that is, long before we need to acknowledge that today much of science has become inextricably intertwined with business and politics. In other words, the deep-seated implication reaches beyond Leiss and Chociolko's (1994, p. 21) observation that 'there is no hope of insulating science and its idealized neutrality with respect to social interests once it enters the realm of economic and public policy choices where interests do contend'.[14] Recognising this deeper level implication, we already acknowledge the observer's effect on the observed, that context, desire and the framework of observation feature in what we see.

Such an appreciation of the mutual implication of observer and observed, clearly runs counter to perceived wisdom which assumes the empirical world of facts to be external to and distinct from the scientists making the observations. Such 'scientific objectivity' in both classical science and every-day terms means first that the position of 'observers' is irrelevant to what they see and, second, that the object of observation is the same irrespective of context, that difference in time and space do not affect the observation in any way. The scientific observer and investigator, it is suggested, casts no shadow. This conventional belief is deeply rooted in Enlightenment thought which starts from the premise that there is an external reality that exists independent of and uncontaminated by the knower, a world that is amenable to objective investigation and can be matched, mirrored and represented in theory. Derrida (1982) designated this presupposition the *'metaphysics of presence'* and showed it to be untenable. As this quest for uncontaminated (scientific) knowledge has been effectively deconstructed from a wide range of theoretical positions,[15] it seems pertinent for this paper to briefly touch on the substantive issue of global time-space distantiation as just one temporal contribution to the debate.

As human beings, scientists active in the fields nuclear physics or genetic engineering, for example, are not only the effectors of change but also the affected of the changes brought about by those technologies. Scientists are personally implicated in their research by the very fact that they are living organisms, that their cells are responsive to nuclear radiation or susceptible to the designer viruses associated with genetic modification. When the effects of such research have become time-space distantiated across the globe and beyond, there is no outside or external position, no time(and)space for the uninvolved spectator and voyeur. This means, scientists as knowers, doers and creators are both implicated in and affected by their research: nuclear physics, genetic engineering, the chemical sciences all operate in a recursive and reflexive universe of manufactured uncertainty and implication. Scientific activity no longer offers a let-out clause from such reflexive engagement. Irrespective of our intentions, we are implicated participants. This makes the aspired position of the unbiased, objective scientist a contemporary misfit, a contradiction in terms, an anachronism; and it makes the spectator position and the window ethic which underpin the belief in the uninvolved and non-implicated observer a figment of the scientific imagination, an illusion shattered on a daily basis by events that impress on us the complex irreversible, reflexively constituted connectivity of contemporary existence. Moreover, 'facts' about the contemporary world are neither external nor distinct from cultural activity, neither expressible exclusively through conventional cause-and-effect relations nor tied to specific times and spaces. Instead, they are both everywhere and nowhere, some time and all time, material and immaterial, visible and invisible, external and internal to the system of observation. The networked, time-space distantiated connections are subject to vast past and future influences, structural reflexivity, and amplification. The simplistic notion of objective observations of empirically accessible factual causal relations is thus highly inappropriate for contemporary process-phenomena such as radiation, released genetically modified organisms and the impact of industrial activity on the environment more generally. Weber's 'facts' therefore are strangely out of tune with the contemporary condition. Not objectivity but explicit engagement and acknowledgement of responsibility therefore need to be reflected in the self-understanding and public expectation of science.

In the traditional objectified discourse of fact-value distinction, the observer and narrator are always outside their respective subject matters. They are free-floating in some mythical hallowed space in which participants are transformed into neutral observers who pronounce on differences between 'others'. Weber recognised the futility of this understanding but like his contemporary Einstein in the natural sciences was unable to follow his insights to their logical conclusion. He sought complexity and the morally committed scientist but clung to the dualisms which kept his theory tied firmly to the scientific and philosophical thinking of the eighteenth and nineteenth century.

With the globalization if industrial culture, principle assumptions and frames of meaning are in need of reassessment. The world-wide impact of the industrial way of life has dissolved, fractured, permeated and crosscut the clear-cut boundaries between nature and culture, science and politics. The characteristics of this new imperial power are thus at odds with the dualistic conception of reality pursued by classical social theorists and promulgated in Weber's fact-value, means-end, is-ought, subject-object science-policy/politics distinctions. In a globally networked world where the 'effects' of everything we do are reflexively and irreversibly dispersed across time and space, touching the lives of earthworms and algae, impacting upon the upper stratosphere surrounding our earth and influencing successors thousands of generations hence, in such a world the thinking in either-or terms has lost its pertinence. De-temporalized and de-contextualized dualisms have lost their accustomed purchase on situations where actions in one place can emerge as symptoms at different historical times and distant places. More importantly still, this inescapable connectivity irrevocably ties personal concerns and desires to collective responsibilities, present hopes, plans and fears to the long-term future and the presents of successors. If everything is connected and if everything makes a difference – if for example, something as gentle and insignificant as the flapping of a butterfly wing can cause a thunderstorm in distant places and times – then the issue of personal implication, values and responsibility becomes not something that can be turned on and off at will but an inescapable accompaniment of action.

## Temporal Reflections on the Value Sphere of Science

When the temporal silences begin to get expressed and the invisible is given form, the visible/material is no longer equated with veracity and the Real. Reality begins to resonate with the immanent process-world beyond empirical accessibility. Facts and values take on a different hue. We see connections where previously antinomies and contradictions reigned supreme. Sensitized to the temporal we can build bridges and bring together what has become disconnected in western theory and most particularly with the Enlightenment project.

Concern with values in the cultural timescapes of science therefore focuses attention on the connectedness of things and the artificiality of abstraction. Whilst abstraction fixes things and processes in time, focus on connectivity and mutual implication attends to the fundamental temporality of being. It highligts that everything affects and implicates everything else in an unending recursive, rhythmic, irreversible, value-impregnated process. A timescape perspective, moreover, brings the importance of context to the forefront of our attention – context meaning the fusion of time and space into time-space, with time and space being neither opposites not separable. Furthermore, it fosters an awareness of irreversibility – that there is no going back even if there is the possibility of repair which could bring the system forward to a condition similar to the one prior to an intervention. The distinction between a belief in reversibility and the knowledge that every action makes an irreversible difference is acknowledged as an important one since belief in reversibility is rooted not only in an implicit trust in the magic powers of technology but also in the illusion of control. As such, it encourages the deferral of responsibility to some future technology: `mastery', as Giddens (1991, p. 202) points out, 'substitutes for morality'.

Recognition of time-space distantiation, irreversible and reflexively constituted connectivity, as well as of past, present, and future interpenetration alters the background assumptions and the theoretical context within which the socio-cultural sciences are conducted. This means, the assumptions that underpin the fact-value, is-ought and means-end schema are in need of revision. Such reconceptualization has not only to take on board the simultaneity of the material and immaterial as well as visible and invisible constitutive forces but also to acknowledge that in our every-day and professional lives we are personally and collectively involved, that we are inescapably responsible for known and unknown effects now and for an unlimited future. This means, as scientists and theorists we need to take account of the future not just as a realm of predictability, known goals and values but, equally, in terms of unknown and unknowable, im/material futures.

The classical approach to values and the associated schema of distinctions are clearly inappropriate to that task. When instead we recognise ourselves as temporal beings that create histories and futures here and now for ourselves and others dispersed in time and space, we enter the realm of values and responsibility. When we accept the constitutive nature of knowledge and scientific 'discovery', we enter the realm of values and responsibility. When boundaries, certainty and control, are destabilised we enter the realm of values and responsibility or, to turn Giddens' (1991, p. 202) statement on its head, when mastery fails, morals become a necessity. When there is no position outside the framework of observation and when we as scientists (of whatever kind) are therefore not objective spectators, not uninvolved observers but embodied, contextual participants implicated in the creation of our world, we enter the realm of values and responsibility. When we are compelled to respond to the future-creating actions of predecessors and are forced to make irreversible choices that count, then we as private and professional persons are inescapably operating in the sphere of morals: thus, re-enters for science a late twentieth century version of Kant's (1781/1966) *moral imperative*.

*Acknowledgements. The research for this paper was conducted during an ESRC Fellowship under the auspices of the Global Environmental Change Initiative (1994-6, L32027312593). It is more fully reported on in my 1998 book Timescapes of Modernity.*

# Notes

1. For an excellent exposition of this relation please see Romanyshyn (1989); also Arendt (1958).
2. On the conventional theoretical distinctions and contemporary critiques , see Adam (1988, 1990) and Macnaghten and Urry (1998, chapter 5).
3. For more a detailed argument and an extensive elaboration of the temporal complexity of the industrial way of life, see Adam (1990, 1995, 1998); Kern (1983); Lash and Urry (1994, chapter 9); Nowotny (1994); Rifkin (1987); Young (1988).
4. There is extensive popular science literature on this subject. Among the most interesting are: Prigogine and Stengers (1984); Prigogine (1997); Shallis (1983); Zohar (1983).
5. For an in-depth discussion on the economic practice of discounting and its relation to value and the future, see Price (1993). For early elaborations of time in economics see Marx (1857/1973, 1967/1976). Contemporary treatise include Biesecker (1998); Held and Nutzinger (1998); Sharp (1981).
6. This applies not just to critiques emanating from every-day and public perspectives but to conceptual revisions arising from cultural, feminist and social theory, philosophy and the social studies of science.
7. On this question, see also Adam (1996, p. 99); Beck (1992, p. 28); Giddens (1991, pp. 215, 223).
8. With the focus on values and the future, this paper develops arguments that were first touched upon in Timewatch and my 1996 paper 'Re-vision: The Centrality of Time for an Ecological Social Science Perspective'.
9. See Weber (1949) and more specifically Weber's essays on objectivity (1904/1949), on ethical neutrality (1917/1949) and on science as a vocation (1919/1985)
10. For Weber's discussion on the question 'How should be live our lives', see (Weber, 1919/1985, pp. 143, 152-3).
11. Pertinent critiques of scientific objectivity have been established in such diverse academic fields as feminist, postmodern and social theory, the philosophy of science and the social studies of science. None, however, brought time to the centre of their analysis.
12. Im/material because they are both material and immaterial in more than one sense; in/action because both action and inaction have consequences.
13. For a detailed elaborations of this assertion, see Adam (1998) and Beck (1992, 1995).
14. As is the case with genotechnology which is big business at every level of its scientific activity: not only are all the transnational chemical giants involved – Monsanto and Ely Lilly, Zeneca and Shell, Upjohn and Bayer, Hoechst and DuPont – but scientists are creating businesses for the sole purpose of reaping benefits from this potentially lucrative activity.

15. This interpenetration and mutual implication has been effectively theorised in philosophical works from Kant (1781/1966) to Derrida (1982), feminist and critical theory by scholars such as Hayles (1990) Ermarth (1992) and Flax (1992), as well as treatise in theoretical physics from Einstein to Bohm (1983) and Prigogine (1996). I have theorised the relation with reference to time in Adam, (1990, 1995 and 1998).

# References

Adam, Barbara 1988: Social versus Natural Time: A Traditional Distinction Re-examined. In Young, M. and Schuller, T. *The Rhythms of Society*. London: Routledge.

Adam, Barbara 1990: *Time and Social Theory*. Cambridge: Polity Press.

Adam, Barbara 1995: *Timewatch: The Social Analysis of Time*. Cambridge: Polity Press.

Adam, Barbara 1996: Re-vision: The Centrality of Time for an Ecological Social Science Perspective. In Szerszynski, B. Lash, S. and Wynne, B. (eds.) *Risk, Environment and Modernity: Towards a New Ecology*. London: Sage, pp. 84-103.

Adam, Barbara 1998:*Timescapes of Modernity: The Environment and Invisible Hazards*. London/New York: Routledge

Arendt, Hannah 1958: *The Human Condition*. Chicago, IL: University of Chicago Press.

Beck, Ulrich 1992: *Risk Society. Towards a New Modernity*. M. Ritter trans. London: Sage.

Beck, Ulrich 1995: *Ecological Politics in an Age of Risk*. London: Polity.

Biesecker, Adelheid 1998: Economic Rationale and Wealth of Time: In Pursuit of a New Economy of Time, *Time and Society*, 7, pp. 75-93.

Bohm, David 1983: *Wholeness and the Implicate Order*. London: ARK

Derrida, Jacques 1982: *Margins of Philosophy*, A. Bass trans, Brighton: Harvester.

Ermarth, Elizabeth 1992: *Sequel to History. Postmodernism and the crisis of representational time*. Princeton, NJ: Princeton University Press.

Flax, Jane 1992: The End of Innocence. In J. Butler and J. W. Scott (eds.), *Feminists Theorize the Political*. London: Routledge, pp. 445-63.

Giddens, Anthony 1991: *Modernity and Self-Identity. Self and Society in the Late Modern Age*. Cambridge: Polity.

Hayles, Katherine 1990: *Chaos Bound. Orderly Disorder in Contemporary Literature and Science*. London: Cornell University Press.

Held, Martin and Nutzinger, Hans G. 1998: Nonstop Acceleration. The Economic Logic of Development towards the Nonstop Society, K. Cross trans, *Time and Society*, 7(2) forthcoming.

Ingold, Tim 1993: The Temporality of Landscape, *World Archeology*, 25, pp. 152-74.

Kant, Immanuel 1781/1966: *The Critique of Pure Reason*. F. M. Müller trans. New York: Doubleday Anchor.

Kern, Stephen 1983: *The Culture of Time and Space 1880 – 1919*. London: Weidenfeld and Nicolson.

Lash, Scott and Urry, John 1994: *Economies of Signs and Space*. London: Sage.

Leiss, William and Chociolko, Christina 1994: *Risk and Responsibility*. Montreal/London: McGill-Queen's UP.

Marx, Karl 1857/1973: *Grundrisse*. Harmondsworth: Penguin.

Marx, Karl 1867/1976: *Capital, Volume I*. Harmondsworth: Penguin.

McNaghten, Phil and Urry, John 1998: *Contested Natures*. London: Sage.

Nowotny, Helga 1994: *Time. The Modern and Modern and Postmodern Experience*. Cambridge: Polity.

Price, Colin 1993:*Time, Discounting and Value*. Oxford: Blackwell.

Prigogine, Ilya 1997: *The End of Certainty. Time, Chaos and the New Laws of Nature*. New York: Free Press.

Prigogine, Ilya and Stengers, Isabelle 1984: *Order out of Chaos: Man's New Dialogue with Nature*. London: Heinemann.

Prigogine, Ilya 1996: *The End of Certainty*. New York: Free Press.

Rifkin, Jeremy 1987: *Time Wars. The Primary Conflict in Human History*. New York: Henry Holt.

Romanyshyn, Robert D. 1989: *Technology as Symptom and Dream*. London: Routledge.

Shallis, Michael 1983: *On Time. An Investigation into Scientific Knowledge and Human Experience*. Harmondsworth: Penguin.

Sharp, C. 1981: *The Economics of Time*. Oxford: Martin Robertson

Weber, Max 1904/1949: Objectivity in Social Science and Social Policy. In E. Shils, and H. Finch H. (eds.), *The Methodology of the Social Sciences. Max Weber*. New York: The Free Press, pp. 50-112.

Weber, Max 1917/1949: The Meaning of Ethical Neutrality in Sociology and Economics. In E. Shils and H. Finch (eds.) *The Methodology of the Social Sciences. Max Weber*. New York: The Free Press, pp. 1-49.

Weber, Max 1919/1985: Science as a Vocation. In H. Gerth and C. W. Mills (eds.), *From Max Weber: Essays in Sociology*. London: Routledge and Kegan Paul, pp. 129-58.

Weber, Max 1949: *The Methodology of the Social Sciences. Max Weber*. (eds.) E. Shils and H. Finch, New York: Free Press.

Young, Michael 1988: *The Metronomic Society*. London: Thames and Hudson.

Zohar, Danah 1983: *Through the Time Barrier*. London: Paladin.

**Barbara Adam** is Reader in Social Theory at Cardiff University. She is founder editor of *Time and Society* and author of numerous books and articles on the subject of social time. Her books include *Time and Social Theory* (1990), *Timewatch: The Social Analysis of Time* (1995) and *Timescapes of Modernity: The Environment and Invisible Hazards* (1998).

# Time, Baroque Codes and Canonization[1]

Boaventura de Sousa Santos
University of Coimbra and University of Wisconsin - Madison

## The Modern Equation between Roots and Options

Roots and options are two of the most basic references of social action. Roots are references that operate by backward linkages; options are references that operate by forward linkages. Social actions may be said to be root-oriented or option-oriented. The specificity of Western modernity resides in the equation between roots and options. Such an equation confers a dual character on modern thought: on the one hand, it is a thought about roots, on the other, a thought about options. The thought about roots concerns all that is profound, permanent, singular, and unique, all that provides reassurance and consistency; the thought about options concerns all that is variable, ephemeral, replaceable, and indeterminate from the viewpoint of roots. The two major differences between roots and options are scale and time. Roots are large-scale entities; options are small-scale entities. Because of this difference of scale, roots are unique while options are multiple.

Roots and options are also distinguished according to time. Societies, like social interactions, are built upon a multiplicity of social times, and differ according to the specific combinations and hierarchies of social times that they privilege. Drawing freely on Gurvitch's (1969, p. 340) typology of social times, I want to understand roots in terms of a combination of a) long duration time and time *au ralenti*; b) cyclical time, the time that *danse sur place*; c) belated time (*temps en retard sur lui même*), time whose unfolding keeps itself in wait. Options, on the other hand, are characterized by a combination of a) accelerated time (*temps an avance sur lui même*), the time of contingency and discontinuity; b) explosive time, the time without past or present and only with future. In a continuum between glacial time and instantaneous time, modern roots tend to cluster around glacial time, while modern options tend to cluster around instantaneous time. If in roots the tempo tends to be slow, in options it tends to be fast. The root/option duality is a founding and constituting duality, that is to say, it is not subjected to the play it itself institutes between roots and options. In other words, one does not have the option not to think in terms of roots and options.

In this equation of roots and options, modern society views medieval society and distinguishes itself from it. In medieval society the primacy

246 Boaventura de Sousa Santos

of roots – whether religion, theology or tradition – is total. Medieval society evolves according to a logic of roots. Its opposite, modern society sees itself as dynamic evolving according to a logic of options. The equation may have emerged in the Lutheran Reformation. Here it became possible, starting from the same root – the Bible of Western Christianity – to create an option vis-à-vis the Church of Rome. By becoming optional, religion as root loses in intensity, if not in status as well. In the self-same historical process through which religion goes from roots to options, science goes the opposite way, from options to roots. Giambattista Vico's (1961) 'new science' is a decisive landmark in the transition that started with Descartes and would be completed in the nineteenth century. Unlike religion, science is a root that originates in the future, it is an option which, by radicalizing itself, turns into a root, thereby creating a wide field of possibilities.

This shifting of stances between roots and options reaches its peak with the Enlightenment. In a large cultural field, which includes science and politics, religion and art, roots clearly presume to be the radicalized other of options. Thus reason, turned into the ultimate root of individual and collective life, has no other foundation but the creation of options. This is what distinguishes it, as a root, from the roots of the *ancien régime* (religion and tradition). It is a root which, by radicalizing itself, makes possible a wide range of options. In the event, options are not infinite. This is evident in the other great root of Enlightenment: the social contract and the general will sustaining it. The social contract is the founding metaphor of a radical option – the option to leave the state of nature and inaugurate the civil society – which itself turns into a root that makes everything possible, except to go back to the state of nature. The contractuality of roots is irreversible, such being the limit of the reversibility of options. That is why, in Rousseau (1973, p. 174), the general will cannot be challenged by the free men it creates. Rousseau says in the Social Contract: 'whoever refuses to obey the general will shall be compelled to do so by the whole body. This means nothing less than that he will be forced to be free'.

From the nineteenth century onwards, the mirror play of roots and options consolidates and becomes the *idéologie savante* of the social sciences. The twin examplars are Marx and Freud. In Marx, the base is the root and the superstructure the options. In Freud (and in Jung) the unconscious is the deep root that grounds both the options of the ego and their neurotic limitation. In a world that had long lost its 'deep past' (the root of religion) science becomes in both the communist revolution and the revolution of subjectivity the only root capable of sustaining a new beginning. On that basis, good options are the options legitimated by science. This is what grounds, in Marx, the distinction between reality and ideology; and in Freud, the distinction between reality and fantasy. In this distinction also resides the possibility of modern critical theory.

Thus Horkheimer (1972, p. 208): 'Reason cannot become transparent to itself as long as men act as members of an organism which lacks reason'. In our century, sociology and the social sciences have subscribed to the new roots/options equation, converted into the master model of social intelligibility: structure and agency in sociology and anthropology; the *longue dureé* and *l'événement* in history; *langue* and *parole* in linguistics.

In the political field, the nation-state and positive law turn into the roots that create the wide range of options in the market and civil society. In order to function as a root, law must be autonomous, which means it must be scientific: the juridical root, as a radicalized option, consecrated by codification and positivism (Santos, 1995, p. 55-109). The liberal state, in its turn, constituted itself as a root by imagining homogeneous nationality and national culture. The state becomes, then, the guardian of a root (ethnicity, language, culture) that does not exist beyond the state.

## Entering a Post-Equation Era

The modern equation of roots and options, on the basis of which we have learned how to think social change, is undergoing destabilization that seems to be irreversible. This has three main forms: turbulence of scales; explosion of roots and options; interchangeability of roots and options. As regards *turbulence of scales*, the root/option equation rests on the stabilised difference between large-scale roots and small-scale options. Today this is thrown into confusion. Urban violence is in this paradigmatic. When a street kid is looking for shelter to spend the night and is for that reason murdered by a policeman, or when a person who, approached in the street by a beggar, refuses to give money and is for that reason murdered by the beggar, what happens is an unpredictable explosion of the scale of the conflict: a seemingly trivial phenomenon seemingly without consequences is equated with another one – now dramatic and with fatal consequences.

Bifurcation occurs in unstable systems whenever a minimal change can bring about qualitative changes in an unpredictable and chaotic way (Prigogine, 1980). This sudden explosion of scales creates a tremendous turbulence and leaves the system in a state of irreversible vulnerability. The turbulence of our time is of this kind: its vulnerability affecting forms of subjectivity and sociability, from labour to sexual life, from citizenship to the ecosystem. This state of bifurcation reverberates upon the root/option equation, rendering chaotic and reversible the scale difference between roots and options. The social contract itself is shaken by turbulence. The contractualization of modernity's political is being destabilized. The social contract is a root-contract based on the commonly shared option of abandoning the state of nature. Two hundred years later, we are faced with structural unemployment, the return of supremacist ideologies, the increase of social and economic inequalities between and inside the world's countries. We seem to be opting to exclude from the social contract a large percentage of the population, forcing it to go back to the state of nature. The deradicalization of the social contract as a master political root implies that the social contract can no longer sustain the range of options it once purported to sustain. As the scale of the root shrinks, the suppression of options that goes with it appears justified as if sustained by an alternative root (the state of nature). Thus the moderate option of the welfare state in advanced capitalist societies appears today to be an extremist position, as extremist and utopian as the socialist option it sought to replace.

The second manifestation of the destabilization of the equation of roots and options is the *explosion of roots and options alike*. 'Globalization' has given rise to a seemingly infinite multiplicity of options. The range of possibilities has expanded tremendously, as legitimated by the very forces that make possible such expansion, be it technology, market economy, the global culture of advertising and consumerism, or democracy. Options appear limitless. And yet, we live in a time of localisms and territorializations of identities and singularities, genealogies and memories. In sum, the time we live in is also a time of limitless multiplication of *roots*.

The explosion of roots and options does not occur merely by means of the endless multiplication of both. It also occurs in the process of searching for particularly deep and strong roots capable of sustaining particularly dramatic and radical options. Though the range of possibilities may be drastically reduced the remaining options are dramatic and full of consequences. The two most telling examples of this explosion through intensification of roots and options are fundamentalism and DNA research. Fundamentalism is an extreme form of identity politics. Indeed Eurocentric universalism may be sen as an extreme form of identity politics. This hegemonic fundamentalism is signalled by its capacity to designate other forms of identity politics as fundamentalism. Neo-liberal fundamentalism is particularly intense. The 'market economy' has become the new social contract: the universal economic base or root which forces the majority of countries into dramatic and radical options. Here for many countries, the option is between the chaos of exclusion and the chaos of inclusion.

DNA research, in the human genome project, signifies culturally the transformation of the body into the ultimate root whence sprout the dramatic options of genetic engineering. The booming neurosciences and brain research also convert the body into the ultimate root. We began the century with the socialist and the subjective revolutions. We are closing it with the body revolution. The centrality then assumed by class and the psyche is now being assumed by the body, itself now converted, like enlightened reason before, into the root of all options.

There is a new *interchangeability of roots and options*. We live in a time of unmasking and deconstruction. Today we see that many of the roots in which we have been mirroring ourselves were but disguised options or perhaps rather underexposed options. We see this in the option of primatology (Haraway, 1989), in the sexist and racist option of the welfare state (Gordon, 1990). We see this in the option, denounced by Martin Bernal (1987), to eliminate the African roots of Black Athena so as to intensify its purity as the root of European culture, and the in option to whiten the Black Atlantic so as to hide the syncretisms of modernity (Gilroy, 1993). We realize that the roots of our sociability and intelligibility are, in fact, optional, and address the hegemonic idea of the future that gave them meaning, rather than the past which, after all, only existed to function as the anticipated mirror of the future. In sociology, in general, the explosion of roots and options in recent times has taken the form of the proliferation of revisionisms concerning the founders of the discipline (Collins, 1994).

The interchangeability of roots and options has become constitutive of our life trajectories and histories. Consider, for example, debates on adoption and the negotiation of motherhood (Yngvesson, 1996). The wall of secrecy that for many years separated the birth mother (root) from the adoptive mother (option) has been questioned by the 'open adoption' policy. The interdependence of birth and adoptive mothers gives the adopted child the possibility to opt between biological and socially-constructed genetic roots or even to opt to keep both of them as a kind of bounded root life contingency. In the new constellation of meaning, roots and options are no longer qualitatively distinct entities. Roots are the continuation of options in a different scale and intensity; and the same goes for options. The outcome of this circularity is that the right to roots and the right to options are reciprocally translatable.

The mirror play of roots and options reaches its climax in cyberspace. On the Internet, identities are doubly imagined, as flights of imagination and as sheer images. People are free to create roots at their pleasure and then reproduce their options ad infinitum. The same image can be seen as a root without options or as an option without roots. It no longer makes sense to think in terms of the root-option equation. The distinction between backward and forward linkages that sustained the equation becomes a matter of clicking. Actually, we come to realize that the equation only makes sense in a conceptual, *logo*centric culture which speculates on social and territorial matrices (space and time), subjecting them to criteria of authenticity defined in terms of scale and perspective. As we move on to an *imago*centric culture, space and time are replaced by instances of velocity, matrices are replaced by 'mediatrices', and authenticity discourse becomes incomprehensible gibberish. There is no depth but the succession of screens. All that is below or behind, is also above and in front. Here Deleuze's (1968) 'rhizome' gains a new up-to-datedness. For media philosophers Mark Taylor and Esa Saarinen (Taylor and Saarinen, 1994, p. 9), 'the imaginary register transforms roots into rhizomes. A rhizomic culture is neither rooted nor unrooted. One can never be sure where rhizomes will break new ground'.

## Transitions and Baroque Codes[2]

The trivialization of roots-options distinction entails the trivialization of both. In this lies our difficulty today in thinking social transformation. The *pathos* of the roots-options distinction is constitutive of our way of thinking social change. The more intense the pathos, the more easily the present evaporates into an ephemeral moment between the past and the future. The most eloquent version of such pathos is the Communist Manifesto. In the absence of this pathos, the present tends to be eternalized, devouring both past and future. Such is our present condition. We live in a time of repetition. The acceleration of repetition provokes a feeling of vertigo and stagnation at the same time. Because of its acceleration and mediatic treatment, repetition ends up subjecting even those groups that assert themselves by the pathos of roots. It is as easy and irrelevant to yield to the retrospective illusion of projecting the future into the past, as to yield to the prospective illusion of projecting the past into the future. The eternal present renders the two illusions equivalent, and neutralizes both. Thus, our condition takes on a Kafkaesque dimension: what exists can be explained neither by the past nor by the future. It exists only in a chaotic web of indefinition and contingency. While modernity deprived the past of its capacity for irruption and revelation, handing it on to the future (Benjamin 1968, pp. 253-64), the Kafkaesque present deprives the future of this capacity. What irrupts in this present is erratic, arbitrary, fortuitous, and absurd.

Because we are in a period of transition, this condition cannot be accepted as a normal state of affairs. It is either confronted as a dangerously deceiving condition or understood as a borderland of relatively unmapped opportunities and uninsurable risks. The strategy of confrontation and denunciation is premised upon the continuing validity of the dualism of scales (large/small) and the dualism of times (times of roots/times of options) that underlies the modern equation of roots and options. The collapse of these dualisms gives way to new servitudes and compulsions which, by virtue of the subsequent hiatus of codification, may easily present themselves as new auroras of liberty. Thus, the explosion of roots that has been the outcome, whether intended or not, of identity politics, does not merely trivialise roots. It brings along the risk of ghettoization and refeudalization – the proliferation of differences which, because they are incommensurate, render coalitions impossible and lead ultimately to indifference. The explosion of roots provokes a rootlessness that creates choices at the same time that it blocks their effective exercize. On the other hand, the explosion of options, far from doing away with the determinism of roots, brings about a new, perhaps more cruel, determinism: the compulsion of choice, of which the market is the utmost symbol and reality (Wood, 1996, p. 252).

Is our condition indeed a question of transition or borderland? To presume so presupposes that the dualist codes that sustained the modern equation of roots and options have been finally sublated. The present hiatus that seems like a gap or absence of codification, is actually a fertile field where new synthetic codes are emerging. At issue are baroque codes in which scales and times mix, and in which underexposed options act like roots and overexposed roots act like options. What is most striking and original about these codes is that, though intrinsically provisional and easily discardable, they have, while they last, great consistency. They are, therefore, as intensely mobilizing as convincingly replaceable. The hiatuses, or gaps, among codes render sequences among them inapprehensible as such. Therefore, sequences have no consequences as consequences have no sequence. The experience of risk is thus much more intense. Since the causes are apprehensible only as consequences, there is no insurance against this kind of risk.

These post-dualist baroque codes are discursive formations that operate by intensification and *mestizaje*. There is intensification whenever a given social or cultural reference is exposed beyond its limits – whether through overexposure or underexposure – to the point of losing its 'natural' quality (e.g., a root turning into an option or vice-versa). There is *mestizaje* whenever two or more autonomous social or cultural references mix together or interpenetrate to such an extent and in such a way that the new references emerging therefrom, however autonomous they may appear to be, bear witness to their mixed heritage (Santos, 1995, pp. 499-506).

*Mestizaje* is of two kinds: *mestizaje* resulting from overexposure and *mestizaje* resulting from underexposure. *Mestizaje* resulting from overexposure concerns constellations of roots and options that proliferate in a chaotic manner, changing places in an irregular and unpredictable way. This kind of *mestizaje* occurs in many of the struggles conventionally termed new social movements: feminist and ecological struggles, the struggles of the indigenous peoples, struggles for human rights, and so on. *Mestizaje* resulting from underexposure concerns constellations of roots and options that concentrate on exemplary, ideally unique reproductions, whereby options become so intensified as to become roots.

*Mestizaje* resulting from overexposure is proper to baroque codes in which roots are subjected to the logic of options. There are roots only because there are options. Risk, a dominant presence in all baroque codes, is, in this type of code, confronted by creativity of action, by appealing to autonomy, self-reflexivity, individuation, extra-institutionality. In baroque codes that operate through overexposure, *mestizaje* preside over the social processes of creative dispersal and networking. The most consistent example of a baroque code bearing the form of overexposure is Beck's (1995) concept of subpolitics. At the antipodes of Foucault, Beck starts from the idea that the institutions of industrial modernity have created subjects they can no longer control. Science and law, the two megaroots of industrial modernity, have created such a wide hiatus between the individual and the State that the political options brought about by modern institutions have become a vast void. Politics needs, therefore, to be reinvented as subpolitics, that is to say, by proceeding to politicize what industrial modernity considered nonpolitical. Feminist and ecological struggles are the examples privileged by Beck to illustrate the new synthetic codes capable of sublating such dualisms as public/private, expert/lay person, political/economic and of shaping society from below by means of reflective rule altering.

The second type of baroque code is constituted by *mestizaje* resulting from underexposure. In this case, options conform to the logic of roots, that is to say, there are options only because there are roots. Here, risk is confronted not by the creativity of action but rather by the sustainability of action, by appealing to options that are intense or shared enough to allow for the sustained reproduction of an increasingly wider range of options. This kind of baroque code presides over *canonization* processes. By 'canonization' processes I here mean processes of particular intensification of references, whether they appear as backward or forward linkages. Intensification can either be produced by strict imitation (or reproduction), as in the musical canon, or by extreme difficulty, if not impossibility, of imitation, as is the case of Christian canonization. Intensification, whatever its process, confers to the object of intensification a particular exemplarity, strangeness, value, and soundness, which make it adequate to function as condition or ground for multiple exercizes of choice, whether permitted or forbidden. Ideally, the process of intensification is consummated when the choice of the object of intensification foregoes justification as choice to become, itself, justification for other choices. The baroque codes that operate by means of underexposure *mestizaje* and preside over the canonization processes are perhaps the most intriguing and complex and therefore require more detailed reflection.

# Baroque Codes and Processes of Canonization

Amongst many canonization processes under way in this period of transition, I distinguish three: the literary canon, the common heritage of humankind, and the world cultural and natural heritage.

## The literary canon

By literary canon is meant the set of literary works that, at a given historical moment, the dominant or hegemonic intellectuals and institutions consider to be most representative, of greater value and authority in a given official culture. Thus Harold Bloom (1994) proffers twenty-six major authors (novelists, poets, dramatists) that he institutes as the Western canon. The role that the church played in the constitution of the biblical canon, has been played by the school and university as far as the literary or, in general, the artistic canon goes (Guillory 1995, p. 239). In the literary canon, baroque codes of underexposure *mestizaje* operate: the works chosen to integrate the canon are the ones that stop being exposed to the logic of options and become the foundation or root of the literary field. The intensification process that these works undergo endows them with the cultural capital necessary to allow them to display the exemplarity, the uniqueness, and inimitability that sets them apart.

As a baroque code, the literary canon is a synthetic code, a code that is also structurally ambivalent since, to subject options to a logic of roots – as befits underexposure *mestizaje* – it must begin by opting among several alternatives so as to deny, at a later stage, the status of root to every alternative that has not been chosen. Thus Bloom (1994, pp. 2-3) asserts with not a little irony: 'the choice of authors here is not so arbitrary as it may seem. They have been selected for both their sublimity and their representative nature'. He continues, after asking rhetorically what makes a particular author or work canonical: 'The answer [is] strangeness, a mode of originality that either cannot be assimilated or that so assimilates us that we cease to see it as strange'. The literary canon is particularly contested in the Anglo-Saxon world. The positions become extreme between those who defend the canon such as they find it, investing it with the function of guaranteeing the national and cultural identity and stability, and those who attack it by questioning precisely the (elitist, partial) conception of identity that it imposes. The discussion of the process of canon formation and reproduction (Kamuf, 1997) in itself sheds light on the historical nature of the canon and its volatility, as well as on the social forces and institutions that shape it one way or the other. Equally important is to note the canon's capacity for resistance, the ease with which it creates solidity and imposes itself as authority, routine or mere inertia. The intensity of the debate, in its institutional, political, and mediatic repercussions, is easily appropriated by the intensification process at the basis of underexposure *mestizaje*. The very debate about options and their alternatives intensifies the submission of options to the logic of roots. Up to a certain point, canonization feeds on decanonization.

The Biblical canon, the texts that together are considered to be the Holy Scripture in the Judeo-Christian tradition, was formed very early on and kept quite consistently; even deviations from it have shown remarkable persistence. 'Given the character of the Church as an institution to which one either does or does not belong, the process of canonical selection in this context must take the form of a rigorously final process of inclusion or exclusion (on dogmatic grounds). Every would-be scriptural text is included or excluded once and for all' (Guillory 1995, p. 237). In the literary canon, things are different by virtue of the different institutional practices of churches and schools. Even in the ecclesiastical field there are differences. While the Biblical canon reveals great stability, canonical law, though far more stable than the secular law of the states, has undergone some changes in the course of the centuries. These changes are due in part to the internal heterogeneity of the different normative elements that constitute the canonical law: divine law, natural law, regulatory positive law.

Unlike the literary canon, the historical canon does not so much concern texts and authors, as rather events and contexts. Though in some countries less visible than the literary canon, the historical canon also exists and consists of the foundational narrative of the nation-state, as well as of such historical events as are considered to have the utmost importance and, for that reason are said to be canonical. In the past decades the historical canon in some countries has been under the same kind of turbulence that has affected the literary canon in the Anglo-Saxon cultural world. Suffice it to mention the controversies generated by the historical revisionism of François Furet (1978) on the French Revolution or Renzo de Felice (1977) on Italian fascism.

## The Common Heritage of Humankind

The *common heritage of humankind* is a doctrine in international law and international relations. The concept was formulated for the first time in 1967 by Malta's Ambassador to the United Nations, Arvid Pardo, in relation to UN negotiations on the international regulation of the oceans and the deep seabed. Pardo's purpose was:

> to provide a solid basis for future worldwide cooperation ... through the acceptance by the international community of a new principle of international law ... that the seabed and ocean floor and their subsoil have a special status as a 'common heritage of mankind' and as such should be reserved exclusively for peaceful purposes and administered

by an international authority for the benefit of all peoples. (Pardo, 1968, p. 225)

Since then, the concept of common heritage has been applied to other 'common areas' such as the moon, outer space and Antarctica. The idea is similar to the idea of the social contract: the construction of commonly shared ground upon which differences and divisions can flourish without compromising the sustainability of social life. However, contrary to the social contract, and as befits a baroque code, common heritage is not a once-and-for-all choice but rather an ongoing process of selection. Whatever becomes heritage has always been there. The instant of nomination creates the eternity of the nominated. The nominated are those natural entities that belong to humankind in its entirety. All people are, therefore, entitled to have a say and a share in the management and allocation of their resources. Common heritage, as J.M. Pureza (1993) notes, involves 1) nonappropriation; 2) management by all peoples; 3) international sharing of the benefits obtained from the exploitation of natural resources; 4) peaceful use, including freedom of scientific research for the benefit of all peoples; 5) conservation for future generations.

Although formulated by international lawyers, the concept of common heritage transcends law, inasmuch as both its object and subject of regulation transcend states. Humankind emerges, indeed, as a subject of international law, entitled to its own heritage and the autonomous prerogative to manage the spaces and resources included in the global commons. Common heritage is a baroque code operating through underexposure *mestizaje*. The natural resources of common heritage undergo a process of intensification converting them into the foundation of the survival of life on earth. As with the literary canon, the options are so intensified that whatever is selected becomes exempt from the game of roots and options. As long as the selection is sustained, it becomes a root without options. The exemplarity, uniqueness, and precious value of the resources that constitute the common heritage is sustained via the insistence that life on earth depends upon them for its existence.

Like the literary canon, the doctrine of the common heritage of humankind has been contested. However, unlike in the literary canon, canonization of common heritage has been attacked by hegemonic groups, especially the US. Instead counterhegemonic groups, such as peace and ecological movements, as well as Third World countries, are the ones engaged in the struggle for the doctrine's canonization. The common heritage of humankind clashes with the interests of some states, particularly those with the technological and financial means for ocean floor exploration (Kimball, 1983, p. 16). The Law of the Sea Convention, signed in Montego Bay on December 10, 1982 is exemplary. Though the Sea Convention was originally signed by 159 states, it took twelve years to be ratified by sixty states, the number of ratifications needed to bring the Convention into force. The implementation of the Convention started in November 1994. Due to US pressure to correct some of its 'imperfections', the Convention will be implemented with an annex agreement, neutralizing its most innovative features. One of the most revealing characteristics of the common heritage of humankind is its baroque openendedness, the capacity to extend the process of intensification to other areas or resources, thus converting them in further roots of life on earth.

Canonization of common heritage has been extended into outer space, in for example the Moon Treaty of 1979, which became international law in 1984. Article XI of the Treaty states that the moon and its natural resources are a common heritage of humankind. Article VI states that 'the exploration of the moon shall be the province of all mankind and shall be carried out for the benefit and in the interest of all countries, irrespective of their degree of economic and scientific development'. Like the Law of the Sea Convention, it was established in the face of anti-canonization struggles of hegemonic powers. Neither the United States nor the former Soviet Union, China, Japan and the United Kingdom are signatories and thus not legally obliged by the treaty. As regards the already established literary and historical canons, struggles aim at historicizing, relativizing, and decanonizing it. As regards common heritage, the process of canonization itself is the object of contestation. Baroque codes often exist in anticipation of the reality they aspire to.

## World Cultural and Natural Heritage

The third process of canonization I will address is the World Cultural and Natural Heritage. As established by the UNESCO Convention Concerning the Protection of the World Cultural and Natural Heritage of 1972 (ratified by 152 countries as of December 1997), monuments, groups of buildings, sites, and natural formations that meet certain criteria and tests of authenticity will be considered as being of 'outstanding universal value' and accordingly nominated for inclusion in the World Heritage List. Such value may be established from a variety of points of view: history, art, science, aesthetics, anthropology, conservation or natural beauty. As in the other processes of canonization the World Cultural and Natural Heritage operates by means of an exceptional intensification of the selected objects, endowing them with such aura of exemplarity, uniqueness, and irreplaceability that they acquire the foundational status of quality of life on earth. For that reason, in the terms of the Convention itself, their deterioration or disappearance would be 'a harmful impoverishment of the heritage of all nations of the world'. This intensification process can be seen clearly in the criteria defined and applied by the World Heritage Committee.[3]

i. represent a masterpiece of human creative genius; or

ii. exhibit an important interchange of human values, over a span of time or within a cultural area of the world, on developments in architecture or technology, monumental arts, town planning or landscape design; or

iii. bear a unique or at least exceptional testimony to a cultural tradition or to a civilization which is living or which has disappeared; or

iv. be an outstanding example of a type of building or architectural or technological ensemble or landscape which illustrates (a) significant stage(s) in human history; or

v. be an outstanding example of a traditional human settlement or land-use which is representative of a culture (or cultures), especially when it has become vulnerable under the impact of irreversible change; or

vi. be directly or tangibly associated with events or living traditions, with ideas, or with beliefs, with artistic and literary works of outstanding universal significance (the Committee considers that this criterion should justify inclusion in the list only in exceptional circumstances and in conjunction with other criteria, cultural or natural)

As regards the natural heritage, the natural sites or formations (whether physical, biological, geological or physiographic) should:

i. be outstanding examples representing major stages of earth's history, including the record of life; significant or on-going geological processes in the development of landforms, or significant geomorphic or physiographic features; or

ii. be outstanding examples representing significant or on-going ecological and biological processes in the evolution and development of terrestrial, fresh water, coastal and marine ecosystems and communities of plants or animals; or

iii. contain superlative natural phenomena or areas of exceptional natural beauty and aesthetic importance; or

iv. contain the most important and significant natural habitats for in-situ conservation of biological diversity, including those containing threatened species of outstanding universal value from the point of view of science or conservation [.]

In December 1997, 134 cities in 58 countries had been declared world heritage. Since 1993 they have been part of the Organization of World Heritage Cities whose main objective is to foster cooperation, solidarity, and mutual support among the cities so that they can preserve 'the privileged position' invested upon them.⁴ In December 1997 the World Heritage List consisted of 552 properties in 112 countries, of which 418 were cultural, 114 natural, and 20 mixed.

As a canonization process, the World Cultural and Natural Heritage has some similarities with the common heritage of humankind. In both cases, the aim is to define systems of protection and special juridical statuses for resources that are considered to be of exceptional importance for the sustainability and quality of life on earth. However, in contrast with that of the common heritage of humankind (or indeed of literary works), the canonization of the world cultural and natural heritage has been relatively little contested. Since 1978 the World Heritage Committee has been steadily including new sites in the List, approximately 35 new sites per year in the 1990s alone.

Unlike the literary canon, the World Cultural and Natural Heritage is a positive-sum game. The inclusion of a site in the cultural or natural canon does not directly imply the exclusion of an alternative site, especially when the sites are located in different countries. On the other hand, while the literary canon up to a point feeds itself upon the forces that contest it, in Cultural and Natural Heritage the limits of canonization reside in the forces that promote it: a virtually infinite canonization of sites might bring about the perverse effect of decanonizing (i.e., trivializing) already listed ones. Baroque codes operating through underexposure depend on the production of scarcity: intensification demands rarefaction. Unlike the common heritage of humankind, the Cultural and Natural Heritage does not question the ownership, whether public or private, of the canonized site or formation. The 1972 Convention states that acknowledgement of the universal value of a given site demonstrates 'the importance, for all the peoples of the world, of safeguarding this unique and irreplaceable property, to whatever people it may belong'.

## The Times of the Baroque Codes

In the previous section I analyzed two types of baroque codes: ones operating through overexposure *mestizaje* and presiding over the processes of creative dispersal and networking; and codes operating through underexposure *mestizaje* and presiding over the processes of canonization. Both types of codes are synthetic in aspiration. The different kinds of *mestizaje* they produce between roots and options bear witness to the fact that the dualism of roots and options is still present in them, even if only as a ruin, a memory or a discomfort. They are, therefore, ambivalent codes, an ambivalence that is reflected in the social times they privilege. These times are themselves ambivalent, irregular, unrhythmical.

There are, it would seem, three distinct temporalities of today's baroque codes (Gurvitch 1969, pp. 341-43). First, there is the *trompe-l'oeil* time which, though apparently a long duration, conceals an enormous capacity for irruption, of bringing about emergencies and abrupt, unexpected crises. Second, there is the time of irregular beat between the emergence and disappearance of rhythms, a time of enigmatic duration and intervals between series of duration. This is the time of uncertainty, contingency, and discontinuity. Finally, there is the alternating time between belatedness and forwardness, a time of discontinuities between anachronisms and anticipations, a time of struggle between past and future fighting for space in the present. The present is thus evanescent in this temporality.

Each of these times occur in both types of baroque codes, in different combinations. Each of these times has a specific ambivalence resulting from its combining, in a failed synthesis, the elements of a given dualism. This may be a dualism between duration and explosion, between the irregularity of the emergence or the irregularity of the disappearance of the rhythm; or between anticipation and anachronism. The way this ambivalence presents itself may vary according to the slower or faster rhythm that shapes the changes or oscillations. Tempos such as *largo, lento, adagio, andante* and *moderato* tend to prevail in baroque codes of underexposure and their processes of canonization. *Allegro, presto* and *prestissimo* tend to prevail in baroque codes of overexposure and their processes of creative dispersal and networking.

# Conclusion

The equation of roots and options is of crucial importance to understand processes of social identity and transformation in Western modernity. In this essay, after having analyzed the equation, I have tried to identify the factors that have lately contributed to destructure this equation. This destructuring has been so pronounced that the equation may be suffering from a terminal crisis, and we are, accordingly, in an emergent post-equation era. In this period twin processes can be detected. One the one hand, socio-cultural phenomena until now considered as optional forward linkages are so underexposed that they become roots; on the other hand, phenomena until now considered as foundational backward linkages are so overexposed that they become optional. Both the processes of underexposure and overexposure involve mixing, interpenetrating, cross-fertilizing and cross-undermining references up until now unambiguously claimed either as roots or options. It is this *mestizaje* of references that translates itself into what I have been calling baroque codes: discursive formations and formulations of socio-cultural identity and change in which the dualism of roots and options is present only as ruin or memory. These codes aspire to synthesis without reaching it: they are ambivalent, complex, relatively chaotic and contestable. These codes, just like the older equation of roots and options evolve in various types of socio-temporal constellations.

Because of their mixed character, their voracious adaptability and their irregular durations and rhythms, baroque codes are congenial to globalization, to both hegemonic and counter-hegemonic globalizations. Baroque codes offer a common ground of ambiguity, a common ground of bounded incoherence and self-contradictoriness in which conflicting interests and social groups can use to their advantage the relative blurring of the distinction between transgression and conformity, between changing and enforcing rules. The relative strength of the different interests dictate the direction of globalization. The outcomes, however, are indeterminable and always reversible.

## Notes

1. I would like to thank Maria Irene Ramalho for her invaluable comments and editorial help. I am also grateful to Immanuel Wallerstein, José Pureza, Barbara Yngvesson, and Paulo Peixoto for their comments and suggestions.
2. By "codes" I mean discursive formations and formulations that function as common language and shared rules in struggles concerning identity and social transformation.
3. These data can be looked up on the Web. See UNESCO, World Heritage Committee, on <http://www.unesco.org:80//whc/criteria.htm>.
4. See the statutes of the Organization of World Heritage Cities adopted in Fez on September 8, 1993. Other institutions concerning the world heritage are the International Center for the Study of the Preservation and Restoration of Cultural Properties (ICCROM), the International Council on Monuments and Sites, and the World Conservation Union.

# References

Beck, Ulrich 1995: The Reinvention of Politics: Towards a Theory of Reflexive Modernization. In U. Beck, A. Giddens, and S. Lash, *Reflexive Modernization*. Cambridge: Polity Press, pp. 1-55.
Benjamin, Walter 1968: *Illuminations*. New York: Schocken.
Bernal, Martin 1987: *Black Athena*. London: Free Association Books.
Bloom, Harold 1994: *The Western Canon*. New York: Harcourt.
Collins, R. 1994: *Four Sociological Traditions*. Oxford: Oxford University Press.
De Felice, Renzo 1977: *Interpretations of Fascism*. Cambridge, MA: Harvard University Press.
Deleuze, Gilles 1968: *Différence et répétition*. Paris: PUF.
Furet, François 1978: *Penser la Révolution française*. Paris: Gallimard.
Gilroy, Paul 1993: *The Black Atlantic*. Cambridge, MA: Harvard University Press.
Gordon, Linda 1990: *Woman's Body, Woman's Right*. New York: Penguin.
Guillory, John 1995: Canon. In F. Lentricchia and T. McLaughlin (eds.) *Critical Terms for Literary Study*. Chicago, IL: University of Chicago Press, pp. 233-49.
Gurvitch, Georges 1969: *La vocation actuelle de la sociologie. vol. II*. Paris: PUF.
Haraway, Donna 1989: *Primate Visions*. New York: Routledge.
Horkheimer, Max 1972: *Critical Theory: Selected Essays*. New York: Herder and Herder.
Kamuf, Peggy 1997: *The Division of Literature, or The University in Deconstruction*. Chicago, IL: University of Chicago Press.
Kimball, Lee 1983: The Law of the Sea—On the shoals. *Environment*, 25, 9: pp. 14-20, 41-44.
Pardo, Arvid 1968: Whose is the Bed of the Sea? *American Society, International Law Proceedings*, 62: pp. 216-9.
Prigogine, I. 1980: *From Being to Becoming*. San Francisco, CA: Freeman.
Pureza, José Manuel 1993: Globalização e Direito Internacional: Da boa vizinhança ao património cultural da humanidade. *Revista Crítica de Ciências Sociais*, 36, pp. 9-26.
Rousseau, Jean Jacques 1973: *The Social Contract and Discourses*. London: J.M. Dent and Sons.
Santos, Boaventura de Sousa 1995: *Toward a New Common Sense: Law, Science, and Politics in the Paradigmatic Transition*. New York: Routledge.
Taylor, Mark and Saarinen, Esa 1994: *Imagologies: Media Philosophy*. New York: Routledge.
Vico, Giambattista 1961: *The New Science*. Garden City, NY: Anchor Books.
Wood, Ellen Meiksins 1996: *Democracy against Capitalism*. Cambridge: Cambridge University Press.
Yngvesson, Barbara 1996: Negotiating Motherhood: Identity and Difference in Open Adoptions. *Law and Society Review*. 34, pp. 31-80.

**Boaventura de Sousa Santos** is Professor of Sociology at the University of Coimbra and the University of Wisconsin-Madison. His research interests are in political sociology, sociology of law and epistemology. At present he is involved in research projects in Portugal, Brazil, Colombia and Mozambique. His most recent books are *Pela Mão de Alise: O Social e o Político na Pós-Modernidade* (Afrontamento 1993), *Toward a New Common Sense: Law, Science and Politics in the Paradigmatic Transition* (Routledge 1995).

# Index

Adam, Barbara, 11,12,13,160
Adams, Fred, 30
aesthetics, 71, 183, 189-90
Agamben, 62
Agger, Ben, 163
Agnès B., 189
Alexander, Franz, 87, 97
Althusser, Louis, 48
anarchism, 33;
  techno-anarchists, 1
Anderson, Benedict & Perry, 212
Anderson, Pamela, 10
angels, 4, 49, 50-1, 52, 53, 55, 58, 61
Apel, 144
apocalypse/apocalyptic, 1, 116,
  120, 152, 155, 157
Apollo/Apollonian, 131, 132, 133,
  135, 141
Appadurai, Arjun, 144
archive, 57-8, 60
Arendt, Hannah, 151
Augustine, St., 199, 203
authority, 188

Bachelard, Gaston, 48
Baier, Annette, 143
Bakhtin, 139
Balandier, 106
Barber, 163
baroque/baroque codes, 154,
  158, 245, 250-3, 255-60
Barth, Karl, 115-17
Barthes, Roland, 10, 201
Bataille, Georges, 52
Baudrillard, Jean, 76, 150
Bauman, Zygmunt, 62, 113, 145,
  152
Beck, Ulrich, 11, 154, 252
Beckford, James, 112
being, 156, 228
Beker, Jeanne, 184
bell hooks, 185

Benhabib, Seyla, 44, 151
Benjamin, Walter, 53, 148, 154,
  159;
  *Critique of Violence* 37;
  *Illuminations*, 48;
  *Origins of German Tragic Drama*,
  158;
  *Philosophical Forum*, 48;
  *The Storyteller*, 9, 148-51, 153
Bennett, Jonathan, 63
Benveniste, 42
Berman, Marshall, 12
Berry, P. & Wernick, A., 113
Beyer, Peter, 127
Bhabha, Homi, 137, 144, 152
Big Bang, 30, 203
Black Athena, 249
Blair, Tony, 13
Bloch, Ernst, 119
Bloom, Harold, 253
Blumenberg, Hans, 119
body, the, 16, 18, 28, 62, 80, 113,
  122, 124, 139, 157, 190-1, 192,
  193, 248;
  disease and, 98;
  mind and, 17, 88, 92, 96, 123, 228,
  229,
nature and 231;
performance and 67, 73-5
Boethius, 115
Bordo, Susan, 10, 182, 184, 193
Borges, 205
Boyarin, 61
Boyne, Roy, 4
Brody, Howard, 99
Buñuel, 205
Butler, Judith, 141, 142, 195
Butterfield, Herbert, 203
Busino, 107

Campbell, Colin, 186, 190
Canclini, Néstor, 136

.

Printed and bound by CPI Group (UK) Ltd, Croydon, CR0 4YY

09/06/2025

14686107-0002